Perspectives on Southern Africa

1. THE AUTOBIOGRAPHY OF AN UNKNOWN SOUTH AFRICAN, by Naboth Mokgatle (1971)
2. MODERNIZING RACIAL DOMINATION: *South Africa's Political Dynamics,* by Heribert Adam (1971)
3. THE RISE OF AFRICAN NATIONALISM IN SOUTH AFRICA: *The African National Congress, 1912–1952,* by Peter Walshe (1971)
4. TALES FROM SOUTHERN AFRICA, by A. C. Jordan (1973)
5. LESOTHO 1970: *An African Coup Under the Microscope,* by B. M. Khaketla (1972)
6. TOWARDS AN AFRICAN LITERATURE: *The Emergence of Literary Form in Xhosa,* by A. C. Jordan (1972)
7. LAW, ORDER, AND LIBERTY IN SOUTH AFRICA, by A. S. Mathews (1972)
8. SWAZILAND: *The Dynamics of Political Modernization,* by Christian P. Potholm (1972)
9. THE SOUTH WEST AFRICA/NAMBIA DISPUTE: *Documents and Scholarly Writings on the Controversy Between South Africa and the United Nations,* by John Dugard (1973)
10. CONFRONTATION AND ACCOMMODATION IN SOUTHERN AFRICA: *The Limits of Independence,* by Kenneth W. Grundy (1973)
11. THE RISE OF AFRIKANERDOM: *Power, Apartheid, and the Afrikaner Civil Religion,* by T. Dunbar Moodie (1975)
12. JUSTICE IN SOUTH AFRICA, by Albie Sachs (1973)
13. AFRIKANER POLITICS IN SOUTH AFRICA, 1934–1948, by Newell M. Stultz (1974)
14. CROWN AND CHARTER: *The Early Years of the British South Africa Company,* by John S. Galbraith (1975)
15. POLITICS OF ZAMBIA, edited by William Tordoff (1975)
16. CORPORATE POWER IN AN AFRICAN STATE: *The Political Impact of Multinational Mining Companies in Zambia,* by Richard Sklar (1975)
17. CHANGE IN CONTEMPORARY SOUTH AFRICA, edited by Leonard Thompson and Jeffrey Butler (1975)
18. THE TRADITION OF RESISTANCE IN MOZAMBIQUE: *Anti-Colonial Activity in the Zambesi Valley, 1850–1921,* by Allen F. Isaacman (1976)
19. BLACK POWER IN SOUTH AFRICA: *The Evolution of an Ideology,* by Gail M. Gerhart (1978)
20. BLACK HEART: *Gore-Browne and the Politics of Multiracial Zambia,* by Robert I. Rotberg (1977)
21. THE BLACK HOMELANDS OF SOUTH AFRICA: *The Political and Economic Development of Bophuthatswana and KwaZulu,* by Jeffrey Butler, Robert I. Rotberg, and John Adams (1977).
22. AFRIKANER POLITICAL THOUGHT, by Hermann Giliomee and André du Toit (1978).
23. ANGOLA UNDER THE PORTUGESE: *The Myth and the Reality,* by Gerald Bender (1977).
24. LAND AND RACIAL DOMINATION IN RHODESIA, by Robin Palmer (1977).
25. THE ROOTS OF RURAL POVERTY: *Historical Essays on the Development of Underdevelopment in Central and Southern Africa,* edited by Robin Palmer and Neil Parsons (1977).

Black Heart

Gore-Browne in 1964.

"You've a black heart under a white skin!"

E. M. L. Mtepuka to Gore-Browne
1 May 1946

Black Heart

*Gore-Browne and the Politics
of Multiracial Zambia*

ROBERT I. ROTBERG

UNIVERSITY OF CALIFORNIA PRESS
BERKELEY   LOS ANGELES   LONDON

Other books written and edited by the same Author:

Black Homelands (Berkeley, 1977); *The African Diaspora* (Cambridge, 1976); *Rebellion in Black Africa* (New York, 1971); *Joseph Thomson and the Exploration of Africa* (London, 1971); *Haiti: The Politics of Squalor* (Boston, 1971); *Christian Missionaries and the Creation of Northern Rhodesia* (Princeton, 1965); *A Political History of Tropical Africa* (New York, 1965); *The Rise of Nationalism in Central Africa* (Cambridge, 1965).

University of California Press
Berkeley and Los Angeles, California

University of California Press, Ltd.
London, England

Copyright © 1977 by
Robert I. Rotberg

ISBN 0-520-03164-4

Library of Congress Catalog Card Number: 75-40666

Printed in the United States of America

1 2 3 4 5 6 7 8 9 0

091674

for
JOANNA
whose book this is

Contents

Foreword by Kenneth D. Kaunda   xiii

Preface   xv

    I "The Spring of Life"   1

   II To the Lake of the Royal Crocodiles   29

  III The Shells of War   60

  IV The Creating of Shiwa Ngandu   94

   V "Lorna, dear and bright"   131

  VI Politics in a Changing Society   170

 VII Realizing the Dreams of Boyhood   210

VIII The Last Hurrah   254

  IX The Triumph of the Majority   290

   X The Contribution of a Multiracial
       Initiative   330

Bibliography   337

Articles by Gore-Browne, 337
Books and Articles about Gore-Browne and His Times, 338

Interviews   341

Index   343

Illustrations and Maps

ILLUSTRATIONS

Gore-Browne in 1964, from *Horizon* (July, 1964), with permission of RCM, Ltd. of Zambia. Frontispiece

Gore-Browne as a young soldier, c. 1902. 31

Gore-Browne (third from left) feeding the pigeons in Paris, 1918. 86

Gore-Browne beside a life-size portrait of Dame Ethel Locke-King, from *Horizon* (July, 1964), with permission of RCM Ltd. of Zambia. 120

An aerial view of the manor house at Shiwa Ngandu, from *Horizon* (July, 1964), with permission of RCM, Ltd. of Zambia. 140

The manor house from the front, 1962. Photograph by the author. 142

Gore-Browne and Henry Mulenga, 1964. 264

Gore-Browne at Harvard University, 1962. Photograph by the author. 319

Gore-Browne listening to Kenneth Kaunda, candidate for president of Zambia, at Shiwa Ngandu, 1962. Photograph by the author. 322

Gore-Browne at Chisamba, 1967. Photograph by the author. 328

MAPS

Colonial Zambia: Major places and physical features. Drawn by Joanna H. Rotberg. 3

The Shiwa Estate, 1920–1940. Drawn by Joanna H. Rotberg. 101

Foreword

KENNETH D. KAUNDA

I readily agreed to write a foreword to this book not because I have absolute knowledge and experience of Sir Stewart Gore-Browne from his childhood to his death at Shiwa Ngandu, but because from the time I knew him in his private life at Shiwa Ngandu and the time we closely worked together in the struggle for the freedom of Zambia, he left in me an indelible impression of his greatness and wholeness. He proved to be a firm believer in the dignity and worth of man. He was a humanist crusader.

As Professor Rotberg points out in this book, Gore-Browne was a man of many roles while he lived. He was a man of fortitude, moral courage, vision, and adventure. These qualities I discovered in him during the time I knew and worked with him and they explain candidly the many roles he played in life. They unfolded with each role that he played and accomplished.

Gore-Browne was one of the rare white people at the height of Zambia's battle for national independence who stood on the black man's side to struggle shoulder to shoulder for freedom and justice. He fought with the black majority, not because they were black, but because they were right and their cause was just. They deserved to win. He heroically challenged the colonialist and racist structures of power and worked relentlessly for their total destruction even at the risk of his own life.

Gore-Browne, apart from the leading part he played in both the politics of Northern Rhodesia and the new nation of Zambia, whose birth he helped to hasten, also sought to tread the unbeaten path of social integration and interaction with the "native." He chose Shiwa Ngandu, in the land of the Bemba people of northern Zambia, as a place to live and work for the realization of his goals. People flocked from all corners of the province to dine and interact with the Gore-Brownes. They felt at home in the company of the Gore-Brownes and the Gore-Brownes in turn enjoyed the social and cultural life of the people. A new civilization was born out of this fusion and integration developed and was bequeathed to the generations yet to come.

Gore-Browne is thus a legend in Zambia—a country which he helped to construct, a country he loved, a country in which his spirit will long live. Zambia's history will, I believe, not be complete without the mention of Gore-Browne's contribution to its making.

The readers of this biography will understand why I have a deep admiration for Gore-Browne's rare qualities of leadership, morality, and dedication to the service of his fellow men. One can only discover what type of man Sir Stewart Gore-Browne was and where his greatness and wholeness lie by reading this book. I commend it to students of history and to all humanistic crusaders who still feel a sense of mission in this world.

K.D.K.
12 August 1977

Preface

There were two Gore-Brownes. The official Gore-Browne was Central Africa's premier statesman during the difficult years of World War II and that hectic half-decade which preceded the establishment of the Federation of Rhodesia and Nyasaland. Gore-Browne led the white Legislative Council of Northern Rhodesia before Roy Welensky. He represented African interests as well, and in a manner unparalleled in any British African colony. He was responsible for significant pro-African legislation and for informal action which improved the lot of Africans as subjects of a distant Crown and laborers for local white settlers and industrialists. Likewise, Gore-Browne's representation of Northern Rhodesia at conferences or colonial meetings in London, Capetown, Salisbury, and Nairobi advanced the interests of Africans in the imperial sphere.

The second Gore-Browne was an ex-artillery officer of aristocratic connections and mien. He farmed a twenty-two thousand-acre estate in a remote section of what is now northern Zambia. There, to his impressive Italianate mansion, he welcomed titled travelers, influential politicians, and, long before other whites felt comfortable doing so, Africans of different backgrounds.

In Northern Rhodesia Gore-Browne was a rural squire as well as a cultural and political leader. But few of his Rhodesian acquaintances knew of his brilliant record in World War I, his first introduction to Africa before that war, or his growth in an eccentric and imaginative family which included former governors-general, bishops, generals, admirals, inventors, and jurists. Few comprehended the depth of his attachment to an inspiring aunt, the genesis of his marriage to the daughter of his first love, or much else of the man behind the monocled façade.

A settler who began life in Africa as an army officer, Gore-Browne became a white politician with rare pro-African ideals and ideas. Finally, he opposed white political control of Northern Rhodesia and wholeheartedly supported the triumph of African nationalism. This book combines a study of the official and the private man. It explains the drives behind his many rôles and analyzes the motivations which prompted someone of his background to work so devotedly and decisively for better race relations, equity, justice, and—finally—the independence of an African-run Zambia.

Only rarely in tropical Africa have whites, in life or after death, managed to earn a revered place in the memories of their successors. Almost alone of Central African immigrants, Gore-Browne accomplished both, being esteemed as a parliamentarian and a patron, as a defender of indigenous rights, and as a campaigner for African political growth.

On three well-separated occasions, Gore-Browne encouraged my wife and me to examine the numerous trunks and boxes of letters then stored in two dark back rooms in the Shiwa Ngandu mansion house. Much of the contents he gave to us, although we copied and returned his diaries and some directly political papers. The corpus of the entire trove, exclusive of the yearly diaries, amounts to about twenty thousand folios spanning the years of Gore-Browne's youth and adolescence, his army career, and forty-seven years in Zambia. The major portion of the whole consists of long weekly or twice-weekly (during World War I, daily) letters exchanged between Gore-Browne and Dame Ethel Locke-King, his aunt. These are no ordinary letters. More epistles, they are reflective, extended, and well-crafted in a style that has sadly gone out of favor. A great many of the total deserve publication as chronicles of pioneering times past or political moments preserved. As a body they express a relationship between individuals and a feeling for events and people which this biography can but strive to recapture.

Gore-Browne's life was so enmeshed in the fabric of Northern Rhodesia and Zambia that official correspondence and records now in the archives of the Republic of Zambia, Rhodesia, and Kenya, and in the British Public Record Office, have valuably supplemented the exchanges between aunt and nephew, Gore-Browne and Lady Gore-Browne, Gore-Browne and innumerable local and imperial officials and citizens, the records of the Shiwa Ngandu estate, Gore-Browne's diaries and jotting books, and the memories of persons and relatives who knew or worked with Gore-Browne during the phases of his several careers.

My wife and I saw Gore-Browne a number of times in Africa and the United States during the last eight years of his life, and corresponded with him throughout a critical period in all our lives when Northern Rhodesia was being transformed agonizingly into Zambia. This prolonged contact nurtured my respect and admiration for a towering contributor to a modern Africa. Gore-Browne wanted me to write about him, but because of our mutual insistence upon objectivity and candor—on "the warts and all"—this is no hagiography. It is the life of a man who rose to the challenge of his surroundings and his era, and realized all of his gifts for the benefit of an adopted people. Many great men live too early or too late to capitalize upon their inherent abilities. Gore-Browne was in tune with his times. Had there been more like him who were responsive to its rapid rhythms, the shift from colonial to indigenous rule might have been more routine than traumatic.

Many of Gore-Browne's relatives, friends, colleagues, and acquaintances provided me with helpful reminiscences, ideas, and suggestions. I am particularly grateful for the opportunity to interview Ronald Bush, Andrew Cohen, Lt. Col. H. P. McC. Glover, Robert and Margaret Gore-Browne, Sapphire Gore-Browne Hanford, John Harvey, Rowland Hudson, President Kenneth Kaunda, Cyril Pearson, Audrey I. Richards, and, on several occasions, Lady Gore-Browne. A number, especially Professor J. O. Bailey, Maj. Victor Delaforce, Nadine Gordimer, Elspeth Huxley, Arthur Creech Jones, the Hon. Justice Sir Austin Jones, Brig. Gen. E. H. Kelly,the Dowager Countess of Lovelace, Violet Vincent Monro, Maj. Gen. R. H. Studdert, and Sir Roy Welensky kindly corresponded with me at length about Gore-Browne. Patricia Norton generously lent me a number of Gore-Browne's letters.

I gratefully acknowledge permission to quote Thomas Hardy's "Lorna the Second" from his *Collected Poems* (Copyright 1928 by Florence Hardy and Sydney E. Cockerell, renewed in 1956 by Lloyds Bank Ltd.). The trustees of the Hardy Estate and Macmillan London and Basingstoke gave permission for the British Commonwealth, and Macmillan Publishing Co. Inc., of New York gave permission for the United States.

Lady Gore-Browne read and commented upon an earlier, longer version of this book. Her criticisms, and those of Audrey I. Richards and Peter Stansky, were of major importance. I am particularly grateful, too, for the research assistance of Nancy Seasholes, who' came to know the Gore-Browne story, and his letters, in intimate detail. Jane Tatlock valiantly transcribed the laconically-taped versions of the Gore-Browne diaries; Evalyn Seidman typed many of the chapters, and Donna Louise Rogers assisted mightily in the final transformation of a typescript into a book. A timely grant from the American Philosophical Society permitted some of the Gore-Browne materials to be recorded permanently. Without the advice of Raya Dreben, much of this effort would have been wasted. Jeffrey Butler supplied some important ideas. Denis and Oenone Acheson and Trevor and Carol Coombe were there when problems arose and provided the kind of sorely-needed support which is so often lacking. All, in their individual ways, contributed significantly to this biography. The debt of gratitude is large, and the list of particulars long.

No one, however, was more involved with the biography in all of its stages than Joanna H. Rotberg. From Cambridge and Chocorua to Shiwa Ngandu, Chisamba, Lusaka, Archway, and Beaulieu the quest for the real Gore-Browne has been shared. This especially is her book.

R. I. R.
4 February 1976

I

"The Spring of Life"

STEWART GORE-BROWNE was born in the spring of 1883, an ordinary Victorian year. The sun of Britain was at its imperial zenith. Her soldiers had won victories in Afghanistan and were proceeding to consolidate their hold on Egypt. In tropical Africa, where the scramble for colonial territory had already begun in undeclared earnest (and from which exertions Gore-Browne was later to benefit), officers and local levies were forcibly extending the Queen's writ to regions as removed from each other as the hinterlands of the Gold Coast and Lagos and the Shire Highlands region of Malawi. The Mahdi was seriously weakening the hold of the Egyptian Khedives and their British advisors in the Sudan, and the Germans were unexpectedly establishing outposts in Kamerun, Togo, and Southwest Africa. Cecil Rhodes had begun to gain control of the world's greatest diamond mines and had entered the parliament of the Cape Colony. Joseph Thomson was in the throes of his epic journey across Masailand. Zambia had been entered tentatively by missionaries, although the area around Gore-Browne's future home at Shiwa Ngandu was still firmly controlled—as it had been for many decades—by the chiefs of the powerful Bemba nation. In the Americas, too, British merchants were active, advancing money to build railways and purchase the products of an expanding frontier. At home William Gladstone governed at the head of a strong Liberal government. A serious recession was beginning and landowners and industrialists long accustomed to having their own way were starting to experience the first major constraints of legislation. A mere five weeks before Gore-Browne's birth a Liberal fired the opening salvo in the electoral battles which, as the century wore on, increasingly employed the ammunition of class warfare. Conservatives were labelled representatives of a class which neither toiled nor spun, and took money from real workers. A new Britain was slowly emerging.

The Gore Brownes were thoroughly representative of and integrated with that thin layer of elite energy which provided the main outward thrust of Victorianism and gave to it an image of responsi-

1

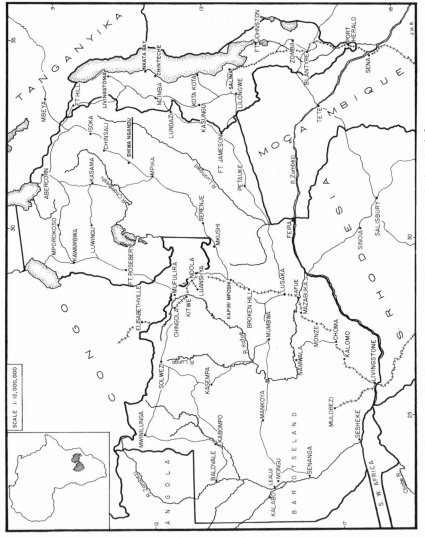

MAP 1. Colonial Zambia: Major places and physical features.

bility, accomplishment, order, and noble morality. The Brownes (Gore was a middle name incorporated by Stewart's branch into the surname only from about the 1850s, and joined indissolubly by a hyphen to the Browne only in the twentieth century; Stewart hyphenated or did without according to whim, but mostly hyphenated) were of Anglo-Irish background, and on little evidence claimed descent from Sir Anthony Browne, one of the closest associates of Henry VIII. In the eighteenth century this branch of the Brownes had an estate in Co. Wicklow presided over by John Browne, an artillery officer who had fought under the Duke of Marlborough at Blenheim. His son Thomas, Stewart's great-great-grandfather, lived in Dublin and was a merchant and an architect of great energy. He gained much worldly success and had four sons. Gore (1763–1843) became an officer, gaining victory and fame in the West Indies, in Uruguay, in Holland during the Napoleonic wars, and later in Afghanistan, before becoming successively governor of Plymouth and general of the 44th Regiment. Thomas joined the navy and rose through the ranks to become a vice-admiral. William became a barrister. Robert Gore (b. 1754) was Stewart's great-grandfather. A well-to-do military officer like the first two of his brothers, he served and then profited by the attentions of the Marquis of Buckingham, Lord Lieutenant of Ireland. When Buckingham left Ireland for England, Robert followed, holding various offices of distinction including the deputy lieutenancy of Buckinghamshire. He also served as colonel of the county militia and justice of the peace, and was described as a man of "ample means, fine presence, and courtly manners, much liked and respected in those parts."[1] He died in 1836, leaving five children, Louisa, Maria, Captain John William Barrington, Edward Harold, and Stewart's grandfather, Thomas Gore Browne (1807–1887). The most distinguished was Edward Harold (1811–1891). After Eton College and Emmanuel College, Cambridge, where he won several prizes and was elected into a fellowship and became senior tutor, Edward Harold joined the Anglican church and was ordained into the priesthood in 1837. In 1854, after writing a definitive treatise on the Thirty-Nine Articles of Anglican faith, he was appointed Norrisian professor of divinity at Cambridge.[2] Ten years later, after publishing somewhat conservative theological sermons and gaining public attention, he was offered the bishopric of Ely. In 1873, after Samuel Wilberforce's death, Gladstone gave him the see of Winchester.

1. G. W. Kitchin, *Edward Harold Browne, D. D. Bishop of Winchester* (London, 1895), 4.

2. *An Exposition of the Thirty-Nine Articles* (Cambridge, 1850; London, 1853), 2v.

For Stewart, grandfather Thomas proved a source of emulation. Born in 1807 at the family seat near Aylesbury to Robert and Sarah Dorothea Steward, the daughter of a Dorsetshire politician (from Melcombe), Thomas automatically entered the governing class with the advantages of the day, including money. At 16 he became an ensign in the 44th Foot Regiment, soon transferring to the 28th Foot Regiment in which he became a lieutenant in 1826 and a captain in 1829. From 1832 to 1835 he served as an aide-de-camp to Lord Nugent, British High Commissioner in the Ionian Islands. Becoming a major, he transferred into the 41st Foot Regiment in 1836 and soon saw action and command during the Afghan War of 1842. Guarding the retreat to India, he distinguished himself in suitably martial ways and was promoted to Brevet Lieutenant Colonel, being awarded the insignia of Commander of the Bath. After service with the 21st Regiment and another promotion to become a full lieutenant colonel, in 1851 he retired on half-pay in order to spend three years as governor of St. Helena. There he extended the water supply system of Napoleon's arid exile and proved himself sufficiently to obtain the significant colonial governorship of New Zealand.[3] On the way, during a period of leave in Britain, the bald governor with the bristly mustache married Harriet Campbell of Craigie, Ayrshire. The daughter of the advocate James Campbell (an heir to a family fortune made in India) she seemed "a woman out of a Book of Beauty . . . [with] ample white muslin flounces and fine long dark tresses."[4] She was then twenty-five, a full twenty-two years younger than the governor.

Thomas and Harriet Gore Browne arrived in New Zealand in 1855, when white immigrants had begun to outnumber the indigenous Maori and local responsible government by settlers had been tentatively introduced. The incipient dominion's colonial and settler institutions were moving into conflict, the 1853 constitution had included no provisions for the representation of the Maori, and race relations between light and dark were perceptibly worsening. Land was at issue: The settlers coveted Maori-owned land; most Maori were loath to sell, and few possessed the privilege of selling communally-owned territory. Governor Browne was the weak fulcrum balancing these dangerously opposed interests. On the one hand, he sought to strengthen the colonial, imperial interest against settler importunities. On the other hand, he and his gifted young wife were, like so many later British governors in colonial Africa, comfortable at the center of immigrant society. Gregarious by na-

---

3. Philip Gosse, *St. Helena, 1502–1938* (London, 1938), 321.
4. Journal of C. W. and Emily E. Richmond, 12 April 1856, Auckland, in Guy H. Scholefield (ed.), *The Richmond-Atkinson Papers* (Wellington, 1960), I, 210.

ture, Gore Browne found friends and conviviality among the settlers. "He was the centre of the social life of the capital, popular with crowds, regular at church. He loved his musical evenings in Government House and the society of gentlemen politicians."[5] Harriet Gore Browne was even more popular and, it seems, equally dynamic and influential. She had the instincts of a natural politician. "Remarkably energetic and clever, without being in the least strong minded," a contemporary wrote, she is "on the contrary very feminine and lady-like. She really governs the country as much as the Governor, for he does nothing and writes nothing without consulting her first . . . She seems to know and remember every-body, having something to say suited to the person and adapted to draw out his or her peculiar gift; perhaps this tact is her most re-markable quality and fits her for the post so well. . . . I have seldom seen a woman I could more respect and admire; one could soon love her too I have no doubt."[6] When Stewart Gore-Browne visited New Zealand in 1950, he found that this appreciation of his grand-parents was still strong. "I won't pretend," he wrote afterwards to the Prime Minister of New Zealand, "that I was not deeply gratified to find myself specially welcomed as 'Our Governor's grandson', nearly a hundred years after he had left . . . I did not know such hospitality could exist anywhere."[7]

The Maori, however, would have remembered Thomas Gore Browne with far less affection. Although he wanted his policies to be humanitarian, and was mindful of the underlying conflict be-tween whites and Maori, he tended to underestimate the depth of indigenous grievance and the extent of their determination never again to be wronged without protest. Gore Browne neglected and misunderstood Maori interests, failed ever to learn their language, and too indecisively tried to resolve opposing Maori, settler, and imperial conflicts.[8]

Unfortunately, the overweening attitudes of the local whites and their insatiable hunger for land, together with the stubborn refusal of Wiremu Kingi and his Maori followers to forfeit their own lands in Taranaki (near New Plymouth), led in 1860 to the first of a decade of Maori wars which only a more astute governor could have pre-vented. Perceiving affronts and challenges where none were in-

5. Keith Sinclair, *A History of New Zealand* (Harmondsworth, 1959), 116–117.

6. June Maria Atkinson to Margaret Taylor, 3 October 1960, in Scholefield, *Papers,* I, 641–642.

7. Gore-Browne to S. G. Holland, P.C. 16 February 1951.

8. Keith Sinclair, *The Origins of the Maori Wars* (Wellington, 1957), 142, 203. For a more vitriolic opinion of the governor, see Alfred Saunders, *History of New Zealand* (Christchurch, 1896), I, 319–320, 334–343.

tended, Gore Browne flung down the gauntlet intemperately. His "show of force" became a battle which unnecessarily embroiled an entire colony and led, with much loss on both sides, to the further subjugation of the Maori to immigrant importunities. Although Stewart Gore-Browne grew up appreciating and seeking to emulate a grandfather known within the family for his "enlightened" attitudes toward subject races, the governor bumbled more and achieved less than even he then understood. "In a situation of great stress, which called for energy, impartiality, and discernment," Thomas Gore Browne "possessed none of the requisite qualities."[9]

After leaving New Zealand, Colonel Gore Browne became governor of Tasmania, then an infant Antipodean outpost, where he exercised his gift for personal relations from late 1861 to 1868, being awarded a long overdue knighthood in 1869. Aside from a subsequent year (1870–71) as governor of Bermuda, Sir Thomas Gore Browne and his six children lived thereafter for the most part in London, spending parts of their summers and autumns at Craigie reliving the nostalgia of empire. Stewart's father, Francis Gore Browne, was the fourth born. Mabyl had been followed by Harold C. Gore Browne (1856–1938), who joined the King's Royal Rifles and saw action in India before becoming a colonel and enduring both the siege and the defence of Ladysmith during the Anglo-Boer War. Wilfred Gore Browne (1858–1928) went to Harrow like his brother, spent two years in the army, but then went up to Trinity College, Cambridge, where he took his degree in 1881. Ordained the next year, he accepted Anglican curacies in the north of England before being appointed rector of Pretoria in 1902. He became dean and then, in 1912, was consecrated the first Bishop of Kimberley and Kuruman, a diocese of 275,000 square miles which included most of what is now Botswana. Mabyl, who never married, lived with him. Francis was born in 1860, being followed by Godfrey Gore Browne, (1863–1900), who joined the Royal Navy at 12 and became a commander. Then there was Ethel, born in 1864, with whom Stewart was to develop a strong and special relationship of love.

Sir Thomas lived to see Francis do well at Harrow and New College, Oxford, to be called to the Bar from the Inner Temple, and to marry Helenor, daughter of John Archibald Shaw-Stewart, second son of the sixth Baronet Shaw-Stewart and lineal descendant of Sir John Stewart, illegitimate son of Robert III of Scotland, and Helena Margaret Angela, only daughter of Boyd Alexander of Bal-

9. Sinclair, *History,* 117. See also Alan Ward, *A Show of Justice: Racial "Amalgamation" in Nineteenth Century New Zealand* (Toronto, 1973), 104, 119, 123–124.

lochmyle. Helenor's father was deputy-lieutenant and justice of the peace of Renfrewshire. Helena was 24 and Francis (known as Frank) 22 when they married. Both had private means, but insufficient to maintain their accustomed standards of living without Francis doing well at the Bar. Frank was serious and scholarly about his work, even after Sir Thomas died in 1887, shortly before Stewart's fourth birthday, and financial resources became available.

When he learned of his grandfather's death, Stewart, the putative heir to the family name, responded quietly. "We must get gamme a new Husband."[10] Gamme was grandmy, alias Lady Harriet (d. 1906) and, as Stewart grew older and more estranged from his mother, so he turned more and more to her (his maternal grand-mother having died before his own birth), and to Aunt Ethel, for support and reassurance. But at first his young life went well. A healthy redhead, he was well looked after by a nurse and was doted upon by his many relatives—the Campbells, the Shaw-Stewarts, and the other Brownes and Gore Brownes. Sapphire Helenor, his sister, was born in 1887, but her arrival apparently caused no per-ceptible or lasting dislike. Only the arrival of Robert Francis, a brother, in 1893, his incessant feelings of alienation from his mother, his father's long hours and frequent absences from home because of important cases, and being sent away to boarding school, upset the even tenor of Stewart's childhood.

For the likes of her first-born, Helenor Gore Browne was too acidic about others and overly demanding of him. She cared little for matters of the spirit—for the mysteries of the church and the delights of the country—which early attracted Stewart. She fussed much, and complained, and was frequently "inconvenienced." For her elder son, at least, she lacked compassion. They were attuned to different beacons from the earliest periods of nurturance; whether or not she resented him unconsciously, or was somehow displeased by his appearance, manner, or habits, to him her antipathy seemed plain. The earliest evidence of his feelings are boyish letters penned on ruled notepaper to his Aunt Ethel. He was about eight at the time, and made it perfectly clear—in a style perpetuated for the remainder of his life—that his mother was incapable of giving to him, that Aunt Ethel did, and that they must carry on a clandestine correspondence lest his mother become horribly jealous. "If you answer this," one letter reads, "please inclose it in a letter to Grandmy as if it arrived alone Mother would see it . . ." In a later letter he told her of his love: "I do *so so so* love you. You are *so* kind to me. I cannot tell you how I love you. I shudder to think of that

10. Helenor to Frank Gore Browne, 18 April 1887.

horrid London. If you have time I should like a private interview of
a few minutes. Your *very very very very very* loving and *extremely*
affectionate dog."[11]

For the rest of his life Stewart preferred going to Ethel rather than
his mother during school holidays—and periods of leave from the
army, or Africa. Brooklands, the house and almost perpetual social
scene in Weybridge presided over by Ethel and her husband, Hugh
Fortescue Locke-King (they married in 1884), was more congenial
to him than the Gore Browne houses in London, in Stroud,
Gloucestershire, or near Woking, in Surrey.

The Locke-Kings were interested in him as a person, and in what
concerned him. Like Stewart, his uncle was a man of common
sense, practicality, and generosity. Far more than Stewart, however, he had an ability to work with his hands, and to contrive
practical solutions to mechanical and structural problems. A grandson of the seventh Lord King and a nephew of the first Earl of
Lovelace, he had means, and used them to support his own inven-
tions and innovations. His father, Peter John Locke-King, was for
many years member of parliament for East Surrey. Born in 1848,
Hugh was called to the Bar from Lincoln's Inn in 1873. Twelve
years later both his father and elder brother died, and he inherited
Brooklands, the family estate on the River Wey. In addition to
serving as a magistrate for Surrey and Sussex, he travelled widely in
Europe and the Middle East, building and owning the Mena House
Hotel near the Giza pyramids in Egypt, and observing local practices wherever he visited. At home, after initially farming the vast
estate, he felled the pine trees at Brooklands to lay out the New
Zealand golf course, one of southern England's finest. He was remembered primarily for being among the earliest promoters of
automobiles in Britain, and the earliest to sponsor racing as a means
of encouraging improvements in automobile performance.

Ethel was seventeen years younger than her husband. Her
mother's daughter, she had a warm briskness, a strong ambition, a
robust faith in her own capabilities (which were great), a feeling
(which she and Stewart shared) for the romance of life, a
concern—which was very Victorian—for the "big" things; firmly
rooted, if conventional, convictions and ideals; and an infectious
gaiety. A witty story teller and a superb hostess, she ran what—had
she been interested in ideas and things of the mind, rather than
doers, and had she not been so caught up with the idle rich—would
have been called a salon. Ethel, attractive, prepossessing and, in later

11. Stewart Gore-Browne to Ethel Locke-King, 7 March and 3 May 1891. A
cartoon appended to the back of the letter indicated Stewart's willingness to slay
dragons for his aunt.

life, "formidable" in the manner of a *grande dame,* also had maternal and possessive streaks. She cared for and cosseted Hugh, who was tubercular, if active, until his death, was an official of the local county chapter of the British Red Cross, and found, or created (as did Hugh), a son in Stewart.

Ethel was Frank's favorite sibling, and Stewart's mother may have felt—justifiably—that she had unfairly to compete with Ethel and her winning ways both for Frank and, later, for Stewart. Yet there is no evidence that Frank and Helenor were otherwise than thoroughly devoted to each other, and to their children in their own ways. Frank was very supportive of Stewart as a boy and a man, and had a quiet pride in his youthful accomplishments. But whereas Helenor betrayed her ambivalence about her son by always imagining the worst, and worrying interminably about his health (yet keeping him away from home—for fear of infecting Sapphire and Robert—when he came down at school with measles and scarlet fever), Frank was steady, sure, kind, and strong in the manner of the best fathers, but always distant and involved in his growing legal practice. Stewart grew up respecting his father, but gaining no more than a standard filial affection. "Father," Stewart later remembered, "I think of as nearly always busy or tired."[12] It is hard to discover the extent to which Frank ever involved himself with Stewart during infancy and adolescence. There were always nurses and governesses, cases in court, and a trip to South Africa in 1889–90 to settle questions concerning the Transvaal debt. Uninterrupted holidays or weekends, with his own family only, were rare. Then, too, Stewart was no ordinary boy. He was a romantic, not really an intellect, wore glasses, disliked sports because he wasn't very good at them, and had little feeling for his father's professional life.

Stewart could later claim no wretchedly unhappy adolescence. Yet he felt that it had been "purposeless," and had lacked the warmth and the richness of the comparable periods in the early lives of his sister and brother. He always regretted that there had been a want of closeness between his parents, and particularly his father, and himself. He felt that his mother neglected him in favor of Robert. Even before Robert's birth, "Mother . . . all the time [was] finding fault & criticising & keeping me in a narrow, dull, groove."[13] The ultimate betrayal in his young life, however, came immediately after his ninth birthday when he was sent off to the Wixenford boarding preparatory school at Wokingham. E. P. Arnold, the headmaster, ran a traditional school for upper-class boys. He and the masters instilled the fundamentals of Greek and Latin,

12. Gore–Browne to Ethel Locke–King, 13 August 1912.
13. Gore–Browne to Ethel Locke–King, 13 August 1912.

taught some mathematics and history, and a little English, and built character in the usual athletic and bullying ways. From the first, Stewart was naturally unhappy at being thrust into a strange, rather forbidding environment. His parents, playing their roles without any intentional unkindness, urged him to buck up, to do his duty, and, essentially, to keep a stiff upper lip. "I am very sorry to hear," his father wrote, "that you are not feeling happy, but you must be plucky and try not to mind . . . I was so sorry not to come with you last Saturday but I was very busy and had to stay in Chambers . . . " And his mother urged him to "take comfort in the thought that you will gradually get happier. Try to take an interest in your lessons and in your play and then you will forget yourself. Remember . . . Nelson's . . . 'England expects every man to do his duty.' Now it is your duty to try to be brave. You have been a good boy at home and we are all sorry to lose you but you will now be a good boy at school and we shall all be so happy when we see you again in the holidays. I cannot go to see you both on Wednesday and Saturday."[14]

Gore-Browne felt that Wixenford "broke" rather than built character. "We weren't allowed out of a master's sight for fear we should get into mischief, we were never allowed to make a noise or laugh, it was called "Fooling" and made a punishable offence, we were taught to lie and to tell tales about each other, and . . . the most rigorous 'decency', bathing-drawers for boys of ten, was an essential part of the training."[15] In later life, Gore-Browne could remember nothing redeeming about the school where he was "prepared" for life.

Yet, academically, he performed unexpectedly well. As Stewart reported, his Latin prose gave his tutor "apoplectic fits," but he was doing the irregular verbs in Greek and reading from Xenophon's *Anabasis.* His father commented appropriately, but woodenly, about every report. The tone of each must have reassured without bolstering the ego of young Stewart, and nothing was ever sufficient or good in itself. Like most parents, his father seemingly withheld full approval, or any approval without strings. The carrot of the farthest conventional middle-class future always dangled. And Stewart sometimes tired of pursuit. "If you keep on steadily doing well . . . " Frank wrote to his son, "you will be a successful man in life for I know you have mastered some work which you found difficult and did not much like. You will have to earn your own living someday so it is very important you should know how

14. Father to Stewart, 17 May 1892; Mother to Stewart, 16 May 1892.
15. Gore-Browne to Ethel Locke-King, 13 August 1912.

to stick to work whether it is pleasant or not."[16] There were few letters from his father, either at this period or later in life, which did not contain a similar homily—all of which Stewart seems to have taken with good grace, and only mild exasperation.

In 1897, like his father before him, Stewart passed into Harrow. In common with the other leading public schools of its day, Harrow, under the expansionist leadership of the Reverend J. E. C. Welldon, emphasized a severely classical education, the molding of character by adversity, fagging, bullying, and games, loyalty to imperial Britain and the Queen, and the glories of the Church—not necessarily in that order. School was where boys blossomed, if they could overcome their loneliness and shyness, where they came finally to discriminate between various status levels, and to mix only with their own kind. They learned how to lead, or how to follow, and gained experience in (and were socialized into) the social and political affectations of the British ruling classes. As his father wrote early in Stewart's first year at Harrow, "I am afraid you are feeling rather lonely, but you will get over that a bit as you get friendly with more boys. Do not go and meditate in the Church Yard. Byron did . . . but you are not a poet . . . [Harrow] is one step more towards the full responsibility of life."[17] With these admonitions in mind, Stewart studied more Latin and Greek. He was said to be deficient in an understanding of the rules for gender, "and things of that kind," but "shewed promise enough in the more important work of translation and style."[18] He was tutored in history, did some mathematics, but little science, and no modern literature. (In those days, the six hundred Harrow students had to choose between science and history and French and mathematics. No one taught German, which Gore-Browne particularly wished to learn.) He participated in the debating society, avoided sports as much as possible (but avidly watched cricket), won a prize for music, and moved painfully through the lower into the upper school.

Most of the time at Harrow Gore-Browne was desperately unhappy. Many years later, he vividly remembered crossing the road to avoid meeting a crowd of schoolmates, fearing being kicked for fun each time he went up to classes on the hill, and counting the quarters desperately in the hope games of football would end. "I'll never forget my very first Sunday afternoon," he wrote long afterwards, "Hamilton Grace . . . Lyon who made my life miserable for

16. Father to Stewart, 18 June 1893.
17. Father to Stewart, 5 March 1897. For Harrow, see E. A. Laborde, *Harrow School: Yesterday and Today* (London, 1948), 60–62.
18. F. Rhys Jones to Gore-Browne (n. d., but about 1897–98).

3 years . . . and R. G. Clarke . . . came into my room & ragged me, much as a dentist with that whirly thing could if he would, in a way you'd hardly credit."[19] Gore-Browne was painfully shy, near-sighted, clumsy at games, and—at least for a time—the complete "worm." Even as late as 1914 he was still mortified and ashamed to be reminded of those grueling agonies of youth.

Nevertheless, worm or no, Gore-Browne was slowly developing a capacity for leadership. Toward the end of his Harrow experience, he became the center of a small but devoted claque of friends. For each of their number, he had juvenile charisma as well as an important sense of purpose and social maturity. He also looked physically much older than his years and had developed the kinds of aesthetic sensibilities (or overtones) which pleased similarly minded schoolmates. Among his favorites were several who, despite their very different careers, were to remain life-long friends and regular correspondents. Foremost was Cyril Pearson, as playful as Gore-Browne, fuller of mischief, and a Harrow prefect; he became an Anglican missionary in India, serving mostly in Bengal, and was finally appointed Dean of Calcutta cathedral. J. H. "Jack" Prioleau, with whom Gore-Browne carried on an intense correspondence in code until World War I, eventually became a journalist in Egypt and Britain. With others, they clowned together and were occasionally serious, jointly put out one issue (seven hundred copies sold) of a scurrilous "independent" school magazine called "The Toad beneath the Harrow," and shared a not unusual interest in matters pruriently male. Gore-Browne, Prioleau, and Pearson wrote letters of intimacy to each other for a decade or more after leaving Harrow. Pearson was the more effusive and open, although Gore-Browne appears from Pearson's replies (his letters to Pearson do not survive) to have reciprocated warmly. After Harrow, Pearson went up to Balliol College, Oxford, and continued to ogle boys old and young. "All last term," he wrote, "I was enamoured of a young Scotchman, something of a river blood, who is more beautifully made than anyone I have ever seen . . ."[20]

The serious business of educating themselves also merited occasional attention. On an ordinary day in summer term, when

19. Gore-Browne to Ethel Locke-King, 30 April 1914. Stephen Tallents was an exact contemporary of Gore-Browne. He, too, hated games and longed for the compulsory football competitions to end. He was better at his books than Gore-Browne, however, winning English and other prizes. Yet after a distinguished career in the civil service (and a knighthood) he recalled Harrow with affection as a place which emphasized sports more than learning, and all-around character building most of all. See his *Man and Boy* (London, 1943), 98–116. Gore-Browne pronounced the account of Harrow very true, and similar to his own experience.

20. Cyril Pearson to Gore-Browne, 31 July 1903.

Stewart was in the lower sixth form, he was called at 6:45 A.M. by a "funny" Irish footman, rushed downstairs and had a cold "tosh," ran a third of a mile up to the school, and did Latin and Greek construction (Sophocles' *Electra,* as a start), the first school lasting from 7:30 to 8:45. Then he went back to his rooms to have breakfast with Pearson—"a very good sort"—and . . . [Young] Coward, an "awful little ass." The rest of the day was spent with Roman history or Latin prose, music lessons on the piano, lunch in hall with Frank Marshall, the "slack" housemaster and a former tutor of his uncles, trigonometry, some English poetry, French, tea, Italian drill on the cricket pitch, followed by study hall, supper, and prayers. In July, 1899, he was examined over an eight day period in Euclidean geometry, Greek poetry, Latin prose, English composition, Greek prose, Sophocles, *Galatians,* algebra, Livy, trigonometry, Roman history, Horace, Euripides, Ovid, Plato, and Cicero. For his free-form composition he wrote a paper on "civilisation" after a thorough reading of all of Scott's Waverly novels. When the results were announced at the end of the month, Gore-Browne was ninth in the second sixth form and twenty-ninth in both sixth forms combined. "So," he prayed in his diary, "I ought to get a remove next term," which he did—into the upper sixth.

During the long summer holidays, Gore-Browne amused himself in the company of women as well as men belonging to his spreading, but mostly family-oriented, social nucleus. In 1899, for example, he began a July retreat by taking Muriel Campbell, his "mightily pretty" cousin, to Lords for the Harrow/Eton match, gaining entrance, according to his diary, with "last year's ticket." That same weekend, he saw *H. M. S. Pinafore,* a "very good comic opera," and *Trial by Jury,* ate innumerable cherries in the garden at Brooklands, rowed on the Wey, bicycled twenty or thirty miles on some days, several times from Weybridge to central London, took Uncle Goff's gun and learned to shoot rabbits—with intermittent success, played hilarious bicycle polo on the grounds of Brooklands and, constantly, fives on the billiard table (it was, Gore-Browne confided, a good game but bad for the table and hardening on the hand).[21] This was the summer that he smoked his first cigar ("I smoked it all and was not sick . . . though I did not feel quite happy some time afterwards"), and was very exercised over the wretched way in which the French were treating Alfred Dreyfus (who was

21. There is a vignette of social history in bicycle polo, but Gore-Browne's description defies comprehension. "The game consists of making a strike as you run through the goal post, a tennis ball with a walking stick, and then riding round the ground kicking a post with your stick on the way. If you can get round the ground before the other players and hit the ball between the goal posts, he scores one. Otherwise he's out."

being retried). Gore-Browne learned how to take and develop photographs, a skill of which he made good use in Africa. He played golf as often as possible with his father who, however, spent most of his own September vacation at Brooklands revising the standard treatise on company law. "Every morning after breakfast," the diary learned, Father "goes upstairs and writes his book, a beastly thing."[22] Meanwhile, the younger Gore-Browne read Charlotte Brönte to himself and Rudyard Kipling, "a grand writer [and] the only modern man with any go in him," to his aunt and uncle. He attended church regularly, dutifully noting and commenting upon the sermons with worldly-wise proficiency.

Motor cars became his particular thrill during this summer. Few could go faster than about twenty miles per hour on the flat, but sped down hill—"a glorious feeling . . . the very vibration makes it nicer." The highlight of that summer, however, was the period of weeks Gore-Browne spent in the Lake Country. It was on this trip that Gore-Browne saw country seats sufficiently sumptuous for him to wish ardently for land and a decent house of one's own. "Why didn't anyone ever leave me a place? I'm sure I'd manage it well and it would be ripping to own it and a little land to take a real interest in."[23]

Some of his school holidays were colored by a less welcome tinge. In London, especially at Christmas and Easter, his mother would send him out calling, to a museum or a gallery, or to a concert, usually with someone for whom he had no liking. All day long he was told how unsatisfactory he was, how much better Robert was, and that he was a liar. "I couldn't have a latchkey because I wasn't to be trusted out at nights as there were undesirable people about," were his mother's instructions. Unfortunately, he did not then really understand why he was forbidden to go out. "If I'd been told there [were] whores in the street . . . it wd. have put me on my honour not to have anything to do with them." But he was never allowed at this time to do things on his own. When he was nearly seventeen, two years before being commissioned in the army, the family nurse was given money to purchase a train ticket for him from Paddington to Torquay. He was sent out for walks

22. Diary, 12 September 1899. Francis Gore-Browne published six important texts on Company Law, but the one that bothered his son was the standard *Book on the Formation and Winding up of Joint Stock Companies,* which had originally been written by William Jordan, with Gore-Browne as a co-author, but which came out with Gore-Browne as principal author in 1902 (London). This was the twenty-fourth edition. It was in its thirty-fifth edition by Francis Gore-Browne's death. It was still being published in 1972. Gore-Browne took silk in 1902 and became a master of the Bench of the Inns of Court in 1911.

23. Diary, 31 August 1899.

with his baby brother and the nurse pushing a perambulator. "I did want to run wild a little . . . drive a horse, shoot off a gun now & then, but beyond being . . . eventually allowed to bicycle there was nothing out door that ever came my way." In whatever he found joy, his mother found harm. Neither of his parents could do more than confuse him about sex, an area about which he clearly needed information. When he was seventeen, a "dirty minded person" who "specialised in warning boys & young men of the dangers of sexual inversion" frightened him "horribly."[24]

Young Gore-Browne had already sought an appointment to the Royal Navy. Although he had not yet been abroad, and had not even crossed the English Channel, the fleet arm of Her Majesty's forces, with its aura of Nelsonian glamor and faraway places, and perhaps the tales of his Uncle Goff, had seemed his youthful calling. He would initially have trained at Harrow, with other naval cadets, so the attraction of the navy was not simply a release from school or a way of fleeing home. But, if premature, it was meant to be a serious career choice, and Gore-Browne was bitterly annoyed when a naval medical board said his poor eyesight rendered him unfit. (In fact, as his inability to withstand even the calmest channel crossing without becoming seasick later testified, the naval physicians unwittingly saved him from much agony and inconvenience.) Gore-Browne had also been considering the church as a career. The law held out no appeal, medicine was (as he and Pearson agreed) overcrowded, and to become a teacher was—somehow—insufficiently active. In any event, entering the professions entailed going up to Oxford; the atmosphere of that great university always attracted him, but the idea of further schooling held out no especial appeal, and training there, although it might have qualified him for the Indian Civil Service—one of his several possible career choices—would not otherwise have furthered his romantic desire to see the world and save the empire. A subsequent, self-deprecatory commentary by Pearson illuminated Gore-Browne's motives, and image of himself. "Can you honestly imagine me saving my country? . . . I think it will be safer to leave you to stamp round in the lime-light and bring back the golden age, while I sit in one of the back seats & join in the applause."[25]

These various ways of making his adult life meaningful, all of which merited and received serious (and mature) consideration, ultimately proved irrelevant. War supervened during Gore-Browne's final year at Harrow. The other choices were quickly subsumed in the consequent agitation and patriotic fervor, espe-

24. Gore-Browne to Ethel Locke-King, 13 August 1912.
25. Pearson to Gore-Browne, 18 May 1903.

cially in the school, and the sixth-former for whom a remove to the upper part of his class constituted a sufficiently worthy goal now bore the burdens of duty to Queen and country (Rhodes, Milner, and Chamberlain were never mentioned). "We had hardly been back a month [at Harrow] before the Boers sent their ridiculous and impertinent ultimatum and declared war on us," the schoolboy wrote. His Uncle Harold, commanding the first battalion of the 60th regiment of the King's Royal Rifles, was invested in Lady-smith, and every movement of General Sir Redvers Henry Buller to relieve the town, Field Marshal Lord Methuen's movement to-ward Mafeking, the British defeat at Magersfontein, and so on, were followed earnestly at Harrow. "Nobody who was not in En-gland at the time," Gore-Browne wrote after the event, can realize the tremendous excitement with which every bit of news true or untrue was received, [or] the keenness of all classes to volunteer for the front when disaster after disaster was announced.[26] Before the end of the first term of his final year, when it was clear that Britain had underestimated the capabilities of her Afrikaans-speaking op-ponents and that the war would drag on, Gore-Browne decided that he would seek admittance to the Royal Military Academy at Wool-wich ("the Shop"), the artillery training college then comparable in esteem to Sandhurst. "With that end in view," Gore-Browne ex-plained, "I went to . . . the occulist to find out whether my eyesight . . . was good enough. He said it would be the merest chance I did pass, but father said he thought I might try so I made arrangements to join the Army Class at Harrow . . . and to get some coaching in Chemistry, of which I knew absolutely noth-ing."[27]

For the remainder of his time at Harrow, Gore-Browne studied chemistry privately, usually in back rooms in Paddington, London—even getting "quite keen" about the subject. He con-tinued with his mathematics and his French, both subjects becom-ing more meaningful in view of his decision to try for Woolwich, and the usual Greek and Latin. Most of the time, he was preoccupied with preparations for his army examinations. Then he prepared to leave the folding beds of Harrow, perhaps, but not necessarily, for the last time. "I expect to go back," he wrote pessimistically, "either from having failed to pass my literary or else my medical exam."[28]

About his languages, however, he had fewer qualms. A few days after his exams, he dressed himself in a new dark green flannel suit and went up to London, to the offices of the Civil Service Commis-

26. Diary, 23 April 1901.
27. Diary, 23 April 1901.
28. Diary, 5 July 1900.

sioners, there to be tested in colloquial French. Here Gore-Browne's charm and ability to ingratiate himself were put to good use. "Ours was a very easy bit about Robespierre, given us by a very clear voiced old man with a white beard. Then we were sent in one by one for 10 minutes conversation. The other chaps said they could not understand what the old man said, but I managed fairly well. We bowed a lot to each other, he said he was enchanted to see me, I said I could not conceive how I had managed to live so long without knowing him, he said he felt sure my French was excellent and . . . expressed great surprise . . . [when I told him I had never been to France, but had learned everything from *Cyrano de Bergerac*]. Then I got on to Daudet, which was a mistake for the old man was himself a Provençal, and screamed Daudet c'est un traitre, so I shut up and talked about Harrow . . . Finally he said that he hoped my other subjects equalled my French (the old hypocrite) and regretted the necessity [of] having to cut short our interview . . . but still hoped we might meet unprofessionally."[29]

"Mother had telegraphed to Harrow to stop my coming home to Onslow Gardens so was not pleased to see me, particularly as the cook was ill, so we did not speak to each other till dinner time!"[30] On this rather jarring, but not atypical note, young Gore-Browne began his last free months before possibly taking on—in his eyes—the responsibilities of maturity. During this time of anxious waiting, Gore-Browne's life was actively idle and socially comfortable. He followed the inclinations of class and family in the manner born; they were to prove close to the core of his life for many years. He played croquet on the grounds of various large houses, bathed often and early in the Wey, ate innumerable family dinners, usually at Brooklands, and met a range of diverting people in the process.

In nearly all respects, however, it was a summer of appropriate frivolity. He was still young and his mind was constantly on his examinations. Finally, in August, the results arrived. He had done well in basic mathematics, English, English history, Latin, and French, and poorly in chemistry, freehand, and geography. But he passed. As the final hurdle, however, there was a medical probe, with a test of his eyesight. "If I fail tomorrow I don't much care what happens," he wrote. "I don't think," he remembered afterwards, "I've ever felt so bad. It was better when they told one to come upstairs into a big room with doctors and weighing things. First they made me pick out bits of coloured wool which I managed all right, and then came the eyes. There were four cards . . . and with my worst eye I could only manage the first two rows. The

29. Diary, 7 July 1900.
30. Diary, 5 July 1900.

doctor told me to sit down and compose myself and stood in front of me and took the other fellows. So I put on my glasses and learnt off the beginning letters of two of the cards. Then he took me again and gave me both the cards I had learnt! I could hardly believe I was through at last."[31]

His father was nearly as pleased as Stewart himself and Robert had decorated the gates at the Woking house with flags. "Its all," Stewart admitted, "too ripping for words," Before the month was over, he received a formal appointment as a gentleman cadet to Woolwich. His Harrow housemaster's congratulatory letter summed up the achievement neatly: "How did you bamboozle your med. examiner? It is really not good for you to get your own way in such impossible conditions . . . If you could know how often in the last two terms, when the leadership of the house has not been all that I could wish, I have consoled myself with the thought that I should have in you one by whom I should be understood, and whom I should understand—you would know how disappointed I am." Then, knowing Gore-Browne, he proffered prudent advice: "Keep your independence of mind in a profession where it is much wanted, keep your enterprise in striking out new lines for yourself, but remember that they must be followed up to their ends."[32]

Gore-Browne made the most of his two years at the Shop. He earnestly wanted to become a good gunnery officer, and paid close attention to the traditional drills and tactics taught at Woolwich as well as some of the newer ideas appreciated after the British defeats in South Africa. He learned how to command a battery, and found—it would later become his hallmark—that with a modicum of imagination and tact he could get on with and, at times, even inspire ordinary soldiers. He directed shooting at Shoeburyness and horse-drawn maneuvers at Okehampton and Amberley. He performed well in his classroom subjects, and particularly in military engineering and practical geometry, artillery fire, military topography, and electricity and magnetism. He faltered slightly in mathematics, but his general conduct was pronounced very good, and Maj. General R. A. Jelf, the Academy governor, recommended Gore-Browne for appointment to the Royal Field Artillery. He is, Jelf reported, "keen and painstaking, and will make a good officer."[33] Everyone seemed to like him, and Gore-Browne was excited to have made so many "pals." He had begun to play poker and roulette, and to win (to his father's horror) substantial sums. He drank a lot of champagne too, especially when he was with his

31. Diary, 11 August 1900.
32. Frank E. Marshall to Gore-Browne, 14 August 1900.
33. Official report, autumn 1901.

messmates. Gore-Browne discovered pleasantly that he was no longer considered a worm. "I was as popular as anyone in my term of 86 cadets & as well regarded," despite continued shyness and the perpetuation of what he later called sentiments priggishly religious. "I don't think," he told his aunt, "you can . . . realise . . . the change when one suddenly got self-respect."[34]

Learning to be a gentleman officer was not very arduous, and Gore-Browne was able to spend holidays and vacations—at Brooklands, in Woking, at Rowner Mills (Lady Harriet's estate near Billingshurst), at Newton Manor (the Falcon Steward estate on which coal had been discovered in Yorkshire), and at Craigie, the Campbell headquarters in Ayrshire—in the leisurely manner to which he had become accustomed.

He enjoyed visits to Oxford, to Pearson at Balliol and to Prioleau at Christ Church, and was particularly taken by its atmosphere of gentility and antiquity, and the unique flannel trousers and Norfolk jackets of Balliol, but he had consciously chosen a different way of readying himself for the demands of the twentieth century. "It is a strange life these men lead," he wrote of Oxford, "but awfully nice I should think. In most ways I feel years older than they are"—which spiritually he was.[35]

This was all a preparation for a kind of life. It was rushed, rather narrow, and not very intellectually or aesthetically oriented, but suited the man Gore-Browne then thought he was, and the kinds of humanitarian general service he hoped to perform, with the possibility, not as yet very clearly focused or articulated, of somehow doing good for Britain, the Empire, and the world. His military employment came in early 1902, when the fresh second lieutenant was posted to the 141st Battery at Kilkenny in Ireland. Later in the year, he accepted an exchange which transferred him to the 4th Battery, then in South Africa. In November, dressed in a new green service kit and a sun helmet, he boarded a train at Waterloo and went down to Southampton, there to board the S. S. Nubia, along with forty-nine other officers, a draft of constabulary, and several score of emigrants bound for South Africa. He had never before left Britain, and was wearied by the thought of seeing the last of "everyone" for many years. Yet, he was finally on his own, away from family and friends, bound for the closest possible theatre of conflict (though the Boer War had just ended). "The last two years have been very pleasant," he told himself, "the freedom of the Shop & all one's pals, house parties at Brooklands, Rowners, and Craigie, the weekends [in London] and . . . the hunting . . . but there's also

34. Gore-Browne to Ethel Locke-King, 30 April 1914.
35. Diary, 25 October 1902.

the feeling of having wasted one's time and not really done anything to deserve such a good time, and so I'm glad to be off for I think there's more chance."[36]

As an officer, he always sought "more scope"—more responsibility, more power, more freedom to create for good. In conditions of growing peace, however, young subalterns had little to do militarily. "O why wasn't I born a couple of years earlier, so that I could have seen and done [warlike] things myself, I suppose there never will be such a chance again," he moaned.[37]

At the Mooi River Remount Depot, in the hills of Natal, where the 4th Battery was stationed under a slack colonel, Gore-Browne, as the most junior subaltern, found that what little he had to do consisted of watching the men care for the battery's sickly horses. They watered them, grazed them, and did drills, but restoring discipline to men who suffered in peace time from being war heroes, and whose contact "with colonials . . . would have sapped the discipline of Cromwell's Ironsides," proved an unremitting task. (Gore-Browne's early view of "colonials" was scathing: when "you meet a perspiring & eminently respectable white man who looks as if he had stepped straight out from behind the counter of a haberdashery shop in Broadway Woking . . . he would probably tell you—doubtless correctly—that he is the backbone of the British Empire, but he does look so out of place and so incongruous."[38]) There was crime and drunkenness to contend with; Gore-Browne soon found himself "shoving" men into the guard room for one serious offence or another. "It's sickening work and then when the men are brought up the colonel won't punish them, so things go from bad to worse. Had a man falling out from exercising order the other morning to pick mushrooms."[39]

He had achieved oblivion, not "more chance." Although he tried unsuccessfully to play polo, hunted birds and rabbits, and got on well with the one or two fellow officers who appeared congenial, the weariness of Mooi River soon depressed him. So did South Africa, where everything was "mercenary & immoral."[40] He passed some of the time writing political essays for possible publication in England (none of this genre was, in fact, accepted), mused about the problems of "native labour" in South Africa—whites were too expensive, blacks too lazy, and yellow too dangerous—and began to wonder what he was doing in the army, in South Africa, and in life. At his period of deepest gloom, however, an opportunity to exercise command—and he was not yet twenty—occurred. A man

---

36. Diary, 15 November 1902.   37. Diary, 7 December 1902.
38. Diary, 16 December 1902.   39. Diary, 28 December 1902.
40. Diary, 31 March 1903.

in the 4th battery came down with scarlet fever and Gore-Browne was detailed to take the entire battery across the river, set up a quarantine cantonment, and wait. No one was allowed near: "The pleasure of the whole thing is that it is entirely my own command to do what I like with." He instituted physical drill parade at 7 A.M., gun drill at 9 A.M., and an afternoon parade. Soon he felt that the men had become "quite smart" and "changed out of all recognition."[41] His father, who, as a result of several publicized fraud cases, was becoming famous, urged him "to take every chance you get of doing something on your own account—and taking pieces, even if only small pieces of responsibility—so as not to rust."[42] This he had done, with the added joy and enhanced self-esteem of discovering that he could command, and easily and well. It was about this time, too, in the loneliness and pomp of the fever camp, that Gore-Browne began articulating—in letters to his friends in England— the romantic vision which he saw for his adult life. Like the heroes of G. W. Henty's many popular novels for boys, Gore-Browne hoped himself to discover and rule a new land in peace and equity. "Where," one of his skeptical correspondents replied, "will you find the vacant land? And assuming that you find it and have dispossessed the rulers, how long will you be allowed to hold it? . . . I cannot help thinking that your common fault is to evolve theories without looking into the practicality of details."[43]

For the balance of his military tour in Africa, Gore-Browne, successful with his fever camp, managed to avoid any but brief stretches back at Mooi River. Much of the time he spent attached to the Royal Engineers doing survey work in and around the farthest reaches of Natal. Everyone locally assumed that there might soon be renewed hostilities in South Africa, at least against Africans: Gore-Browne's assignments, some of which he contrived for himself, were to reconnoitre the least well-known country, taking trigonometric compass bearings, sketching, mapping, and generally providing intelligence sufficient to update or supersede existing cartographical representations. First he went to Pondoland, for more than a month, then beyond the headwaters of the Mooi and Bushman's Rivers and up into the ten thousand foot Drakensberg mountains on the Basutoland/Natal border, both times with no more than a pony and a black servant.[44] In the process, he began to

41. Diary, 31 March 1903.
42. Father to Gore-Browne, 13 March 1903.
43. Benskin (?) to Gore-Browne, 17 March 1903.
44. A slight, discursive account of a portion of this journey later appeared as "Notes on the Section of the Drakensberg Mountains from Giant's Castle to Cathkin Peak," *The Alpine Journal*, XXII (1905), 362–369. It was Gore-Browne's first published article.

appreciate Africans a little more, being particularly taken by "a splendid nearly naked Zulu with a long spear in his hand and a dash of red" who stepped out of the river "looking like a God."[45] He met some young white farmers who were doing well by working very hard; one told him, as a kind of *leitmotiv* for Gore-Browne's future, that if "you put your guts into your work you will do ten times what you could in England but that if you expect to have nothing to do but order black men about you won't succeed any more out here than at home."[46] Contrastingly, he encountered an old white seaman who had married an African, and emerged from "a wretched hovel . . . almost in rags with a dirty table knife stuck in his trousers. It gave you quite a shock to see him talking like a gentleman and to see decent books on his table . . . It was a pitiful sight"[47] which he was to remember in the African years to come.

The remainder of Gore-Browne's formative year overseas was spent readying the battery and himself (by trying to learn Hindi) for its expected transfer to India, avoiding the settler "flappers"—what he called "poodle faking"—and dances presided over by Sir Henry and Lady McCallum at Government House in Durban. Gore-Browne was keen on seeing the world, and looked forward with his usual enthusiasm, to India. He had as yet developed no great love for Africa. But all of these serene plans were abruptly altered on Christmas Eve. His horse balked at a jump and Gore-Browne fell on his head. He was delirious, delivering to the assembled company a half hour discourse in fluent French, a recitation in Latin which included some scraps of Horace (always his favorite), and the speeches of the Shop's elaborate "Public Day" ceremony. He took the role of battalion commander, lustily singing the right tunes for the band at the right places, and making the commander in chief's speech for him, "with a good many irregular comments thrown in."[48] After a period of hospitalization in Natal and the Cape Colony, Gore-Browne, feeling hardly the worse for his experience, was invalided home to England.

It was an ignominious way to leave his battery, but Gore-Browne was very keen to complete his dreary duty, and to return home to his friends and extended family, and also to the possibility of being offered more auspicious professional opportunities. "It was funny," he confided after at last reaching Britain, "to be civilly spoken to in a shop after South Africa where every man thinks he is as good as you."[49] At home, during a sick leave which he extended

45. Diary, 9 June 1903.
46. Diary, 24 June 1903.
47. Diary, 9 June 1903.
48. Gore-Browne to Father, 1 January 1904.
49. Diary, 12 February 1904.

for a full year, he returned to the idle social life of his late 'teens, hunted, went grouse shooting, ferreted, began endless confrontations with the dentists of London, went to Paris with family, renewed acquaintances with Prioleau, Pearson, and army "pals," saw more and more of Aunt Ethel, and, gratefully receiving many expensive presents and much hard cash, came of age in May.

With his new riches, he bought himself a single cylinder 8 h.p. Renault, soon nicknamed "Bird," and devoted the summer of 1904 almost exclusively to her care, feeding, and frequent resuscitation. Bird had no side doors, no windshield, and heavy brass acetylene lamps for illumination. One long trip in her took him through the lake district to Scotland, especially to Craigie and then on to Crawfurdland Castle in Kilmarnock, where he spent many happy hours with Violet Vincent, to whom he was soon familiarly and affectionately "Goat." In October he paid his first visit to Bingham's Melcombe, the imposing Dorset manor house of Reginald Bosworth Smith, his father's housemaster at Harrow, where Gore-Browne had also had him as a tutor.[50] In December, he began a month-long tour—his first of many—in Bird through France to the Riviera and north into Italy as far as the River Po, Turin, and Novara through snow and over icy roads, with frequent stops for mechanical repairs and the viewing of cathedrals. The total distance to and from Italy covered 1724 miles. "Probably," he wrote, "had a better time . . . than ever before."[51]

Gore-Browne was especially taken by Bingham's Melcombe. Although it had an atmosphere and a heritage which could never be recreated elsewhere, its essence lodged securely in Gore-Browne's memory and gave him much subsequent pleasure. The manor house lies in a sheltered cove on the southern side of the Purbeck

---

50. Reginald Bosworth Smith, the son of an Anglican canon, was born near Dorchester in 1839. He was head boy at the Marlborough School and matriculated at Corpus Christi College, Oxford. There he obtained a first-class degree in classics, becoming president of the Union and being elected into a fellowship at Trinity College, Oxford. Subsequently, he became an assistant master and later a house master at Harrow, where he taught from 1864 to 1902. He became an authority on natural history and ornithology, and made his name in the 1870s as an appreciator of the character of Muhammad and Islam. He published *Carthage and the Carthaginians* (London, 1878), and a massive, influential *Life of Lord Lawrence*, viceroy of India (London, 1883), in two volumes. It became a best-seller and went into seven editions. He meanwhile became an articulate and widely known pamphleteer and promoter of liberal causes. After Harrow, he became a magistrate for Dorset, a member of the county educational council, and vice-president of the Dorset Field Club. See J. J. Foster, *Wessex Worthies* (London, 1920), 86–88. For Bosworth Smith at Harrow, see C. H. P. Mayo, *Reminiscences of a Harrow Master* (London, 1928), 60–69; Tallents, *Man and Boy,* 108.

51. Diary, 13 January 1905.

Hills, ten miles distant from any town or railway station. In Gore-Browne's time, the house stood substantially as it would have appeared during the reign of Mary (1555–1558). A two-story dwelling of grey stone, it was entered past a gate house with walls nine feet thick. The chief wing of the house opened out onto a flagged courtyard—"a place of mullioned casements and quaint gables, where pigeons strut on the stone terrace or perch on the pinnacles above the great oriel window." Bosworth Smith himself described the house as neither grand nor grandiose. "It is simply restful and homelike; but the oriel projecting from the old hall, with its lofty gable, its weathercock . . . its mullioned windows, its delicate traceries, its graceful finials, half revealed and half concealed by Virginian creeper and topped by eagles ready for their flight, its massive and deeply chiselled coat of Bingham arms, all in warm Ham Hill masonry, is a very dream in stone, an ideal of Tudor domestic architecture."[52]

Not until May, when he joined the 10th Battery, Royal Horse Artillery, at Aldershot, was Gore-Browne returned to active duty. Emotionally, however, these early months of 1905 were among the most unsettling of his adult life. Almost for the first time, he looked seriously at a woman, warmed to her, and approached that state of transcendence which—had Gore-Browne then been the marrying kind—would have been described by the hackneyed "falling in love." Early in February he took a train down from London to Dorchester in order to attend a dance of the kind his mother staged once or twice a year in London for four or five hundred guests. He disliked the atmosphere of these large society balls, and was usually uncomfortable dancing. Why he deigned to attend is unclear, but he admired and respected his hosts, the Bosworth Smiths, and perhaps could hardly have refused an invitation from such kind friends of his family. "The ball," he wrote afterwards, was "neither better nor worse than most of its kind." However, he did dance once with Lorna, the Bosworth Smiths' eldest daughter. A year older than himself, she was small, frail, and possessed an incisive, whimsical charm of her very own. She was the prettiest girl there, he reported. After the dance the Bosworth Smiths and their large party of guests drove home to Bingham's Melcombe, obtained an "odd" meal in the kitchen at 5 A.M. and, as Gore-Browne recalled, "after filling hot water bottles for the ladies, to bed."[53]

52. Frederick Treves, *Highway and Byways in Dorset* (London, 1906), 102; Reginald Bosworth Smith, *Bird Life and Bird Lore* (London, 1905), 76. For the house and its history, see also Rose E. McCalmont (ed. C. R. B. Barratt), *Memoirs of the Binghams* (London, 1915), 26–40; John Hutchins (ed. Richard Gough and John Bowyer Nichols), *The History and Antiquities of the County of Dorset* (London, 1815; 2nd ed.) IV, 200–203.
53. Diary, 3 February 1905.

The days after the ball were a compound of Lorna, her friends, and a series of prominent visitors. Although rarely alone with Lorna, Gore-Browne was transfixed. They walked to the Dorchester Gap, through lonely, sparkling country, went on horseback to Milton Abbey, talked of car touring abroad, played the piano for one another, rode to the hounds, picked flowers near the fish pond, arranged books in the gatehouse prior to its occupation by the Thomas Hardys, and gradually came, it is difficult to ascertain precisely how well, to know each other's temper. There were too many diversions, and too many people, for complete absorption, however. Thomas Hardy, after all, had a certain *éclat,* and demanded appropriate attention even as a family friend. Gore-Browne thought him charming and Mrs. Hardy "awful." "He talked about his books quite naturally and most interestingly." He said that he wrote *Tess of the D'Urbervilles* "unconsciously." He reported that he still read Walter Scott with pleasure and that Browning had written too much. After dinner he regaled the company with droll Dorsetshire stories.

There was another set of significant visitors, too, Major and Mrs. Charles Sydney Goldman. A South African millionaire (1868–1958), he owned *The Outlook,* a sporting magazine, and was "dreadful to look at but very interesting." Agnes Mary Goldman, Gore-Browne noted, was the daughter of Arthur Wellesley, Viscount Peel, speaker of the House of Commons. She apparently liked Gore-Browne's manner and appearance, and his conversational ease, for she invited him many times thereafter to dinner in London.

That first long weekend stirred Gore-Browne. Yet he did not see Lorna again until mid-March, when they were both invited to a dinner and an amateur play rehearsal in London. Together with her sister Joan, they went down to Rowner Mills, and then to Cambridge, where Neville Bosworth Smith was sitting an examination at King's College. In the evening Gore-Browne drove the small party via Ware to London in the moonlight. Two days later he fetched Joan and Lorna from the Goldmans, where they had been having lunch, and took them calling on a variety of people. With Lorna he danced in the Chelsea town hall. That Sunday, he took her to early church in Billingshurst. Then they had breakfast on the river. Finally, after some drives to and from Rowner in the darkness, Gore-Browne returned her across country to Bingham's Melcombe.

The notations in Gore-Browne's diary are prosaic, and reveal little of the emotional charges which she undeniably exploded. Nothing of the sort ever quite moved him as much; no woman (except her own daughter) ever touched him and gave his head, as well as his heart, such serenity. Only Aunt Ethel and Lorna then knew how she affected him. A letter written in the penumbra of nostalgia captures, far more than his diary, or the memories of survivors, what those precious early weekends were for Gore-Browne. "She's all the spring of life to me," he recalled. "That first day in February on the downs behind Melcombe when we went after the hounds together in the warm, kindly, air, damp with rain, and with prim-roses everywhere & brown fields and hedges not yet awake. And then later in the year at Rowner she & I walked across the fields to early church, it was March, but it must have been an early year for I remember daffodils (yes & violets by the railings in front of the porch) and green everywhere in all the promise of spring; and then a day we spent together at Cambridge when I drove her (& Effie [Bosworth Smith Grogan] & that little idiot Joan) down through the Hertfordshire country . . . and the spring glory was beyond any words to describe, the willows behind the colleges on the backs & every kind of spring flower daffodils & bluebells in all their magnificence—and she & I sat in King's Chapel for a while; and the drive back was wonderful too, the long evening & the dusk, & the little car pulling in the fresh cool air as I sometimes pretend no other car has ever pulled since."[54]

He was with Lorna again in July, at Bingham's Melcombe, driving over from the South Camp at Deepcut where he was with the battery. "There was just that one short blaze of summer glory—the July day that I spent alone with her at Bingham's Melcombe, I could tell you every hour of it from the moment I saw her in church before she knew I'd come, to the evening when we sat on the hill the monks used to climb, looking over the house, and she told me [Edwin] Goldman [Charles Sydney's brother] had asked her to marry him, and the moment when we said goodbye in the dark on the old bowling green by the yew hedge."[55] It was almost the end, and there is no contemporary record of Gore-Browne having pressed his claims ahead of Goldman's, or of having tried to over-take Goldman, as Lorna may well have wanted.[56] Ethel was instru-mental in, and later took full responsibility for, having dissuaded him from pursuing this first golden ray of glory. Her arguments are not known, but they made sense to Gore-Browne, a young officer

54. Gore-Browne to Ethel Locke-King, 1 January 1922.
55. Gore-Browne to Ethel Locke-King, 1 January 1922.
56. The only hint that Gore-Browne may formally have proposed is contained in a reference to a conversation in the 1960s with Mrs. Joan Cochrane, Lorna's sister. Encouraged by her family, she told a Hardy scholar, Gore-Browne asked Lorna to marry, but was rejected. Mrs. Cochrane died before more could be discovered about the circumstances of the proposal. Neither Gore-Browne nor Ethel Locke-King ever referred to anything as specific as an offer of marriage. For the note about Mrs. Cochrane, see J. O. Bailey, *The Poetry of Thomas Hardy: A Handbook and Commentary* (Chapel Hill, 1970), 613.

with few prospects of competing financially with an established professional. "I've never for one moment doubted," Ethel wrote later, "that it would have been ruin for you to marry her . . . not entirely because of your 'career' perhaps more by what they call our 'woman's' intuition."[57] Gore-Browne agreed—seven years later. "I don't go about pretending my life is ruined," he reassured Ethel. "I most certainly think a young soldier's got no business to marry; & I fancy you were absolutely right, & at the worst . . . it was bad luck we should have met when & how we did, seeing that things made it impossible, and at the best that we'd not have suited and can both go on idealising the other all our lives."[58] Ethel's counsel had been decisive.

The open avowal of ardor was less common then, too, and Gore-Browne, accustomed to keeping some emotional distance (as befitted a young officer), and having had little experience in matters of the heart, may have been too paralyzed to proceed rashly without formal encouragement. Lorna herself clearly radiated warmth and wanting, but her signals were mixed. Gore-Browne's comparative youth and circumstance may also have limited his comparative advantage. Goldman, after all, was older and established. Born in South Africa in 1862, he had been educated in Germany. In 1892 he had become professor of surgery at the University of Freiburg, after working in Frankfurt with Paul Ehrlich on a cure for syphilis. He perfected a technique for the staining of living tissues which revolutionized the study of microbiology and had begun work on the pathology of cancer.

"My dear Stewart," Lorna tried to explain after that Sunday alone. "I know that you will have been kindly thinking of me now when I told you Mr. Goldman was coming. Well, he came . . . and I knew on Sunday that nothing else could happen . . . I hardly know that it has happened but we are engaged. You won't expect me to say the usual things but I think you may understand that there are *more* than the usual things to be said. I feel all is well with the world. The morbidness you complain of is flying . . ."[59] For her, Goldman's decision to seek her hand, and her acquiescence, were somehow fated. At least she seems then and later to have regarded the marriage (unless Gore-Browne took the kind of drastic steps he was ill-equipped to attempt?) as akin to one arranged. She was a fatalist, and remained so during her difficult later life, when she and Gore-Browne reopened their relationship by correspondence.

Only Ethel and Lady Harriet, his grandmother, knew how

57. Ethel Locke-King to Gore-Browne, 15 August 1913.
58. Gore-Browne to Ethel Locke-King, 28 September 1913.
59. Lorna Lawrence Bosworth Smith to Gore-Browne, n.d. (July, 1905).

Lorna's engagement stilled and saddened something deep within. Lorna herself may not have known, for Gore-Browne's righteous decision to forego pursuit would have kept his eyes unblinking, his back straight, and his manner correct. He was with her again in early September, after the engagement was announced, in order (as a friend of the family) to help raise money for Mrs. Bosworth Smith's local nurses fund. With Lorna, Joan, and Neville they performed scenes from *School for Scandal* and *Sweethearts*; the fund grew by twenty pounds. That same weekend they played tennis, which Gore-Browne did badly, bicycled, and went off together to Milton Abbey. The next, and last, time he saw her was in February, 1906, after months at Deepcut with the 100th Battery, R. H. A., many maneuvers as far as High Wycombe and Oxford, a sketching course at Chatham, the purchase of a new 24–36 h. p. Fiat called Ug, and a journey in it with Prioleau to and from Monte Carlo (where they played the tables successfully) and Menton. On the evening of 24 February he drove down to Bingham's Melcombe, where Lorna came to meet him at the gate. Later, while he was eating a late supper, he met Edwin (of whom there is no diary description). Two nights later, after assisting in the preparations for the marriage, and even helping convey Edwin into Dorchester for shopping— what could be more "manly?"—he sat next to Lorna at a small table at dinner, and danced with her afterwards. In the snow of the next afternoon, a Tuesday, Lorna became Mrs. Goldman. The diary entry is bare. But later, for Gore-Browne, it was a day of "winter's winterest, snow in patches, & rain . . . I saw her for the last time as she passed me to get into the car that was waiting by the Gate House."[60]

60. Gore-Browne to Ethel Locke-King, 1 January 1922.

II
To the Lake of the Royal Crocodiles

UNSETTLING though Lorna's marriage must have been, it was the only serious interruption in the even flow of Gore-Browne's private life and professional development. And she, for all her unique and enthralling properties, was still, somehow, an exotic export into the ordered confines of a world populated largely by family and army. As such, especially given an absence of overt commitment or deep entanglement, his loss, in some ways his failure, and the memory of what she had appeared to be during a few precious days, could be relegated with comparative ease to the mind's compartment reserved for honorable explorations of human involvement. In later years he refused to pretend that he had suffered a broken heart. His defenses had been too well raised, and, with Aunt Ethel's assistance, secured, for the wraith of Lorna to have caused damage more permanent than the faint scar which was visible in subsequent years only to those few who knew the young adult as well as they knew the soldier of European combat and the statesman of African maturity.

Lorna had drawn out and shared Gore-Browne's instinctive eye for and love of the beauties of nature. The country, whether on the small scale of southern England, with its rolling downs and stately churches, or the more forbidding sombre scapes of Scotland and Africa, attracted and warmed him. He preferred heritage to modernity, and throughout a long life cherished the glory of the old without disparaging the kinds of progressive devices which eased daily existence. A positive feeling for history (with an eye from the early days of keeping diaries on his own place in its later compilation) coincided with fully assimilated notions of the responsibilities and appropriate behavior of someone born into and nurtured within the upper stratum of a socially divided society. Together with class allegiances and a strongly felt loyalty to the church, not

29

necessarily, though primarily, to the Established Church of England, Gore-Browne shared many of the assumptions, attitudes, and prejudices of his kind. Some he was to outgrow. Others fell to the challenges of new information or changing circumstances over the course of a hectic and politically active career which spanned generations and brought him fame and power at a time when most men usually begin to lay down burdens of authority. There was a residue, however, which he retained, and which gave definition and a certain characteristic style to the Gore-Browne of both twenty-three and eighty-four. He was well bred and proud of being so. Occasional lapses of his own, and the transgressions of others against the set of conventions commonly ascribed to by his class, earned harsh condemnation. There were only certain ways to dress, certain kinds of subjects which could be discussed with women, and certain kinds of behavior which were appropriate. There were special rituals to be followed in the performance of one's duties and pursuits. Port, for example, could only be passed in accord with particular forms to which Gore-Browne rigorously adhered—as would any young man of his background. Drinking in general, however, signified poor breeding, and Gore-Browne imbibed moderately, and with no special pleasure. He had no love of society, and felt most formal appearances, like balls, more obligatory performances of duty than sources of enjoyment. In his twenties he played bridge, gambled, went to horse races, and so on, but more as a part of the doings of his "set" than any obsessive fascination.

He believed in all of the usual verities of his kind. Premarital intercourse, divorce, and so on, were only indulged in by the sinful, and best discussed covertly. Politics was only mildly interesting, and, except for "front-page" issues of some drama, Gore-Browne's youthful diaries and letters betray little concern for the national and international issues of the day, except insofar as they directly impinged upon his prospective career in the service. He clung, too, to stereotypes—"drink-besotted Irish navvies" and "Jewish moneylenders;" "uncouth foreigners" and "hustling Americans." He suffered real fools little, but could make people of the lower orders feel at ease—if they remained respectful and maintained social distance. He was basically anti-semitic and anti-papist, writing and mouthing the usual sentiments of prejudice and, when he himself was occasionally mean with money, critical of his own "Jew-like" tendencies. But in these, and in so many other ways, he was simply at one with his peers.

There were other, more important aspects of English upperclass life which Gore-Browne had internalized by his twenty-third birthday. Being superior to others was insufferable without benevolence and kindness; the masses had fewer advantages, and he

Gore-Browne as a young soldier, c. 1902.

and his ilk were ordained to improve their lot. Respectability, appearances, and "place" would be maintained throughout, but the
gift of being born to lead and rule could not be exercised without
doing something for others. This was no inherited masochism, but
a sacred trust of the kind which had rationalized empires and given
purpose to the lives of aristocratic reformers. This was the mold
from which Gore-Browne was also formed. Respect came through
doing something for others, no matter how few. For psychological
reasons, too, Gore-Browne needed the reassurance that came with
being accepted, sometimes to the point of making friendships
awkward. He was sentimental and conscious of remembrances, and

was close to a select few as well as being acquainted with and relied upon by many.

Yet, as much as he interacted in person and in correspondence, there was also a reserve which blocked almost everyone from glimpsing the inner Gore-Browne. Before World War I only to Prioleau, Pearson, W. W. Gillum (known as Peckham), Cecil Kerr, and especially Aunt Ethel, did he ever give of himself in any sustaining manner. There were a host of other men with whom he embraced the vagaries of military life, some segments of his far-flung family with whom he shared an affinity, and many others upon whom the impress of his personality was decisive, but the shyness, stillness, romance, and bearing of the youthful soldier who became in turns a successful staff officer and politician were known by few. With the exception of Aunt Ethel, who hid a similar romantic ardor and poetic eye beneath the practicality and dash of a woman of society, and for whom writing letters also fulfilled a cathartic need, only Lorna and Violet Vincent were more than surface distractions before the War. It was during his late twenties, too, when Gore-Browne's alienation from his mother was at its height, and before age had mellowed their estrangement, that Ethel and Stewart began to see more and more of each other. During the years from 1906 to 1911 most of Gore-Browne's free weekends and leaves were spent at Brooklands, not at his immediate family's different homes.

Between Stewart and Ethel much was still unspoken, but less and less so as Gore-Browne approached thirty. They both dreamed vividly, Gore-Browne having the clearer and fuller recall, and deriving more pleasure from recounting and reliving his revealed inner world. He, in this way akin more to Uncle Hugh, also believed in parapsychological phenomena. The older he became the more faith he had in extrasensory perception and his own ability to receive messages and premonitions through dreams. Only with the Locke-Kings could Gore-Browne ever discuss these matters, and to Ethel as to no other—ever—he spoke the unspoken and gave the confidences of a young adult. Each fulfilled great needs in the other, the one for a mother, the other for a son, and each, as the affair of youth bloomed with increasing age and greater self-assurance, became the other's distant, unobtainable lover.

Aunt Ethel and Uncle Hugh reciprocated Gore-Browne's passion for motor cars. Their correspondence back and forth, Gore-Browne's diaries, and letters to Gore-Browne from his male friends from 1905 to 1911, all discuss cars incessantly. They compare makes and speeds, anthropomorphize particular models, give them affectionate names, and lavish upon them, and upon the business of speeds, records, accessories etc., the kind of attention they devoted to little else during these Edwardian years. The vehicles were, ad-

mittedly, constantly breaking down and having to be repaired by
the owners; a one-to-one relationship, man to machine, was therefore more natural than in an era of mass consumerism. In a select
upperclass English circle, the newfangled motor monsters were all
the rage, and Gore-Browne was unusual only in having a forty-
year-old aunt who cared as much as he did, and who fueled his
enthusiasm incessantly. On two occasions they dashed off across
the Channel together on spurs of the moment to watch the Grand
Prix road races in France.

Most of Gore-Browne's continental touring (the diary recording
in laborious detail every occurrence to the car, if not its passengers)
was done in the company of one or more of his male contemporaries. First with Prioleau, who was even more obsessed than
most of the smitten crowd, and who owned Katinka, and later, after
he had gone off to Cairo to write for the *Egypt Morning News,* with
Peckham and Kerr, Gore-Browne organized and orchestrated annual and sometimes twice-yearly month-long motor safaris across
France to Tuscany or the Piedmont, up into the Haut Garonne and
the sub-Pyrennean districts of southwestern France, or down the
Loire to discover the many glorious chateaux that startled him so.
He and Peckham slept two to a bed, for warmth, whenever it was
cold, and, aside from the inevitable disagreements about the choice
of "booths", i.e. hotels and inns, and which sights to see (Gore-
Browne preferred churches and battlefields), all of the long odys-
seys seem to have proceeded without major personal clashes.
Gore-Browne vastly preferred harmony to discord, and often acted
as peacemaker, compromiser, and smoother of ruffled feathers unless and until matters of high principle became involved. Peckham's
taste for the Follies, and for sitting in the fashionable cafés of Paris,
had frequently to be indulged despite Gore-Browne's own aver-
sions. Some of the others had little patience for the frequent repair
stops and endless nursing of sick vehicles from one rudimentary
dealer to another. But for Gore-Browne, perhaps even more than
the others, just being with them in France, free, and driving an open
car at twenty or thirty miles per hour down snow-slicked roads was
satisfying and sufficient for a gentleman soldier in times of peace.

In addition, by way of enhancing his lust for automobiles, driving, and improving the performance of these machines, Gore-
Browne was associated through the Locke-Kings with the very nub
of incipient British motor and motor-racing activity. Hugh
Locke-King's inventive mind had early appreciated the need for an
arena where the country's fledgling motor industry could test its
products to the limit (the roads of Britain had a speed limit of
twenty miles an hour until 1934), and where drivers could race cars
competitively for sport as well as for experimental reasons. He had

owned motor cars and trucks since the mid-1890s and had tinkered
with them incessantly. Unlike many members of the Gore-Browne
extended entourage, Uncle Hugh refused to let practical or structural obstacles deter the realization of any of his visions. But of all
his large-schemes, the making of Brooklands, Britain's first true
motor-racing track, took the kind of prescience, courage, innovation, and determination (even when supported morally by Aunt
Ethel and advised legally by Frank) that few acquainted with automobiles then possessed. In 1906 he began to construct a vast
amphitheatre, almost three miles in length and 100 feet wide. Not
the least of his bold decisions was the use of concrete for the track's
surface. Although Americans had been using concrete on road sur-
faces for more than a decade, the first British road was to be fabricated in concrete only in 1912, and durability of concrete was as yet
imperfectly known. No expansion joints were provided, and the
vast circuit was preponderantly composed of 200,000 tons of six-
inch-thick plain mass rather than reinforced concrete. The two
curved ends of the track were steeply banked so that cars travelling
up to speeds of 120 miles per hour could follow the curve around by
centrifugal force; higher speeds would require drivers to counteract
centrifugal force by steering. The combination of the banks and the
pioneering but insufficient use of concrete necessitated almost continual repairs and repaving throughout the track's thirty-year existence. There was also a finishing straight which branched off from
the shorter of the two level stretches of track. The whole, which
cost about £250,000, provided a model for less ambitious copies at
Indianapolis in the United States and at Montlhery in France.

More than 13,000 people watched the first races at Brooklands in
July, 1907. Gore-Browne drove a 30 h.p. Thorneycroft and finished
third in one heat. Until about 1911 when society amateurs, with
their jockey colors and other accoutrements borrowed from horse
racing, were thoroughly superseded by a new breed of professional
drivers, he participated in nearly all of the races, sometimes in special competitions for military officers on regular service, and occasionally as the driver of large cars owned by wealthy friends. In the
early years of the track, too, he spent many hours on it testing his
own cars or matching his own with those of the Locke-Kings or
their friends. On one occasion he managed to average more than
eighty miles per hour. Gore-Browne was also concerned, along
with the Locke-Kings, in making a financial success of the track. It
depended first on quarterly auto races (all-night endurance racing
having been stopped after irate neighborly protest) and then on
airplane races (the inner circle of the oval being used as a landing
ground with Uncle Hugh's encouragement), including the first
from Brooklands to Brighton, 1911, the first 1,010 mile Circuit of

Britain race, also in 1911, cross-country out-and-home handicap races, which began in 1912, and so on. Motor and air races continued throughout the 1920s and 1930s, the Vickers company ultimately using the track and its surround for the production of aircraft during World War II.

Competitive motor racing fit Gore-Browne's temperament. It gave him a sense of achievement and provided public testimony to his manhood. It pleased a mediocre athlete who had hated games at Harrow to accelerate around the two steeply banked turns at ever-increasing speeds, to produce the fastest possible times from machines meant for more staid performances on the earth roads of the day, and to be among the pioneers of Britain's newest sport. No dare devil, he nonetheless enjoyed the thrills of rapid driving, the brushes with danger, and the resultant acclaim. During the Easter meeting, 1908, for example, Gore-Browne drove a 47.6 h.p. Gibron in a race for military officers. Although the betting was two to one against him, and snow fell sharply throughout the race, making the various cars almost indistinguishable, Gore-Browne won the Roble Military Cup with an average speed of sixty-four miles per hour. "Got a very good start owing to watching the man's hand at the gate," Gore-Browne explained. "Car pulling really strong but rain soon turned to snow. Pretty severe. Lead all the way and go extremely fast down the Big Bank and faster still on the Oyster Curve. Cutting into the straight begin to miss badly presumably owing to wet getting at the magneto. Suffer quite considerable pangs all the way down as I expected to be passed any moment. However eventually the flag line comes into sight. Considerable content afterwards."[1]

Motoring also gave Gore-Browne a new field in which to exercise his literary abilities. Prose came easily to him, and at first flowed even more smoothly than it did for his brother Robert, who tried to live by the pen. The newspaper at Harrow was evidence of early interest, and in South Africa he began writing not only the article published in the *Alpine Journal,* but a book composed of episodes in the life of a young officer. He recounted some of his European tours for *Autocar* (1904), and wrote of racing with and for Prioleau when the latter became automotive correspondent for the *Daily Mail* (London). In 1908 he published the first of several essays on artillery and other military matters in the *Royal Artillery Magazine.* Throughout this period, and until 1910, he worked periodically on a book, regaling his friends and colleagues with chapters which nearly all thought amusing and worth publishing. Despite the intervention of novelists like his friend Humphrey Neville Dickin-

1. Diary, 20 April 1908.

son, however, Gore-Browne never polished it sufficiently to show it to a publisher. His diffidence may have inhibited its completion, and Dickinson's quiet criticism may have also had a deterrent effect. "Seriously," Dickinson wrote on one occasion, "I advise you to go on with your writing—to confine yourself to quiet subjects like mountains and battles and histories, and to impart into them all the freshness and epigrams which in your own good taste you *dare*. And don't forget that fiction is a fascinating pleasure which *might* any day bring you off with success. . . . However, the probability is that a quiet historical subject is your most promising field."[2]

By the time of his second departure for Africa in 1911, Gore-Browne had developed into an accomplished writer of letters. This was his real métier: his pen quickly sketched in a scene, provided a vignette of a daily or weekly activity, had the gift of making the homely and banal come alive with their mundane force intact, and deftly established a smooth rapport with a correspondent. His was an eighteenth-century talent generally unappreciated in the twentieth except by a close circle of male friends, all of whom complained, deprecated themselves, and feared the loss of his affection whenever letters were delayed.

Aunt Ethel's pleasure in long, lavishly-rounded descriptions of places and people equalled his; together they sustained a delight in what an earlier age called sentiment—the shades of feeling evoked by misfortunes and successes, encounters, the process of dreams, and the interaction of mind and mystery. Theirs was a mannered, but nonetheless real and effective correspondence which ripened with maturity into one of the delightful recorded personal interchanges of the day. Gore-Browne also kept diaries virtually always (except for the war) from 1899 to his death, and was commended officially for accounts of pre-war maneuvers, but most of the entries are matter-of-fact, unrevealing, and disappointing except as bare records of events. It took Ethel to elicit the best. Their readable dialogue, which continued voluminously until 1956, is as much his memorial as any political or human accomplishment.

Soldiering consumed only a small portion of his energies during the years in Britain between periods of service in southern Africa. For much of the time he was stationed at Colchester with the 18th Brigade. Once each year there was a month of serious maneuvers, either along the downs of Sussex, or in the slate country of mid-Wales, and Gore-Browne and his fellow subalterns then became exceedingly busy. For the rest of the year, however, his and their duties were light. The batteries were drilled weekly in firing and

2. H. N. Dickinson to Gore-Browne, 5 July 1905. Dickinson had only begun to break into best-selling print. His *Things That Are Caesar's* (London) was published in 1906, to be followed by six other novels.

tactics, the horses were exercised, but with no wars or invasions for which to prepare, the routine was fairly undemanding. Weekend leave was easy to obtain, and as much time was spent by Gore-Browne and his friends in the fancy dining places of London—the Trocadero, Oddinos, and Lauriers—as in the mess at Colchester. There was leisure for visits to the scattered homes of his family and acquaintances, for long summer and winter holidays, and for the enjoyment of concerts, opera, and the theater.

When on duty, Gore-Browne frequently lectured to his troops and the staff college on military history, sat long examinations for promotion and qualification as a French interpreter, and almost once each year was sent on a short course of further instruction. In 1905 he gained the highest grade in the School of Military Engineering for field sketching and route reconnaissance. The next year, in Southampton, he spent a month learning the techniques of ordnance surveying. According to the commandant, he "acquired a good knowledge of the method of conducting a trigometric survey in exploration work and the manner of running trigometric traverses in forest country." He possessed only a fair theoretical knowledge of the application of field astronomy to surveying, and required "further experience in the [art of] practical observing."[3] In 1907, he obtained his certificate in signalling at Aldershot, and was thereafter qualified to instruct others as well as to lay telephone lines for maneuvers and worry about his battery's communication systems. Despite these accomplishments, and the generally good notices he received regularly from his superior officers, Gore-Browne's eyesight prevented his transfer from the field to the horse artillery. "I am sure," an official in the War Office wrote, "you will agree that nothing but the best and the quickest sight is enough for the RHA. It is about as essential as any quality can be. There is nothing whatever against Gore-Browne but when I took his name up [the Adjutant General] would not have it and rightly if I may say so."[4]

Gore-Browne was never completely content with this effortless, comparatively placid life. He sought more scope, preferably abroad where there might be an earlier chance of holding minor commands, despite his already recognized intellectual abilities and the opinions of his friends that he would soon be sent to the staff college. Through contacts in the War Office, in 1907 he attempted to secure posting to the military mission in Uganda; there the process of pacifying indigenous inhabitants was still underway, and in the public eye. But thrice this kind of preferment was refused him. Instead, in 1910, when his brigade, with Kerr, his then inseparable

3. Colonel R. G. Hellard, report on Gore-Browne, 23 November 1906.
4. F. Mercer to Montgomery, 22 April 1909.

friend, was sent to South Africa, he was posted tentatively to the outer Siberia of Glasgow, and then mercifully reprieved to run the artillery section of the university officer training corps at Oxford. Gore-Browne wanted very much to remain with his battery, but training nonetheless proved a congenial assignment, Gore-Browne liking the young men and the challenge of readying students accustomed to privilege for the more disciplined life of the army. The culmination of his year as a training officer was a summer's week of strenuous field attacks when he was in sole charge of the divisional artillery. At the end of it, and his year with the aspirant officers, Gore-Browne had proved to himself, and probably to others, that he had that subtle quality with which good officers were born, and which they could not be taught. Gore-Browne was good with men. He could lead, and inspire others to give of themselves and to perform military tasks to the best of their ability. He was a stickler for discipline, and willingly "gave tongue" when seized with displeasure. But he was no rigid martinet, and men responded appropriately.

The opportunity of again commanding men preparing for war, and soldiers in combat, would come sooner than he or anyone else expected. Immediately, however, Gore-Browne's peace-time progression from minor to major responsibilities was interrupted by a secondment of his own preference. In January a friend in the Royal Engineers who sat in the War Office told him of a military commission which was being sent out to survey the boundary between Northern Rhodesia and the Belgian Congo. Kerr was in the Transvaal, a thousand miles away from the wild frontier where the survey was to take place, but he and Gore-Browne were already separated by 6,000 miles. Each missed the other, and hoped that being closer together would at least permit them to share vacations and a hunting trip or two. "Your news," said Kerr, "is the best I've heard for a long time."[5] So Gore-Browne, who also saw it as an opportunity to do something unusual and exciting, requested appointment to the Commission, met and liked Maj. R. A. Gillam, the leader of the survey, and Capt. Walker, his deputy, and was soon accepted as its third officer. After trying times with the dentist and a shopping spree—"Heavens knows what I am not spending on buying things for this expedition, most of which I shall probably lose or not want."[6]—he said goodbye to G. Lowrey, his faithful batman, had tea with Ethel, and sailed from Southampton for South Africa.

The borders between the Belgian Congo and Northern Rhodesia were then established only imprecisely. They had been specified in

5. Kerr to Gore-Browne, 19 March 1911.
6. Diary, 25 July 1911.

an agreement concluded between Britain and King Léopold II, Sovereign of the Independent State of the Congo, in 1894, but the resulting document was primarily concerned with the leasing of British territory north of Lake Albert along the Nile River. Léopold coveted access to that river for geopolitical reasons. The southern Rhodesian borders of his kingdom were of less immediate interest, and the portion of concern to Gore-Browne was delimited by part of a sentence only. The line between the two jurisdictions was to run southwards from Lake Bangweulu to its junction with the watershed separating the Congo and Zambezi Rivers. This it was to "follow until it reaches the Portuguese frontier," more than five hundred fifty meandering miles away.[7] The Portuguese eastern frontier, the result of a different treaty, had been established arbitrarily on the meridian 24° E. Although these vague parameters bifurcated indigenous groups and made little cultural or linguistic sense, their existence permitted cartographers, the wielders of brightly colored inks, to tidy up the maps of Africa. They also were a logical outgrowth of the insensitive manner in which the continent had been partitioned by and among the colonial powers. As treaties, however, these awards represented theory rather than reality, and would remain subjects for potential dispute until detailed surveys on the ground translated the sense of the agreements into concrete detail. It was the task of Gore-Browne and his colleagues, therefore, to discover the actual watershed, and to fix the location of and build beacons on the highest points separating the Congo from Rhodesia.

Technically, the Boundary Commission's work was simple and straightforward. Once the high points between the two river systems were established, the new beacons had to be seen from at least three other sites in order to furnish acceptable triangulations for the mapmakers. Ordinarily theodolite surveying sufficed, the local inhabitants could guide the commissioners to the ridges, and, in time, as quickly as the commissioners could traverse the terrain on foot, erect beacons, and obtain sufficient observations despite haze in dry season and clouds in the wet, the Commission would reach the 24th parallel in the west and Lakes Mweru and Tanganyika in the north and east. Since it was an Anglo–Belgian commission, and each side's observations and beacons were presumed to be checked by the other, the task was expected to move along steadily. At the western limit, the commission would link up with a comparable Anglo-Portuguese commission.

Delimiting borders across a largely untrodden terrain (Africans

7. Edward Hertslet (ed.), *The Map of Africa by Treaty* (London, 1909), III, 578–579.

usually travelled along the rivers, not upon the separating ridge) proved rather more taxing in practice, however, than it seemed in theory. Europeans, especially men on active service, required supplies in considerable quantity if they were to subsist for weeks, if not months, distant from even the creeping outposts of Westernized Rhodesia. At this time, one or two farmers, a very few mission stations, one mine, and two bomas (administrative stations) were the only outward manifestations of imperial Britain west of the line of rail. Moreover, large quantities of labor were required to erect beacons, make camps, and carry provisions from the line of rail (effectively Ndola) to the commissioners. These men also had to be fed, and could hardly expect to be able to live off the land. Ensuring adequate supplies of labor, and logistics more generally, were thus foremost among the trying problems faced by the commission as a whole, and by the commissioners working individually, separated as they were by long distances from one another. Equally, the commission could hardly hope to function well if its relations with laborers and villagers were less than sound, or if the commissioners themselves interacted antagonistically.

Frontier conditions breed loneliness, the consequent isolation encourages paranoid delusions and alcoholic tendencies, and, among some Europeans at least, the different rhythms of Africa prove sufficiently unsettling to elicit and enlarge any other incipient personality abnormalities. Thus Gillam, under whom Gore-Browne worked directly on the delimitation of the border from Ndola northwest to the 24th parallel—Walker, Capt. Everett, and Lt. Wynne being sent to establish the northeastern perimeter separately—turned to drink and irrationality. He proved incapable of making up his mind, would give urgent instructions and countermand them later, alternately praised and distrusted his subordinates, felt threatened by the administration of Northern Rhodesia, with which he quarrelled, and by the Belgian component of the commission, with the members of which he had little to do. He made no effort to understand or deal with Africans, and could in no way cope with the organizational requirements of his far-flung retinue. Gore-Browne, though a subordinate and a subaltern, and a gunner among engineers, was therefore compelled to make his own way despite Gillam's incompetency, personality problems, and contrary orders. He was forced to try—sometimes single-handedly—to mollify the Belgians and the Rhodesian administrators, win the cooperation of Africans, find the border, and, generally, to accomplish the aims of the commission expediently, and without subverting Gillam's authority.

The experience of the commission was the making of Gore-Browne. Because of Gillam, and the nature of the survey, he was (in the white sense) often on his own amid the glories of Africa. Purely in terms of sensate realities, Africa offered the climatic warmth which mattered so much to Gore-Browne, and which England obviously could not equal. He even enjoyed the stifling October heat before the yearly intertropical convergence brought rain, the months of intermittent downpour, and the hazy dry days of spring. The bitterly cold nights of plateau winters were more reminiscent of Europe, but at least the weather was then dry and Gore-Browne endured occasional frosts easily. He was pleased by the scrub deciduous forests, the wet valleys, and the undulating low hills of much of northwestern Zambia. More attractive were the people, especially his carriers and employees, most of whom happened to be Bemba from northeastern Zambia, and the Lamba, Kaonde, Lunda and other related peoples of the border area west from Ndola to Mwinilunga.

The majesty and simplicity of Africa greatly excited him. He could teach and gain respect by demonstrating those virtues of class and breeding which were in him innate. He could achieve esteem by being himself, and without the kinds of artifice which caused him pain in European circles. Being a bwana, or master, could not but have helped to gratify his ego. And, as with so many Britons of his generation, rural Africans uncontaminated by "civilization", vigorous, masculine, robustly pure, proud (particularly the Bemba), martial, and touchingly loyal as clients, proved attractive.

In their eyes, and therefore in his own, he could prove himself. He showed an ability to take and delegate serious responsibility. He learnt to make his way in the bush with the assistance (not always easy to obtain) of the local inhabitants (where there were any in this thinly populated part of Rhodesia) and his followers, to do his particular job with despatch and without the complications which beset his compatriots, and, amidst this verdant, in some positive ways lonely setting, to come to know himself in a manner which would permit him largely to avoid crises of generativity during the decade of his thirties. He also became a hunter. Since most meat was for the pot of his carriers, killing big game daily and regularly was no mere sport. It lifted the ego, enhanced self-esteem, gained prestige among his men, and demonstrated, not only to himself, that Gore-Browne was a man. Without such accomplishments, he could not have grown in Africa, nor learned to be so at one with it and its inhabitants.

From the commission's earliest weeks in Northern Rhodesia, when Gore-Browne was plunged into the bush without interpreters or guides to begin doing the kind of surveying which he had never tried before, he reacted positively, consistently praising the country, its indigenous population, and all aspects of his task and his physical surroundings. Nature enveloped him and with it he felt content. He responded particularly to the feelings of space and limitless growth that strike most sensitive first-time visitors to the high Central African plateau. "The day before yesterday," he wrote in December 1911, "the sun rose so that the sky was all one mass of deep crimson slashed with bars of solid gold and edged by a dark violet coloured Earth, a very mantle for God."[8]

Going off alone with carriers and a black military escort was pure joy. Describing an early hunting expedition away from the commission's base camp at Ndola, he explained that "to begin with, you send on a long string of carriers. . . . They take everything, tent, bed, bath, stores, etc. on their heads, about 50 to 60 pounds weight each. About two hours afterwards you start yourself, on a bicycle, with a man running behind carrying your gun or rifle, and another ready to carry your bicycle across streams or to take it when you stop to shoot. Of course, bicycling in this country is not what it would be in England indeed it alone is quite exciting. The track is only about two feet wide, full of holes and tree roots, winding in and out of the thick forest . . . with often a tree across the path." But life on continual safari was not always blissful. There were times, he assured his aunt, when a steady march began at 5:30 A.M. and, although "exquisite for the first five hours", proved longer than expected. Yet the path "winds on and on and on through the blind bush with the tree crickets making that noise like hissing steam coming out of a pipe, and ones throat is so dry it hurts to go through the motions of swallowing, and the dambo [watery plain] when it does come turns out to be nothing but the bed of dry river, and the carriers are tired and straggling so that even when you do reach the end of the journey there is a two hours wait till your stuff comes up during which time you sit on the hard ground."[9]

Gore-Browne's servants, messengers, soldiers, and 140 carriers worked out well from initial acquaintance and his admiration eventually made the homeland of the most dominant among them—the Bemba—his own. "My hunter, [Peter]" he told his mother, "is rather a dream, he carries an assegai, & a zebra's tail for a whip. . . . In the morning he greets one [in the Bemba fashion] by kneeling down & clapping his hands which is very picturesque but disconcerting at first."[10] Moreover, he was "beautifully made with shining black limbs, a purple loin cloth and a yellow vest. . . . He [had] the vivid beauty . . . which seems to be the first thing the

8. Gore-Browne to Ethel Locke-King, 11 December 1911.

9. Gore-Browne to Father, 15 September 1911; Gore-Browne to Ethel Locke-King, 10 November 1911.

10. Gore-Browne to his mother, 20 September 1911.

native loses when he comes in contact with civilization. Ugh, why will these missionaries put the women into print dresses and make the men wear trousers?"[11] Meniane, his cook, was also picturesque—"the most evil looking villain with a puzzled kind of expression into the bargain, and he swings a bright red blanket over one shoulder & swaggers along *exactly* like a Spanish villain in Grand Opera."[12]

Chikwanda, the head messenger, had been a corporal in the police, was about 35, and was a little wizened man—something, Gore-Browne imagined, like a Gurkha. He was also of the elite Bemba elephant clan. Kakumbi, the second messenger, was one of the best looking men Gore-Browne had ever seen, being tall and graceful. A Bemba, he had "gentle and pretty" manners, but basically was an "idle ruffian . . . of the sort that it is difficult to be angry with." A small boy, Bulaya, who had once worked for a drunken doctor, was Gore-Browne's personal servant, doing everything at all times. About twenty-five carriers were required for Gore-Browne's personal belongings and another eighty hauled the loads and grain and stores for the full party. Together they progressed about fifteen to twenty miles a day through open country and occasional villages where Gore-Browne's hunter made the startled inhabitants lie on their backs and clap hands abjectly for the big man. "I live like a king, a supply of live fowls going with me."[13]

For enduring a life he found pleasant and more invigorating and interesting than isolating, with all of the hunting and marching he could want, excursions to the tops of hills, the erecting of beacons, and the possible tedium of triangulations, the army paid Gore-Browne £850 a year. But they forced him—as he rapidly discovered—to associate with men, especially his fellow commissioners, for whom he could develop no respect. Gillam, in addition to being muddled, and indecisive, was a prig. He fouled the official air despite his evident personal liking for Gore-Browne (who obeyed despite a feeling of great contempt). When Kerr came up to Northern Rhodesia to spend several weeks with Gore-Browne, Gillam refused to let him come within four miles of the Ndola base camp for fear Kerr would somehow discredit the official mission. Gore-Browne never saw Walker, Everett was killed by a lion, and the non-commissioned officers, all engineers, were, as far as Gore-Browne was concerned, tolerable if dense. More intolerable were most of the whites on the line of rail, with their South African-like racial attitudes, their uncouth manner, and their inability to treat

11. Gore-Browne to Ethel Locke-King, 29 September 1911.
12. Gore-Browne to Ethel Locke-King, 29 September 1911.
13. Ibid.

Africans humanely. He judged the Belgians, despite their love of good parties and wine, and their comparative openness with Africans, similarly wanting. They were slovenly. They took advantage of and cheated their African subjects, and were now and again wantonly brutal toward them. He excoriated their "unending beastliness . . . to natives, the attitude which is often cruel and often maudlin and often sloppily sentimental and often brutally inconsiderate, but never dignified or even logical." Gore-Browne wanted the Belgians to treat Africans as people, and "not as a convenience like the trees one burns for firewood."[14]

Gore-Browne minded the Belgian failure to set a good example—to administer even-handed justice to their subjects, to gain African respect while keeping the Africans in an appropriate place—and to provide appropriate discipline. The Belgians, he said, "will laugh at a boy who is waiting on them, and perhaps throw food at him, & in any case talk about him in his presence . . . After that they will give the boy cigarettes . . . & allow him certainly to lounge about in the hut with his boots on & perhaps to wear a hat." In contrast, when he and his own party visited the Belgians the Bemba "played up" well. For instance, Gore-Browne wrote, "the look of surprise on one of the Belgian officer's face when, as he & I passed near my 50 fellows who were sitting around camp fires, they all stood up & I asked him if they might sit down again, was curiously satisfying." Then, after a "dinner orgy" with the Belgians, Gore-Browne, on being escorted home to his own encampment, found all of his people, who should have been asleep, waiting for him. Gore-Browne asked "what the blazes they wanted, & my policeman said 'You can't be too careful, with people like the Boula Matari [the Belgians] about.'"[15]

"The ordinary white man," Gore-Browne observed as he did and could for decades after, "seems afraid to be really strict & afraid to be really kind, & in any case is never consistent." Servants and Africans, Gore-Browne found himself asserting, were to him more than so many machines, still less so many animals. His particular followers were friends for whom social distance and reserve was natural. It occasioned no strain when accompanied by affection, strictness, scrupulous honesty, and confident leadership. These attributes Gore-Browne had, or developed. Sometimes he lost his fearsome temper, and the men ran, but he prided himself on punishing (usually flogging) only when Africans understood their offenses. One of the worst sins, he preached, was hitting an African in a temper. Yet most of the local whites, especially the miners, the

14. Gore-Browne to Ethel Locke-King, 2 October 1912.
15. Gore-Browne to Ethel Locke-King, 10 January 1912.

inebriates, and the Belgians, all tossed their weight about, caroused, whored in the expatriate way by taking women in villages and towns by force, thoroughly demeaning what Gore-Browne thought of as Europe's God-given task of uplifting its colonial subjects and "setting a good example." Gore-Browne took a turn observing the Ndola court and was scandalized. "When you see a white man come up and perjure himself in the witness box for half an hour in order to score off a miserable native, you feel a bit sick."[16]

Gore-Browne cherished rather old-fashioned sentiments, even in 1911 and 1912, but for him if not for Britain or the local British South Africa Company administration, these truths, and the hoary Kiplingesque imperialism of late Victorian England, had a meaning which was exemplified daily in his contact with Africans and the stray whites of Northern Rhodesia.

Fortunately for his sanity, there were a few fellow countrymen who understood and shared Gore-Browne's prejudices and fundamental integrity. Frank Melland, the native commissioner and author, was one, the medical officers and one or two military escort officers attached to the commission were others, but most of all, during the first two years of the commission, there was Tony Watson. A twenty-four-year-old Englishman whose father had joined the Royal Navy after losing all of his money, Watson enlisted in the Cape Colony Police at sixteen and transferred to Northern Rhodesia, where at nineteen he became an assistant native commissioner. He was a crack shot with a reputation for killing lions and leopards. During what Gore-Browne later remembered as "those damnable days" at the onset of the commission, when he and his unpleasant compatriots sat at Ndola and waited for something to happen, Watson, then the native commissioner, "was the bright spot." He was "the only soul in the whole place who spoke our language," he told Ethel, "& who was one's own sort. Do you know what I mean? . . . He wore, when I first saw him, old clothes that had evidently been made by a good tailor; he asked me to lunch and didn't apologize for the food (which was beastly) beyond saying that his cook had left . . . he didn't say a word about his shooting exploits . . . ; he treated his natives like a gentleman & a thing which attracted me more than any of the others his manners were equally good with the Chief Commissioner & with the half drunken railway brute." After inviting him to a Christmas meal in the commission's camp at Kafulafuta months after this initial encounter, Gore-Browne and Watson became inseparable and affectionate friends. Whenever Gore-Browne could break away from survey duties, which were not too taxing during the rainy season,

16. Gore-Browne to his father, 18 January 1912.

he left his tent and trekked in to sleep in Watson's Ndola house. "You don't know how pleasant it was to be in a house again, after 4 months of tent, & to listen to the rain on the roof," he told his aunt early in 1912. Moreover, he challenged her to conceive of how "one's whole outlook on life is changed by having a companion who takes the same view of the things that we do—after being for months either alone or with people whose every utterance jars and with whom you are always holding yourself in." Watson had "the exact balance on the subject of natives". He knew an indigenous language thoroughly, and proved an inspiration to Gore-Browne, who soon spoke Cibemba well. Watson could thus talk to Africans, not merely give instructions. His sympathy with Africans was gentle and merry, he read Jane Austen and Charles Lamb, and yet had a good sense of discipline and propriety with his servants.[17]

It is clear from Watson's letters to Gore-Browne (his to Watson do not survive) that whatever warmth Gore-Browne felt toward Watson was reciprocated in kind, and then some. Throughout 1912 he wrote assiduously to Gore-Browne in the code Prioleau had earlier employed, accompanied him as often as possible on safari, shared and understood Gore-Browne's difficulties with Gillam and Capt. R. G. Steel, the newly arrived second-in-command, and gave of himself openly. Every letter carried the impress of intimacy. "Dear thing," he wrote reassuringly in July when Gore-Browne was out well northwest of Ndola. "I have written to you every time I have had a chance to send in—so do not get depressed. I will *always* write, even a short note, when there is an opportunity. It is fucking that we shd. have not been able to come up to the Muliashi [River] together but we must try to arrange to meet at least on my southward way. Deg degongot," he lapsed into their private cipher, "thegink egl deont legove yegou, cegause yegou knegow I dego (Dont think I dont love you because you know I do)". And he concluded with a coded "Love dear", sometimes it was "Love and Kisses, Thine Tony."[18] It is clear that Watson and Gore-Browne had a manly relationship, and that each meant much—at least in the lonely positions in which each found himself—to the other. Watson must have also welcomed and enjoyed the attentions of the older, well-bred young gentleman, and Gore-Browne revelled in Watson's youth and courage.

Watson and Gore-Browne were devoted to one another. On one occasion in April, 1912, when Watson heard a rumor that Gore-Browne was ill with malaria, he gathered carriers and set out from Ndola at 1 A.M. to trek the forty miles that separated the two.

17. Gore-Browne to Ethel Locke-King, 10 January 1912.
18. Watson to Gore-Browne, 29 July 1912.

Without stopping—despite the grumbles of the carriers and his own aches—Watson walked for fourteen hours to bring help, if needed, which on this occasion it was not. Fortunately, Gore-Browne's survey work kept him within a hundred miles or so of Ndola and Watson for much of the first half of 1912, and he was thus able to bask in this affectionate glow comparatively often. During this period the commission was proceeding northwestwards in stages by first reconnoitering 100 miles of frontier, then putting up thirty to forty foot high beacons, each of which took two to six days to build, depending upon the extent of clearing needed on the hilltops, and then measuring the angles from and to the beacons, which usually took about ten days each. The resulting calculations consumed a week, and then a 100-mile-long segment was completed.

The commissioners reached Chinsenda on the railway in June and Baya, farther northwest, in September, before striking westward for the to-be-determined border north of Kansanshi mine. In this vicinity Gore-Browne spent the sultry spring months of October and November trying to complete his observations of the last beacons near the source of the Kafue River. But the haze of the season, a product largely of African fires (which provided fertilizing ash before the onset of the rains) usually inhibited clear sight, particularly of a hill called Selano. This, when seen, would close up his own forward reconnaissance and make good the 100 miles which he was doing on his own. Working rapidly at this final stage before going with the rest of the Commission on home leave, Gore-Browne was attempting to see across the broad, heavily-treed plain of the upper Kafue, hoping somehow that his beacons east and west of the Kafue basin would prove intervisible. He had planned to use heliographs to penetrate the haze, but at the last minute Steel, ever jealous of others, commandeered the heliographs and their operators. So Gore-Browne, with time running out, was forced to gamble on some clear weather to see Selano from Chipushi, and thus close the remaining major gap in his triangulations. Doing so at first seemed impossible, so Gore-Browne had to find a new hill to the north, clear and beacon it, and then try to see Selano from it and it from Chipushi. "Later," Gore-Browne concluded a long letter home, "I . . . went up the hill for the evening light, & saw and observed Selano" at last. "Can you guess what it means and the black men are as pleased as I am. Have seldom been so delighted about anything in my life."[19]

Gore-Browne's work for 1912 was finished, and he could catch

19. Gore-Browne to Ethel Locke-King, 18 November 1912. See also the quotation in Stewart Gore-Browne, "The Anglo-Belgian Boundary Commission, 1911–1914," *The Northern Rhodesia Journal,* V (1964), 325.

the mail train to Capetown and a ship home with pride and much relief. Yet he was still seeking the most appropriate role in life for himself. Kakumbi, Chikwanda, Bulaya, and the other Africans, and Watson and Melland, had pointed him in one or two directions, but at home there was Ethel, and a military career which had at least four more years to run before he could qualify for a pension. About himself he had learned more than he may—even in his most reflective moments—have appreciated. The army, he knew, could contain him no longer. Almost anything would be better than returning, still a subaltern, to a regiment. Even captains watched the meal ration issued to horses and turned out at night to hear sleepy sentries mouth ill-understood orders. He dismissed the bar as a possible career—"Oh the purposelessness of that; to wrangle on, and search after subtleties not caring really whether they make for good or evil." So, he asked, "shall I go into Parliament?" With £180 a year from his father, an M.P.'s pay of £400, pension from the army and £250 of his own, he had the prospect of about £1000 a year. It seemed sufficient. And his thirtyish age would be about right. Moreover he could speak clearly and decently and was not afraid of the sound of his own voice. "I don't fancy I'd be an obscure member anyhow. Is it a scheme? I've always had it in the back of my mind . . . The only way to rule in England is to go through politics."[20]

Even more enticing was carving out a place for himself in Africa. Certainly, as he confessed to Ethel, he did have a special capability of "pulling men together and making them play up." He contrasted this talent, however, with what Ethel called being an overseer. "I am about as little of an overseer as anyone who ever worked with natives I fancy as all the time I am trying to make them do things *without* supervision."[21] In his mind, therefore, he had begun thinking of combining the most congenial parts of his present life. He liked the way Watson played David and numbered villagers, guided them, and looked after their welfare in a manner distant but concerned. He would have liked a district of his own, especially if he could have combined such a position with both secondment from the army—"as Lugard and those sort of people were lent to the Niger Company"[22]—in order to retain his pension rights, and the proprietorship of ten-thousand acres (owned nominally by the Locke-Kings) somewhere in Northern Rhodesia. At first he contemplated an estate in the great Hook of the Kafue River region, but Kakumbi, Chikwanda, and the others painted such inviting descrip

20. Gore-Browne to Ethel Locke-King, 16 August 1912.
21. Gore-Browne to Ethel Locke-King, 16 May 1912.
22. Gore-Browne to Ethel Locke-King, 2 April 1912.

tions of Bemba country, and Melland, once a commissioner in Mpika, confirmed so many, that, as early as mid-1912, he had fixed in his own mind upon a settlement somewhere in northeastern Rhodesia. He envisaged that Kerr would help him manage the estate, and that Aunt Ethel, increasingly his soulmate in ways Watson could not hope to be, would live there with him. Then too, Gore-Browne had his dreams. He wanted something on his own—"I don't much care whether the world [he meant his father and mother] thinks it a good job or not"—and he thought that Rhodesia had possibilities.[23]

Certainly he was attracted by the idea of recreating a feudal demesne in Africa, where the indigenous people already believed in a sort of autocratic socialism, and owning land with "your own natives living on it more or less dependent on you."[24] "I can't help thinking," he told his uncle, "that a straight Englishman, who took things quietly and didn't rush people (& who was pretty severe when necessary and very far from a sentimentalist) would be able to be in some sort of relationship to them" similar to that of their traditionally aristocratic chiefs who punished with utmost severity offenses against the common good and held "absolute and entire control of everything." Such a life would, he thought, take the place of the very English upperclass life which was being "crushed out of existence."[25]

By the time that Gore-Browne and the commission, now commanded by Steel, returned to Northern Rhodesia in April 1913, Gore-Browne had passed his examinations for promotion to Captain, tested his so recently strengthened spiritual and romantic bonds to Ethel, and moved closer to Uncle Hugh (Nunk). He was ecstatic to be back in Africa with his own people. Among his first tasks was finding the source of the Kafue which, thanks to a Kaonde headman and an especially delegated guide, he accomplished speedily in May and in which he took a ceremonial bath. Fortuitously, too, but pleasantly so, Gore-Browne's last beacon of 1912 was nearby, and in the clear light of approaching winter, he saw eleven other beacons and could thus confidently begin examining the next 100-mile stretch of frontier beyond Kansanshi. During the winter months, after walking sharply northwestward beyond the searching tributaries that flowed into the Kapombo River, and skirting its own headwaters, Gore-Browne went due north around the source of the Lunga River, which ultimately also joined the Kapombo, and then followed the watershed in a gentle southwesterly direc-

23. Gore-Browne to Ethel Locke-King, 16 May 1912.
24. Gore-Browne to Ethel Locke-King, 15 March 1912.
25. Gore-Browne to Nunk, 21 October 1912.

tion before it turned steeply northward to form the jutting pedicle of Rhodesia's farthest northwest and reached the junction with Angola. He made his usual forward reconnaissance, climbing likely hills, erecting beacons and so on. He and his men built a medium-term camp on a bend in the upper Lunga (fairly close to the administrative *boma* at Mwinilunga) of which Gore-Browne was proud, cut a path along the uppermost ridge for a ponderous steam-driven traction engine which theoretically was hauling their sixteen tons of supplies from Baya via Kansanshi at about three miles an hour, all the while flopping into streams and ditches and floundering its solitary way through the bush.

At the end of August, with the forest receding and the upland plains becoming more frequent, Gore-Browne crossed the Zambezi River near its origins and, twelve miles from the 24th meridian and with scant warning of its existence, came upon Kaleñe Hill, one of the great outreaches of missionary penetration of Rhodesia from the west. In 1906 Dr. Walter Fisher and other Plymouth Brethren from England and Scotland had established Kaleñe as a sanatorium for and extension of their long-existing evangelical exercises along the upper reaches of the Zambezi in Angola.[26] "For days past," Gore-Browne wrote from Kaleñe, "I've been hearing of a hill on the top of which lived Totoro, some said he was a Portuguese, some said he kept a store, some said cattle." Finally, after climbing the hill at midday, Gore-Browne and company discovered a mission station. He had never seen one before, "but you couldn't mistake it." He couldn't quite describe the atmosphere, but there was something about it he found distasteful. "The people weren't rude, but they weren't courteous, & they looked apathetic, & the whole place was slack & untidy & slovenly; they'd too many clothes on & yet not enough." The Fishers and their teenage children he found hospitable but reserved, their food nasty (except for strawberries), and the atmosphere of continual piety rather trying. Gore-Browne found asking a blessing before meals in fundamentalist fashion funny, and missed reverence for the Church as sacred mystery. "Lost in wonder," Gore-Browne's diary recorded, "at the pluck, narrowness, and faith of these people."[27]

These were the halcyon days. With the exception of serious and increasing differences with Steel, the survey was proceeding smoothly with Gore-Browne far in front doing the kind of pioneering which he found so acceptable. Although Bulaya had proved trying in April, he and the other members of his Bemba-speaking

---

26. Robert I. Rotberg, *Christian Missionaries and the Creation of Northern Rhodesia* (Princeton, 1965), 93–96.

27. Gore-Browne to Ethel Locke-King, 31 August 1913; Diary, 31 August 1913.

staff were now giving Gore-Browne pleasure and loyalty as well as performing their tasks well. Kakumbi, who travelled like many of the others, with his wife, and was "tall, beautifully made, swaggering . . . with a [ready] smile . . . & a temper as quick as lightening," had become even more of a favorite than before.[28] And Gore-Browne liked the warm way in which he was accepted, respected, and admired by his personal followers and even the carriers and soldiers attached to the party. Concern on their part was constant and always touching. One night, when Chikwanda and Gore-Browne returned unexpectedly late from a hunting foray, they were greeted with relief by sixty unexpectedly alarmed Africans. They had sent out search parties and fired guns and lighted fires. "When we walked into camp . . . the whole 60 flung themselves on me exactly, but absolutely & literally, like sixty Johnnies [a dog] welcoming Nunk in the hall after a day in London. They jumped up, fawned, nuzzled, stroked me shyly running away frightened & coming back, & then they all made a ring around me & the fire & while the rest sang & clapped in time to the music an old man danced before me, & then another & then another running out of the circle. The first was grotesque [and] when he finished a lithe young Apollo ran out. . . . I've never seen anything quite so magical, so Pan-like, & it was pure delight to watch."[29]

He was at last wholeheartedly and openly at one with Ethel, too. Although never physical, their relationship had grown and matured by correspondence in 1911 and 1912, was enhanced by the months on leave that Gore-Browne spent as much at Brooklands as at the Gore-Browne house near Oxford, and during 1913 lost all pretense of being that customary between aunt and nephew. Doing so was but a long overdue acknowledgement that artifice was unnecessary. They began explicitly to vow what each meant to the other, and what had been evident from their more formally contrived communications for years. Symbolically important, too, Gore-Browne and his aunt in mid-1913 both dropped the employment of formal nominative salutations. Their letters thereafter easily began "My dear" or "My very dear." "As usual," the 30-year old wrote to his 50-year old aunt in one typical letter, "I just can't say how I want to come & talk to you. There's nothing on earth to say, but merely that I want to sit in front of your fire, or on the blue sofa & just tell you the different happenings and discuss them with you. . . . You've been [a helpful personality and soulmate] pretty well all my life to me, but I didn't know I was that to you in any way. It's really a bit like the sun—without it I'm the same person I suppose as far as flesh

28. Gore-Browne to Ethel Locke-King, 7 May 1913.
29. Gore-Browne to Ethel Locke-King, 6 July 1913.

& blood is concerned, but life & the power of living are at a lower level. . . . When the sun's shining, everything's easier and fuller, the compression is better; and it's just the same when there are two of us. . . . We're a power together."[30] Being with Ethel (and with his black cohorts) gave him the self assurance and psychic well-being he sometimes lacked, and which he never derived from dealings with his family. "I want *you* every minute of the day, to help & to scheme & to criticise," was the common combination of sentiments.[31] He told her everything, fantasied what he must have known could never have been realized—a future together in a house constructed to her taste (and his) somewhere in the heart of Bembaland where his blackmen would wait on her as they did on him, and where their very remoteness would prevent the interference (and prying eyes) of other whites (and his parents). Nunk would somehow come along and be a part of things, but she would be his. They would have a chapel in the house, a hall, and a library, and it would center around an Oxford-type courtyard and would be in an Italianate style, rather Tuscan. Of the local dark wood their carpenters (and a large circular saw was probably required) would make massive furniture. "It does make such a difference to the house don't you think, & prevents it looking cheap & suburban."[32] He pictured great doorposts and fireplaces, and a broad black staircase with immense bannisters. Letter after letter contained sketches of the whole and its parts.

On her part, Gore-Browne was no longer "dearest lad". He became "my dearly beloved." His letters to her were her hidden life to which she turned in thought whenever weary or laden with cares. When your letter came, she wrote of an unexpected Sunday morning delivery, "it went to my bath & sat there with me pretending that it had some affinity with the warmth of the water."[33] His letters turned everything to gold for her. She wanted him as much, if not in the same way, as he desired her. "Dear, who are more dear to me than I can ever show you . . ."[34]

"Oh my dear," Gore-Browne wrote to Ethel in 1914, "I think we could do great things together. I suppose it's all to do with the subconscious, & the very imperfectly understood powers that make up mind & memory. . . . I do feel that you and I are nearer to each other and more use to each other than any other is to either of us. . . . I feel as if nothing could ever really come between you and

30. Gore-Browne to Ethel Locke-King, 21 May 1913.
31. Gore-Browne to Ethel Locke-King, 30 June 1913.
32. Gore-Browne to Ethel Locke-King, 20 October 1913.
33. Ethel Locke-King to Gore-Browne, 15 August 1913.
34. Ethel Locke-King to Gore-Browne, 19 December 1913.

me. . . . I do feel I want your share in anything I do, and you tell me it's the same, and that I help you. I don't really know what the world would be like if you weren't in it . . . the very thought of having to live without you gives me a sort of chill feeling of all the joy, & half the power gone."[35]

By this time circumstance, the escapades of Nunk's cousin Peter King, a soldier in India, and Nunk's generosity had brought Ethel and Gore-Browne tangibly close in a way that at last gave more hope of permanence. Peter had fallen in love with a married woman and made known his plans to marry.[36]

He promptly plummeted from family grace, Gore-Browne replacing him as heir and, virtually, adopted son. Ethel insinuated this possibility late in 1913 and Nunk himself came around to making his choice all but known a little later. "If I died I know you'd stick to Nunk & he'd feel you were his son—& if Nunk died it wouldn't make any difference between you & me—we should be just what we have always been to each other."[37] Brooklands, heavily in debt, would henceforth be Gore-Browne's as well as the Locke-King responsibility, and any African venture could more legitimately be shared. "Think," he thanked his aunt, "what it means to me suddenly to find the place, & the people I've all along, & all my life almost, thought of as home, and as my nearest & best (that's not true of Nunk till lately of course, but you know what you've been to me all my life) becoming that in real truth, without any imaginings or chance of a snub." The experience was "as though one had suddenly discovered a missing parish register making one the legitimate son of parents one had known all one's life & loved & yet never been able to own. Oh my dear its too good to be true. . . . Think of belonging to you really . . ."[38]

Before Christmas 1913 Gore-Browne had committed himself and, what is more, promised his African retinue that he would buy land in Lubemba and put cattle on it before going back to Europe. But it was still unclear whether or not he would go back to a battery in September 1914, or whether he should try to find a slack station so that he could cram for entrance to the staff college. Or should he try for an administrative position in an African territory? Unfortu-

35. Gore-Browne to Ethel Locke-King, 8 February 1914.

36. Peter King's given name was Frank Jerome Maitland King (1884–1941). His father, George Henry Maitland King, was the grandson of the sixth Baron Peter King, and a descendent of the first Baron of Ockham, Lord King, who was Lord Chancellor in the early eighteenth century. George King (1853–1937) married Maud Giffard, and their son Peter entered the Royal Engineers, eventually becoming a colonel.

37. Ethel Locke-King to Gore-Browne, 19 December 1913.

38. Gore-Browne to Ethel Locke-King, 16 March 1916.

nately, he would probably have to start at the bottom, which ruled out that alternative. Anyway, he wanted to be in Central Africa among his own people, the Bemba, and near the estate on which he and the Locke-Kings would, he hoped, settle and "be powers in the land." "Oh for a job of my own with a bit of power, & a bit of responsibility, & a bit of construction in it," he implored.[39] He thought that he was well past any major turning points in his life's path. If his Africans abandoned him, then he would scurry home and face a dark future. Until that happened, and he doubted if it ever would, he knew that "more and more and more" he had come into his own in Africa. "How I want you to come and share it," he wrote.[40] It was an honest and full assessment even if Gore-Browne could not then have discerned the exact shape of his own immediate or long term futures, and if no crystal ball could have revealed the vigorous role which he was to play in Northern Rhodesia.

Steel was then the only blot on the otherwise bright horizon. Only two years older than Gore-Browne, he was already a major in the Royal Engineers. Although he had few of Gillam's more obvious failings, and could give orders, he had a better taste for comfort than work. Even for a four-month stay, the huts at temporary camps had to be whitewashed, meals were incomplete without several courses, and breakfasts were habitually late. Gore-Browne would have commented upon, but not really minded, any of these traits if Steel had done his fair share of the work, or if he had at least refrained from being critical of everything Gore-Browne did. "Himself he's done nothing. He gets up between 9 & 10, sometimes does a page or two of accounts, or drafts a letter which I type. One whole afternoon he hemmed the breeches of the messengers (true), another day he watered the garden."[41] Steel could speak no African language, and must have felt rather lost beside Gore-Browne. Their temperaments were as opposite as their classes and behavior were distinct. But it was breaking faith with carriers that led to an irreparable rent between them. In July 1913 Steel refused to let 150 carriers, dismissed by Gore-Browne after completing their three-month contracts, go home. When they refused to work without pay, he tried to starve them into submission, and promised to flog every twentieth man. He finally relented a month after they should have been paid off. "Thus," commented Gore-Browne with venom, "is the faith of the black man in an Englishman's word upheld by the senior representative of the Imperial Government."[42] Later, Steel

39. Gore-Browne to Ethel Locke-King, 12 November 1913.
40. Gore-Browne to Ethel Locke-King, 27 December 1913.
41. Gore-Browne to Ethel Locke-King, 10 October 1913.
42. Gore-Browne to Ethel Locke-King, 15 October 1913.

felt oversupplied with carriers, and dismissed them before their time was up without paying the full, agreed-upon wages. Even then, he suddenly found that more carriers were in fact needed. Gore-Browne gnashed his teeth.

The parting of the ways was occasioned by more of the same kinds of behavior in 1914. Steel spread and told lies about Gore-Browne and other whites and acted in a manner that bordered on the paranoid. He complained about camps made by Gore-Browne and the district commissioner, sent several of his noncommissioned officers home unnecessarily, and set about working himself for the first time in months with a great burst of flurried activity. What made Gore-Browne's blood boil further, however, was his attempt to make a profit for the commission by selling its grain at outrageous prices to others—the Belgians, the Anglo-Portuguese Commission, and so on. Finally, in January, he went so far as to order Gore-Browne, camping some distance away on the Myafunshi River, to do the same. This Gore-Browne naturally refused to contemplate, and paid off his men. "I expect an explosion," Gore-Browne wrote. "He is behaving so outrageously that you can only believe it possible when you think of him as insane, with a madman's cunning flashes of apparent sense."[43] Gore-Browne did not consider himself "justified, even with your sanction," he wrote Steel, "in using force to compel carriers to stay . . . not because I wish to 'pander to native custom' . . . but as a simple matter of right and wrong." As a result, Steel's next letter carried a curt note of dismissal from the commission for "wilful disobedience."[44] And so Gore-Browne was no longer Assistant British Boundary Commissioner. "I don't think I could have done other than I did," he wrote Ethel. "I was determined not to have a row over personal matters . . . but I think I was bound to stop him going on doing down the natives. . . . Ugh! he's a nasty beast as well as a mad one."[45]

It was a sad ending to Gore-Browne's part of the commission. In his own eyes he had done right. It was in keeping with his breeding and his sense of how he would be judged by his peer group in England—and his aunt. Equally, his men meant much more than Steel. Yet by, as Steel accused, thus "currying favor with the Awemba", Gore-Browne risked the kind of official bad marks which might—depending upon which kinds of men were serving in the personnel section of the War Office—curtail any hope of a

43. Gore-Browne to Ethel Locke-King, 18 January 1913.

44. Gore-Browne to Steel, 18 January 1914, quoted in Gore-Browne to Lord Herbert John Gladstone, H. M. High Commissioner in South Africa; Steel to Gore-Browne, 22 January 1914.

45. Gore-Browne to Ethel Locke-King, 30 January 1914.

profitable future in the army. Moreover, his dismissal coincided with the arrival of a letter from Livingstone informing him that the company could offer him no commissionerships in Northern Rhodesia. Shortly before, he had learned that an Anglo-German commission to delimit the borders of the Southwest African Caprivi Zipvel, which Gore-Browne had hoped to command, had been cancelled. Thus far there was no negative word about his application for ten thousand acres in northeastern Rhodesia, however, so Gore-Browne, at least welcoming his unexpectedly early freedom to travel (the commission would anyway have concluded its work by June or July), broke camp, Chikwanda going ahead, and set out across country with about seventy Bemba-speaking followers for the promised land.

Unhappily, the company was not giving away the promised land to young subalterns merely for the asking. The chief surveyor said that he had authority to allocate acreage on or near the railway line, where everyone else was trying to make Northern Rhodesia prosper, but not up somewhere in the wilds, where Africans held sway. In a state of some anxiety and agitation, Gore-Browne therefore had to detour smartly southwards to Livingstone to employ his undoubted charms on the administration. There, his existing good relations with many official whites, and a reputation for aristocratic gentlemanliness, performed wonders. The police met his train, and everyone appeared kind. The treasurer asked him to lunch, the public prosecutor to dinner, and the secretary put him up for the local club and helped him to attend to his affairs. If he could find someone, i.e. someone white, to occupy his land in his absence, he could have an estate in the Abercorn, Fife (Isoka), or northern Kasama districts where there already were a handful of settlers. But since there were no other whites in the Mpika and Chinsali districts (the heart of Lubemba) he could not settle there. (The company feared being forced to supply groups of settlers with a physician, a school teacher, and other expensive personnel.) Even so, Gore-Browne was satisfied, for he had heard that the Mpika and Chinsali districts might well be infested with tsetse fly, and from all accounts Abercorn was a veritable paradise. "Anyhow it's all better than I'd feared," he wrote.

Northeastern Rhodesia would be as remote as possible, Gore-Browne believed, from the baleful influence of the South (Southern Rhodesia and South Africa), its racial policies, and Africans corrupted by towns, by mines, and by the poor breeding of most whites in Rhodesia. "Of course, the native isn't perfect, he's very far from it, & he's very trying, & he's got a good share of vices, but for us deliberately to take him and put him in the way of learning lots more without an effort to do anything for his good beyond seeing that he is not unduly crowded in the railway carriage or any other place where inconvenient comments might be made by some outside observer, seems to me pretty rotten. Every Boma tells the same tale, at every village where I stop & talk the head man complains that all his men are carried off to the mines, leaving the women to become whores, the fields uncultivated, the villages tumbling down, and when they come back full of cheap trash bought in the stores, they merely drink & idle & are rude & uncivil till their money is all gone, when they go back again to the mines. It's rather pitiful."[46] He implored his aunt to help him stem the tide of unwanted progress in at least one part of black Africa. "Oh do let's come out here & try & keep the little corner we can influence decent & upright and uncontaminated." He described Chilanga, on the railway, where he stayed with James Moffat Thomson, the magistrate. "Here . . . are 900 settlers, ¾ of them Dutch, & if I told you the things they do & the life they lead & the cruelties and injustices & meanesses, it would spoil all the picture & make you utterly sick."[47]

On Good Friday 1914 Gore-Browne reached Lake Young, the traditional name for which was Shiwa Ngandu, or Lake of the Royal Crocodile clan. "Step out of the tent now and look at the lake a strip of blue silver with clumps of dark, deep-green trees, and behind purple hills coming down to the water side," he told his aunt.[48] Gore-Browne liked the site very much, having seen nothing as dramatic and appealing during the course of the long march from Ndola to Serenje, Chitambo Mission, Chilonga Mission, and Mpika boma. Furthermore, within hours of his arrival Gore-Browne had killed his first rhinoceros, a black, sullen beast "straight out of Wagner," and obtained his African name—Chipembere, Cibemba for rhinoceros, the animal with the fearsome temper. The omens were thus good and his feeling was right. He set up house on the lake, there and then. But the soil looked sandy and poor and there was rumor of tsetse fly.

A few days later, having meant to push straight on, Gore-Browne was still camped by the side of the lake. "I kept wondering if it wasn't to be our home." On the other side of the lake the soil looked better, the villagers swore there was no fly, and Gore-Browne saw women bringing in bundles of grass from which to distill a substitute for sea salt, a rare commodity in Africa. He also noticed a stream, the Katete, which washed out of the hills and would probably bring alluvial deposits with it. When he explored the stream he saw that its fall would be steep enough for power, and

46. Gore-Browne to Ethel Locke-King, Good Friday, 1914.
47. Gore-Browne to Ethel Locke-King, 8 March 1914.
48. Gore-Browne to Ethel Locke-King, 10 April 1914.

for the running of pumps and a circular saw. There was a "delicious" valley, snug and sheltered with palm trees. "I pictured the valley ablaze with fruit trees, anything in the world ought to grow there." Then he located a site for a house above some natural terraces, about four thousand seven hundred feet above mean sea level, with a good view of the lake and the distant hills. The villagers were also very welcoming.[49] Gore-Browne had found his fairy kingdom.

He could hardly contain his excitement. In good conscience, however, he had to examine other possibilities. First he consulted with Robert "Bobo" Young, after whom the lake had been named. Young, a legendary native commissioner, was credited with singlehandedly taming the Bemba in the 1890s. He was based at Chinsali, sixty-five miles north of Shiwa Ngandu, and had been cautioned by a fellow native commissioner to ready himself for Gore-Browne's arrival. "I have warned . . . Young," E. H. Cholmeley wrote to Gore-Browne, "that a man will be coming along with a window pane in his face, and a plausible manner, with subtle and alluring schemes and propositions, and while leaving him free to take his own line with him, have suggested that he use the greatest discretion."[50] Young and Gore-Browne took to each other immediately, and Young naturally agreed that there was no better spot in the northeast than Shiwa. Nevertheless, he urged Gore-Browne to look elsewhere before opting for an estate there. He pointed him toward Mirongo, the old boma, potential cattle ranches in Fife district, several sites on the Chambezi River, and obvious places on the highlands near Abercorn. (In Abercorn there were already settlers, and bound to be more, however, and Gore-Browne wanted no part of other whites.) There were better places for cattle than Shiwa, but there was really no suitable market nearer than the Congo or Southern Rhodesia, so Gore-Browne, who was anyway less interested in agricultural potential than amenity, had little reason to be tempted by the other possibilities.

All roads led back to Shiwa. During May and a part of June, after looking at other sites, he camped by Shiwa Ngandu and began readying a more permanent house, felling trees for seasoned timber, planting and preparing irrigation works for fruit trees due from the White Fathers at Chilonga, and buying cattle and clearing pasture land. He also tried teaching Chikwanda as much as possible of the rudiments of Gore-Browne's type of farming. Everything went well, the chief and the 100 villagers were excited when he returned

49. Gore-Browne to Ethel Locke-King, Easter Sunday, 1914.
50. Cholmeley to Gore-Browne, 2 March 1914. Cholmeley had examined Gore-Browne at Ndola in Cibemba and said that he passed the test set for commissioners.

and delighted when he told them of his plans. They also helped with the building, unasked. "The women . . . turned out . . . to mix the mud [for house plaster] and carry it from the kneading pit to the house. They made a jolly sight walking with that classic grace our folk have lost . . . singing the while . . . It seems to me a wonderfully right state of affairs & a very desirable kind of socialism. I am clever and better equipped than these people, & so they all work to provide me with what I reasonably want, a roof & a garden; but I get them meat, & protect their crops from marauding eland, & find them money for their tax & a few luxuries they can't get otherwise. . . . Also in trouble, if an enemy came and burnt their houses or carried off their women, they'd expect me to take up their cause." Moreover, they did not presume equality and, when Gore-Browne passed through the village, they fell down and clapped their hands in true Bemba fashion, shouting his praises continually. "But if I tried to presume on my side . . . & take their crops or rape their women, or make slaves of their children, they'd very soon rise up."[51]

Alternative employment for the local Bemba, as Gore-Browne well knew, meant being recruited to labor in a mine in the Congo, Northern Rhodesia, or farther south. There, he said on many occasions, "they are as well looked after as machines, and . . . a . . . drunken dago, or perhaps an Englishman roars 'pick up the bloody pickaxe you black bastard' and when the man looks at him inquiringly, not . . . having understood a word, he hits him with a red hot iron."[52] Gore-Browne had witnessed such an incident at Kansanshi. For the hundredth time Gore-Browne fantasied on paper about making "a life work of the black people." "We'll write a book," he told Ethel, and the care and administration of our own black people "will keep us from becoming cranks." Shiwa would be their "royal park."[53]

With Bulaya and Kakumbi Gore-Browne set out for England in July (Bulaya would learn to cook, Kakumbi would see the soldiers and fine sights, and both would for the first time meet decent white women who were "chiefs" and even tempered.) He had found his future home, and had made a start at taming it. He was unhappy at leaving. But Ethel, and Brooklands, unpleasantness with his mother and father—his father thought farming a bore and feared that Gore-Browne would some day become a hateful colonial politician—and much else of which Gore-Browne was blissfully unaware, awaited. He was 31, with prospects more unusual than he knew. It was a perfect moment to go home.

51. Gore-Browne to Ethel Locke-King, 25 May 1914.
52. Gore-Browne to Ethel Locke-King, 25 May 1914.
53. Gore-Browne to Ethel Locke-King, 18 May 1914.

III
The Shells of War

"OH MY DEAR, life is so glorious, and this world is so beautiful, and its inhabitants are so nice, and every single moment is so worth while!" At the apogee of his powers—full of healthy self-esteem—Gore-Browne was writing to his aunt from Dar es Salaam after a strenuous but rewarding journey from Shiwa Ngandu en route to England.[1] Life was for once capable of being taken at the flood: The choice of Shiwa Ngandu had been confirmed; likewise his love of Africa and the Bemba had been tested and reiterated. Nunk had decided to "adopt" Gore-Browne as heir in place of Peter King and Gore-Browne was on his way "home" to Brooklands to claim the inheritance and, most of all, his beloved Ethel. As he travelled across German East Africa, northwards around Cape Guardafui and up the Red Sea on a balky German freighter to Port Said, and thenceforward to Marseilles on a Union Castle liner, in his own mind he made definite plans to serve another three years in the army—until he could obtain a pension—before returning to Africa in order to establish Shiwa Ngandu "on a good footing." Serving in the peacetime army at home would somehow be endured. The quarrelsome boundary commission was at least behind him.

Gore-Browne may have sensed a pulsating tempo of war in the casual utterances of remote servants of the Kaiser in Dar es Salaam, but he gave little thought to its coming crescendo, and to how the guns of August might change the future of a regular officer. On 28 July, aboard the *Emir* as it steamed slowly into the Suez Canal, he learned that Archduke Franz Ferdinand had been assassinated and that Austria and Serbia had gone to war. The remainder of his diary entry is terse: "11:30 off again and into the canal. Very interested." Only on 1 August did he and others steaming across the southern Mediterranean past an eruptive Stromboli appreciate the onrush of danger. They learned of Russia's ultimatum to Austria and the widespread mobilization in Europe. An English fleet raised steam in

1. Gore-Browne to Ethel Locke-King, 9 July 1914.

Portsmouth; another went on maneuvers. Finally, on 3 August, the liner docked unexpectedly in Marseilles. There, however, passenger trains had stopped running, the city was ominously quiet, and Gore-Browne's British currency was everywhere refused. Crossing France to the Channel was a necessity, especially for an officer suddenly aware of how one set of fantasies might abruptly supersede another.

Gore-Browne managed to obtain train passages for himself and several other shipboard acquaintances with military engagements to keep. Boarding a late afternoon train (and leaving Bulaya and Kakumbi to sail to London) he reached Paris the next morning, finding the Place de la Concorde draped in flags and the shops of the Rue de la Paix shut tight. The streets were empty but people surprisingly calm. Another late afternoon train took Gore-Browne to Boulogne. As he crossed the Channel, Britain declared war on Germany.

It was the auspicious fifth day of August. Southeast England was awash with rain. Gore-Browne had been away a year, but it seemed like a decade or more. Leaving in peace, he found himself unexpectedly part of a nation at war. As the train from Folkestone pulled damply into Charing Cross station he went straight to the War Office nearby. Unfortunately, the first ranks of the British Expeditionary Force were full. So Gore-Browne went down to Brooklands.

Gore-Browne's war began in earnest three days later, after fretful reunions with Ethel and Nunk, with his brother Robert, with his mother and father, and with Kerr. Lt. Gore-Browne joined the 32nd Brigade of the Fourth Division at Woolwich. Like so many others, he foresaw a comparatively brief conflict and a rough but salutary victory for Britain and her allies. As his initial contribution, Gore-Browne went off with a part of the ammunition column to a small village near Norwich to join a flying column protecting the eastern coast of Britain until the territorials were ready to take over.

After a week of these preparations, the Fourth Division was rushed to the Continent. After "concentrating" at Harrow, Gore-Browne and the remainder of the division steamed across the Channel, guns, horses, and all, to land on French soil: for the first time in many centuries, a British army was in France to assist rather than fight the French. For Gore-Browne, the moment for which he had long prepared had—from a professional point of view—at last come. He doubtless contemplated war, imagined some of its horrors and many of its glories, but the manic mood was still very much with him. He remained euphoric, sentimental, conscious of mortality, and almost melodramatically at the kinds of heights he had reached earlier—and virtually only with Ethel. Whatever might have occurred between them during the brief days he spent at Brooklands before going off to war, Gore-Browne had lost none of his fervor. "This is to be a last letter," he began after reaching France, "for tonight as ever is we're off, into the very thick of it, I fancy, and it's likely to be a while before I get another chance. And if it should be never, well, you'll know that all is well and that we'll still belong to each other for ever and ever and ever. . . . Oh my dear thank you for all you've been to me all through."[2] This was a constant theme throughout the war, and each rendezvous in Europe and the occasional leaves at Brooklands only matured his reverence.

Soldiers, even officers, need love objects, particularly in wars. And for Gore-Browne, who had numerous acquaintances of both sexes, many close male friends, a family (whom he kept distant), and a great (paternal) affection for particular Africans, there was only Ethel on whom he could lavish the kind of love usually reserved for someone more physically accessible. "My dear I love you," he wrote after a particularly trying three days on the Belgian front. A week later, after being made captain and posted to a particularly static and not very dangerous part of the line, he continued: "You know you are all the world to me and bound up with my whole life and that I long for you as I suppose a husband longs for his wife when they are really one."[3] Only to Ethel, busy then and throughout the war with the Red Cross hospital work for which she later received her title, could Gore-Browne write openly about his fears, his ideals, and his dreams (often of returning under clear, sunlit skies to Shiwa).[4] To her, too, he transferred responsibility for his close wards, Bulaya and Kakumbi. They had finally reached London by sea and were at first employed at Brooklands—much to the resentment of the English employees—as members of the domestic staff. "P. S.," Gore-Browne ended what he feared might be a testamentary letter, "be kind to the black men . . . And if anything happens to me they are very much my bequest to you."[5]

Gore-Browne found himself (although he could not have appreciated its dimensions fully at the time) almost immediately (from 24 August 1914) part of a desperate rearguard action covering the British retreat to Le Cateau, in and around which a major battle

2. Gore-Browne to Ethel Locke-King, 22 August 1914.

3. Gore-Browne to Ethel Locke-King, 3 November, 10 November 1914.

4. Throughout the war Ethel was assistant county director and vice-president of the North Surrey Division of the British Red Cross Society. For much of the time she administered twelve makeshift hospitals in large private homes, three of which were her own.

5. Gore-Browne to Ethel Locke-King, 22 August 1914.

was fought two days later.[6] He was second-in-command of the ammunition resupplying column for the three field gun units of the 32nd Brigade, Royal Field Artillery. Most of the 150 men under him were comparatively raw recruits; Gore-Browne's responsibility was critical. He saw that gunners scattered over a wide radius were never without shells, that his horse-drawn wagons (caissons) were always where they were needed, that the horses were fit, and that "turn-around" and "down" times were progressively reduced.

Gore-Browne's first tastes of war were a compound of continuous cacophony and psychedelic lighting, of major bombardments, the pitiful streaming of refugees, stories of German atrocities, and intense, even hallucinatory, lack of sleep. During his first night he slept on a doorstep for forty-five minutes, then found himself in the middle of a battle—something similar to "sitting on the piston head of an internal combustion engine running at about 200 revs." There was "ceaseless noise and . . . spurts of fire, and . . . bits of wood and bullets flying about, with everywhere clouds no bigger than a man's hand as the only outward and visible sign, and the air literally full of the screaming of the things as they pass, all this is so comically out of place in a peaceful . . . French landscape with the crucifixes standing up by the roadsides, and a church bell calling desperately the while."[7] That night, after the battle of Ligny, he slept two hours and then beat a hasty retreat, marching virtually for two days without any sleep whatsoever.

It was at Ligny, southwest of Le Cateau, that Gore-Browne was closest to the Germans. "I was absolutely the last Englishman (or Frenchman) to leave the village, with my wagons, and I'd had to watch all the infantry come through, and then the last battery, and then get my push away." They marched "back and back and back—three times all night through and on into the next day, and then on again." They hallucinated, Gore-Browne seeing doors opening into lovely gardens. And everywhere, as they fell back toward the Aisne River, "always there were these wretched people fleeing from their homes, more pathetic than I can possibly tell you—all women and old men, and children who'd no business to be hurt, and whose men were all at the war." A little later, as the British counterattacked along the Marne, Gore-Browne saw how the Germans had devastated town and country. "It's quite beyond description. Whole towns deliberately and wantonly sacked." Houses

6. For the full context, Barbara W. Tuchman, *The Guns of August* (New York, 1962), 234–262; J. E. Edmonds (ed.), *History of the Great War: Military Operations, France and Belgium, 1914* (London, 1922), 53–140.

7. Gore-Browne to Ethel Locke-King, 4 September 1914.

were thoroughly pillaged. "It's a beastly sight when every single private belonging is pulled out and smashed or spoilt. . . . Before leaving they nearly always use the rooms, and sometimes the cupboards or cooking pots, as latrines. This isn't pretty to tell you, but I've seen it all with my own eyes."[8] By the end of his first three weeks at war, Gore-Browne had learned how unpleasant, degrading, and dehumanizing modern wars were. The glamor that he had once expected to find on the front had vanished. He had not known warfare to be so indecisive, squalid, and expensive of the lives of bystanders. "I'm afraid its the senseless waste that oppresses me most of all," he wrote weeks later, "when you see splendid bridges blown up, huge factories demolished, the glare of burning towns lighting up the sky, and everywhere and on all sides private property demolished . . . ruthlessly."[9]

Gore-Browne was part of a hasty flight southwards ordered by the frightened British General Staff. Staving off defeat at Le Cateau, the British abandoned St. Quentin, reassembled at Noyon on the Oise, abandoned their allies, and retired across the Aisne. For much of the critical battle of the Aisne, Gore-Browne and his men ferried ammunition across the river and the canal, past a destroyed sugar factory, and on up to the batteries on the heights on the northern side of Aisne. Until early October Gore-Browne would go up the ridges two or three times a day to resupply the batteries, or at least to see what they needed. It was much the same when they moved the column to Braine on the Vesle River. Gore-Browne's column —indeed, his entire brigade—played an important but definitely supporting role in a war which was almost never again to see hot pursuit over many leagues of enemy territory, desperate rear-guard stands, rapid maneuverability, forced marches, and the like. Remembering it all a year later, when the war had become a confrontation of opposing fortresses, Gore-Browne said, "I don't say war was precisely what we expected, but it wasn't so very far off, and anyhow we did do more or less what we'd been trained to do all the many years—we galloped into action, and we limbered up & went off, and we marched, & halted & marched again, and had sudden alarms, & cavalry jingled by, and infantry deployed across green fields in great swinging lines, and war was more or less war."[10]

Although Gore-Browne saw little of the infantryman's front in 1914, the artillery batteries being emplaced on the high ridges well behind, the trench warfare which was to be such a dulling characteristic of the long combat began along the northern banks of the

8. Gore-Browne to Ethel Locke-King, 16 September 1914.
9. Gore-Browne to his mother, 22 October 1914.
10. Gore-Browne to Ethel Locke-King, 22 September 1915.

Aisne where the armies remained immobilized for the last weeks of September and the first days of October. There were early frosts, and much rain. The deep mud, which prevented guns from being shifted more than 15°, for example, and which virtually entombed the troops for the duration of the war, was a feature of the slog on the Aisne and the long front that gradually developed during the autumn of 1914 northwestwards through the Somme to Ypres.

During the first days of October, the entire British army was gradually and stealthily shifted away from the Aisne to the Allies' far left flank in Belgium. Supply (and evacuation) lines would be shorter if the Britons were fighting with the Channel at their backs, and Field Marshal Sir John French and the other British commanders felt greater comfort in resuming their position on the French left. There they could bring all of the scattered British units back into contact with one another. Gore-Browne's unit marched for four bitterly cold nights into Flanders.

Gore-Browne was proud of his organizational achievements in Flanders. Each dawn he went to see the horses fed, returned for a good farm breakfast with his brother officers, went back to the stables to see that the horses were groomed properly, unless "there's a lot of amm. wanted at the guns, in which case I go off with wagons and perhaps do not come back till dark." His fellow subaltern supplied the needs of the infantry. After a regular lunch he went "for a ride round the different batteries getting the news and finding out the situation."[11]

What he wanted was a job with more scope. After all, he was well and expensively trained, and had the qualities and skills necessary for a good staff officer. Also, he knew that he had real gifts of effective communication and leadership. "I'm eating my heart out for a job to spread myself in a little. That's not a complaint," he told Ethel, busy with her new hospital, "but I feel I could do more somewhere else."[12]

Instead, on 10 November, Gore-Browne became a captain and second-in-command of the nearby 135th Battery. "I've in a way less responsibility even now . . . and less of a free hand, so I'm not overjoyed at the change . . . but . . . I'm a sod to complain," Gore-Browne wrote. The battery took up a position near Nieppe, northwest of Armentières and southwest of Messines, and Gore-Browne fired away at the Germans for the remainder of the month, during which time he was never able to take off his clothes. "It's not really a hard life . . . and not comparable to that the infantry lead for either hardship or danger—but oh for the end and for quiet—for

11. Gore-Browne to Ethel Locke-King, 26 October 1914.
12. Gore-Browne to Ethel Locke-King, 10 November 1914.

peace, the noise continues almost ceaselessly, only becoming worse when we fire ourselves or when shells burst near us." There were the black and yellow fumes of 11-inch shells, and continual sniping, too.

One of the growing problems was German forward air support. Occasionally, despite what Gore-Browne took to be expert concealment, a German pilot would find the 135th, drop "a long trail of shiny stuff" to give the line and range to the German guns and, a few minutes later, high explosive shells would arrive in the midst of the British pits. "In the old days all you worried about was cover from the front, and I fancy doing that was considered rather cowardly till the Boer War. Now you have to think about cover from above, and it only wants a machine that can come burrowing under ground at about 120 miles an hour to make the thing complete."

Gore-Browne was in charge of the horse lines—their feeding, watering, exercise, and grooming; he was commended for good arrangements and results, but the work was "infinitesimal," and he was easily bored. "Of course it's immensely important that these things should be done," he lamented, but "I've really painfully little to do . . . and less than no responsibility."[13] He wanted to be working eighteen hours a day on something that mattered, rather than three on horses, when there was combat all around him.

Suddenly, the snow, his chilblains, the bursting shells, the horses, and the war fell miraculously behind him. Gore-Browne returned to Brooklands on 2 December. Abcessed teeth and septic crowns, which had pained him since August, needed attending in London. He had much to do, Ethel and Nunk, his family, and Bulaya and Kakumbi to see, and some jockeying in Whitehall for a more suitable position. There was also the future of Shiwa, which had never, even in the darkest moments of the war, left his mind. But he was a soldier disabused, like so many others, of the romance of war, of the quest for honorable easy victories, and of the character-building utility of combat. He had been frightened, and had seen too much to make him believe that war could uplift spirits. Too many hapless civilians and solid soldiers had been killed. There was brutality, wantonness, and, despite the respect that he had for the British infantry, a realization nevertheless that theirs was a monumental exercise in futility. He had also come to know himself a little better. Certainly he knew how he longed for Ethel, for a decent staff position leading to some kind of command, and for the end of it all so that he could take the triad back to the lake, the bright skies, and the people—his people—at Shiwa Ngandu. Most of all, Gore-Browne

13. Gore-Browne to Ethel Locke-King, 10 November, 18 November, 24 November, 1914; Gore-Browne to Nunk, 23 November 1914.

had tested himself. He had known fright and he felt that he would not now be killed in the war. Nor did he think that his closest male friend, Kerr, would perish. Gore-Browne was a man who clung to simple, direct, and—in his mind—noble certainties.

Like Gore-Browne, the cabinet had abruptly and belatedly realized that warfare was no longer a duel between professional armies on figurative open fields. Static defenses were useless. Nor, it had rapidly become clear, would superiority on land be decided by power at sea. Whole nations had to bear arms; rural Britons might need to defend their familiar fields as townsmen their crowded streets. Even the expeditionary force, the largest army ever sent overseas from Britain at the outset of a war, was realized to be puny in comparison with the continental levies and inadequate for the real needs of the new, life-intensive warfare by attrition. Five regular divisions had gone to France in August and a sixth reached the front in September. The dominions and the colonies were sending troops—Gore-Browne had fought in Belgium beside lancers and fusilliers from India—and divisions of territorials were also bound for the front. But, as Horatio Herbert Kitchener, the war minister, had realized earlier than his generals, Britain needed hurriedly to raise another "new" army, the first 100,000 men of which were organized during the autumn of 1914 into six divisions—numbers nine through fourteen. As the implications of the long retreat from Mons became apparent, a further six divisions, numbers fifteen through twenty, were planned and men recruited.

The armies of Europe in the past had never achieved much success with hastily mobilized batallions and divisions. The Germans confidently expected the Britons to end up as *Kanonenfütter*. Kitchener, however, felt that rigorous and lengthy training under experienced supervisors could turn raw recruits into comparatively disciplined soldiers. He even had the faith (or wisdom) to think that the instruction of months could make of these men the gunners and drivers needed for highly mobile field batteries. Many of his regular army contemporaries were prepared to see callow youths and aged cityfolk transformed into something resembling an infantry. But to think that some of them could even be turned into artillerymen seemed beyond credibility. There was particular skepticism with regard to the second 100,000; at least the first six divisions could count on a leavening of older territorials and men with some martial experience. By the time the Seventeenth Division was organized, this pool of volunteers had evaporated and supplies of all kinds were virtually non-existent. Uniforms, guns, blankets, tents, etc., arrived only months later. And most of the men were recruited from the towns of northern England. Few knew how to "make do" out-of-doors. Fewer still, as Gore-Browne was to discover, had ever seen a horse or could imagine how riding, harnessing, and so on, could be accomplished.

Gore-Browne was assigned to help train the Seventeenth Division's artillery at Swanage. "Two hours ago," he wrote to Ethel, "I emerged into the damp and dark and groped my way to the C[ommandant] R[oyal] A[rtillery]'s Office. Up two flights of stairs I found a somewhat elderly general who shook me by the hand, & (politely) asked me what I wanted. He said so many officers came that he couldn't keep them all in mind! We talked for awhile, & when he discovered I was a regular his face lighted up, & when I told him I'd come from the war he beamed, & booked me for a lecture [to the troops]." After some desultory conversation he asked about Gore-Browne's posting. " 'I've got to make 4 new batteries,' [he said] 'so I could give you one, or . . .' " Then he inquired whether the War Office officials had said anything specific. Gore-Browne said that everyone hoped and expected that General Purvis would give him a staff job. " 'Oh that's first rate, I was going to lead up to that.' . . . So I suppose all is well [but] don't take it as settled." Gore-Browne ended the report: "Think, if at last I really have red tabs on my shoulders."[14]

All continued well for a while. "Very satisfactory so far. My old man is a dear, & seems prepared to lean on me." Gore-Browne was working ten if not eighteen hours, but the activity was ceaseless. As *the* staff officer, he was constantly on the telephone, organizing, settling and "making crooked ways smooth." On the side he organized some lectures for the would-be gunners. They were a "rum lot"—"The Lord knows how they are to get trained in time."[15] But they presented an even greater challenge for an energetic staff officer and his compatriots. Unfortunately, the halycon days were destined to be brief. In late January, as Gore-Browne's diary puts it: "About 6:30 the General came round and produced a bombshell. Bad night." Although Purvis had never stopped commending Gore-Browne to the War Office, the personnel managers there sent a proper brigade major to supersede the younger captain. Off came the red tabs. "He seems nice, though rather languid," Gore-Browne wrote of his replacement."[16] And Gore-Browne retreated one rung to staff captain, expecting at any moment to be relieved there, too, despite Purvis' protestations to the War Office. But the official gazetting of his rank as staff captain finally came in March.

Gore-Browne meanwhile decided to leave the local hotel for a small house in the town. Bulaya and Kakumbi were summoned to

14. Gore-Browne to Ethel Locke-King, 4 January 1915.
15. Gore-Browne to Ethel Locke-King, 7 January 1915.
16. Diary entry, 24 January 1915.

be his servants, an arrangement which persisted only for a brief period before Kakumbi suffered a stroke and had to be rushed to a hospital near Brooklands. Bulaya also became more and more cantankerous. Whatever these difficulties may have been, they seem to have been meliorated. And Kakumbi recovered rapidly, rejoining the ménage. During February, March, and April Gore-Browne did what he could to introduce them to English life. "I wanted them to see and learn what the very best of our things were . . . and how we really live. Something to set against the mining town which is what passes [in Northern Rhodesia] for the height of English habits and living. I wanted to educate them, & not spoil them."[17] Whenever Gore-Browne managed to get leave, to drive to Abingdon to see his parents, to Brooklands to see the Locke-Kings, to Salisbury or Winchester for the army or to visit the cathedrals he loved so much, or whenever he went off to find his old male friends, and even when he visited Lady Grogan (sister of the first Lorna) at Bingham's Melcombe, Bulaya and Kakumbi were along, both to "do" for him and also to join him and others for meals and outings and to "see" England. It certainly was a success at some levels. Gore-Browne missed them later, when they had gone, particularly Kakumbi's "utter simplicity and faith in a God whom he knows even less about then we." "I miss the fellow more than you'd think possible," he told Ethel. Kakumbi, for his part, probably revered the young master for whom he had hunted, and with whom—on a level for those days of reasonable equality—he had seen England. "If you do not see me when you [return to Northern Rhodesia]," he parted from Gore-Browne, "you will know that I am dead."[18]

Bulaya was a more complicated personality, and what he felt about Gore-Browne is not completely clear. With Gore-Browne soon to return to the front and R. S. M. Tagart, a native commissioner, about to leave Britain for Northern Rhodesia, it seemed opportune in May to send them both back home. The war was clearly going to be of a longer duration than originally imagined—Kitchener was now prophesying three years—and Kakumbi's heart problems would probably be eased in familiar surroundings at Shiwa. The decision made good sense to Gore-Browne, and probably also to Kakumbi. On the eve of May they therefore booked into a hotel in central London, prior to taking a ship from Tilbury. By 5:30 the next morning, when Kakumbi burst in upon Gore-Browne, Bulaya was gone. He had "bolted." Kakumbi knew nothing. Later Gore-Browne found a letter saying that he was going to "get other work." And that was the end, for

17. Gore-Browne to Ethel Locke-King, 24 November 1914.
18. Gore-Browne to Ethel Locke-King, 3 May 1915.

Gore-Browne at least, of one African experiment. Bulaya, whether afraid of Tagart or fascinated by England, certainly then had no intention of returning home. Yet, although Gore-Browne lost track of him and for a time the police could discover nothing, it was not the end of Bulaya. [19]

Gore-Browne suffered a more crushing personal blow in early May, when Captain Cecil Kerr was killed in Belgium by a bullet through the head. No man had been closer to Gore-Browne. Losing Kerr, though he seemed to take it reasonably well at the time, hurt bitterly and was never forgotten. Grateful he was to God, "Who even if he took him away, and I suppose he can do what he likes with his own, let me know him." A year later, when Gore-Browne was

---

19. About a month after Bulaya left Gore-Browne, the police discovered that he was washing dishes in a London hotel. Later, after holding other menial jobs, he served in the Middlesex Regiment and the 2/19th London Territorial Battalion as Private Samson Jackson. Released in late 1921, he worked in a military canteen in France and saw some service in Palestine. Thereafter he drew unemployment pay (until February, 1922). A few months later he asked the British South Africa Company to send him back to Northern Rhodesia. As a former soldier, this was rightfully the responsibility of the army, and the company refused. So Gore-Browne and Dame Ethel offered their assistance and the company was prevailed upon to provide a free third-class passage by ship. On the eve of his departure in May, however, Bulaya found a job and refused to go home.

Subsequently Bulaya became an actor and married a white English woman. He held a succession of minor theatrical rôles before appearing in 1924 in a successful West End play, Leon Gordon's neatly titled *White Cargo*. An analysis of the predicament of white Britons isolated and stagnating on an alien and corrupting West· Africa rubber plantation where whiskey flows freely and the principals lust for a mulatto woman, it received favorable reviews and was made into a movie. Bulaya played Jim Fish, a servant. (*White Cargo* first opened in New York, then moved to London. For a synopsis, see Mary James, "The Play that is Talked About," *Theatre Magazine*, XXXIX [March, 1924], 26 ff. See also *Spectator*, CXXXII [24 May 1924], 834.)

Bulaya's altered status profoundly embarrassed those colonial officials who feared the rise of an African middle class. His new condition and his refusal to be repatriated occasioned a remarkable dispatch from Governor Herbert J. Stanley to the secretary of state for the colonies. "I feel grave doubt," said the governor, "whether it would be in the interests of the man himself, or of any relatives whom he may have in this Territory in the Kawambwa district, to encourage his return after a period of ten years spent among the class of Europeans with whom he is likely to have consorted in Europe. He could hardly be expected to readjust himself to the ordinary conditions of the life of a native village, nor could he continue to live like a European in this territory. It is just possible, however, that he may have learnt some useful trade or be qualified to support himself in some other way but . . . I should . . . be very reluctant to take the risk of employing him in the service of the Government." (Stanley to L. S. Amery, 13 March 1925.)

involved in the battle of Somme, he recalled that "when Kerr died [I thought] I couldn't care for anything again, but I do care for this [Fifth] division & this work, and it's as it were part of him & for him, for it's so exactly what he would have wanted it to be. You were right," he told Ethel, "when you said that he would not die, but go on being and helping and caring." Even ten and more years later Kerr's spirit burned brightly in his memory and featured frequently in his ever realistic dreams. "Oh my dear," he wrote from Shiwa, "if Kerr were here now how peerless it would be—I can't imagine an element he'd be happier in, and I believe this place would have given him all he wanted in life." For Gore-Browne, Kerr had been one of the "priceless things."[20]

In April and May, 1915, 18-pounders and howitzers finally began arriving for the batteries of the Seventeenth Division. They and the gunners were railed to Salisbury Plain for shooting practice. The guns were still without sights, but some arrived on the eve of training maneuvers, and these and other necessary equipment were assembled by mid-June, when the gunners trained at Okehampton and the rest of the division began to assemble in its full strength near Winchester. By then Gore-Browne marvelled at the transformation—the unkempt, ill-disciplined roughs of February had become soldiers, or at least reasonable facsimiles thereof. "Considering that they got [American] horses in January, harness in March and guns in April, sights the day they went to practice (& then only 4 for 48 guns!) they were wonderfully good—their keenness and zeal was delightful to watch. . . ." But as for being ready for service, they made mistakes which would have cost commissions in an earlier era. Their guns were sometimes 26° out of line (i.e., the shells fell a whole mile off target at a medium range of 3600 yards). They set fuses to burst at the muzzle instead of on percussion at target—all things which would destroy their own infantry in a real battle. "They will learn in time, but we haven't got that time."[21]

Anyway, he was frantically busy, going whole days without eating more than a sandwich and rushing everywhere to prepare the artillery for its final muster and, too soon, the departure for France. It was a way temporarily to avoid thinking about Kerr. He saw too little of Ethel and less of his parents. The war was closing in again. Early in July the division left for the front. "I'm not humbug enough to say . . . that all is easy," he confessed, "or that I'm looking forward to the fear that I suppose is bound to come my way again. Only I do know, now, [especially with Kerr dead] that all is

20. Gore-Browne to Ethel Locke-King, 28 May 1915, 9 July 1916, 13 May 1925.
21. Gore-Browne to Ethel Locke-King, 10 June 1915.

well and that there's nothing to make a fuss about in all this as I used to do."[22]

The war had become far more widespread, and its orchestration and tactics far more complicated than when Gore-Browne had left. The Germans had broken through in Galicia, capturing hordes of Russians and forcing a widespread retreat which was soon to result in the capture of Warsaw and a broad swath of Polish, Ukranian, and Latvian land 150 miles deep. The Allied assault on European Turkey—Gallipoli—was already proving a fiasco despite the commitment of 100,000 troops. It was to be ignominiously abandoned at the end of the year. The Italians had joined the Allies and were about to tie down ten Austrian divisions in Trentino and at the many desultory battles of Isonzo, in eastern Venetia. The Allies were continuing to do well in Mesopotamia, and the Russians had come out of the Caucasus to conquer a large part of northeastern Anatolia. The South Africans had wrested control of Southwest Africa from the Germans. The *Lusitania* and other neutral vessels had been sunk by German U-Boats, but Britain was about to demonstrate its naval superiority off Dogger Bank, in East African waters, and in the Baltic and North Seas. France and Britain had also started mining and wiring the Channel and other access routes. Pressure from the United States would soon slow German submarine aggression. Airplanes were still being used for reconnaissance, some had begun to drop bombs, and the Germans had introduced monoplanes capable of firing a machine gun through a whirling propeller.

Despite all of this activity, however, the critical theater of operations was still centered on an arc of territory dipping from Belgium south of Ostend through Flanders and ultimately passing east of Reims and Verdun. There, one bitter winter in the sodden trenches had passed. The Germans had used gas for the first time; the British were becoming proficient with new versions of older hand-bombs, called grenades. Some British commanders had demonstrated the effectiveness of anti-aircraft fire from the new machine guns. The Germans had scaled heights, and battered British defenses with flame throwers. Both sides had tried desperately to burrow forward and undermine each other's trenches. It was a war which depended on the dogged determination of an infantry which suffered as many casualties from the new malady, trench foot, and from the old scourge, dysentery, as it did from the German attacks. One company of the Seventeenth Division set some kind of record for being in the trenches for forty-two consecutive days. Others, although not individually in the trenches continually, had served collectively

22. Gore-Browne to Ethel Locke-King, 6 July 1915.

—like the Third Division—on the main front without relief since Mons, nearly a year before. The gunners had become more important, even if they spent most of their time shelling German lines from fixed emplacements. During the autumn and early winter months—the remainder of 1915—the British joined the abortive French attempts to break through in Artois and Champagne, and resisted a determined German assault—with chlorine and phosgene gas—on the salient east of Ypres.

For the six months that Gore-Browne helped to run the artillery side of the Seventeenth Division, the British army was essentially on the defensive. The Seventeenth returned to Gore-Browne's old Fourth Division sector east and south of Ypres, a little to the north of Messines, which was in German hands. This was the flat territory (with its few strategic low hills) which Gore-Browne knew so well, and liked so little. Although the Seventeenth Division participated in only minor skirmishes, it nevertheless bore the brunt of the kind of daily German battering which might have been considered a major attack elsewhere on the Western front. No other "static" theater of war had so many alarms, false hopes, bad dreams, and so great an experience of being gassed, phosgene particularly lingering for days and reaching well behind the lines.

Gore-Browne was responsible for oiling the fighting machine— for the care and feeding of 3,500 men and 3,700 horses, for the movement of ammunition to all of the units scattered along a 7,000-yard front, and generally for the well-being and martial readiness of the artillery side of his still-inexperienced division. As staff captain, one of his more onerous but necessary duties was not only the provision but the accounting for of every round of ammunition expended in whatever circumstances by the division. On the distribution end Gore-Browne looked after seventeen batteries, some of which fired field guns, some howitzers, and some trench howitzers. There also were three infantry brigades to be furnished with rifle and machine gun requirements. "I think they eat it or light the fire with it, judging by the quantities they require," he said.[23] Additionally, there were 12 kinds of grenades in use, all of which required careful handling and packing, and then rapid dispatch to the front. In one attack a single battalion of the Seventeenth Division used 9,000 in an hour.

There were endless conferences and other time-consuming tasks. He dealt with all personnel matters, replacing casualties, promotions, postings, reports on officers, complaints, courtsmartial (men were fined and tied to gun wheels for insubordination, or sent home to spend years in a stockade), censorship of the mail, and so

23. Gore-Browne to Ethel Locke-King, 15 August 1915.

on. He concerned himself with the equipment for his artillery brigades, with the provision of stores and clothing, the repair of guns, and all of the corresponding impediments of gunners in war. By mid–October, after two months at war, there were still not enough sights for all of the guns. Gore-Browne and his commander, General H. L. Jackson, tried to obtain some from Expeditionary headquarters and to beg or borrow them from divisions elsewhere, without success.[24] Fortunately, in these and in other supporting roles, Gore-Browne's abilities and energies were appreciated by his superiors. "No one knows better than myself," the commander of the 81st Brigade wrote, "the enormous work you have done for the seventeenth division and how wonderfully you have managed to oil the wheels of this jerry-built engine of war." As far as his taciturn commanding general was concerned, Gore-Browne had "carried out his work to my entire satisfaction. Has very good abilities, is energetic, and had shown considerable tact and a good deal of organising power in carrying out his duties."[25]

Despite these formidable administrative accomplishments, Gore-Browne was hardly an administrative automaton. As the third link in the chain of artillery command, he always needed to know what was happening on the tactical side. If a battery were shelled, or the Germans attacked *en masse,* he could hardly afford to respond to frantic telephone inquiries with a plaintive, "Oh, I'm just the staff captain . . ." So, in addition to regular tours with Jackson, and his own visits in the afternoon to the batteries and the columns, he tried to remain informed of tactics overall, and how the front fared each day. Rows of field telephones hung in a little hut outside of his office, and all morning one or another rang with inquiries for various British- or American-manufactured field pieces. There were calls about the explosion of an enemy's mine on the Seventeenth Division's front or the discovery of German gun flashes in such and such square on the map. All of this activity, with orderlies rushing to and fro and motorcyclists roaring up on their machines, the telephone jangling, and files being blown open by the wind, occurred for the most part in a black hut knocked up by the engineers.

Although the righteous battles in which he longed to play a part never occurred, Gore-Browne was busy running the "show" he felt eminently qualified to run. "If only my work is good," he said

24. For the national deficiencies and problems, see James E. Edmonds, *A Short History of World War I* (London, 1951), 96–98.

25. Col. R. S. Hardman to Gore-Browne, 9 August 1915; Gen. H. L. Jackson, confidential report on Gore-Browne, quoted in Gore-Browne to Ethel Locke-King, 22 August 1915.

in constant refrain, "I'm entirely content. It is so hard to draw the line between being efficient & keeping other people up to the mark, & being naggy & 'Prussian,' or just sloppy & slack on the other hand. [W. W.] Gillum tells me his Sergeant Major said . . . 'We mustn't have the wagon piled up like that, Sir, if the Staff Captain sees it he'll have it off at once.' "[26]

Sometimes the war came close. "This is nothing but two great fortresses set up against each other," he wrote describing the battle for the trenches of Hooge (30 July) at the farthest point of the Ypres salient. "There must have been 790 [guns] shooting at the same moment . . . At 2.50 it was timed to begin, & at 2.50 there was noise like an immense orchestra all drums, rolling out . . . Over all a crescent moon, & drifting clouds, and the ceaseless brilliant flashes round a third of the horizon." A few weeks later the Germans found the division's 9.2s. and pounded the zone with seventeen-inch shells. "You've no idea," Gore-Browne told his aunt, "what a 17 inch is like. We are 3 or 4 miles from those particular 9.2s, but things fall off the shelves with the concussion . . . after all, it's a *ton* of high-explosive going off . . . and a bit of the shell fell 1600 yards from the burst. . . . It's almost incredible but . . . no harm was done . . . beyond that the [guns] were covered with mud. . . . They say, too," he concluded, "that as the smoke cleared away the sentry on the guns was seen, still standing at ease."[27]

He came to know the nastiness of the growing use of gas. The French had perfected a shell which combined vitriol (sulphuric acid) and phosphorus, and in September it began blinding Germans. "To think that we've come to that, that that's part of our duty . . . I think [it's] incomprehensible." Indeed, he admitted, "I don't think about any of it, I'd sooner not, and its much better not to."[28] When the French bombarded the Germans with this mixture, enemy soldiers fled in thousands to a nearby lake. Later both sides kept gas masks, and special respirators, at hand in the trenches.

The inefficiency of the military machine as a whole, and the numbers of casualties and vast expenditures of money which might have been halved with more efficiency, frequently depressed Gore-Browne. The British army, he realized, had its share of brave fighters. More to its credit, however, was the ability of its ranks to endure misery stolidly, dependably, and for long. Given the fighting ability and efficiency of the Germans, Gore-Browne felt that only a stolid army could ever hope to emerge successful from the kind of slogging to which the great world war had degenerated.

26. Gore-Browne to Ethel Locke-King, 11 October 1915.
27. Gore-Browne to Ethel Locke-King, 15 August, 22 August 1915.
28. Gore-Browne to Ethel Locke-King, 19 October 1915.

"There's no fight at present," he said in November—although it could have been almost any month—"only the ceaseless hammering away & killing & getting killed, the wear & tear that only shows in the casualty lists.[29]

This was Gore-Browne's war, but he was about to undergo another major metamorphosis. Much as he liked his present job, and had a paternal affection for the raw division which he had helped to mold into a reasonable fighting force, he felt ready (and knew he had twice earlier in 1915 been recommended) for promotion to brigade major and divisional staff work rather than artillery work alone.

Fortunately, Gore-Browne's qualities of leadership and initiative, and his undoubted organizational gift, had at last been recognized. Early in January 1916 he was posted from the Seventeenth to the Fifth Division, as a brigade major. "So I shalln't go to a Battery & I'm now definitely on the staff," he crowed. "It's really a big step, and I suppose a bit of a compliment, for Brigade Majors are usually Majors." It was a return, too, to the regular army of which he still felt a part. The move to the Fifth Division provided an opportunity to participate at the divisional level in policy making and policy implementation, gave him increased and significant responsibility of a continually challenging kind, and gave his ego a healthy injection of gratification. The year as brigade major of the Fifth Division became Gore-Browne's happiest and most rewarding.

As the Fifth Division moved from the front at Arras to the great, ultimately decisive battles on the Somme, and on to the line at Bethune, so Gore-Browne's reputation grew among its men and commanders. "The Capt usually gets to bed between one & two a. m. after being out best part of the day," his orderly wrote to reassure Ethel, "usually returning smothered in mud. . . . The Captain's work . . . is never finished even when he does go to bed, he is often woke up 2 or 3 times, either with messages or to speak on the telephone to someone . . . "[30] He mapped, made sense of and coordinated the ceaseless flow of intelligence reports, translated orders from GHQ into specific directions for the brigades of his division, went to conferences, accompanied his commanding general on visits to the artillery batteries, and, unlike those many other brigade majors who let themselves become overwhelmed by the flow of paper and imprisoned in their offices, made it a rule personally to provide a visible link between the batteries and the men and headquarters and higher authority. This responsiveness to the needs of the components of a division proved a valuable and most meaningful part of Gore-Browne's routine on the Somme (and elsewhere), and contributed greatly to his growing reputation as an innovative and caring staff officer.

By April Gore-Browne knew that he was "making headway." He was keen on his work, feeling it "the very job" for which he was suited. This was a sentiment which ripened, with reason, as the peaceful spring turned into the wrathful and aggressive summer and the casualties of attrition at Arras became the slaughter of the Somme. Already—even in his most ebullient letters, however, he expressed (but only to Ethel) inner, depressive thoughts about war which must have come painfully to a regular officer. He wrote once of a conference: "The sun was shining, & the chestnut tree we sat under was beginning to come out, & birds were singing. There were 20 of us, all keen, & young, & I suppose picked for some kind of ability, & we might have been [brought] together to advance the progress of the world. . . . Instead we were there to kill. Why has it got to be? Or if it has got to be why mayn't we all be swallowed up, you & I & everybody else, & begin afresh in a New Heaven & a New Earth, if this one is all so cock-eyed and topsy turvey?"[31] Particularly disturbing to him were the ways in which the war destroyed persons for whom he had special affection. Rupert Brooke's poetry was much on his mind. Kerr, of course, had been the first great loss. Then at Arras, a lieutenant, one "of the very best of all we've got . . . curiously like Kerr . . . & as good as they make them," was killed by fire after having been through Gallipoli. "I don't know when I've thought so much of a fellow on a short acquaintance," he confessed. He was of the kind who made Gore-Browne feel good—he diffused kindness and gentleness and good cheer. Later, in heavy shelling on the Somme, another—as "good a youngster as we'd got in the show"—was killed. He'd been sleeping for some days in Gore-Browne's hut. A few weeks later, a third was lost. "If there was one out of all the lot of the youngsters . . . that I'd have asked to keep it was he. It's about all one can bear when they go down like this."[32]

Gore-Browne's rôle in the battles of the Somme was a heavy mixture of his usual logistical and tactical oversight and the kind of energetic and morale-boosting intervention so necessary in times of crisis. On 26 July he spent five hours amidst shelling worse than even he had experienced. "I really rather enjoyed it. It was truly a bit of a lark—one had to dodge so much. One shell or rather two knocked us down." A few days later he wrote orders all night for an attack [on Longueval] that began the next day and lasted for two.

31. Gore-Browne to Ethel Locke-King, 13 April 1916.
32. Gore-Browne to Ethel Locke-King, 14 May, 26 July 1916; 7 August 1917.

"It's quite easy to [write orders] peacefully in a library with plenty of time and books of reference. It's another matter when the corps orders they are based on come in at the last moment, are possibly obscure, involve a great many other units & arms of the service, and have to be digested and applied to all our own brigades in an hour or two."[33] "It was always your sympathy in little things," a fellow officer recalled. "It kept one going . . . My dear old boy, I'd give *anything* to have you back & I'm afraid everybody else feels [the same] . . . . Your sympathy . . . made you the best B. M. that ever stepped . . ."[34]

Gore-Browne could say little to Ethel about his daily activities, but throughout August and September 1915 he wrote nightly, indicating exhilaration with the trials he was being permitted to share, heightened anxiety, and fears of the imminence of death. "My overpowering feeling," he wrote early, "is why, why, why is it necessary? Can the Lord demand this really? And couldn't He do it more simply with a pestilence?" Proud as Gore-Browne was of his battery commanders and their men, the glamor of war had fled. "Now," he wrote in mid-August after being under intensive fire for nearly three weeks, it's "merely . . . a case of keeping the teeth in."[35]

The third great British assault on German positions began on 15 September and lasted for the rest of the month. It was fought on a ten-mile front from Combles to Thiepval, the guns having been concentrated one per twenty-nine yards, and ordered to bombard the enemy solidly for the first three days. There were standing and creeping barrages, tank assaults (forty-two tanks were available), and the usual infantry dashes across muddy, cratered land from one wire to another. Only toward the end of this battle did the usual slogging stalemate for a brief moment resemble open warfare. The gunners at last had a chance of blazing away at Germans running, at batteries in the open, at wagons driving away, "and at all the targets one dreams of and never gets."[36]

After the main and decisive battles, which had given the British army several miles of territory and several key villages, had ended, but before the entire odyssey of the Somme had concluded with the onset of winter and the German decision (after 370,000 fresh casual-

33. Gore-Browne to Ethel Locke-King, 26 July 1916; Gore-Browne to Father, 6 August 1916.

34. Gore-Browne to Ethel Locke-King, 30 July 1916; Lionel to Gore-Browne, 22 May 1917.

35. Gore-Browne to Ethel Locke-King, 25 July 1916, 10 August 1916.

36. Gore-Browne to Ethel Locke-King, 22 August, 14 September, 1916; Gore-Browne to Nunk, 20 September 1916.

ties) to retreat to more easily defended positions fifteen to thirty miles eastwards, Gore-Browne was sent back with his tired batteries once again to Bussy-les-Daours, near Amiens.

Despite the lull, he was as busy as before. He had perfected the art of keeping in touch, and, because of the extensive distance covered by the Fifth Division, it was a full day's work even to call upon a few batteries. He tried systematically to visit every brigade headquarters, each battery, every battalion, stop in the trenches (of which there were miles and miles), and go on to the ninety-eight observation posts. In addition, there were the flying corps, heavy artillery, balloon men, and the mappers with whom to maintain contact. There was the usual paper work—defence schemes, attack schemes, reports, promotions, intelligence, and the rest. There was also the heavy responsibility of reorganizing the staff of the division. So many officers had been killed during the Somme that new recruits had to be trained and others promoted. For a time, too, Gore-Browne dashed back and forth to army headquarters lecturing to army brass about his experiences, how artillery was best organized during major battles, and the like. It was his life, and in many ways a reasonable climax to his first tour with the Fifth Division. "Really," he wrote about his time on the Somme and with the Fifth Division generally, "I am one of the luckiest men . . . I've had work to do that was wholeheartedly & entirely what I enjoyed & what, I fancy, I was suited for . . ." His commanding general concurred, being unable to speak too highly "of the Services which this officer has rendered. His untiring energy, zeal, & tact, & the instruction he has given to young officers, have conduced very greatly to the efficiency of the Divisional Artillery." There was also the fond appreciation of his brother officers, and the special praise of Captain Robert H. Studdert, a battery commander. "It is difficult to thank you for all you do for us, and you are quite indefatigable," he wrote in the middle of the Somme battles. "Everybody's cure nowadays for any worry they have is 'Oh, tell Gore-Browne about it and he'll fix it up all right.' " Later he reminded Gore-Browne that he had never known anyone of whom people thought so much, or who was so liked and respected by all ranks and officers, a conclusion borne out by the many letters which Gore-Browne received when his transfer from the division became known.[37]

Austin Jones was in the divisional artillery before Gore-Browne arrived, and knew how poor the relations had been between the regimental and staff officers. "You altered the character of those relations and changed antipathy to friendship." Many years later

37. Quoted in Gore-Browne to Ethel Locke-King, 23 October 1916; Studdert to Gore-Browne, 19 August, 15 September 1916.

Jones, by then a retired high court judge, was still unstinting in his praise: "He was much more than just an excellent Brigade Major. He was an outstanding personality, a 'character' and a great 'morale raiser.' He visited the batteries constantly, and by his wit and humour and inexhaustible store of really amusing stories created an atmosphere of confidence, cheerfulness and merriment which was always welcome and was of particular value in the grim conditions of the Somme. . . . "[38]

It was his personal touch, his interest in the welfare of the division, and his ability to cut through red tape, which were most appreciated. "In times of stress," wrote a junior officer, "there is nothing that helps so much as the feeling that there is someone at court who is taking a personal interest in the welfare of each officer and man."[39] Gore-Browne loved the praise, sheepishly thought it deserved, and knew at last that he belonged, and that he could command men at war. Then, too, in January, 1917, he was awarded the Distinguished Service Order—welcome recognition from above.

Gore-Browne was at the top of his form. Under conditions of great stress he had performed not only creditably, but exceptionally. Best of all, his humanity had been as well appreciated as his matchless ability, and by the ranks as well as officers. For the men of the Fifth Division he had demonstrated that the machine of war somehow still cared, that it could ensure equity, make exceptions when necessary, extend sympathy, reward real performance (in the form of honors for exceptional bravery), and, at the same time, suffer no loss in fighting trim. As far as the divisional artillery was concerned, this was to a measurably large extent all Gore-Browne's doing. They knew they were better off in many ways than other divisions (and during the Somme they had had an opportunity to see how other outfits functioned), and they—if the numerous unsolicited testimonials are a fair sample—gave Gore-Browne much of the credit. As far as he was concerned, he had done what was necessary, and out of no prissy sense of obligation to some higher sense of duty. It was simply his way. He was a regular army officer, he had a gift for human rapport, and—simply put—he cared mightily about making the machine (or any organization) function well. His good memory, knack for remembering faces and personal details, cheerfulness (the melancholia and fits of depression were forced below the surface), tidy mind, practical sense, and the un-

38. Capt.—later Sir—Austin S. L. Jones to Gore-Browne, 6 January 1917; Hon. Justice Sir Austin Jones to R.I.R., 30 September 1963.

39. Col. E. Harding Newman to Gore-Browne, 2 January 1917; W. D. Morgan to Gore-Browne, 26 December 1916.

questioned ease with which he articulated lucidly, were advantages. But needs of his own gave greater definition to these gifts. He wanted desperately to be wanted, and craved the affection only Ethel, and Kerr, had ever really offered. Being known as G. B. or "old Gorey" was important. Being accessible and generous in giving was an essential part of being Gore-Browne—of being a leader by virtue of warmth and energy (for he worked hard and well) rather than by sheer force of character or intellectual flair.

What could have been better—for the war effort, for the thorough utilization of talent, for the division, for Gore-Browne— than to have left him with the Fifth Division or to have given him greater responsibility within it or the British forces on the front? However, armies are, no less bureaucracies, subject to prevailing institutional rules. The great bureaucratic arm reached out from London at the turn of the year, when Gore-Browne was at the very height of his expectations and powers, and transferred him away from his comrades, away from everything which then had meaning for him. To his consternation and utter disgust, Gore-Browne found himself, in early 1917, posted as second-in-command of a small British liaison unit responsible for introducing the expeditionary force of Portugal, a newly mobilized ally, to its role on the western front. In theory, the liaison unit had wide and important responsibilities, and that Gore-Browne was seconded to it presumably indicated a respect for his abilities. Unfortunately, however, the scope of command of the unit had never been defined clearly. The Portuguese were allies, not subordinates, and Gore-Browne, the commanding colonel, and the specialists attached to the unit were advisors who wanted to instruct but could only suggest. What was equally if not more frustrating was the extent to which the unit was, during Gore-Browne's months with it, largely removed from actual combat.

The Russians were revolting and leaving the war, the Americans were entering it, the Italians were winning on the Isonzo and subsequently losing severely at Caporetto, the Salonika offensive was still stalemated and King Constantine was about to resign, the Germans were taking Riga but being punished by the French and the British, and throughout these momentous months Gore-Browne wallowed in frustration with the Portuguese. For much of the time he was so "fed up" and "evil," that he even stopped writing to Ethel. Part of the trouble was that there was never enough to do. In early January he arranged for the Portuguese to be housed and fed, and then waited for days until the Portuguese, "looking in their long cloaks like part of an opera," finally arrived by train. Then began the long process of indoctrination via lectures and personal discussions with the Portuguese commanders. There were a few interpreters attached to the mission, but Gore-Browne and his fellow officers were compelled to discourse constantly in French, which Gore-Browne could do with ease only if his ideas had been sorted out beforehand. On the whole, since Gore-Browne went through life being a great labeller—and a man of ingrained prejudices despite being tolerant—he felt that the Portuguese were pretty superficial, unreliable, and lacking in application. The Portuguese, he told his uncle, were "not much catch."[40] And though they listened to what he and his fellow British officers had to say, and diligently took notes, for the first few months Gore-Browne felt that he was having little impact on their training and tactical appreciation of modern trench warfare.

He hated being cut off from action, and from his pals. "I wonder if you know what a difference you'd make if you were here," one battery commander wrote from the front. "You don't know how you kept us going at the Somme . . . . I believe you'd be perfectly happy living in the mud with us here."[41] He "pottered about," and even when the commandant went on leave and he was in charge, did little more than draft some papers and, once, make a momentous decision about a consignment of boots for the Portuguese gunners.

From mid-1917, Gore-Browne served as artillery staff officer general in charge of staff training schools in England. He was also made GSO 2, which was a special honor for a gunner. Based in Cambridge, at Gonville & Caius College, where artillery officers were being instructed, he was in charge of organizing classes and, since the commanding general gave him his head, doing whatever he felt most appropriate for both the senior and junior courses, each of which lasted three months. Reconciled at being away from the front, he consoled himself with the feeling that at least he was in a position of influence and could spread the gospel, as he knew it, "to as wide a crowd as [he was] ever likely to encounter." He was also strenuously busy, a welcome change, in touch with interesting people, and was not hurting his possibilities for advancement by instructing the real cream of the army.[42] Gore-Browne also managed to steal away to London now and again, and to see Ethel, now Dame Ethel (her tireless work in the hospitals having been recognized with the award of a D. B. E. in the 1918 New Year's honors) for brief, cheering lunches or snatched evenings at Brooklands.

40. Gore-Browne to Nunk, 2 March 1917.

41. Lionel G. H. to Gore-Browne, 18 April 1917.

42. Gore-Browne to Ethel Locke-King, 21 October 1917. Edward Grigg, editor of the *Round Table,* later governor of Kenya, and the first Lord Altrincham, was a Guards officer in one of the courses. Gore-Browne found him "both encouraging & discouraging on the larger issues of life" (Gore-Browne to Ethel Locke-King, 8 January 1918).

The army wanted him to take the "very finest job I've ever had a chance of," as an artillery liaison officer with the French army, but the War Office refused to part with him, the Cambridge courses apparently then being too important. Meanwhile, the Germans attacked boldly in the spring in Flanders, later on the Aisne, and near Metz, everywhere pushing back the tired Allies, and worsening relations between the French and the British. The Germans were then a mere thirty-six miles from both Abbeville and Paris. The onset of the great influenza epidemic also laid low men on both sides, but the Allies, at least, were being bolstered almost daily by fresh reserves from the United States, and by a few minor but significant victories. In mid-July the Germans concentrated what turned out to be their final, last-ditch effort on the Marne from Argonne to Chateau-Thierry. But this failed, and by August the French, British, and American armies had forced the Germans back to an old front along the Vesle and Aisne Rivers. Few knew it, but the outcome of war had at long last been decided. The Germans, having lost about one million men since the beginning of 1918, could no longer replace them. And by this time, indeed by the beginning of the battle for the Marne, Gore-Browne was back in action, having been returned to the Fifth Division initially as G. S. O. 2 to Major General John Ponsonby, late of the Coldstream Guards and the new commander-in-chief of the Fifth.

"God & G. H. Q. are very good," he wrote.[43] The Fifth Division was then deployed on the edge of the Forest of Nieppe, in French Flanders. Aside from sending clouds of irritating mustard gas onto the British lines, the Germans by mid-July had assumed a purely defensive posture. The mosquitoes were aggressive, the weather was warm, and their accommodations poor, but until August, the division encountered the Germans only in a desultory way. Nevertheless, Gore-Browne was hard at work again, fully enjoying his increased responsibility. "I doubt if there's a happier man in France."[44] He was acting G. S. O. 1, a job he used to dream of "in the old days." "I feel as though I'd be content for the rest of my life, having once had this chance." There were friends everywhere (including Cambridge contacts), people pleasing him by being pleased to have him back. Fortunately, his duties did not prevent him from doing what he did so well. Each early morning he made the rounds of the advanced posts, bolstering morale, dealing with minor irritations, gathering information. Now, instead of the ten artillery batteries, he had thirteen battalions, thirteen field companies, the service corps, signallers, and other ancillary units to coordinate. And he had become a lieutenant colonel.

43. Gore-Browne to Ethel Locke-King, 29 June 1918.
44. Gore-Browne to Ethel Locke-King, 22 July 1918.

There was much more to do when the Fifth Division moved south to take part in the victory offensive of August and September. It pushed rapidly forward toward familiar territory through Achiet and Bapaume in the direction of Le Cateau. Such rapid advancing meant continuous juggling by the staff. Before each attack there were six to seven thousand men to be detailed across miles of unknown country in the dark, and as the battle progressed Gore-Browne and his staff had to know where they were, what they were doing, and how the assault could be assisted, advanced, or modified. During the first two weeks of steady fighting the Fifth advanced nearly five miles and captured 4,000 prisoners, their disposition being added to Gore-Browne's many other responsibilities. Their advance throughout September was comparatively rapid considering the way the war had been fought since 1914, but still a bitter matter of forcing the Germans grudgingly to give up a fortified hill here and a beleaguered village there. It demanded the orchestration of artillery (working out their complicated barrages at night in dark dugouts), aircraft, infantry, and cavalry, and the Anzac and British troops working together as a part of the Third Army thrust.

Soon the Third (of which the Fifth Division was a part) and Fourth Armies recaptured Cambrai, their troops crossed the Escaut River, managed to avoid shelling a number of villages which had been in German hands since the dark days of 1914, and even marched into one major center, Caudry, to the strains of the *Marseillaise* and the joyous crying of the local inhabitants, most of whom managed to find a secreted tricolour to wave from the shattered but secure housetops.[45]

To Gore-Browne's annoyance, Sir Julian Byng, now commanding the Third Army, took him away from the division in mid-October and attached him to his own general staff. He had been promised a chance to remain with the Fifth, where he had become such a critical factor in the division's success. Certainly Ponsonby needed him, and uncharacteristically bemoaned his loss in a hastily pencilled note. "A great gloom has come over all of us," he wrote to Gore-Browne. "I really cannot confess all I feel about your valuable help to me . . . You have helped me to understand and know gunners better than I have ever done before and you have told me exactly everything that is going on without saying a disparaging word against anybody. Your splendid energy in going up to the front line at all times of the day and night has been a marvel to me —Well I have been very lucky and I still fervently hope that we

45. A. H. Hussey and D. S. Inman, *The Fifth Division in the Great War* (London, 1921), 248, includes an account of this pleasant day which Gore-Browne's eye-witness report contradicts (Gore-Browne to Mother, 15 October 1918).

may soldier again together before long. . . ."[46] No officer could have asked for a better encomium from his superior.

"Instead of being a bit of a dog in my own house I'm really only a superior clerk," Gore-Browne wrote of his promotion to the Third Army staff.[47] He was confined to an office, which irked him, particularly since the times were glorious at the divisional level. He was also no longer virtually his own boss. A Major General and a G. S. O. 1 were his superiors. There was not all that much work, and Gore-Browne was able to get it done in a few hours. Some of the rest of the time he read newspapers or novels. He was a coordinator, meshing troop movements by train and road, the arrival of supplies, and the availability of billets. Tact was needed, a tidy mind, and an awareness of how divisions operated, but— particularly at the end of a war—it was not a job for Gore-Browne. He asked regularly for a transfer back to the division.

Although the Allies gained important victories on the Italian and Balkan fronts during the autumn of 1918, the western front was the decisive arena. On 10 November, having been on duty during the previous night when the final confirmation came, Gore-Browne wrote frantically to Dame Ethel that men would no longer be smashed in the line, civilians battered, and youngsters deprived of a life of peace. "They're shouting & singing, down the road, but one doesn't feel much like that." "My dear," he ended the letter, "you, & Nunk, & Kerr."[48] The next day he signed a "Secret" duplicated order to all corps and brigades of the Third Army: "Hostilities will cease at 1100 hours on November 11th. Troops will stand fast on line reached at that hour which will be reported by wire to Third Army. Defensive precautions will be maintained. There will be no intercourse of any description with the enemy." At home, as Nunk described it, everyone had a grin on his face, the High Street of Weybridge was full of cheering and shouting citizens, all of whom waved their union jacks feverishly. "One very respectable old Lady had a paper parcel under her arm & a flag round her neck making a sort of apron." "Half a dozen soldiers joined hands & danced a ring round 2 quite upper class ladies who quite appreciated the compliment." "All I feel," Ethel wrote, "is I want to put my head on your shoulder & beat you & cry out."[49]

"Yes it's beginning to be peace now," Gore-Browne managed to write a few euphoric days after the armistice. "One can't quite believe that never again will one have to wait & watch anxiously to

46. John Ponsonby to Gore-Browne, 16 October 1918.
47. Gore-Browne to Nunk, 24 October 1918.
48. Gore-Browne to Ethel Locke-King, 10 November 1918.
49. Ethel Locke-King to Gore-Browne, 13 November 1918.

Gore–Browne (third from left) feeding the pigeons in Paris, 1918.

hear that [one's pals] are all right."[50] He was happy and satisfied, for the end of combat, of course, but also because he was going back to the division. For a time the renewal of hostilities remained a possibility and the division had to be maintained in a state of preparedness. It moved, or, rather, 15,000 troops, their arms, horses, and wagons, transferred themselves for ten days according to Gore-Browne's complicated plan. Finally, at the end of December, he had them all housed over an area of 140 square miles near Namur in Belgium. The first major crisis was Christmas dinner, the Service Corps being short of men, supplies, and transport. "I personally spent the early hours of Christmas day . . . buying bloody sausages in Namur."[51] Thereafter, and throughout January and early February, Gore-Browne had his administrative hands full dealing with the comfort of the troops in an area of overcrowded billets rapidly filling up with refugees. The local Belgians were also sullen, at least at first, and transport grew increasingly more complex to organize. The men, too, were naturally restless. In order to keep them entertained and non-mutinous, he began a divisional school, with classes in each unit. He wanted particularly to "get intellectual fellows together for discussing subjects of imperial & social & general interest." They would examine the latest economic and historical theories, and focus on problems of postwar reconstruction. Dutifully, Dame Ethel sent £20 worth of books and pamphlets from a London bookstore, and he plunged wholeheartedly into the educational business, radically mixing officers and men together in the classes so that each could learn to appreciate another point of view. By the end of January more than 5,600 men were attending these voluntary classes, taught by men from within the division and some special recruits. He also appointed games masters, set aside recreation rooms, planned concert parties, and coaxed the cinema into his cantonment. Although he described his pursuits as those of "county magistrate," he was beginning to behave like a chief purser of some transatlantic luxury liner of the 1940s. No magistrate or purser, however, had to cope with the rapid wastage of his clientele. Throughout the latter half of January and most of February, the division began to disappear in inconvenient ways. Demobilization occurred in the service corps and the administrative staffs as rapidly and as suddenly, and with even more disruption, as it did in the fighting cadres. His drivers, cooks, and teachers were on the trains home before he could replace them and keep the remaining men supplied and amused. Even his own office emptied without

50. Gore-Browne to Ethel Locke-King, 15 November 1918.

51. Gore-Browne to Ethel Locke-King, 10 January 1919. See also Gore-Browne to Ethel Locke-King, 5 February 1932.

much noise. It was maddening. And, because the division had and still meant so much to him, it "hurt" to see them go. The life he had known—and he was almost never as busy as he was in the twilight period between armistice and full-scale peace—was fast disappearing. By March almost all of the men were gone; in April the division was no more than a cadre, and in May the very last troops left Charleroi by train. The Fifth Division was no more, being reborn, for other purposes, a year later at Curragh, in Ireland.

The future began to intrude. The demise of the division forced him, very much against his prevailing mood, to return to the kinds of speculation which had preoccupied him—those days seemed so distant now—before the war. A lieutenant colonel who had been decorated with the D. S. O. and twice mentioned in dispatches, Gore-Browne had achieved an enviable war record. His commandeers praised his discretion and expertise, and, with the war over, made the most of his undoubted administrative talents as well as his extracurricular social skills. (How he hated, but endured, all of those dinners and bridge-parties in the postwar military lull!) But the enormous British army contained a flood of generals and full colonels who might want to stay on in the shrunken regular regiments. They were the ones who would have priority in the race for responsibility, and would cancel the "brilliant future" which Gore-Browne's father confidently predicted for Stewart. He was likely to be given a humdrum office job in London, which for him would be most unsatisfactory. Yet in February it seemed likely that he would be selected for a plum posting, as an instructor in the Staff College at Aldershot. There was even a letter from the headquarters of the Northern Command, in York, telling him confidentially that the director of staff duties had said that he was to be so appointed. "I strongly advise you to take this job, and to make up your mind to remain in the Service. . . ."[52]

Although Gore-Browne thought that he would in fact take the position if offered since it would place him near Dame Ethel, would be "extremely high class & wd. mean goodish pay & a comfortable fairly strenuous existence"—all welcome attributes in unsettled times—he was in fact ambivalent since it would tie him down and close off the other options toward which he had slowly been directing his thoughts. Certainly he wished to do something which gave him "a full days' work" and held some human interest. But he could not bear to think concretely of these alternatives, wanting a quiet time of leave to recharge his batteries. He thought that he might like to travel lazily for a while, "to sort of clear one's brain," and mentioned Africa as one of the places to which he might go.[53] In these

52. R. W. Hare to Gore-Browne, 17 February 1919.
53. Gore-Browne to Ethel Locke-King, 10 February 1919; 18 November 1918.

early months after the cessation of hostilities, however, Gore-Browne could not and did not revert immediately to his Rhodesian vista. Too much had happened in the interim. He had gained a knowledge and faith of his own particular abilities—an important and fulfilling degree of self-esteem—and had a robust, if uncertain, view of what the future might hold for himself, and his kind.

The war had loosened many emotional links and strengthened others. Everyone and everything, except Ethel, for whom his rather adolescent love had ripened into a mature and transcendent, almost synergistic warmth, competed for a time with the "unbreakable bonds" to the Fifth Division. His relations with his mother had, if anything, deteriorated, and those with his father were on a flat, satisfactory, but not especially rewarding plane.

The African side of Gore-Browne's life at first seemed trivial compared to his experiences with the division, and he did not immediately turn for sustenance to the great vision (nurtured by Hentyesque ideas so long ago) of a peaceful roost to rule in the country of the Bemba. Instead he thought of Kerr, and some of the men whom he had known too briefly, before they perished in Arras, at Ypres, or on the Somme. But no man then, or for many years after, could capture his attention the way Kerr had. Aside from Ethel, too, in the aftermath of war women played an even smaller part of his life than they had before he went out on the Boundary Commission. A few unattached ones wrote regularly, and Lady Diana King's sauciness rather amused him, but his feelings were not then directed to marriage.

During the first months of the war a desultory and restrained correspondence had begun with Lorna Goldman, his first and far off romance. She and Edwin Goldman had lived in Berlin, where their daughter Lorna was born in 1907. A second child, Bosworth, was born in 1909. During these years Goldman experimented with radioactive isotopes in his laboratory. He sought medical applications, his work paralleling that of the Curies in Paris. In 1913, however, after enduring months of acute suffering, he died, apparently of cancer. "His spirit dominated the body" to the end, Lorna's mother wrote. Her mother also described Lorna's courage and thoughtfulness for others in time of stress. Yet she was very frail, very worn, and desolate. "They were just all in all to each other." To his aunt, Gore-Browne remarked: "Poor Lorna . . . whether she loved him or no she'll suffer most dreadfully." After a decent interval, moved by a mixture of fond memory and common commiseration, he wrote a warm letter of condolence and she, after carrying the letter around for more than a year, answered it on her way from England to South Africa, where she and her children hoped to find "health and hope." I don't believe," she picked up the threads of years past, "you will mind my silence, it was not very easy to write about my loss, especially after I had waited a little. The first mood is very different to the second. . . . In the first one is almost carried along . . . into another world and sees glimpses of it, and then one gets landed into a bad quagmire." "Are you in the war?" she asked. "I expect you are and glad to be there, doing something and being brave among the great negative deeds of the age."[54]

Lorna had lived with her brother Reginald on a Paris Evangelical Mission station in Basutoland (Lesotho), and then, her own health deteriorating, had moved to the supposedly better climate of Graaff Reinet in the eastern Cape Province. She wrote of the children, who waxed robust and vowed themselves colonials forever. "And what are you doing? Carrying out the deed for which all your past years have been a training—and carrying it out well I know." Gore-Browne replied occasionally of his part in the great war and she rejoined with descriptions of life on an isolated farm. She urged him to paint the colors of the war vividly, and welcomed his eloquent if somewhat restrained replies with effusive, avant-garde but never cloying philosophy. "You have fed a mind that was hungry," she began one letter. She shared his feeling for Africa, and wrote evocatively of the land and its smiling peoples. She also responded to the omnipresence of death on the battlefield, herself being sufficiently unwell to have thought about its open door. "We do not get to that door when we most want it," she said. "It seems to me we get there just when we have first learnt to love this world's loveliness and begun to wish to stay in it. . . . [We] show [our] ripeness to pass on by vivid joyfulness in things of this visible world." Two years later, after at least one operation and a dramatic, last-minute recovery from its consequences, she told Stewart that she "ought to have died long ago, but now have every prospect of living till 90."[55] She had to make plans, and took herself and her children to the Plumtree School in southwestern Rhodesia. There her health again failed, and, in September 1919, after a second operation, she died in South Africa.

"She didn't have much happiness in this life," Gore-Browne wrote to Dame Ethel. "It seems a week or two," he recalled, "but it's really fourteen years. She was so wonderfully beautiful & frail. . . ." "Do you remember the [first] morning . . . I ever saw her? I think I can remember every moment we were together afterwards. . . . We walked to church at Billingshurst through the fields

54. Mrs. Reginald Bosworth Smith to Gore-Browne, 25 August 1913; Gore-Browne to Ethel Locke-King, 28 September 1913; Lorna Goldman to Gore-Browne, 11 January 1915.

55. Lorna Goldman to Gore-Browne, 31 December 1915; 6 September 1917; 16 February 1919.

all gloriously golden with buttercups. And that morning we went on the river in the canoe, & talked such nonsense. . . . And then the last time of all at her wedding, & our dinner side by side . . . and all that happened." Selfishly, he said, "one is awfully lucky to have had this in one's life once anyhow. And as for her, she's happy now anyway." He was not pretending, nevertheless, even to himself, that he'd been going about heartbroken for fourteen years, but Lorna was "a very precious & a very sacred memory & now it can't ever be anything else . . . no doubt it's best so."[56]

The army still remained his life, and a reasonably satisfactory, ego-boosting, and challenging one at that. His last assignment was not to the Staff College, which might have kept him permanently in the army, and eliminated this biography, but to the staff of the British Army of the Rhine, based in Köln. At first, under Brig. Gen. C. G. Fuller, he was responsible for what was still called War Organization, and ran "his own show" with the help of a captain and a cypher clerk. He coordinated rather than initiated, tried to mesh central and field interests, and to maintain some semblance of liaison with similarly placed French and American units. Occasionally, before the peace was signed in June 1919, he had official dealings with the German military. His months on the Rhine were also punctuated by the opera, when in season—he learned to appreciate much of Wagner and some newer compositions, like Richard Strauss's *Der Rosenkavalier,* with its "scandalous" libretto.

On the whole, Gore-Browne's life with the Rhine Army was very good, and somehow rather empty. During the first half of 1920 he remained busy, and wholeheartedly enjoyed a visit to Berlin, "thrilling" Warsaw, and Danzig (which he thought had more character of its own than any town he had ever seen), and official dealings with the British embassy in Paris, the American army in Koblenz, the German army in Dusseldorf, and so on. He had friends in cities scattered up and down the Rhine, but the days of occupation were drawing to a close, an overriding purpose was lacking, and Gore-Browne began to look forward to "being out of it, & settling down to a definite job . . . of hard work & constructive work." Soldiering, he thought, was dead for at least ten years. "I'm itching," he concluded, "to be running a show again & dealing with men."[57]

He settled on a return to Northern Rhodesia, and received the enthusiastic moral and financial support of the Locke-Kings. (His parents were less excited.) Frank Melland had been among the many acquaintances in Rhodesia to have kept him informed of

56. Gore-Browne to Ethel Locke-King, 19 October 1919.
57. Gore-Browne to Ethel Locke-King, 13 May 1920.

doings there during the war. In 1919 Melland had also discussed
Gore-Browne's agricultural prospects at remote Shiwa Ngandu
with Josselyn de Jong, Northern Rhodesia's secretary for agriculture. Melland suggested that roses could be grown there commercially and quickly, and that they would keep their scent. They were
thinking of Damask and Rose de Provence, and of distilling the
essence and shipping the result with its high value and low bulk to
perfumeries in Europe. Gore-Browne thought that such a scheme
made sense and planned his return to Northern Rhodesia for 1920,
on a trial basis while on long leave from the army.

By 1920, after talks with the Locke-Kings over Christmas, he had
become more and more determined to try to farm Shiwa Ngandu.
Having received assurance in 1915 and again in 1919 that the British
South Africa Company would provide him with 10,000 acres at
nominal cost (one shilling), in 1919 and 1920 he took advantage of a
scheme to settle ex-soldiers in the colonies, specifically in Northern
Rhodesia, on very favorable terms. He brought together a number
of his military chums, Charles Austin, Captain E. A. Smith, M. C.,
and Major Walter Cowie, and obtained a promise of a series of
adjacent land grants from the company. Then he set about introducing the men vicariously to Africa, preparing a plan for the joint
working of a large estate devoted to the manufacture of essential oils
and the cropping of grains, and drawing up legal memoranda of
understanding between the various partners. Even so, not all of the
preparations were smooth. One of the original men backed out and
a replacement had to be found. The company took months to answer letters, having to refer matters of decision to Livingstone for
the advice of the administrator. But Gore-Browne threw all of his
considerable energies into the task, pulled strings and eventually
made the company see things sensibly—from his point of view. He
had a vision of a special kind of community where black and white
would live together in productive harmony, the whites instructing
the blacks benevolently. This was a paternal proposition, but he had
seen how badly Africans were ordinarily treated by white settlers,
and wanted—if he really were to settle and farm experimentally and
profitably in Rhodesia—to create an oasis of black and white co-
mity. For these kinds of reasons he was drawn to Melland's proposal
for a united Central Africa north of the Zambezi, a confederation of
British territories as far as Kenya. "One wants to do anything to
further the right views as regards natives."[58]

The pictures of Shiwa that Gore-Browne drew for his fellow

58. Gore-Browne to Ethel Locke-King, 30 August 1919. The proposal was
contained in Frank H. Melland (using the pseudonym "Africanus"), "A Central
African Confederation," *Journal of the African Society,* XVII (1918), 276–306.

recruits cannot be recaptured. Nor do we know what he and they discussed during the months of 1920 when the settlement scheme was in embryo. His enthusiasm must have been infectious, almost irresistible, however, for he always had the power to be elegantly persuasive about the schemes to which he himself was drawn. Although he was taking soldiers along, the return to Shiwa Ngandu constituted a sharp psychological break with the army which had been his home, with England, with his family, and—although they would continue to correspond and he would always hope that she would come out to Shiwa to live—with Ethel. The pull of Shiwa marked the end of a war and the beginning of an adventure into maturity.

IV

The Creating of Shiwa Ngandu

NORTHERN RHODESIA was still a remote, impoverished, and comparatively unpromising corner of the British Empire. There about a million Africans, speaking more than 30 languages, inhabited a kidney-shaped territory the size of France and the Low Countries. For the most part they grew maize and manioc, pulses, and a few exotic vegetables in the manner of their forefathers. Some, in the eastern and western portions of the country, herded small, humped zebu cattle. There were fatty-tailed sheep and goats, but few pigs and domesticated fowls. For agricultural use, the digging stick predominated, the heavy hoe was used in the wealthier areas (where it was now imported from Europe), and in one or two favored sections missionaries had introduced the oxen-drawn plough. But the soils of Northern Rhodesia were almost uniformly ill-adapted to anything so mechanized and massive as the plough. They were light, poor in nutriments, and susceptible to easy leaching. Many areas were also prey to the tsetse fly, which vectored the trypanasomes so fatal to horses and cattle (and humans). Many Africans, particularly the Bemba, had hunted extensively, but the coming of the Europeans and the widespread slaughter of game during the nineteenth century had lessened the supply of protein regularly available by these means to ordinary tribesmen.

Only a comparatively small handful of Africans, about four thousand, had stepped forward from the ranks of "ordinary tribesman" to become teachers, evangelists, or civil servants. In about 1920 another thirteen thousand were employed on European farms, there were about three thousand house servants, two thousand or so on the then small mines, and about the same number were employed as unskilled artisans. The many thousand other Africans grew cash crops (maize, mostly) along the line of rail from Livingstone to Katanga or subsisted on the produce of tiny gardens,

94

small-scale trading or bartering, occasional hunting and fishing, and—but only in the areas where there were settled whites—on the cash they could obtain for their labor. The copper mines which were to transform Northern Rhodesia economically, and to provide a livelihood for many thousands of men, were not then of proven and exploitable quality, there were no plantations, the soils, high altitude, and very uneven and stingy rainfall having minimized the possibility of growing tropical crops requiring intensive cultivation or harvesting. In addition, and equally important, Northern Rhodesia lay at least a thousand miles from the sea and lacked rivers navigable (as David Livingstone had ascertained) to the ocean. There was a railway, which had bisected the country in 1910, but many of the territory's most populous areas were 500 or 600 miles from the line. Finally, off the main line of rail, there were tracks, and a few roads, but much of Northern Rhodesia was criss-crossed by no more than the paths of porters. Only a primitive telegraph system and a very rudimentary telephone network connected Livingstone, the capital, with the distant remainder of the colony.

Despite its drawbacks economically, Northern Rhodesia was still widely but not exclusively regarded as a white man's country. The British South Africa Company was approaching the last years of its stewardship but it encouraged white settlement, especially of ex-soldiers, and still hoped for the kind of agriculturally-based economic growth which would provide its shareholders with dividends. In 1920 Northern Rhodesia could count only about three thousand whites, roughly twelve hundred of whom lived on farms, three hundred resided at Christian missions, and another three hundred were involved in the administration of the country. Although the missionaries had established themselves predominantly in the rural areas, the farmers and administrators were clustered on and about the line of rail, which had become the country's economic fulcrum. There were the railwaymen and the miners, both of whom swelled the white population of the colony's geographical waist. The governor and his immediate subordinates constituted a tiny, wealthy, white upper class. The remaining nonindigenous employees of the Company, native commissioners and high-level clerks in the secretariat in Livingstone, and the missionaries, largely constituted the white middle or upper-middle class. The white-workers—artisans, locomotive drivers, farmers, etc.—comprised the lowest stratum in a highly stratified, scattered, and fragmented colonial outpost society. Most of the farmers were inexperienced and their hopes of making money from tobacco or maize were hampered by the high cost of transport after the war, by rising (if still low) costs of labor, by what they thought of as the fickleness of employees, and by the sharp slump in prices for agricultural commodities which began in 1921 and continued throughout that decade.

These were not auspicious times to try to begin a self-sustaining agricultural experiment in Northern Rhodesia. The company's days as an administering body were coming to an end. It had little incentive to undertake the kind of agricultural investigations and incur the other heavy infrastructural and developmental costs which might have encouraged the investment of private capital and effort and the immigration of serious settlers from Britain and South Africa. In the northeastern section, where Gore-Browne intended to make a home, these limitations on the part of the company were particularly evident. Shiwa Ngandu was within the orbit of the native commissioner in Chinsali, sixty-five miles distant, but before Gore-Browne established an estate there, the various commissioners (and therefore the company) knew little of its problems or particular possibilities. Moreover, no roads ran to Shiwa Ngandu; nor did they extend beyond Mpika, sixty-four miles to the south, or Kasama one hundred eighteen miles to the northwest. The closest mission stations were those of the Roman Catholic White Fathers at Chilonga (south of Mpika) and the United Free Church of Scotland at Lubwa, a few miles south of Chinsali. Both had themselves been established only recently, Chilonga in 1899 and Lubwa in 1905. No one, not even the local inhabitants, knew much about the qualities of Shiwa's soil (the territory's first scientific soil analyses were undertaken in the 1930s), rainfall, climate, or even the productivity (were that really measurable) of the local people. If Gore-Browne were to grow saleable crops everything —perhaps even expertise—would have to be imported and exported on the heads of porters from and to the line of rail, 600 miles away, and thence by rail a thousand miles or so to Beira or Port Elizabeth. Or it might prove economic to follow a route by water from a point on the Luapula River only seventy miles from Ndola on the line of rail and sixteen days by canoe from Shiwa Ngandu. Gore-Browne could rely on no assistance, especially in sudden emergencies, from neighboring whites. Least of all could he expect to take advantage of the experiences of earlier homesteaders. Except for a man who grazed cattle sixty miles away, there were none for vast distances, and no one in the territory who had tried to produce essential oils commercially on his kind of land. From the beginning Gore-Browne was *sui generis,* intentionally so.

Gore-Browne's scheme ultimately depended, although even he probably failed to realize this truth until much later, on the abilities, adaptability, and receptivities of the local people, and on those many others whom he might expect to attract to his estate. Shiwa

Ngandu was within the chieftaincy of Nkula, a senior but subordinate chief of the traditionally powerful raiding and hunting Bemba. The company had "subdued" the Bemba a mere 22 years before. The memories of the elders of the tribe therefore encompassed a comparatively lengthy era of the nineteenth century when they ruled nearly all of the high plateau of northeastern Rhodesia, being challenged before the whites only by the passage of Ngoni in the 1840s and by Swahili-speaking slavers (including Tippu Tib), with whom they exchanged slaves and ivory for guns in the three decades before the first Europeans began to nibble at the Bemba kernel. (David Livingstone had camped on a hill near Shiwa in 1867.) Among the less powerful peoples on the northern and eastern flanks of the Bemba, and subject to periodic raids, were the cattle-keeping, patrilineal Mambwe and Namwanga. Within the vicinity of Shiwa Ngandu, the Bemba both conquered and partially assimilated the Bisa, matrilineal agricultural people like the Bemba themselves, but with a trading rather than the Bemba reputation for martial success. The Bisa under Chief Chibesakunda occupied much of the land northeast of Shiwa Ngandu toward the low-lying but distant valley of the Luangwa River. At Shiwa itself, and in all of the other directions, there were Bemba owing allegiance to Nkula and, ultimately, to the great chief Chitimukulu, who resided near Kasama.

When Gore-Browne returned to Shiwa to settle, the Bemba, the largest Northern Rhodesian ethnic group, probably numbered about 100,000. They lived in small, scattered communities under headmen responsible to the district chief and, because of the deficiencies of the soil and the character of their own implements, they shifted their fields, and hence their villages, at multi-year intervals. They practiced the *citimene,* or slash and burn, method of preparing gardens before each rainy season, clearing the brush and pollarding the limbs of trees, burning the slash, and sowing millet, sorghum, maize and—by Gore-Browne's time—planting manioc in the ash-fertilized bed. This technique, with its enforced alternation of crops, showed great ingenuity but, when compared to their northern neighbors and other Northern Rhodesians, was less complex and innovative. Fortunately, their land was well watered, with many perennial streams flowing either into the Chambezi River, and therefore ultimately into the great system of the Zaire, or over the nearby escarpment and into the Luangwa, and thence into the Zambezi River. Freestanding lakes, like Shiwa Ngandu, were comparatively rare. Most of the forest cover, however, was common deciduous *brachystegia,* the scrubtree which did its best to cover the territory. Near Shiwa there also were a few patches of *mushitu* evergreen groves, the only parts of the country to remain lushly green when winter came in April and the grass browned.

Around Shiwa, at a height above sea level of nearly 5000 ft., the nights and some of the days from May through early August were bitterly cold, with ground frost common. Then spring came, and September and October were the months of hot, dry, relentless heat which abated only with the coming of the rains in November. The rains remained, more or less with showers daily, until March or early April, contributing about thirty inches on average to the plateau around Shiwa. This amount traditionally enabled the Bemba to cultivate a single crop, harvesting it between April and July. But the averages conceal droughts and the anxieties of a hard life and a slim diet supplemented by the success of the hunt. It is from this comparatively harsh base, with its disdain for the decorative arts or other than governmental or militaristic attributes, that the Bemba built a hierarchically-organized political institution sufficiently stable to withstand the company's administrative intervention and its introduction of direct rule by commissioners. It could also absorb new lairds, with their many pretensions, like Gore-Browne.

By the time of the arrival of Gore-Browne the Bemba had gradually grown accustomed to the ruling ways of whites. From 1901 the Bemba had been required to contribute financially to defray the Company's administrative and military expenses. They were assessed per hut, so that a polygynous male paid according to the number of his huts (each housing a wife and her children). At first they paid in kind, the bomas resembling a farmyard at harvest time. Then, as ablebodied men were induced to seek employment on the line of rail, in Southern Rhodesia, South Africa, or the Belgian Congo, or even on mission stations closer at hand, the cash economy slowly reached outlying villages. "Poor villagers," Gore-Browne wrote shortly after his arrival, "their tax [has been] put up from 5/- to 10/- a year as a reward for being loyal. It's the good old policy of exploiting the black man, in this case it's intended to drive him down to the mines in Southern Rhodesia, 1600 miles away, where they're short of labour."[1] Fairly often, too, Africans could only satisfy their financial obligations to the government by working without pay on the roads or in the gardens of the nearest native commissioner. There was some forced labor for community projects, too, but in Bemba country this kind of excessive abuse of authority was less frequent than in colonial Kenya or in Tanganyika under the Germans.[2] Later the migration of men from villages, in large part the result of heavy taxation, was to denude Bemba vil-

1. Gore-Browne to Ethel Locke-King, 15 June 1921.
2. For a discussion of this system, and its abuses, see Rotberg, *Rise of Nationalism*, 41–47.

lages, transform the countryside, and destroy a traditional way of life, but by 1920 the exodus had not yet appreciably begun to alter the area around Shiwa Ngandu.

The company, and the governments of Britain and Northern Rhodesia, had become intimately identified in Bemba eyes with the heavy burden of taxes and their attendant consequences. Tax collecting was the major preoccupation of the provincial administration. Native commissioners routinely toured villages counting huts, registering taxable males, drafting men for stints of unpaid labor, and—on occasion—burning the huts of recalcitrant defaulters. Debtors were also imprisoned. None of these actions could have endeared the administration of the territory, or whites in general, to people like the Bemba. As a native commissioner commented in 1920, "There are causes for unrest: The Native is getting nothing out of the white man; we give him no education, nothing, and screw 10/- out of him. The wages are usually 6/- per month . . . and calico you cannot buy."[3] In addition, the Bemba and others had been subjected to the arbitrary rule of aliens. Their chiefs had been deprived of traditional executive and jural powers, and in their place had been substituted an unfamiliar collection of English laws and methods of weighing evidence which to them made little sense. But these new regulations and their interpretation were less onerous than the humiliation and feelings of inferiority which accompanied white governance. This was more a problem of the towns and bomas, but even the villagers quickly learned to behave in a subservient manner to whites in rural areas. The ordinary villager learned that equal protection of the laws was a fiction and that there were certain kinds of public establishments which he, as a mere African, could not enter, certain levels of power to which he could no longer aspire, and a prescribed place which it behooved him to keep. By 1920, too, the government had provided neither hospitals nor many schools for villagers like those in and around Shiwa Ngandu. As a missionary concluded in 1921, Africans say that they are "practically all *akapolo,* or slaves, whereas the slave raiders, of whom the government has freed them, always left the great majority free."[4]

Shiwa Ngandu, fortunately for Gore-Browne, had, being especially remote, remained relatively isolated from many of the currents of discontent then beginning to affect Northern Rhodesia. Although the final battles of World War I had occurred within the heart of Bembaland, and General Paul von Lettow-Vorbeck's march southwards had only been halted on the banks of the Cham-

3. Interview with Peter Cookson, 30 May 1920, B 1/8/2. Lusaka archives.
4. D. K. van Oesterzee, in the *Nyasaland Times,* 17 March 1921.

bezi by the armistice in Europe, the people of Shiwa Ngandu had played no particular role in combat besides supplying a few carriers. Similarly, in the aftermath of the war, when adherents of the African Watch Tower or Kitawala movement had preached a millenarian message of dissidence in the Abercorn, Fife, and, indeed, Chinsali districts of northeastern Rhodesia, they had apparently found few followers, and made no especial attempt to spread the message of revival as far south as Shiwa Ngandu. The Kitawalans spoke persuasively of the imminent end of the world, when oppressed Africans would rid themselves of colonial government and inherit the earth. They urged their followers to cease laboring for whites and for chiefs.[5] But in the rather special enclave of Shiwa Ngandu, the coming of Gore-Browne elicited more expressions of joy than displays of obvious antagonism.

A few Africans had anticipated his return since the balmy days of 1914. Chikwanda, the local Bemba headman, had increased the size of his village, most of the newcomers presumably looking forward to whatever employment Gore-Browne could afford them. Mali-mali and ten or so other men had continued to look after Gore-Browne's small herd of cattle and his hut. But aside from a rough cattle enclosure, Shiwa Ngandu was no more developed physically in 1920 than it had been before the war.

There Gore-Browne arrived, ready to begin his great agricultural and human experiment, in September 1920. En route from England he had stopped in Johannesburg, "the beastliest place in the whole world," where his brother Robert lived. Public affairs in South Africa, he said, neither for the first or last time, "make you want to vomit—our people at home seem altruistic by comparison."[6] With Robert's help he was able to obtain equipment for the estate, and suggestions that peppermint and geraniums might be grown profitably for their oil. With Robert, too, he shared some of the fantasies about what Shiwa could mean—in terms of race relations and agricultural self-sufficiency. Amateurishly, they talked about the kinds of practical matters about which they knew hardly anything. Both he and Robert planned for Shiwa on the basis of assumptions which—as they both later discovered—were far removed from reality. Information upon which to base the kind of decisions and preparations which Gore-Browne had to make almost everyday were simply lacking. In one respect, though, certainty was possible. Shiwa would at first have no place for white women: "So we'll still be able," he gleefully wrote, "to pee out of the window."[7]

5. See Rotberg, *Nationalism* 136–139.
6. Gore-Browne to Nunk, 16 August 1920.
7. Gore-Browne to Robert Gore-Browne, 22 August 1920.

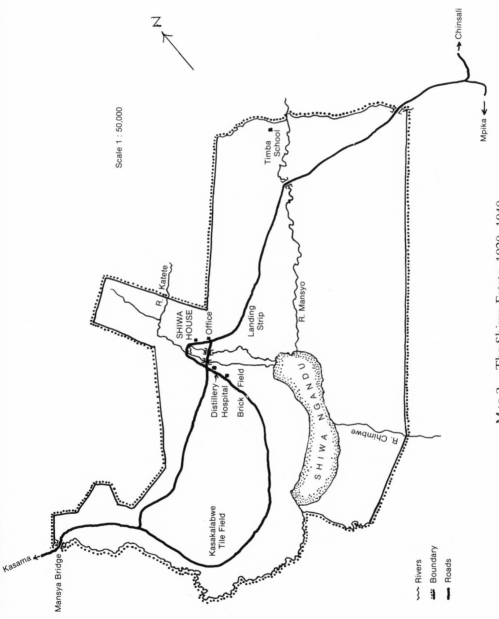

MAP 2.   The Shiwa Estate, 1920–1940.

Gore-Browne could hardly restrain his enthusiasm when his train passed through the spray of the Victoria Falls and chugged up the narrow-gauge rail line to Livingstone. "It was really like being home again . . . Every soul in the place is as nice as they can be from the Administrator [L. A. Wallace] down to the store-keeper."[8] Several of the African *askari* even remembered him from the days of the commission, and immediately gave him the comfort—without which he always felt awkward—of having his own orderlies.

Wallace cooperated warmly. Gore-Browne and his three partners were each to receive the standard ex-serviceman's free grant of three thousand acres. Gore-Browne's would be at Lake Young, but the others would wait to choose the land until they knew more about the area. Gore-Browne was also promised ten thousand more acres at the pre-war, now very inexpensive, price of a shilling an acre. "So far so good," he remarked. But as he proceeded northward along the railway line his successes were more mixed. The secretary for agriculture was on tour and no one at the company's experimental station at Chilanga could provide good advice about the likelihood of growing the exotic flowers and fruits with which he intended to experiment. He spent two days in and around the Lusaka farming district north of Chilanga, but rejected it, despite its lower costs of transport, as an alternative place of settlement. The land near the line, he wrote, is "damnable even if it is rich. I'd sooner have a villa at Brixton."[9] At Chisamba he found Cowie, the partner who had gone out ahead to learn about farming, brickmaking, and much of the heavy work, managing a rundown farm and fending off a drunken white bricklayer who beat and frightened off the available African laborers. (Cowie had ploughed eighty acres, sunk wells, made roads, fabricated 250,000 bricks, broken oxen, etc.)

Gore-Browne slept poorly in Cowie's single hut on a cold bed of straw. About daybreak, whilst lying awake, the open door was darkened by a tall figure. He thought it was someone for Cowie. "Ni Kakumbi, Bwana," the figure in the door uttered. "You know the gentle voice and the smile," Gore-Browne wrote. "He bent down clapping his hands." It was Kakumbi, corporal in the King's African Rifles in Nyasaland, who had walked 400 miles from Zomba across the heart of Northern Rhodesia to keep his wartime vow. "I could almost have cried," Gore-Browne remembered.[10]

Kakumbi made the remainder of Gore-Browne's return journey easier and more enjoyable. Together they stopped in the new lead and zinc mining town of Broken Hill (Kabwe), from which point

8. Gore-Browne to Nunk, 22 August 1920.
9. Gore-Browne to Ethel Locke-King, 27 August 1920.
10. Ibid.

Gore-Browne despatched 250 carriers to Shiwa Nganda via Serenje with all of his bulky equipment. Sixty loads of personal goods travelled with them to Ndola, where Gore-Browne arranged with government assistance to hire seventy-five carriers (at four shillings each) for the trek to Kabunda on the Luapula River. "I can't tell you the joy of giving all the horrors of the rail-head the slip," he wrote soon after their safari had started out for the river. The stationmaster and several others had the DTs, the customs officer was fuddled twice a day with drink, "during which periods he repeated every remark he'd made the preceding day," and there was an assistant magistrate who had been shot through the head in the war and was "not quite all there." Gore-Browne had had enough of the "semi-cultivation of the beastly little townships."

The seventy miles to the Luapala took five days. "Picture us going along, [Kakumbi] in front with rifle, spear, & hunting knife, then myself in helmet, khaki shirt, & shorts, blistering knees, stockings, & burning feet, then Austin, then a boy with a shot gun—and 2 miles behind the carriers."[11] At Kabunda they piled into five large canoes, the one with Gore-Browne and his retinue (and nine paddlers) sporting an awning, and slowly threaded their way up the broad river, into and across swampy Lake Bangweulu to Chilubi Island, and then up the narrow sudd-congested Chambezi River toward Shiwa. "We sit in our deck chairs with a table between us and a thatched roof over our heads," Gore-Browne explained. "With a great swinging stroke we go up the broad placid river . . . sometimes green trees overhang it, sometimes we go through grassy plains, always it's homely & not the least like the African river of fiction & the West Coast."[12] There were hippo to watch, and puku, lechwe, and duck to shoot for the pot. Villages appeared with men and women wearing skins around their middles. Once they met a party of canoe-borne minstrels. Except for a day when the guides lost their way and the paddlers propelled the canoes for seventeen straight hours until the destined village was reached at midnight, the journey was easy, enjoyable, and uneventful. The final sixty-mile stage took four days overland from the long disused rubber factory on the Chambezi.

"It *is* good to be back," Gore-Browne wrote at the end of September. "We'd a great reception—drums, singing, & native dances. They're pleasant, cheery, people." "I can't tell you what it's like here," he wrote a week later to Dame Ethel. Although the weather was as warm and dry as it ever became, "the lake, & the hills, & the

11. Gore-Browne to Ethel Locke-King, 11 September 1920; Gore-Browne to father, 14 September 1920.

12. Gore-Browne to Ethel Locke-King, 14 September 1920.

sky, & the green trees, & the sparkling air" excited him.[13] Twelve headmen of nearby villages had come to pay their respects, and give presents. More than sixty Africans had sought permission to settle on the estate (for which they would have to provide three months worth of paid labor) and more men were asking for employment (at six shillings a month plus food, the equivalent of another four shillings a month) than he could possibly engage. The tenancy relationship conformed particularly to Gore-Browne's own ideal definition of his role as the local laird: "You settle him in happily round you with his wives & children, you help him with his troubles, & in return he works for you, for the regulation wage of course, for a part of the year."[14] The sites for the rose garden had been selected, the houses were being built, and Austin was buying food and keeping accounts. Gore-Browne was thirty-eight, happy, full of visions, and, for the moment, his romantic ideals had not been sullied by the harsh realities of a lonely farming life in the middle of distant bush.

Gore-Browne and his partners intended the development of Shiwa Ngandu to begin immediately, and for the experimental phase to be concluded at the end of the first growing season—in the northern spring of 1921. Gore-Browne fully expected to have a firm basis by then on which to assess the economic viability of his estate. Austin would supply and run a store selling goods to the Africans; the profits from the trading operation would support the agricultural work until it, too, could be made to pay. Austin would also look after the accounts of the estate. Cowie, due to transfer to Shiwa after the rains, would supervise the equipment and construction, and plough and harvest the land. Until he arrived, Gore-Browne would assume these tasks, as well as supervising everything else. The fourth member of the entourage, Smith, of the First Tank Battalion, in Wareham, was to arrive soon with quantities of damask rose plants. It was assumed that the roses would bloom profusely and that attar, a fragrant volatile oil which formed the base for a range of perfumes, could successfully be distilled from their petals.

Freight costs by road to Mpika and on to the railway line were about £50 a short ton, or 3d per pound (9d all the way to Europe). The water route involved two transshipments, and was unsuitable for motorboats. These factors had persuaded Gore-Browne that there were going to be no easy ways, in the short term, of eliminating the high costs of marketing produce. It was immediately obvious that only very high value, low bulk commodities could possibly be grown profitably at Shiwa. An attar, or some other essence—one of the essential oils, anyway—fitted these requirements neatly.

13. Gore-Browne to Ethel Locke-King, 5 October 1920.
14. Gore-Browne to Ethel Locke-King, 10 October 1920.

Rice, which Gore-Browne had hoped to grow, would be too heavy to ship profitably to the railway line or overseas. The same was true for maize and beef, even if chilling were technically possible.

The first weeks before the onset of the rains were thus taken up with hurried preparations. Under the supervision of that "old villain", Chikwanda, 220 unskilled laborers prepared an acre of ground for roses, readied a vegetable garden, and planted tobacco and the maize (although ploughing was difficult without oxen) with which Gore-Browne intended to feed himself and his retainers. They erected a four-roomed, mud-walled, thatched house with a twenty-eight-foot high ridge pole for Gore-Browne and Smith, a small cottage for Austin and Cowie, huts for the servants, a communal kitchen, and a store in which Austin began selling basic foodstuffs, trinkets, and the "most utterly rubbishy cloth you can imagine" for one shilling sixpence a yard. Gore-Browne had praise for his workers. "They are really good . . . when taken the right way, and laugh & sing all day long, and what is more are, or seem to be, really anxious to please one, and keep asking if the work is good. Of course at times they are jolly trying—often it's one's own fault for expecting them to be able to do things beyond their experience—and sometimes one has to fuss around and ginger them up—but on the whole they are wonderfully good, & it's quite amazing how one can control 220 natives & get all the work done without trouble."[15]

Chikwanda was invaluable, but Gore-Browne's instinct for paternal leadership, reinforced as it had been by the experiences of war, also proved relevant. He took a personal interest in the welfare of his men, and, often though he might complain, really enjoyed being pestered for the kinds of services a lord of the manor could render to "his" employees or followers. "One has to keep going round to make sure everything's all right. They require medicine & help of various sorts, & there are always about a dozen men sitting in front of my tent with various needs all of which takes an awful lot of time."[16] There were visits from headmen and other dignitaries, and "much ceremonious chat just when one is busiest." "As it is I'm dead weary at the end of each day," he wrote during those early weeks when his spirits were still resilient and the disappointing contingencies still seemed only temporary, easily surmountable, obstacles to ultimate success.

Each day brought new problems for the protean farmer and estate manager. With Chikwanda's assistance he began castrating

15. Gore-Browne to Ethel Locke-King, 10 October, 24 October 1920. For a memory of the bungalow and of Gore-Browne, see E. Knowles Jordan, "Chinsali in 1920–22," *Northern Rhodesia Journal,* V (1964), 544–545.

16. Gore-Browne to Nunk, 16 October 1920.

bulls in order to obtain ploughing oxen. The dangers of a food shortage were eliminated when Bisa from villages in the Luangwa valley walked in with 4000 pounds of maize for sale. Brickmaking, at first using the method of drying the best mud in the sun, was begun in stiff rich soil near the lake. No one had dared venture onto the "sacred" lake for years, so he had to show his men how to hollow a large dugout canoe. As late as December, 1920, there was still baggage and loads of goods scattered all over Northern Rhodesia—on the trail from Broken Hill, and along the line of rail to Livingstone. It had to be fetched. An unexpected worry was the need to keep vast supplies of coin with which to pay workmen and purveyors of grain; Africans refused to take paper money since it easily burned, and became wet and torn. "It's no good offering 50 black men a cheque on Lloyds!" There was also an annoying stream of visiting whites—hunters passing by, curious administrators, labor recruiters, merchants, and even—one isolated day—a tramp. "One wouldn't mind if most of them didn't infer they were conferring a kindness on lonely settlers by coming to cheer them up!"[17] When the rains came, the roof—like all fresh thatch—leaked, and the process of repair and maintenance, which was virtually never to cease, began. The first acres of virgin land proved unsuitable for gardens, too; at least the initial plantings failed, and all of Austin's expensive fencing was wasted.

Gore-Browne could cope mentally with the vicissitudes of nature, but despite his tact and experience at crisis management, he suffered fools, waste, inefficiency, and slackness—especially by whites—with less than equanimity. Austin, reliable as a subaltern, appeared to have no real head for business. Gore-Browne's may not have been much better, but Austin early evinced an inability to economize and to find inexpensive ways of accomplishing the objects of the estate. Part of the problem was that the operating funds were all Gore-Browne's (and the Locke-Kings). Both Cowie and Austin were full partners, but their input was meant to be labor rather than capital intensive. This made for unspoken sensitivity and, even if Gore-Browne were at first unaware, his approach, and a natural desire to continue playing G.S.O. 1 to his subordinate officers, made a partnership based on unrealizable premises of equality something less, and more paternal. But even before Cowie arrived and subjected the carefully elaborated scenario to additional strain, Gore-Browne was forced to accept the fact that Smith, who had been entrusted with gathering the necessary knowledge about the process of distilling essential oils, as well as shepherding the roses (which could not travel on their own) and geranium plants, was backing out. Without Smith, and the mature roses, the whole

17. Gore-Browne to Ethel Locke-King, 26 November 1920.

essential oils scheme, and with it any hopes of making Shiwa into a paying proposition, had to be abandoned (or deferred) for at least a year. This was a cause of more than insignificant anxiety. Neither the resources of Gore-Browne nor those of the Locke-Kings were limitless, and in those early days Gore-Browne could not assume that he could draw indefinitely upon the Locke-Kings. Although by early 1921 he believed that he could manage Shiwa in great comfort for about £300 a year (his own income from investments and a pension being £800 a year), he could see no possibility of generating any income whatsoever without the distillation of essential oils.

For the next six years Gore-Browne struggled doggedly to make Shiwa pay. The untested assumption on which all of his plans and improvisations rested was that a profitable market existed, probably in Paris, but maybe also in London, for the rare oils which scented expensive body perfumes. (Most of the latter were ten to twenty percent oils dissolved in alcohol.) The major distillers, and the fragrant plants and flowers which provided their raw material, were located along the French and Bulgarian Rivieras. In some of the French colonies, like Algeria and Madagascar, in francophone Haiti, in Italy, and in Australia, there were secondary centers of similar horticulture, but the extent of sophisticated information available for the would-be supplier of essences was limited, and based on the experience of planters in Provence and the Côte d'Azur—not tropical Africa.

The most delicate and expensive essential oils were taken from flower petals. The tiny sacs of fragrant plants also stored substances that gave off pleasant odors, and the essences—the oils—could be expressed from barks, buds, leaves, rinds, roots, woods, or even whole plants. The actual process of obtaining the oil was relatively simple, and called for steam distillation. When steam was passed through a plant material (or, as in the case of flowers, it was boiled) the oils turned to gas, which was cooled to produce a condensate and the liquid essence. The distillation machinery was easily contrived, but keeping the fragrance of a flower or a plant and transforming it, stage by stage, into marketable oil, took—as Gore-Browne learned painfully—skill and judgment. Knowing what to grow best and most profitably also called for the kinds of marketing and agricultural expertise which neither Gore-Browne nor any of his ex-officer colleagues, nor anyone in Central Africa, possessed. Early in 1921 the Northern Rhodesian secretary for agriculture sent Gore-Browne some descriptive pamphlets; the "novelties" which took his fancy included *Eucalyptus citriodora,* the leaves of which provided the oil, and tansy *(Tanacetum vulgare),* a hardy herbaceous perennial with aromatic leaves. Gore-Browne ordered seeds of fragrant scented *Pelargonium geraniaceae,* the common geranium, since it was a source of essential oils which would, he understood, prove sufficiently valuable to withstand the still escalating transport charges. He grew a grass, *Vetivera zizanoides,* popularly known as kus–kus, planted camphor laurel *(Cinnamomum lauraceae),* a 30–foot high tree indigenous to China and Japan, spear–mint, *Mentha pepperita,* fennel, lavender, and coriander. But only the eucalyptus ever took to Shiwa's poor soil.

Gore–Browne and his cohorts also investigated other ways of making money from the soil, and from the country. Africans had responded to his invitation to sell a few banana trees by bringing in 700 or 800, all of which he felt compelled to buy at 6d a time. Could he distill a banana liqueur and thus make a fortune? Or should he try growing rice and making the drug ergot?[18] Unfortunately he had no idea how this fungus disease of cereals was brought about, controlled, and harvested. Cowie arrived, finally, with orange trees, and the magistrate at Mpika gave Gore–Browne some peach trees which immediately began blooming well. (It was possible to express oils from the kernels.) At one particularly depressed point, Gore–Browne also contemplated guiding shooting parties for profit and, at another, transporting goods down the Chambezi for others. He wondered if he could sell fresh produce to the, alas few, whites in Kasama, 118 miles away, or rice to the Belgian mine population in Katanga (the price turned out to be uneconomic, like most things). There were inevitable periods of despondency. Gore–Browne could not bear his visions of a contented community in the rural bliss of Central Africa to founder on the rocks of materialism. Doing good was important, but paternal benevolence had to be justified by a visible businesslike façade.

Fortuitously, at a moment in early 1921 when solutions to his many unanswerable problems seemed difficult and his partners were becoming restless, Gore–Browne came to believe that Robert might be able to provide just that ingredient which would bring about Shiwa's success. Robert's own job was proving less and less promising, especially with troubles on the Rand and the potential in South Africa for racial violence. Additionally, Margaret, his wife, had been delivered of a still–born boy, and longed to leave her surroundings. Robert's other vocational alternative was to read for the Bar, as his father had always hoped, but literature attracted him far more than law, and Shiwa, he anticipated, would provide him with the earned leisure to turn his hand to writing. It seemed altogether an attractive and workable proposition, and Robert set about with accustomed industry to learn the essential oils business. In April Margaret and Robert arrived en route to England. Their initial reactions were favorable, although they both worried about

18. The dried sclerotal bodies (ergot) were used to contract muscle fibres during hemorrhage or for the contraction of the uterus before or after labor.

what they would do if the scheme failed. "It damned well shalln't fail," was Gore-Browne's response, but he kept it to himself.[19] Robert was also concerned about Shiwa being a "blind alley," sentiments similar to wounding ones voiced by his father. "Robert ought to do something of importance in the world," he wrote to Stewart. "I should not like R. to be only a back-woodsman, and you cannot have any assurance that for many years if at all he could emerge from that stage."[20] He wrote with similar and unexpected

19. Gore-Browne to Nunk, 2 May 1921.

20. Father to Gore-Browne, 17 March 1921. Stewart may have been too sensitive to his father's cautionary statements. The two sentences quoted in the text offended him (see Gore-Browne to Nunk, 2 May 1921), but in writing about them to Ethel and Nunk he failed to put them in his father's rather fuller context. After the first sentence quoted, his father went on to remind Stewart that "you have done good service to your country in the war and may say that your share of work for England is well above average—but," and here Stewart felt the knife's twist, "I should not like R. to be only a back-woodsman. . . ." Then he went on, "Moreover, if you shd. find in the end that you have to chuck farming the delay in starting in life wd. have very seriously prejudiced Robert in taking up any other career."

Gore-Browne wrote to Dame Ethel. She, with divided loyalties, told her brother and he directly addressed his son. "I am glad she told me," he wrote, "because now we can have it out. First, and most definitely, I do not think anything of the sort. Let this sink in—I do not think you a waster. . . . If I have had doubts as to how far the work itself will realise all you expect of it, that is only a case of two men forming different opinions on the practical question of how a job will work out. . . . It is quite probable that you will make Shiwa one of the big things in the world. . . . You know that I am proud of you . . . that even before the War I thought you had great possibilities and that during the War I thought you showed a capacity which even I had not realised before. My fear was that I was anxious lest I shd. be too ready to be proud of my own chicken. When the War was over I thought if you waited you might get some big Imperial or international job, and I daresay I thought you would be wasted on Farming even if the farming was on a big scale and was in the nature of developing a district, in fact I thought the Job did not provide sufficient scope for your abilities and Character. You think it does and probably you are right, but do not be sore. . . . I quite recognize that to 'make the desert blossom as a rose' is a great ambition and if you make your corner of Northern Rhodesia a great success you will have proved my fears groundless." (Father to Gore-Browne, 30 June 1921.) This Stewart tried relentlessly to do, both by making the desert bloom and by making Shiwa one of the big things of the world.

His father, who had become Sir Francis in 1921 after being a justice of the peace in Berkshire and chairing the Civil Service Arbitration Board (1918–1920) and the complex Railway Rates Advisory Committee of the Ministry of Transport (1919–1921), died in 1922, leaving a large but indefinable gap in Stewart's life, a widowed mother with whom he could only exchange banalities, and a small legacy. (An inquest declared that Sir Francis had accidentally suffocated himself with his hand while asleep. [*The Times,* 5 September 1922, p. 7.])

tactlessness to Robert & Margaret, but—to Stewart's great joy—
they both decided becoming a part of Shiwa was what they should
and would like to do. "It's the one thing that would make this
scheme entirely blessed," Gore-Browne crowed to his aunt.[21]
Robert went home via Lake Tanganyika and the East Coast route,
stopping in Cannes and Paris to learn something about essential
oils.

Robert and Margaret returned early the next year. In the interim,
however, the relations between Gore-Browne and his two other
partners rapidly worsened. Cowie and Austin saw no immediate
prospect of income, and neither had independent resources. They
knew they could live, but only on Gore-Browne's bounty, and with
his sufferance, though he might not show it. Less and less were they
equals, running the affairs of the estate together, and the accession of
Robert and Margaret, which meant a legal restructuring of the
partnership and a further, even if unintended demeaning for both,
brought suppressed antagonisms to the surface. Gore-Browne also
failed to account for the ways in which isolation and loneliness
affected most men of ordinary character. Both were younger than
Gore-Browne, and neither had his widespread interests, his ability
to plunge himself into books, or anyone like Ethel with whom to
communicate. Early in 1922 the bubble burst. Austin and Cowie
both told Gore-Browne how inconsiderately he had treated them,
how Austin felt that Gore-Browne classed him with "the natives,"
and how Cowie had been slighted in this and that. No single retro-
spective complaint could have been taken seriously, but something
in Gore-Browne had sapped their own vitality. Austin left early in
the year and Cowie was discharged in October.

The partnership with Robert lasted little longer than the original
arrangements. Their approaches to life, and therefore to Shiwa,
were dramatically different, Stewart having a faith in its ultimate
greatness which could be shaken, but never destroyed. Robert, con-
stitutionally and emotionally, was another man, and was unable to
share the especial romantic vision that was at the heart of Shiwa's
vitality. Few persons, no matter how close to Stewart, could ever
see how Shiwa would become a viable entity. Most regarded the
estate and the essential oils schemes as a grandiose indulgence of
Stewart's fancy. Then, too, the cultivation of essential oils demanded the kinds of patience, willingness to defer gratification,
enjoyment of Africa and Africans and contemplative feeling for
loneliness and isolation which, in the case of Shiwa, only its creator
could ever accept.

Nevertheless, they lived and worked together for the balance of

21. Gore-Browne to Ethel Locke-King, 11 May 1921.

1922, and Robert and Margaret directed Shiwa alone throughout all of 1923, which Stewart spent in Europe and North Africa. Three days after his return in early 1924, however, they left for good. Robert's private explanation had validity and long-term relevance: "I came out entirely," he wrote to his sister on his way home, "to push E. oils and also to try and get things on a sounder financial footing. I found, it seems to me, the interests of a more or less ornamental estate always taking first place and S's time and money going into this. (The class of waste . . . was £60 for servants' uniforms the first year—S spending part of his time planting ornamental trees during the E.O. planting which was left to natives, the E.O. trees I had brought out being put in unsuitable but picturesque positions etc. etc.). . . . I wrote my fears . . . to ELK and said if S did not get clear on E.O. I would have to go out. After seeing him she wrote quite definitely—'S does not regard Shiwa as a commercial enterprise,' and in a second letter 'E.O. is the industry but it is not to stand in the way of his Shiwa the jewel of central Africa scheme.'"[22]

Whatever the proximate causes, by 1924 it was apparent that Gore-Browne's infectious enthusiasm for the future of Shiwa Ngandu could be transmitted in no permanent way to other whites. This was a message he received reluctantly, having for long nurtured a lingering hope that running Shiwa might not turn out to be a full time occupation, and that, after establishing the estate on a sound footing, he could spend every other year or so in England with Ethel. Yet only he possessed an overpowering desire to prove Shiwa possible. Other whites were not to be trusted in matters which affected its future.

Although Gore-Browne employed whites in supervisory positions until the 1950s, he relied on them less and less, and slowly turned Shiwa into a full extension of his own, still developing, personality. Rowland Jones, a youthful bank clerk whom he had known in England and Johannesburg, and who had worked in Nairobi, spent from 1922 to 1925 (until he turned to drink and miscegenation) doing the jobs Gore-Browne hated—the bookkeeping, running the store, measuring this and that, and generally everything office-like that Gore-Browne disdained. Hector Croad, a former magistrate, worked off and on for many years as a mechanic and engineer, building roads and bridges, repairing culverts, constructing sheds, and putting together the essential oils distillery. Humphrey Gilkes, a friend of the family and a doctor, came out briefly in 1924 before discovering that he could not bear to be so remote. (Gore-Browne badly wanted a physician for his

22. Robert Gore-Browne to Sapphire Hanford, February, 1924. Interview with Robert and Margaret Gore-Browne, 6 July 1963.

employees and villagers, but Gilkes proved a mistake.) Viscount
Peter Ockham, son of the Earl of Lovelace, was sent out by his
father to become a man under Gore-Browne's general supervision,
and remained six months assisting his host in vague but useful
ways. Young Richard Muggridge spent a year in Gore-Browne's
employ, but proved a wastrel and a liar. There was Frank Boxall,
an employee of the Locke-Kings, who worked well, but was prone
to illness and sloppiness, and went back to Brooklands in 1926.
Finally, there was Joe Savill, an orderly in the 15th Brigade of
the Fifth Divisional artillery, who asked Gore-Browne for help in
finding a job in 1921, worked for a while at Oakley, and then
brought his enthusiasm and practical knowledge to Shiwa in 1925.
Having few pretensions and knowing his subordinate place, he
stayed for more than fifteen years as foreman and chief of works.
For Gore-Browne, ordering employees about was less of a strain
than cajoling partners or maneuvering one's kith and kin. But it also
meant that the whole responsibility for success or failure—
including everything to do with the oils—was Gore-Browne's, that
he would have to attach himself irrevocably to the future of Northern Rhodesia, and look for earthly rewards and moral sustenance
to its black as well as its tiny, crabby white population.

About the last he had few illusions. Most, he frequently told
Ethel, were simply "not of our kind." They lacked class, and there
was nothing that repulsed Gore-Browne more than the manners
and attitudes of "low-class" whites. Their unfeeling treatment of
"the natives" irked him; it dragged more sensitive whites down
into the dirt and unnecessarily polluted the atmosphere of race relations. Their ways were South African, and Gore-Browne feared for
the future if the incubus of racial tension spread northward from the
Union. Fortunately, in these early years the line of rail was distant,
and in the Northern Province of Northern Rhodesia there were
only about 300 whites, with most of whom he at first had little to
do. On the other hand, even with the shopkeepers and road supervisors Gore-Browne managed to get on—to talk their language and
to demonstrate the kind of common touch which had won him so
much warmth in the war. By 1925, when he was even more popular, there were unannounced visitors almost daily—Presbyterian
doctors, provincial and district commissioners, White Fathers, agricultural experts, and storekeepers. He turned himself out of his
room, even his bed, for them, fed them at all hours, even lost his
precious Sunday morning sleep for unworthy strays. Wanting a
certain kind of solitude—especially when there was work to
do—he believed himself sorely tried. But the face was always
brave. He wanted to be wanted, to be liked, but it was more than
those simplicities. As much as he found an excess of visitors trying,

and an unpleasant diversion, his hospitality was lavish, warm, and soon justly famed within the small white community. Partially it was a matter of breeding, but Gore-Browne felt an obligation, a *noblesse oblige,* to provide—to give as he himself had always partaken of good hospitality. On what still was a lonely frontier, too. most whites were drawn to one another, and were naturally freer with their friendship than they would have been in Europe. Nevertheless, feeling rather removed from the problems of the Tanganyika Plateau Farmers Association, he refused an invitation to become a member of that fledgling white pressure group, and, disdaining their fears of "a native rising," also spurned a plea to help found a rural farmer's defence force.

Gore-Browne began to involve himself as a settler in the national affairs of his adopted country after returning from his long leave in 1924. For the first time he knew that Northern Rhodesia would henceforth be home. Secondly, and of equal importance, the Company was relinquishing its administrative presence. On April 1, 1924, Northern Rhodesia became a Protectorate of the Crown, being administered by a governor and secretariat appointed by and responsible to the British Colonial Office. Many of the company's magistrates were asked to stay on, becoming district commissioners, and for several years the shift from one method of governance to another was hardly discernible to the concerned eye. Certainly Gore-Browne, by now heavily involved building roads for and with the government from Chinsali, and from Kasama to Shiwa, experienced no immediate improvement in the efficiency of the bomas. "That damned Chinsali *boma,*" he wrote on one of many occasions in 1925, "promised forty men five weeks ago to finish off the bridges in the Katete meadow where the main road crosses (me to pay, boma to recruit), a day or two ago they wrote to ask Did I still want them. They mean well but they're helpless and hopeless. I'd like," he said finally, "to be a senior official here for just six months, and to stir people up a bit like my Chiefs used to sometimes in the Army."[23]

In fact, Gore-Browne was running a private *boma* of his own, keeping the local peace, disciplining all but the most serious cases, doing many things for the estate which a farmer on the line of rail would naturally have expected the government to provide, and relieving several district commissioners of concern for the large zone around Shiwa.

Within the Northern Province, Gore-Browne had become more than a curiosity. He gave out medals in Kasama, was consulted over this or that problem by the district commissioners or the mis-

23. Gore-Browne to Nunk, 7 July 1925.

sionaries, and was visited by anyone passing within a hundred miles of his still remote and, compared to what it later became (but not the standards of Northern Rhodesia at the time), primitive outpost. He was even beginning to gain a national standing. "The Governor," Gore-Browne's old friend Tagart wrote from Livingstone in mid-1925, "is very interested in your experiments." He hoped that Gore-Browne's initiative would provide a resource base on which to develop northeastern Rhodesia as an African agricultural bastion—as another Uganda. "It would be a triumph if the Plateau could rival Uganda in that line."[24] Indeed, Sir Herbert Stanley, the new governor, who had served previously in Southern Rhodesia and South Africa, proposed to see for himself by visiting Shiwa Ngandu.

The several days that Governor and Lady Stanley spent alone at Shiwa put the serious purposes of Shiwa on the national map, accelerated the process of making Gore-Browne into a leader among settlers, and helped to interest Gore-Browne himself in matters of the entire territory as well as his "own show." The visit went well from the moment on the first afternoon when the Stanleys entered his library to have tea and saw, fingered, and borrowed samples of Gore-Browne's already impressive collection. "They both . . . fell in love with my books, which he tactfully said reflected his own taste exactly, & talk flowed in an easy stream." They talked the chat about books and authors which Gore-Browne, who read omnivorously, could do so well. "Then it was time to go out for a stroll," a pattern which Gore-Browne followed with visitors until his death, to show the Stanleys the extent to which Shiwa Ngandu had emerged from the chrysalis. "The nursery filled them with enthusiasm, and . . . the walk along the canal back through the mushitu is quite exquisite, & they cried out with delight at the broad clear river, & the glimpses of the hills through the trees. They were sensible at the still room, admired the roof . . . & were impressed by the apparent simplicity of everything. Then we walked on back across the new broad embankment spanning the Katete meadow, past the Equipment Store, & Forge, & the new long plough shed, [and] back up to [what was] Government House for the time being."[25] In the open space before the house Gore-Browne's servants, and all the laborers, their wives, and observers from miles around

24. Tagart to Gore-Browne, quoted in Gore-Browne to Ethel, 29 August 1925.

25. "Have I told you," Gore-Browne interrupted his description of the visit, "of one prize idiot of a visitor who seeing this same still room, a great unfinished shed—30 feet high, 70 feet long, & 35 feet broad, with its copper vats & pipes, & locomotives, said in all good faith 'oh is this Mr. Croad's house?' I nearly replied 'Yes, he sleeps in one of those copper things, & has dinner in another.'"

were assembled according to instructions. "The capitaos were all drawn up wearing spotless uniforms, with all their medals shining, & looking as smart as only good native troops can, something of the conscious smartness of Guardsmen; the other ex-soldiers were drawn up, a little apart, bemedalled & in clean native dress; the villagers & women were grouped in the picturesque way that seems natural to them, & the children enchanted Lady Stanley by making mud pies in the flower beds during His Excellency's speech." The speech was translated by James, Gore-Browne's African clerk. It was an admirable interpretation, Gore-Browne reported, "for though he only caught about 2/3, especially when H. E. had warmed up & got on to Duty to one's country & similar sublime conceptions, he never hesitated a moment but put out a flow of good Chiwemba utterances which the multitude loudly applauded. For the Duty to one's country he substituted what I recognized as a Mission phrase equivalent to 'casting off the works of Darkness.'" At the end, after the Governor had invited the multitude to tell him of their problems and grievances, Mwango, another faithful retainer, immediately said "How should we have troubles to speak about when Col. Gore-Browne is our father and looks after us?"

Gore-Browne always excelled as an effortless host, carefully arranging even the smallest details beforehand. "Dinner was a tremendous success. The moroccan lamps all lit, the great brass bowl blazing with petunias, the boys in yellow & white . . ." White soup with new asparagus was followed with fresh lake fish fried, wild duck, and cheese straws, all washed down with champagne. "My dear," the governor addressed his wife, "This is indeed much the best food and drink we've had anywhere." He had two helpings of everything ("give me some more of that wild duck, and then shut me in my sty," he said to his host) and most of two bottles of champagne. The meal the second night was equally successful, soup with little squares of toast, fish soufflé, roast guinea fowl, steamed pudding with brandy cream sauce, and cheese eggs in little pots, again accompanied by champagne. Kalikeka, the cook, had done Gore-Browne proud, even shooting the ducks and the guinea fowl himself.

Naturally, for Gore-Browne excelled as a conversationalist, the discussion between three who were delighted to find others of their own kind in the middle of nowhere, flowed endlessly, one evening well past midnight despite Gore-Browne's need to rise at 5:30. The governor was very keen on developing roads, and transport generally, and found a receptive ear in Gore-Browne. They talked of the desirability of developing the road and lake route to Dar es Salaam, and of the route westward to Lobito Bay along Robert Williams' still uncompleted railway. He talked of a plan for a port at

Mpulungu on the lake, the very spot which Gore-Browne had tried to buy from the company, and of the necessity of bringing the telegraph line to Kasama and Mpika. Stanley also revealed his intention to decentralize the Protectorate, establishing a provincial commissioner in Kasama.[26] These conversations constituted Gore-Browne's introduction to the problems of greater Northern Rhodesia, and on each point Stanley and Gore-Browne shared their experience and ideas. On the overarching subject—race relations, and the development of the indigenous majority—they equally aired their ideals and reflections, and found each other receptive. The governor, Gore-Browne reported, was "intensely pro-native in a sensible way. . . ." "Justice and patience [were] the 2 characteristics required in dealing with the native, & he doesn't expect too much from his Education schemes."[27]

Like the governor, Gore-Browne had a positive approach to and appreciation of Africans. He had come to Africa originally intolerant of inequity, coarseness, and brutality and, despite the social pressures imposed by a peer group which feared and was antagonistic to Africans, managed during the days of the Boundary Commission, and again after returning to settle at Shiwa, to relate warmly and openly to Africans as humans rather than chattels. This was a rare trait in a settler, but it conformed to Gore-Browne's self-definition of his role. Being a benevolent paternalist suited him, and, during the first decades in Northern Rhodesia, when paternalism was believed to be the highest rationale of colonialism, he practiced a form of English squirearchy which elicited warm African responses. Most of the other Rhodesian whites preached benevolence but in practice regarded the welfare of Africans as competitive with and therefore secondary to their own, as a class. Gore-Browne always demonstrated a concern for Africans as individuals, and, with an unusual degree of detachment, altered and modernized his day-to-day responses to them as a group—and his philosophical opinion of their collective abilities—the longer he stayed at Shiwa and the more it became his home.

Establishing Shiwa gave Gore-Browne an inevitable relationship to Africans as employees, as retainers, as personal servants, as chiefs and headmen, and, in one or two special cases, as companions. The

26. Gore-Browne to Ethel Locke-King, 30 October 1925.
27. Geoffrey C. Latham, the new secretary for education, had stayed two nights with Gore-Browne a few weeks before, and spoke rapturously of complicated schemes of uplift for Africans, which Gore-Browne welcomed, but about which he was skeptical. He remembered Bulaya, and still had a lingering distrust of educated Africans.

gradual evolution of his feelings about and regard for Africans was based on these kinds of encounters as well as on a growing understanding of how he might most appropriately affect the future of his adopted country. At no time, however, especially in the beginning, did Gore-Browne give Africans more credit than he thought they deserved. He fancied himself a realist capable of seeing Africans in their true light, and never regarded them as primitive innocents in the manner of the "sentimentalists" of Exeter Hall. There was no simplemindedness in Gore-Browne's dealing with Africans; what is striking, however, is the way in which he gradually broadened his views, changed his perceptions, and enjoyed a one-to-one relationship with Africans individually. Other settlers and most missionaries lacked this ability to modify their prejudices. Once fixed in attitude, and reinforced by the prevailing low local opinion of Africans, they went through life condemning, denigrating, and learning nothing from Africa. Gore-Browne, probably because of his background, his war experiences, his inner-directedness, and the unique quality of his vision, escaped being clamped in the vise of hackneyed prejudice and always trusted a very personal, experience-based knowledge of Africa and Africans.

The shifts in his thinking were never dramatic. It was the cumulative effect of daily dealings with Africans which moved him from the stage of condescension to thorough understanding, from the point of mild concern to the vehement championing of their rights, and from bemused reflections to agonized appeals on their behalf. In the days of the Boundary Commission he had supervised the activities of African workers who performed comparatively simple tasks correctly and well. Most served him for brief periods, and his contact with most of them was mediated by a *capitão*. At Shiwa, however, larger numbers of Africans (more than 1200 different individuals were employed at Shiwa during the first year, at least 1800 in 1925) came into his orbit as an employer. Most resided on his estate, and he was in many ways responsible for the whole of their behavior, not merely the working segment. In the capacity as liege lord, he came to know Africans in the round. After a year at Shiwa his occasional disappointments had cumulated, and plunged him into deep gloom. Living with and in some senses for Africans was proving unsatisfactory. "I am still unhappy about . . . the natives," he wrote home. "I don't feel I can ever really trust them now. Making all allowance for what they are, it seems one must just be resigned to their being liars always, often thieves, and generally untrustworthy. That's a hard saying of the people ones got to live among, & I hope I'm wrong. . . ." "The whole worry," he continued, "is that one doesn't seem to be able to treat them as I think

I've always treated people who worked under me, i.e. with trust & with consideration in return for loyalty & honesty. That sounds awfully pompous & prosy but I don't know how else to put it."

The Africans at Shiwa were not hostile, not idle, and usually charming and cheerful, he said. "I don't think I've ever broken my word to any native about anything." Even, he said, "in little things I'm scrupulous to the point of being silly about it daily." Yet Africans were unable, he felt, "to stick to anything . . . unless it suits." Even faithful Kakumbi had once refused to obey an order from Cowie and later had thoughtlessly practiced the *citimene* form of cultivation, burning trees on the estate without permission. Moreover, Gore-Browne complained, even the most skilled of his African employees were incapable of making a second mat the same size as an original or of making a building or a flight of steps with straight lines. "He simply doesn't see any difference between crooked & straight which makes bricklaying anxious work!" Africans were shrewd, he said, but they also seemed "incapable of connected thought." He ended one long description of these problems on a note of acute anxiety. "It's really worrying me a good bit this native business—I still like them, but I don't see how one can live amongst people when all the giving is to be on one's side. I don't mean only things like medicine & money, but decent treatment & consideration." "All one's ideas," he reported, "of living peacefully & cooperatively . . . were hopeless."[28]

A month later, after investigating incidents and reflecting about some of them—and also after the rains had broken—Gore-Browne was more relaxed about Africans. "Great peace once again with the natives, & apparent understanding. I expect the fault when its otherwise lies partly in oneself. I don't mean that the maddening & rotten things they do . . . are 'not as described,' but one ought to be able to make the necessary allowance—and of course it is true that there are funny underlying causes of which one's ignorant." A sympathetic, but cautionary epistle from his Uncle Wilfred, the Anglican Bishop of Kimberley and Kuruman, may also have reminded him of the regularities of Africa. "We all have to endure a phase of disillusionment with Africans," he wrote, "and I am surprised at the courage of Missionaries, who live permanently with no other surrounding—The quality does not run evenly thru' the whole man & one comes on soft places. . . . There is a sort of give & take & I try to be equable & make it inconvenient to people to be dishonest, or otherwise unsuitable; but never to sulk for that is ineffective and makes one . . . miserable."[29]

28. Gore-Browne to Ethel Locke-King, 22 October, 7 August 1921.
29. Wilfred Gore-Browne to Gore-Browne, 31 October 1921.

Gore-Browne demanded loyalty and devotion from his staff and respect and hard work from his employees. Yet African attitudes towards their responsibilities were not his own. They were casual and he was autocratic, and his remedies at first were forceful. "I think I've got them well in hand again," he reported during his first year, "by a show of severity." He admitted over & over again, especially after his uncle's urging, that endless patience was a virtue and a necessity. One must exercise self-control, he agreed. But Gore-Browne at first had little of either. He wouldn't suffer fools gladly. "At times I know I'm unreasonable & violent," though being "frightfully violent tempered" helped no one.[30] These bouts of real antagonism and chastisement coincided with especial instances of African unreliability and/or what he & other whites called cheekiness. He would allow no black man to show disrespect to himself, or to other whites. When one seemed to sass Boxall, Gore-Browne ordered him beaten. "I think it essential," Gore-Browne explained, "to keep up discipline & white prestige & so on."[31]

"I did hope to be able to be on decent terms with the people & help a bit," he said afterwards. But at first he was short-tempered, sometimes brutal, and too often assumed "at once that a man's lying as soon as he opens his mouth . . . and simply to regard them as cattle which one makes use of, feeds, doctors when sick, & if it's necessary beats when they're over obstinate."[32] This was an exaggeration of depression, however, for only acute exasperation exploded Gore-Browne's ferocious temper. If punishments were meted out, like the fifteen lashes prescribed for a youth who played dangerously with the saw bench engine, they usually resulted from an hour or so of thought rather than precipitous anger. When Boxall began "knocking Africans about" for trivial stupidities or inefficiencies, punching them in the jaw, and generally picking quarrels, Gore-Browne anxiously and repeatedly chastised him. "Please don't do it," he wrote in a note carried by hand across the estate. "I'm never proud of myself if I lose my temper with a native & hit him, though I admit it's often difficult not to." To Dame Ethel he was even more vehement: "The whole thing is the sort of low class, brawling, business that is of daily occurrence in S. Africa, & on the railway line here. . . . Damn my white assistants."[33]

He had no faith in legal remedies and was well aware of the

30. Gore-Browne to Ethel Locke-King, 7 August 1921.
31. Gore-Browne to Ethel Locke-King, 15 September 1925.
32. Gore-Browne to Ethel Locke-King, 22 October 1921.
33. Gore-Browne to Boxall, 31 August 1925. Gore-Browne to Ethel Locke-King, 15 September 1925.

Gore-Browne beside a life-size portrait of Dame Ethel Locke-King.

expediency and counter-productive nature of thrashings. Equally, his first two years at Shiwa made him skeptical about well-intended missionary-promoted panaceas. His uncle Nunk had written to him about the theories of James Arthur Ross, the head of the London Missionary Society station at Kambole, near Abercorn. Ross was promoting the "raising of the native on his own lines," and advocated self-help schemes of all kinds. "Where I'm stumped," Gore-Browne replied, "is how to set about it." "These people just won't be raised." He cited Kakumbi as an example. Although "one of the nicest natured fellows you could have, not one single scrap has he picked up from all he saw in England, & during the war, though his eyes were very wide open & he took a jolly keen interest in everything . . . yet he still lives in a rubbishy hut full of bugs, still stuffs a few seeds into a patch of ashes on ground which he doesn't even trouble to hoe, still brews beer, from such grain as he does grow, in the summer & goes hungry in the winter." Gore-Browne would distribute vegetable seeds, tobacco seeds, high class maize etc. to anyone at Shiwa, but neither Kakumbi nor anyone else could, he lamented, be bothered. "When I hear of people like Ross trying to raise money in England from folk by talking of village industries amongst the natives, I'm inclined to think their zeal must have blunted their sense a bit." Anyway, Africans were happier left alone were it not for the fact that whites had "come along & unsettled them."[34]

"About the natives," and how to handle them, he wrote with the experience of two years, "I quite agree that personality is the thing that tells, and that will win in the long run. But I think what one is apt to miss in the first flush of enthusiasm is that there is a big barrier set up by centuries of a different mode of thought & a different environment, across which or through which personality has got to act. . . . Well in the case of the native you've got to get through that barrier (which is all the more real that a well mannered native doesn't let you see it exists) always remembering that it's reinforced by indolence, fatalism, & a very genuine desire (I'm certain) to be left alone."[35] Movement across the barrier could be made only when, in extremis, Africans saw that the white man's gun was helpful in killing man-eating lions, when the white man could avert famine by distributing grain, or when the level of fear—fear of the consequences of disrespect and doing evil—was high enough. Cruelty for its own sake did not pay, but he advocated reinforcing the admonitions of Western society through chastisement.

It was the belief in being able to "educate them up" which set

34. Gore-Browne to Nunk, 8 March 1922.
35. Gore-Browne to Nunk, 2 August 1922.

Gore-Browne apart from most Northern Rhodesian whites. Although his views at this early stage cannot be said to have been far in advance of his contemporaries, he had not closed his mind to African perfectability. Faults Africans had, and their eradication, and the general socialization of Africans in the ways of the West, would take time, but Gore-Browne's disillusionment had not deepened into hopeless despair. In an ironic aside he told Nunk that were there a local election, his own African community would doubtless elect "the fellow who'd issued out the most meat to the neighborhood."[36] Nevertheless the vicissitudes of the earliest years at Shiwa, which might have turned Gore-Browne into a narrow-minded bigot, instead dampened his romantic idealism and gave him realistic expectations on which to encourage and reward African aspirations. By 1925, too, he had begun devolving serious respon-sibilities to Africans with some success. Driven of necessity to put greater reliance on Africans because of his almost perpetual dissatis-faction with white assistance—"the white staff are such a cursed nuisance"—and the growing scale and complexity of Shiwa's oper-ations, he gave real supervisory tasks to Africans and found, to his excited surprise, that they could do them well. His special find was James Mwanza, who gained credibility by being able to pay the casual laborers at the end of each month, "though one isn't keen on letting any native have opportunities at getting at cash," and could type, more and more assuming the burden of doing the trying (forty or so a week) official letters from Gore-Browne's drafts, keeping accounts, and the other office work.[37] Gore-Browne also turned nearly all of the storekeeping problems over to a locally-trained African, and found that Mulemfwe, the head *capitão,* or foreman, was capable of supervising road work and bridge build-ing to the exacting satisfaction of Croad, who rarely praised. Mushembe, the head gardener, was coping admirably with the mul-titudinous tasks of readying seedlings and cuttings, and also man-aged a large labor force of ninety children with economy.

In 1925 Gore-Browne also added a medical dispenser to his staff. Aaron had been trained by the Presbyterians but had fallen from grace by transgressing their strict sexual code. Otherwise medical assistance from Kasama was now five hours by truck away, but Gore-Browne had long wanted someone to relieve the range of minor ailments from which the Africans suffered. Aaron attended the constipated babies, the men and women with coughs, and all those who had cuts and sores, ordinary fevers, and tummy aches.

36. Gore-Browne to Nunk, 24 May 1922.
37. Gore-Browne to Nunk, 29 July, 22 April 1925.

"Already," wrote Gore-Browne in July, "our people are flocking to the dispensary and claim anyhow to get great benefit."[38]

At about the same time as Aaron began providing medical advice and pharmaceuticals, Gore-Browne also obtained a teacher from the Presyterians and started a school. There were about 150 children of school age on the estate and he felt, despite his anxieties about Ross's schemes for uplifting Africans, that "they ought to get some teaching instead of running wild." He was still suspicious of purely literary instruction, however, and wanted them to be taught to read and write and count only to the point where they could benefit from prolonged instruction in agricultural methods and "crafts."

Almost without long-term planning, and before the estate could be said to have more than the faint prospect of paying its own way, Gore-Browne had made it more than a commercial proposition. For him it was an outpost of white "civilization" in the wilderness. As surrogate-chief, he felt himself responsible for the provision of social benefits to at least the residents of the estate. When Dr. Aylmer May, the principal medical officer of the Protectorate, paid a surprise visit to Shiwa later in the year, his pleasure with the dispensary fell on welcome and proud ears. "Why you're a public benefactor," he told Gore-Browne.[39]

By the end of Shiwa's first five years, Gore-Browne had come more and more to base his plans for its material and spiritual future on Africans. White supervision would still be necessary, but only African cooperation, training, and skill could move the scheme forward within an all-embracing framework of benevolent paternalism. In this last respect, Gore-Browne had not altered his overall approach. It had, moreover, been validated to his satisfaction by the experience of the first quinquennium. "You could hardly conceive a more ideal state of affairs, for the black man has here, I truly believe, all he wants in his present state of development, he's under sufficient discipline for his own comfort but isn't unduly interfered with, he has the opportunity of 'bettering himself' if he likes . . . and he can earn such money as he wants at his own home." Furthermore, Gore-Browne was himself receiving all that's good—"sufficient deference due to my superior intellect or training . . . but not . . . servitude which would . . . undoubtedly be demoralizing to me, as well as the native, however careful I tried to be not to abuse it. . . ."[40] The barriers of social distance were also beginning to slip. When Gore-Browne brought a Ford truck for the first time from

38. Gore-Browne to Ethel Locke-King, 21 July 1925.
39. Quoted in Gore-Browne to Ethel Locke-King, 6 November 1925.
40. Gore-Browne to Ethel Locke-King, Easter Sunday, 1925.

Broken Hill to Shiwa, he was met by excited crowds, including one who hugged him. "I suppose that isn't done really, but one couldn't object."[41]

"Probably I'm only here really because I like being an autocrat over a lot of black men," Gore-Browne ended a long, revealing letter to Ethel in 1925. He had no faith in indirect rule, since the power of chiefs had long ago been destroyed by colonial rule and most of the local inheritors of the imposing titles were weak men whose political vitality had been sapped irredeemably by the British. Equally, at a time when Nyasas and Northern Rhodesians were beginning to found their own schismatic Protestant sects, he was skeptical about the ability of Africans to run their own churches. "I've seen nothing," he wrote, "in these people here that makes me feel they are fit to organize a church. . . . You know how keen I am that they should help themselves, & how I'd like to delegate authority & responsibility, but it simply can't be done" yet.[42] Nor did he think institutionalized responsibility of any kind could be transferred for "ages, if ever." But these pessimistic sentiments were not denigrations of Africans alone. Gore-Browne held very low opinions of democracy, and blamed President Woodrow Wilson for putting ideas prematurely in the minds of many. "How the devil is a modern state to be governed?" he asked. Democracy was impossible, and a contradiction in terms. Some sort of efficient & intelligent tyranny was the only satisfactory solution. After all, wasn't "the world too big for itself altogether?" In terms of Shiwa, he felt capable of ruling the estate and the neighboring villages successfully, and on the whole for the good of the governed, "but then my intelligence is to theirs as 1000 to 1, *and* I should have the material backing of money with which to subsidize the force necessary to keep order & get my own way."[43]

One of Gore-Browne's many ex-military friends sketched an irreverent but insightful parody of the Colonel's new life. Although this correspondent wrote from Morocco, and knew nothing of the life of a Northern Rhodesian settler and squire, he obviously understood Gore-Browne. "I picture you," he began, "in either a wooden shack or a mud & plaster one, consisting of a living room, an office, and a rear. . . . In the centre, looking both to right & left and in front stands Colonel Bluddygore, the world-famed soldier, statesman & priest. Efficiency bristles round him, natives (ever so beautiful in their bronze birth-suitings) rally at his merest bark and scatter at the twitch of his toe. He is alone once more. We who have entered

41. Gore-Browne to Ethel Locke-King, 13 August 1925.
42. Gore-Browne to Ethel Locke-King, 18 February 1925.
43. Gore-Browne to Ethel Locke-King, 31 May 1924.

unobserved and are hiding behind the stuffed rhino watch his every movement. We see him turn to the business-like table, whip out file G22 and without a moment's hesitation proceed to dictate to himself that masterly letter to the Rhodesian government for which he will be so justly famous. No sooner has he finished typing for himself than he leans back in his chair, sniggles to himself & says, 'I *am* a shit.' This evidently opens up a train of thought and he brings down that heavy vellum tome, labelled 'My Memoirs' (for which he will be so justly infamous) and writes 42 confessions off pat. Seized now with a fit of self-chastisement, he squares his jaw, adjusts his eye-glass and strides with grim determination to the third room, the rear. . . . Back again to the office he becomes a boy again, kicks his heels, whistles the Meistersinger Overture without a false note, and picking up a pruning-knife sets foot for the wilds, there to nip rose-buds, gut hippopotami or, if the need occurs play midwife. . . . Oh Gory, what a rum life!"[44]

Gore-Browne indubitably enjoyed living the life of a super staff officer, being an autocrat, certainly. More accurately, the role ideals on which he modelled himself were in many respects those of the English public school, of the neo-Edwardian English aristocracy —of "his class." He tried to perform creditably as a benevolent despot, the first six years at Shiwa being an appropriate test of his character.

Gore-Browne was sentimental in a rather old-fashioned way, his appreciation of African reactions and African motivations in those days being clouded by his own romantic self-image. Then he hardly understood the extent to which wanting to be wanted, and fulfilling those wants easily and without giving away much spiritually, explained his rapprochement with Africa and Africans. He likened himself to a patriarch, but patriarchs had ties of blood. Gore-Browne was a lord of the manor. If decent, kind, and bountiful, he won respect, reverence, and loyalty without sacrificing social distance, or becoming at one with his people—a posture impossible in England for a man of Gore-Browne's ambitions, talents, and means. These personal needs also help to explain his lavish management of the estate—his willingness, indeed desire, to be known as a public benefactor, his inability to turn away almost anyone who wanted a job, and his refusal to economize even though, throughout the first six years of Shiwa's existence, not a penny had been earned, and £18,000 of his own money, some of his father's, and many thousands of Nunk's had been spent (not always wisely) on the estate's capital and recurrent development. In 1923 he had promised Robert categorically that if Shiwa were not a commercial success he

44. Richard Nea to Gore-Browne, from Casablanca, 30 April 1921.

should give it up.[45] But by 1926, when the running of Shiwa cost about ten pounds a day, the estate had become a way of life rather than a simple business venture. Robert's fears had been justified; essential oils were the justification, not the rationale.

There was no early hope of profits, nor even any appreciable cash flow. Samples of geranium oil had merited praise from an English expert.[46] But the stills were not yet ready, the coriander and tansy had failed, termites had eaten the orange trees, and the roses were failing to thrive. Eucalyptus, on which so much hope was based, matured in 1926 and young Africans scaled the trees, stripped the leaves, and tossed them down into waiting carts. He could grow it, and distill it—in small quantities anyway—but could he sell it? These were questions for the future, and reason enough to begin thinking about going home for a second visit (all of 1923 having been spent in England, in Bulgaria during its revolution, and in Morocco).

There were other, more subtle and compelling reasons why he wanted to return to England. Nunk, who had long been invalided, and who had poured his heart (and money) and practical advice into Shiwa and Stewart, had died early in 1926. There were thus two widows, one with whom he could still not come to terms (though he gritted his teeth and invited her to Shiwa), and another whom he wanted much more than ever before. He hoped, even half-expected, that Ethel would spend the rest of her life with him at Shiwa. He prepared a house for her in 1926 and embroidered fantasy after fantasy. Throughout the first six years of Shiwa he carried on a weekly, sometimes twice-weekly dialogue with her about everything that happened. He spoke to her, vividly, via letters, and was communicated with just as desperately by her. Their affection and regard had ripened during the long absences, and after Nunk's death he began to write to her more openly than he had since the dark days of the war, and the pre-war crises in Northern Rhodesia. He longed for her, and "needed her so." Once he complained that of the endless list of guests and the many Africans, only with the Stanleys had he experienced "human converse."

The longing for Ethel was real, and different. He also admitted, on a rather less elevated but nonetheless real plane, to being excruciatingly lonely. Other than his letters to Ethel, and the pleasantries passed with the innumerable unwanted and tiresome guests, there were only books and dreams. He read hungrily, commented assiduously and compared continuously. At meals (when there were no "dratted" guests) he read non-fiction, usually biographies

45. Gore-Browne to Robert Gore-Browne, 25 September 1923.
46. Thomas H. Durrans to Gore-Browne, 4 January 1925.

of worthy great men or discussions of contemporary affairs. On Saturday evenings he read novels, disliking many, especially those that followed Conrad's structural model, or those that gushed, or were a little too sordid.

Dreams and books made his loneliness harder to bear.[47] They revived his ties to the past, to England, to Ethel, to a wider family. What he needed was someone with whom he could share his soul, someone with whom to enjoy the beauties of Shiwa, the qualities of the people, and the growth of the estate. The often irascible, petulant, self-indulgent, impractical squire contained a poet of sorts, and, especially after his hopes of reviving the spirit and fellowship of the Fifth Division had been shattered, a lonely romantic in need of fellowship and warmth. He thought that he needed a wife. It was not a new sentiment, although its expression had become more frequent the longer he had stayed alone at Shiwa. And at times he was ambivalent, extolling the virtues of a wife in one week's letter and drawing back in the next. Shiwa was all-absorbing, and in many ways he had long considered himself wedded to it, and appropriately so. For instance, when his Uncle Wilfred, the Bishop of Kimberley and Kuruman, visited Shiwa in 1924, Gore-Browne criticized himself for being inattentive—for preferring to worry about Shiwa rather than chatting by the fire at night. "When Uncle Will is telling me something about Higher Criticism in its later developments I'm wondering whether I'd better get rid of the 3 villages who want to leave Lukaleshye . . . or thinking about Tansy and its market." Was he fit to have a wife? Would she divorce him, a fate he feared? Would a wife perceive how he felt about Shiwa, "How much one's in earnest, and how one tries not to be an amateur & a dilletante?" A year later, he decided that "it certainly would be a big help to be married"—if, he added the rider, "it chanced to be the right person." The next year, however, after Nunk's death, his queries and musings took on a more positive tone. For the sake of both Shiwa and Brooklands, he did wish he were married.[48]

But to whom? After Lorna Lawrence Bosworth Smith Goldman, and the days of the Boundary Commission, had come the war, with its male fellowship. He had corresponded in a desultory way with Lady Diana Charlotte King, Evelyn Bonner, and Halcyon Wing, three younger girls, but their relationships seem to have been more avuncular or filial than (at least from his point of view) seriously

47. Gore-Browne's accounts of his dreams are rich in atmosphere but impoverished in data, making any analysis of Freudian symbolism difficult and obscure.

48. Gore-Browne to Ethel Locke-King, 20 June 1924, 20 May 1925, 9 April 1926.

romantic. When Halcyon married in 1921, her mother wrote con-
solingly to Gore-Browne that she had always hoped her daughter
would marry a dashing young officer, but dashing young officers
usually had no money, and the successful suitor in fact had private
means. As Gore-Browne said at the time, "she's nothing to me . . . I
wish she could have been, but she wasn't & that's all about it."[49] In
1923, when he was in England, he saw two younger acquaintances
of the family, first Nada Stancioff, and, then, towards the end of his
leave, Lady Katherine Carnegie, the daughter of Lord and Lady
Northesk. Dame Ethel had sagely prescribed someone not too
young, not younger than about 25 or 28, as Gore-Browne's companion, but she and he, and their friends, knew few suitable unmar-
ried women in that somewhat advanced age bracket. His exploration of these and other possible romantic attachments during 1923
does not appear to have been especially thorough or prolonged, but
whatever the length of their acquaintance, Gore-Browne sought
Katherine's affection in those last weeks before his return to Africa.
Enamoured he seems to have been, but not necessarily in love. And
time was against him, for he met Katherine in Scotland in October
and saw her in England only in November and December. "I'm
only sore with fate for not giving me the chance to do my own job
myself," he wrote later. On her part, Katherine appears to have
been intrigued, but unwilling on so brief an acquaintance with a
man so much older to agree to the engagement Gore-Browne
proposed. "I cannot tell you," Lady Elizabeth Northesk wrote to
Dame Ethel, "how sorry I am that Stewart's hopes cannot be. They
had become mine too . . . I am . . . so proud that he should care for
[Katherine] but oh how I hated his being hurt."[50]

As he sailed back to Africa from Marseilles in late 1923 and early
1924, Gore-Browne still hoped that either Nada or Katherine might
remain free until he returned to England. He corresponded with
neither, however, continuing to pour out his emotions to Ethel
only. Nada was the first to defect, becoming engaged early in 1924,
but Gore-Browne had mentally already thought her too competitive with Shiwa. (Even a year later, however, he confessed that he
couldn't stop thinking about her.) A few months later, Katherine, in
whom he had invested more attachment, also became engaged.
Ethel commiserated. "She is very young & she has chosen a partner
of her own time of life, but she has missed a big opportunity & a
very much greater offer to life—the proven man who has kept his

49. Gore-Browne to Ethel Locke-King, 27 December 1921. Lady Diana married Alistair Gibb, son of Sir Alexander and Lady Gibb, in 1927.
50. Gore-Browne to Ethel Locke-King, 20 December 1923; Lady Northesk to
Ethel, 17 December 1923.

ideal. & My dear My dear I mind you so greatly I know you accepted her word & that you did not want any yea & naying—but it has got to be hard to know her clean gone."[51] And it was hard. "There's nothing to be said about it all. Oh, if it might have been. . . ."[52]

Gore-Browne's immediate heterosexual physical and emotional needs, if not his desire for a soul mate, could easily have been satisfied at Shiwa. Openly or covertly, he could have acquired one or many African mistresses, and followed the hallowed local practices of Chirapula Stephenson, who had sired dozens of children, all of whom he acknowledged, or other more discreet administrators and settlers.[53] Suitable matches could have been made, and even sanctioned by blacks, if not officially approved by whites. Jones had lived with an African woman, and even fathered a child, without drawing more than his ire. But for Gore-Browne to have done so would, if nothing else, have transgressed a personal moral code, smudged his image in the eyes of his peers, and—he feared realistically—"lowered himself" in the eyes of both white and black Northern Rhodesians. As he wrote—was it surprising?—"I don't keep a native woman myself, but I've no special views about people who do."[54] There were a few unattached white women in Northern Rhodesia, if color had been a bugbear, and some even in Kasama, which did its best to remain socially lively. But Gore-Browne had little time or energy for merriment, especially with or among "inferior" whites. The gay mess parties in Köln were far behind him. As he wrote to Ethel, "Oh how orgies bore me nowadays."[55]

Any wife who came here would have to be entirely devoted to me *and* to the place," Gore-Browne concluded.[56] Only Katherine, he mused, might really have fit, and survived, but she had been too young. She had to understand how he might, time and again, "like a little peace with his natives," how he needed solitude yet wanted to be wanted. She would have to accept—especially at his age—a fondness for playing staff officer, and degenerating into a sergeant major. There was his frightful temper, too. "When I was raging at some slackness on the part of my servants," he recalled, "I found one of them under the table. . . . 'What the Hell are you doing there,'" I roared. The trembling African answered, "'When the

51. Ethel Locke-King to Gore-Browne, 20 August 1924.

52. Gore-Browne to Ethel Locke-King, 26 September 1924.

53. See Kathaleen Stevens Rukavina, *Jungle Pathfinder: The Biography of Chirapula Stephenson* (London, 1951).

54. Gore-Browne to Ethel Locke-King, 22 August 1925.

55. Gore-Browne to Ethel Locke-King, 17 December 1926.

56. Gore-Browne to Ethel Locke-King, 20 May 1925.

forest is on fire the wise man steps aside.'"[57] Moreover, he was frightfully compulsive, spending every evening for a week cleaning out, sorting, and filing the contents of his small house. He made lists, needed to keep official as well as personal matters jotted down in diaries, fussed furiously about details, and bore disorder of no kind. He was scatalogically minded. And he still liked hearing and telling risqué stories. He looked forbidding, but underneath the Chipembere there was a lonely, sometimes frightened boy whose maturity needed to be winkled out by some magic woman.

Ethel had described the qualities of that woman. "She would have to be . . . very special—not a very young one who dreams of filling the horizon & being of chief account herself, nor one who only goes there because of her personal devotion to you, but one who has a longing after the life for itself & a strong feeling for you added. . . . If she only cared for you, she'd not be able to put up with your absorption in the place."[58] Other than Ethel herself, who could possibly satisfy his many complicated needs in the ideal way? Whether or not anyone could, he concluded that he should *very* much like a wife. "But I don't know how it's to come about."[59]

In late 1926, after Croad had returned to Shiwa following a long absence, Gore-Browne started homeward via Abercorn, Tanganyika, and the east coast route. Shiwa was a reality, even if geraniums had failed to flourish and the economic viability of essential oils was as yet unproven. Moreover, his prospective importers were urging him to concentrate on the geraniums, and neroli, and were rather discouraging about Eucalyptus, the only fragrant plant which had thus far taken at Shiwa.[60] It was hard for Gore-Browne to wrench himself away from the tasks at hand and from his Africans, but Ethel, and the possibility of finding a wife, drew him relentlessly to Britain.

57. Gore-Browne to Ethel Locke-King, 26 November 1926.

58. Ethel Locke-King to Gore-Browne, 30 July 1924.

59. Gore-Browne to Ethel Locke-King, 9 January 1926.

60. The oil of *citriodora* produced a higher yield in Northern Rhodesia (at Shiwa) than in Australia, to which it was native. It was also appropriately high in aldehyde content. For the analysis, see Peter George Carter and John Read, "An Examination of Some Rhodesian Eucalyptus Oils," *Journal of the Society of Chemical Industry*, XLIV (1925), 525–526.

V

"Lorna, dear and bright"

IT IS HARD to be forty-four and in need of a wife, especially if one's standards are high. The monocle was resting more and more comfortably in Gore-Browne's left eye, his hairline had receded considerably, and, although still erect, strong, and wise in the ways of the bush, he had grown correspondingly settled in manner, attitude, and routine. His temper had mellowed, but not much. Then to be considered there was the mystique of Shiwa, and Gore-Browne's plans for its fulfillment and apotheosis. Physically, it was not yet the grand estate it was later to become, and there was still a minimum of creature comfort. For Africa in the 1920s, however, the housing was adequate. Almost no one had done so well with so little so far from a railway or a main road. There were Africans—servants, retainers, employees, chiefs, and a few confidants. There were the officials of the boma, and the scattered and distant settler community. Above all there was the ethos and beauty of Africa, the isolation from previously experienced cues, and the remoteness of a place like Shiwa from medical and other Western facilities. For the right woman, however, this very isolation, and Shiwa's uniqueness, could prove romantic, enticing, and something of a rare challenge in a world which had only recently been tormented by the closing of frontiers, the taming of the wilds and, assaulting other senses, the kinds of unrest and militancy indicated by the British General Strike.

Gore-Browne, his eyes twinkling as he told stories of white, black, and animal Africa, could well have appealed to the senses of unusual women. Some would have warmed to stories about the hunt, especially of rhinoceros and lion, others to his observations about the Bemba, and still others to his talk of the war, of Brooklands and its society, of opera, and generally of the breadth and depth of his experience—something no younger man could have hoped to equal.

All of this, whether or not explicitly offered and discussed, Gore-Browne embodied and brought home during the winter of 1927. He also carried somewhere deep within the organs of his being a well-nourished, unshakeable, and irreplaceable love for Ethel. She remained the lodestar, the beacon of his aspirations, the woman with whom all others would have to share. Gore-Browne and Ethel were too close for another to intervene; each depended on the other for reassurance and a precious, affectionate sustenance which was more than filial. Even in her sixties, Dame Ethel was unflagging in energy, rectitude, and dominance. She was still managing the affairs of the Brooklands and the track. She was the center, too, of the affairs of the clans Gore-Browne, King, Shaw-Stewart, and many others, compelling them all to recognize and pay homage to the force of her personality. Another woman, especially a mate for Gore-Browne and a prospective mother of his children, and thus Ethel's adopted lineage, would have to satisfy her and either accept her role or vie for priority. No equation involving Gore-Browne could ever neglect her sign, demean her power, or confuse her influence with those of an ordinary, if much revered, aunt.

It was to her that Gore-Browne returned in 1927, and with her encouragement that the search for a wife ensued during the early months of the year. Dame Ethel believed that it was "all wrong" that Gore-Browne should depend for emotional sustenance on so potentially perishable an item as herself. She urged him to marry and overruled his protestations that marriage would "spoil everything".[1] With this imperative very much in mind, Gore-Browne and Ethel rendezvoused first in Sicily, where others would not interfere with a private homecoming. From Palermo they travelled to Messina and on to Taormina, still a spa of some repute, and then to the mainland, to Naples and Rome. For him, the joy of seeing her "really alone without a soul to come between . . . was worth anything . . . . It's so true that I've only got you in the world, there's not another soul to talk to."[2]

Only after she had returned to England could Gore-Browne face his own mother, who, rosy and healthy, was exercising her nagging and complaining arts in St. Raphael, an English colony on the south coast of France. Her incessant bridge and many dissatisfactions irritated, and he had to remind himself of filial obligations whenever she disparaged Ethel, Nunk, Shiwa—"the white elephant"—or himself. The benediction came, however, when she declared that Gore-Browne should never marry. "It would be wrong."[3]

Nevertheless, Gore-Browne reached England in mid-February with prospective partners very much in mind. Evelyn Bonner had already been married off, much to Gore-Browne's relief, and of the young debutantes of his previous visit only Nada Stancioff, her

1. Gore-Browne to Ethel Locke-King, 1 January 1933.
2. Gore-Browne to Ethel Locke-King, 26 January 1927.
3. As reported in ibid.

engagement broken, remained a good prospect. Another possibility was Captain Cooper's daughter Ruth, with whom he lunched in Paris, and Esther, with whom he spent many hours in London before, and at Brooklands during, the Easter holidays. Finally, late in March at the funeral of Mrs. Reginald Bosworth-Smith, the first Lorna's mother, at Bingham's Melcombe, Stewart and the second Lorna suddenly met. "He saw me in the drawing room . . . and I was so much of a spit image of my mother that he fell in love with me at first sight." They immediately started talking about Africa. "He was about the only nice person there. And he showed me photographs of Africa."[4]

Lorna Goldman was nineteen. Saucy, aware of herself in some ways but unsure and ambivalent in many others, she was in her last school term at Sherborne in Dorset. A ward of her father's brother Sydney and his wife Agnes Goldman, she had often stayed at Bingham's Melcombe with her grandmother. The Goldmans travelled incessantly, to the Continent and the Orient, and Lorna had only her younger brother with whom to share the distant and early loss of her father, and the recent and still unrequited loss of her mother in Africa. She liked Gore-Browne from the first—at least she liked him better than anyone bar her brother—later confessing that initially she had no thoughts of marriage.

Gore-Browne proposed before the end of that April in England. "We'd gone out after tea with the dogs, and had been talking happily and friendlily. I think she cried for a moment, then she said 'I shall have to think—it's a bit of a shock. I can't say now!'"[5] They were together with Effie, Lady Grogan, at Shropham Hall (Attleborough, near Norwich in Norfolk), having spent Easter and another weekend under Ethel's watchful and ultimately approving eye at Brooklands, and talked about the proposal, on and off, all the several days they were together. Gore-Browne thought of nothing else, but afterwards found it difficult to fathom Lorna's own emotions. She was positive that she did not want to be married immediately, and initially preferred to go out to Africa, which greatly attracted her, as his employee. "I expect," Gore-Browne wrote, "she's too young to feel deeply about anyone yet, and she's all mixed up with bits of ideas partly out of books . . . partly what she's been told or heard, about her duty, and about marriage, and social work, and so on, which mostly just confuse the issue. Poor girl it's a bit rough on her to have to decide."[6] He thought that she should see Africa again before making up her mind. Throughout

4. Interview with Lady Lorna Gore-Browne, Archway, London, 1966.
5. Gore-Browne to Ethel Locke-King, 30 April 1927. Lady Gore-Browne does not remember crying. She was against marriage in principle.
6. Ibid.

Gore-Browne admired her radiance, her willingness to sit or walk with him for hours and seem happy. She was honest and straightforward, particularly when feeling that as a prospective wife she was not clever or knowledgeable enough to be of use to him at Shiwa. Yet he also knew that Lorna was against the idea of marriage—of its physical and mental confines, of its demands, and of responsibilities to another. It would deprive her of an independence that she had never begun to enjoy. But she also needed a protector and a mission. What better than contributing to the happiness and well-being of the man her mother admired and might have married?

"'I do feel its rotten not to be able to say yes or no,'" Lorna told Gore-Browne as they parted at Shropham. "'I'll try not to be vague,'" she said.[7] When, Gore-Browne asked Ethel, could they have Lorna back to Brooklands again? Would Ethel, whom Lorna had said she admired, write to her about marriage and life and decisions and so on? The rhinoceros was acting like a colt in the springtime fields. Something, probably his oft-reiterated need for her, finally made her agree. It was after an evening late in May in London that she wrote affirmatively, and subsequently at his club, before lunch, that she said "yes" in person. Gore-Browne was beside himself with joy.

"She shines," Gore-Browne quoted a Bemba line about a good-looking girl. He gave her a ring and some ivory beads and took her down to Oakley, the family seat. As the day of the marriage approached they endured the endless necessary rounds of family arrangements, the interviews with the Goldmans and Lorna's trustees, and some last days with Ethel.[8] Originally Ethel was to go back to Shiwa with them, not in the capacity of a white lady's maid and companion, which Gore-Browne's sister had insisted was necessary for Lorna's health and mental state, but as the honored guest. These plans ultimately went awry, however, Ethel prudently insisting that she could not leave Brooklands. Both Lorna and Stewart professed to be very disappointed. "We both did want it, and would have enjoyed it. . . . It won't be amusing parting from you . . .". And at the end of the same letter, in Lorna's young, crabbed, upright printing, she endorsed "all of this and do please come because as far as we're concerned you do know you are wanted."[9]

The wedding ceremony took place on 23 July in St. George's

7. Ibid.

8. The marriage was accompanied by an elaborate settlement or financial contract since Lorna was a ward in chancery.

9. Gore-Browne to Ethel Locke-King, 3 July 1927.

Church, Hanover Square, London. Midshipman Bosworth Monk Goldman gave his sister away and Major Studdert, of the Royal Artillery and the days on the Rhine, was best man. The list of guests was a roll call both of their separate and intertwined pasts and of those recently responsible for bringing them together. Many presumably remembered another wedding years before, and marked the irony and reward of a second Lorna substituting for the first. It is not known how the principals felt, in this regard, but for one venerable observer love gained was no certain cure for love lost. Thomas Hardy entitled his poem, in the form of a soliloquy by an amused Gore-Browne, "Lorna the Second."[10]

Lorna! Yes, you are sweet,
But you are not your mother,
Lorna the First, frank, feat,
Never such another!—
Love of her could smother
Griefs by day or night;
Nor could any other,
Lorna, dear and bright,

Ever so well adorn a
Mansion, coach, or cot,
Or so make men scorn a
Rival in their sight;
Even you could not!
Hence I have to mourn a
Loss ere you were born; a
Lorna!

Hardy, whom Stewart and Lorna visited in August, would have known why Gore-Browne chose the Melcombe of so many memories, now empty, as the site of their honeymoon. "Think of it," Gore-Browne wrote to Ethel, "coming back here, married to Lorna, and on our own."[11] He remembered tea in the Oriel with Lorna's mother, and the many times since, especially during the war, when he had enjoyed the atmosphere of calm which embraced the house, its tight courtyard, the splendidly aged yew topiary, and the house's many dark reception rooms. Stewart and Lorna were supposed to stay a few days, and then go on to Vienna, but after the second night they hated to flee a retreat which was proving more idyllic than either had expected. The house was fortunately available for most of August, so, despite the steep cost (about twenty guineas a week, including two servants), they lingered on. As the days passed Gore-Browne became more and more enchanted with his child bride. (He wrote regularly to Ethel throughout this honeymoon period, speaking warmly but not too intimately of Lorna. She also wrote to Ethel, but as a schoolgirl to a new foster parent. Rarely did she mention Stewart.) "It's all been far, far, far better than anything one could have imagined—& than anything one has ever deserved," he wrote a day after the nuptials. Three weeks later, urging Ethel to join them in order to share their bliss, he told her

10. Thomas Hardy, *Human Shows and Winter Words* (London, 1931).
11. Gore-Browne to Ethel Locke-King, 28 July 1927.

that she had "shared everything in all my life, and if you don't come here and be with us for a bit, you'll miss something that still seems too marvelously good to be true. . . . You know how one likes to show off anything very priceless or perfect, to the right person." He was ecstatic. "Lorna is I do truly think one in ten thousand—and each day I think so more, & am better content with my lot. It's jolly to have a wife one's proud of . . . [12]"

Stewart had a wife. But Shiwa was still without a mistress. The newlyweds' relationship had been tested only by repose and the satisfaction of pentup ardor. Each had explored the psyche of the other and had begun to play roles new and potentially unsettling, but their days together were as yet free from the stress of routine and the strain of particularity. Nonetheless, neither hesitated to return to Shiwa, for they were both confident and mutually fulfilled in ways neither could have foreseen nor had previously experienced. After a September of preparations and relative-hopping, they took a train to Venice, and sailed for Egypt, East Africa, and the lake route to Shiwa. They toured the Giza pyramids and saw the Sphinx, staying at Ethel's Mena House hotel, and bathed in the Red Sea at Port Sudan, where the demeanour of the local Africans moved Gore-Browne to comment pessimistically on the ability of blacks and whites ever to live side by side except in a territory like the Sudan, which was simply too torrid for colonists. As far as Kenya and Northern Rhodesia were concerned, he felt that the political climate was already too embittered for positive developments to ensue. Most of all, he bemoaned the lack of a reasonable progressive policy. "It's all very puzzling," he wrote, "and rather depressing. Depressing because no one seems to have any definite, thought out, policy anywhere."[13]

In Mombasa and Zanzibar, where their cargo ship stopped to discharge freight and passengers, Gore-Browne had little incentive to extend his reflection about the stagnation of race relations. In both places they were the guests of the leading whites, and were lavishly feted and guided around both islands. Even in Dar es Salaam, they received official hospitality, stayed with the head of the railway system, and went to grand balls where Lorna was resplendent. Nevertheless, reality was coming closer, first in the form of urgent messages from Croad at Shiwa and then, after a pleasant train journey to Kigoma and an easy passage to Mpulungu in the newest ship on Lake Tanganyika, the two, now united in common purpose, arrived home to cope with the well-being of crops, the maintenance of roads and bridges, the physical expansion and im-

12. Gore-Browne to Ethel Locke-King, 24 July 1927; 17 August 1927.
13. Gore-Browne to Ethel Locke-King, 10 October 1927.

provement of the estate, the morale of employees, the welfare of Africans, and the entertainment of a growing stream of generally unwelcome visitors. Most of all, Gore-Browne knew how necessary it was to incorporate Lorna into, and somehow have her come to share, the fullness of his vision of Shiwa's future. A period of subtle socialization, and tutelage, was required. Fortunately, however, Lorna was eager to throw herself mind and body into a myriad of his projects. She wanted to prove herself, to please her man, and to make herself useful and productive. For Lorna, especially, Shiwa was meant to be the beginning of a purposeful life.

Except for specific separate tasks and her hours with Aaron, the medical dispenser, Lorna worked with Stewart nearly every minute of the first year or so after her arrival at Shiwa. Together they wrestled with the fundamental problem of Shiwa's existence: could the estate be made to show a profit from essential oils? In Gore-Browne's absence in Britain Croad and Savill had continued the lavish spending of the past; they had improved their own residences, and employed large amounts of labor on brick and tile-making, and on several oil schemes. It took Gore-Browne a long time to ascertain the precise amount spent, but it was well over £4,000 per annum, with virtually no income at all, especially since Croad had failed to reerect the distilling apparatus as requested. Of the total, £600 per annum was Croad's salary and £240 Savill's. Another £400 or so was spent on African salaries and wages, the remainder going toward materials and supplies, nearly all of which were still shipped expensively from England. Locally, petrol cost between six shillings eightpence and seven shillings sixpence a gallon, and their Morris sedan and their Ford truck drank fuel with a fervent thirst. Keeping those two vehicles roadworthy was also costly, parts having to be sent from Bulawayo and Johannesburg. Seeds, cultivators, hoes, and almost any kind of farm equipment had to come from afar. Household or personal articles came out from England and even butter (their own herds at first produced too little milk) was fetched from Kasama at three shillings threepence a pound plus freight. They also had to supply much of their own transportation; hauling their fifty-one cases from Mpulungu, for example, took months and several trips with their own truck and a number of ox-drawn carts. But in 1928 the government at last began paying for the maintenance of the roads leading to Shiwa.

The income with which to maintain Shiwa now came from the interest on Gore-Browne's capital—about £1,500 per year until 1932, when interest rates fell—and large, recurrent and frequent special injections of funds from Ethel. Although the Brooklands estate and track were also going through a difficult period, she managed to contribute at least £1,500 a year, and sometimes much more, to the operation of Shiwa. She had inherited the faith of her late husband, and regularly encouraged Gore-Browne not to end his capital-intensive experiments even if the immediate results seemed unprofitable. She and he both poured good money after good in the hope, someday, of turning a profit on essential oils.

From the estate, the Gore-Brownes could never count on more than derisory sources of income. Their trading store was rented out to a Northern Rhodesian firm for £50 a year. During a year of grain shortage, Gore-Browne realized a small profit on £37 worth of maize he purchased from Africans at a shilling a pound, stored, and sold to the government at two shillings a pound. Once he sold geranium cuttings and lemon grass seed to a man who wanted to start manufacturing essential oils in Tanganyika. This brought in £3. He built bridges and culverts on the roads passing through Shiwa for the government (of value to him, too) for far less than cost. Before 1933, Gore-Browne never managed a gross return higher than £135 per year from essential oils.

From the time of their return from England in 1927 the Gore-Brownes tried to trim the estate's expenses in order to live more fully within its income and not to drain Brooklands, and to discover how their funds were, in fact, spent. Using African labor more intensively and wisely, and employing fewer men throughout the year, were among the money-saving reforms instituted by Gore-Browne in 1928. But he could not bring himself to be really mean, so his longstanding practice of giving presents to employees on the slightest pretext—which Croad thought was wrong and wasteful, and responsible for making Africans "cheeky"—continued. He also realized that the key to productivity was close supervision, at first by himself or Lorna, by Savill, and, eventually, after he had come to realize that it was possible, by African foremen and *capitãos*.

The Gore-Brownes could hold down their extravagances and trim personal and estate expenses fairly easily. Stewart refrained from ordering all the good books he read about in the *Times Literary Supplement*. Prodded by Lorna, he attempted to be self-sufficient and to stretch expensive, already overstrained lines of communication a little less than before.

Yet even as the Gore-Brownes effected economies and Stewart established more sophisticated accounting procedures so that he could ascertain precisely how much the production of different essential oils cost per ounce of distilled yield, and thus whether Shiwa was or was not prospering, so one or another unexpected contingency or act of God interfered with the smooth and less expensive running of the estate and their own personal lives. The onset of the Depression was the most decisive of these unforeseen eventualities. Returns on oils and the interest on their securities fell without commensurate reductions in fixed expenses in Northern Rhodesia. In 1931, as the Depression made itself felt in Africa, their total expenditures soared in a largely unrelated way to £5,027. The employment of a new white couple (she to nurse, he to tend the cattle), local building expenses, passages to Britain and back, plus Britain's abandonment of the Gold Standard, were the immediate reasons for such heavy outlays. In 1932, with oils producing an income of £96 and the store £61, Shiwa alone cost £4,100 to run, including £1,650 on the construction of their large house. Their personal expenses totaled £1,388, so the overall yearly outlay was about £5,500. In later years there were unexpected journeys by air to Britain, expensive medical consultations for Lorna, payments for nurses and nannies, and so on, but the overall level of personal expenditures remained about the same except in 1933, when it went up to £2,446. Shiwa, too, held its own level, and expenses there were even reduced after the manor house was completed in 1933. Fortunately, and especially after Gore-Browne's securities became less valuable and dipping into capital seemed imprudent, Ethel remained unstintingly generous. Whenever Stewart and Lorna wrote about their attempts to economize, usually in small things, but also with regard to visits to Britain, she reminded them that they need never scrimp of necessity.

Gore-Browne reluctantly recognized and greatly appreciated this financial lifeline. It gave him a welcome freedom to experiment, and to invest with only a hope of future results. Much as he wanted virtuously to live within his means, he was thus independent to a degree other settlers and agriculturalists in Africa could hardly hope to match. Nevertheless, if the monetary constraints were few, there were fundamental ethical considerations. Nunk knew, Gore-Browne told his aunt. "Even you only think of it as an occupation, in your heart of hearts, I think. You *can't* realise how desperately I want to make it a self-supporting show before I leave it either for the Next World, or for other interests or duties in this. I don't mind if it's not essential oils, and I want to keep abreast of all that's going on, but I do want more than I can begin to say to make it a complete show. I've always believed that what one wants very much," he wrote revealingly, "one's apt to get, and its pretty wonderful the luck I've had here, first Nunk to be everything to it, & you following on; and then to have Lorn what she is . . . There's no point in going on over & over again saying it. What one wants is to have results to point to."[14]

14. Gore-Browne to Ethel Locke-King, 13 May 1933.

An aerial view of the manor house at Shiwa Ngandu.

Gore-Browne continued to expand the acreages devoted experimentally to a variety of potentially remunerative crops. Lemon grass, the first specimens of which he had acquired near Albertville in the Congo in 1926, seemed to grow well in Shiwa's poorish soil; in 1928 there were thirty acres of it, and a seemingly secure market at about 3/6 a pound distilled. Unfortunately, the world price slipped rapidly the more successfully Gore-Browne managed to grow it. The price of geranium oil at first remained high, but Gore-Browne despaired of it ever growing properly at Shiwa. Clumps did well, but the 80,000 fifteen-inch cuttings that were struck each spring rarely rooted consistently, withering in the open fields as the Central African summer turned toward autumn. The supply of leaves was thus always uneconomically small. In 1928 Gore-Browne managed to distill only eight pounds of the oil. *Eucalyptus citriodora* grew more consistently, and produced better yields, one hundred pounds being distilled in 1928, but the price was never very attractive. Bigaradia oranges would eventually supply neroli oil from the blossoms and petit grain from the leaves, and seemed to do well, but before 1933 it was still too early for the oranges to produce blossoms in quantities sufficient to distill. The other citrus trees that Gore-Browne had planted a few years before also seemed to do very well. In particular lemons and limes flourished, and Gore-Browne was initially very confident that limes would—as they were to do so much later—prove to be the salvation of Shiwa. In the West Indies, however, limes and lemons were not distilled. Instead the oil was extracted by delicately pricking the oil sacs in the rinds of the fruits. Savill copied a special pricking gadget, called an ecuelle, and trained several Bemba women to use it. In 1928 ten pounds of oil of lime was thus collected and despatched home to England, with the Gore-Brownes anticipating a good price of forty-five shillings a pound and positive encouragement. Unhappily, however, the spikes of the home-made ecuelle had dug too deeply and extracted juice, not oil.

There were many other irritating obstacles to producing oil profitably. Fields of lemon grass and geraniums had to be weeded; seventy, eighty, or more Africans were employed throughout the wet season just to keep the weeds down. The transplantation of thousands of little *citriodora* seedlings without damaging their long tap roots was an unheralded feat. During the dry season the crops had to be watered, initially by hand, and then, after an elaborate and expensive irrigation scheme was constructed with a barrage across the upper Manshya River and brick sluices leading to the nearby fields, attention had to be paid to the proper direction of the flowing water at the appropriate times. During the wet seasons, and the rains in 1928 were especially heavy, flood waters had to be diverted

The manor house from the front, 1962.

away from roads and nursery beds through a deep canal. The canal, the bridges, which were washed away in 1928, the several fords across the rivers, and the estate's roads and paths all had to be maintained and repaired.

In these early years there was little thought of fertilizer or of countering plant pests and diseases. Thus, if weather and soils permitted, Gore-Browne obtained good crops. Distilling was the next concern, and once Croad had reerected the machinery and managed, after much trial and effort, to make the vats watertight, this process should have been straightforward. Profits were enhanced by careful distillation, however, and in these early years Gore-Browne never really managed to control his own processes to the extent necessary to produce the very best oil. At first he overheated his lime oil, or lost lemon grass oil through undercondensation or letting the grass sit too long before distillation. He and his assistants were still amateurs muddling through and hoping all the time that they would somehow measure up to the standards demanded by their English buyers.

There was another approach to prosperity in oil which Gore-Browne occasionally contemplated and might, with profit, have attempted. He could have stimulated the growing of the oil-bearing plants by Africans on sections of the estate, leaving to them the problems of making the trees and shrubs flourish, the collection of the leaves or the oils, and the attendant costs. Surely this might have proved a less capital-intensive approach and one which could have encouraged the growth of African interest in oils. But to have done so Gore-Browne would have needed to guarantee a price per pound for raw unprocessed crops of a certain quality, and then to have managed to recoup that price by distilling cleverly and shipping the processed materials to a pliant market. He had too little experience and, moreover, too little faith in African abilities to realize that this was a viable method. "The natives just won't do it, and I don't blame them seeing how hard it is to make anything grow here," he said.[15] There is a further explanation of Gore-Browne's reluctance to experiment with village-based productivity. That method would have undercut his pleasure of patriarchy, his need to be the provider and dispenser of employment, pay, and provisions in as direct a manner as possible.

"Lorn and I keep wondering and wondering," he wrote in despair in late 1928, "about the prospects for this place. . . . The whole point of the thing is that it should succeed, just as . . . Brooklands has got to succeed, if [our] stewardship . . . is to be justified." The Gore-Brownes could live pleasantly at Shiwa, he estimated, for

15. Gore-Browne to Ethel Locke-King, 21 September 1928.

about £2,000 a year, keeping up a garden, and cattle, and growing their own food, maintaining the roads and bridges, etc. "But it would be a pretty useless sort of existence." On the other hand, to make the place pay he and they had to continue to spend money without the assurance that Shiwa would ever succeed. Even the farmers at Abercorn and Fort Jameson were going bankrupt, he reminded Ethel, so agriculture in a new country with poor communications was, he admitted, the worst of risks. But, if she agreed, and she did, he and Lorna would continue to struggle in the hope of eventually accomplishing "something truly constructive & of permanent value."[16]

"If," Gore-Browne wrote at the end of 1929, "the geranium grows, and the citriodora seeds don't get washed away by the rain, & the young plants aren't later scorched by the sun, and if white ants leave them alone, and if the lemon grass thickens and keeps down the weeds round it, if, if, if, then we shall do all right this year." That is, they would be all right if the dam held and supplied water for the distillery at the right time, and so on.[17]

Oils were the presumed rationale for Shiwa throughout the 1920s, 1930s, and 1940s, but it was not until 1931 that the unexpectedly prolonged experimental phase came rather decisively to an end. Gore-Browne's impatience with geraniums had mounted over the years; they grew only "so desperately patchy" and required intensive weeding.[18] Nothing he, Croad, or Africans could do would make the plants grow consistently in and around the lake. All of his darkest suspicions were confirmed, too, when the new accounting procedures demonstrated in 1929 that it cost the estate at least five times the gross return on geranium oil to grow and distill it. With the spread of the great Depression, which otherwise began seriously affecting Northern Rhodesia only in 1931, world prices for geranium and other fragrant oils also began slipping dramatically. Gore-Browne therefore gave up on geraniums, once Shiwa's poor best hope, and ploughed under the remaining plants. "I can't say," he told Ethel, "what a relief it is not to have those damned geraniums to see to. It was a perpetual anxiety, and led to nothing."[19]

Shiwa's future would now depend on established, low maintenance crops. The *Eucalyptus citriodora* was already there and growing without demanding more than minimal attention. The lemon grass had established itself in patches, and once Gore-Browne learned to

16. Gore-Browne to Ethel Locke-King, 14 November 1928.
17. Gore-Browne to Ethel Locke-King, 22 December 1929.
18. Gore-Browne to Ethel Locke-King, 20 January 1930.
19. Gore-Browne to Ethel Locke-King, 13 December 1930.

rotate it with nitrogen-restoring beans, weeds became less persistent. In late 1930, too, Gore-Browne received the first unequivocally favorable report from Thomas Durrans, his English oils analyst. The *citriodora* was "a good marketable oil" and the lemon grass had a good odor and was said to be "a good marketable oil of the West Indian type." Durrans also liked tansy. But the market for *citriodora* and lemon grass had virtually disappeared with the worldwide slump; certainly Gore-Browne could not produce and ship at the low prices those oils commanded. And he could grow too little tansy to make it the mainstay of the estate.

Similarly, taking too many leaves from the orange trees in order to distill petit grain would harm the trees and limit subsequent productivity. Only limes and orange blossoms seemed promising. Because of hurricanes and disease in Dominica and Grenada, the market for lime oil had, despite the Depression, actually improved, and absolute prices were rising. Gore-Browne's problem was rather agonizing, however. Although he planted more than 10,000 lime and 3300 orange trees in 1930, and there were another 10,000 or so lime and orange trees from previous years, it would be several years before there could be sufficient limes and orange blossoms to distill in quantity. Only then, by which time the West Indian sources might have recovered, could lime or neroli oil be distilled and shipped overseas. As Gore-Browne murmured in late 1931, "for the moment there's nothing to do but wait."[20]

The oranges were the first the realize their expected potential. In late 1934 they were at last white with blossom like an English orchard in late spring. Bemba women brought in as many as eighty basketfuls a day—enough to keep two steam stills active throughout the week. Under irrigation, Gore-Browne expected to obtain two full crops of blossom a year. In quality, too, Gore-Browne now knew that he could produce neroli equal to the best French kind, the English analysts having already written several letters of encouraging praise. By the end of 1934 the limes were also bearing, and being distilled in greater quantity than ever before. Fortuitously, too, a British firm wanted his *citriodora,* and so in 1933 and 1934 he was able to sell about 500 pounds of its oil. But prices had fallen sharply, the neroli, once worth twenty-five shillings an ounce, now fetched ten shillings an ounce only, and the *citriodora* paid only four shilling sixpence a pound. Thus in the mid-1930s Gore-Browne began succeeding in a modest way; although he sold only £200 or so of oils annually, he did so with reasonable medium-term commercial prospects.

20. Gore-Browne to Ethel Locke-King, 31 October 1931.

Oils were no more, however, than the major excuse for anguish and expense. Gore-Browne's conception of a well-run estate included 300 beef cattle and oxen, and the dairy herd begun in 1932. There were repairs and improvements to roads, bridges, houses, and stores; bricks and tiles to be made by hand and fired in separate kilns; and trees to be felled, hauled from miles away, and converted into sawn lumber.

The projects, large and small, were endless, and probably designed to be so. But the ravages of Africa made most new houses and storerooms essentially temporary. Termites quickly tunnelled their way through ordinary wood, mud, and thatched habitations, and by the late 1920s few of Gore-Browne's early buildings were safe. In 1929 he and Africans therefore erected a one-story termite-proof brick dwelling which included bedrooms for Lorna and Stewart, a dressing room and a separate study for him, a library, a reception room, dining room, loggia, and the usual facilities. It took about eight months to complete and was designed to be but a wing of the large manor to which Gore-Browne had long aspired. Its construction also signified the beginnings of a permanence that Lorna had helped to bring to Shiwa.

Later, in 1931 and 1932 when Gore-Browne waited impatiently for his limes and oranges to mature, he busied himself with preparations for another, much larger dwelling. This was the genesis of the great house toward which he had long been working. The arrival of a second child (the first had come in 1929) gave it a certain rationale, even urgency, and, before he returned home to England in 1931, he laboriously constructed a scale model of wood and clay and prepared a large area so that foundations could be blasted during his absence. Just before the rains fell in late 1931 he also for the first time organized and supervised the construction of a large bridge over the Manshya River (which flowed from Lake Shiwa). The bridge connected the two portions of the road which passed through the estate and which had, for want of another, become the main road from Livingstone, Broken Hill, Mpika, and Kasama to Mbeya, Dar es Salaam, and Nairobi.

With partial support and encouragement from the government (about £100 worth), with a gang of 130 inexperienced laborers, with no concrete or mortar and very little cement (it being prohibitively expensive at £7 a drum) Gore-Browne, who had never designed more than a culvert before, found the necessary specifications in an old Royal Engineers' handbook, and set about spanning the twenty-five foot wide river with brick arches. First 70,000 bricks had to be fired, the waters diverted, tons of stones collected and rammed into the mud for footings, and then the necessary three arches (Gore-Browne wanted four but the government would only pay for three) devised and built. The process took six weeks, and then embankments had to be recut and the road straightened, but finishing such a large bridge gave Gore-Browne more satisfaction than almost anything he had ever done at Shiwa. "I suppose the true delight of building is that what was for weeks and months just a thought in one's own brain suddenly turns into a concrete fact, and exists."[21] Even if he could not yet count on success with essential oils, at least he could wrestle with and defeat torrents of shifting water by building a permanent bridge and thus justify an existence which now and again seemed unworthy of the noble and virtuous ideals with which he had first come to Shiwa. Almost a year before, after trying his hand with a one-arch culvert, apparently the first built of brick in the Protectorate, he told Ethel that if he ever sought another career, he would prefer it to be in the Public Works Department. "I used to think I'd like to be an administrator, a Lord Cromer, or even a Lugard—but nowadays one feels so disillusioned & depressed about the results of all administration & the ruin . . . of the work of men like Cromer . . . ." At least being the means of constructing a "decent bridge on a public road" was a way of serving "the community."[22]

The Manshya bridge was but his first essay at the art of erecting sizeable public works using local materials. In the early 1930s improved methods of communication and transport began gradually to knit Northern Rhodesia closer together. The telegraph reached Mpika at the beginning of the decade, and Gore-Browne's own work on the main road that traversed the estate made possible more intensive south–north traffic, but the real revolution came with the establishment of an air route linking Croydon (London) with Alexandria, Luxor, Wadi Halfa, Khartoum, Juba, Entebbe, Nairobi, Moshi, Mbeya, Mpika, Broken Hill, Bulawayo, and Johannesburg. The route was laid out, landing strips found and made, and the first successful experimental flights completed in 1930 and 1931. Although the obvious line south passed over Shiwa, the estate and the lake providing good landmarks in the days of low-flying single and two-engined biplanes, the bomas at Isoka and Mpika were more obvious stopping places than isolated Shiwa.

Gore-Browne, with his ties to Brooklands, wanted very much to take part in this development by air, but at first all that the new flights meant to him was the prospect of halving the time his letters took to and from England. In early 1932 Imperial Airways began

21. Gore-Browne to Ethel Locke-King, 31 October 1931. For a similar attitude to road-building in Joyce Cary's life and fiction, see Molly M. Mahood, *Joyce Cary's Africa* (Boston, 1965), 178.

22. Gore-Browne to Ethel Locke-King, 6 December 1930.

flying air mail and passengers from Croydon to Cape Town, Gore-Browne and his retainers accustoming themselves to flights each way once a week. (The elapsed time was eight days.) In late January the maiden flight suddenly circled the lake, swooped down low, and landed on a comparatively firm stretch of meadow near the offices and still room. Shiwa had fortuitously provided an emergency landing ground, the pilot being unable to take off the next day until Mulemfwe and 100 other laborers cleared a predecessor to what, in 1933, became an official, government-financed emergency strip with two runways. Gore-Browne very much welcomed the opportunity to design and then to direct the building of his own airport. Trees were felled, the stumps removed and the holes filled in with bricks, anthills leveled (a massive undertaking), and the whole covered with fresh earth shifted from elsewhere on the property in ox-drawn carts. The process, Gore-Browne wrote, looked "very massive & primaeval [with] 130 workers hoeing and singing and carrying buckets of earth . . . ceaselessly day after day."[23]

Aerodromes helped to open up the Protectorate, especially for the administrative and commercial elites. Gore-Browne advocated their construction almost everywhere as easy and productive means of providing work for unemployed Africans. Few other tasks on which large gangs of common laborers could be gainfully employed were as labor intensive, and as inexpensive in terms of white supervision. Yet the cutting of roads through woodlands absorbed even more labor than a string of airstrips and, Gore-Browne argued successfully, benefited more of the people of emergent African territories. Although he had once cherished Shiwa's isolation, and had seen it rapidly erode, he knew the value of good motorways and for many years urged the planning and construction of a modern Rhodesian road system. In particular he promoted a brand new route direct from Mpika to Chinsali, and thence Isoka, Tunduma, Mbeya, and Nairobi—the Great North Road. The main road had for some years meandered from Mpika toward the Chambezi crossing and Kasama, then back through Shiwa, and so on to Chinsali. Gore-Browne's proposed direct line would eliminate the roundabout route, save miles, and, not so incidentally, take Shiwa eight miles off the main road and thus spare the Gore-Brownes many visitations.

The government of the Protectorate began thinking about the Mpika-Chinsali road (the Shiwa "bypass") in 1931, surveyed it extensively in 1932, and in 1933 finally appropriated funds for it, partially as a public works relief measure, and partially because

23. Gore-Browne to Ethel Locke-King, 3 April 1933.

better communications were recognizably needed. Gore-Browne had earlier indicated his willingness personally to supervise the project, to obtain the labor, and to make the necessary bricks, etc. His price, which included no overhead or profit, was also attractive. So in 1933 Governor Sir Ronald Storrs—Lorna described him as a "swollen potato"[24]—came to Shiwa for a ceremonial visit and gave Gore-Browne the welcome news that he could go ahead with the fifty miles or so of road and six large and small bridges. The government would contribute about £1,200 and, wonder of wonders, demand no plans or specifications. Gore-Browne was to be given a "free hand." During the dry months of 1933 he took advantage of this free hand, cut an access route from the estate to the line of the new road, and then worked southward clearing, stumping, and ditching. The return journey northward in 1934 was devoted to construction. After three months of steady work with no power equipment, Gore-Browne could report personally to the new governor, Sir Hubert Young, that the Mpika to Shiwa Junction section of the great Cape to Cairo road was ready to be used for wheeled vehicles. During the actual phase of construction, Gore-Browne each week wrote ecstatically about his life in camp, and the sheer joy of road making. "This road is the most fascinating undertaking and grows and grows on one, as one watches it become a real thing," he said. "Once again its the supernatural joy of creation—bridges, & causeways, hills climbed by driveable roads, swamps crossed—all this at one moment merely in ones mind, & then it suddenly turns to fact."[25]

Finishing the manor house in 1933 gave Gore-Browne satisfaction of the same kind. After all, this was intended to be more than a functional habitation for a remote settler and his family. The scale rivaled even the governor's mansion in Livingstone (Storrs called that establishment an "abbattoir"), but with better, more rococco taste. When Mulemfwe, Savill, eighteen bricklayers, and himself had eventually translated the plans and model of 1931 into a house of startling grandeur, it included a dark but imposing entrance hall, a courtyard of guest rooms, kitchen, pantry, and dining room on the ground floor, a second floor with a large, book-lined library and a balcony, study, and bedroom for Gore-Browne, a bedroom and dressing room for Lorna, bedrooms for the children, a "box" room, and several smaller rooms which could be used for nannies or guests. As Gore-Browne and Ethel agreed with regard to the overall plans for the house, it was "silly to be cramped in Central Africa." A small, cool, groundfloor room served as a wine cellar,

24. Lorna to Ethel Locke-King, 14 October 1933.
25. Gore-Browne to Ethel Locke-King, 4 September 1934.

and another round-fronted room overlooking the broad lawn (trimmed and groomed initially by a servant wielding a blunt table knife) served as an oratory or chapel. On Sundays they played on their hand-hewn tennis court. The whole, which cost in materials only about £5,000, was served by piped water delivered from the dammed-up Katete by an expensive, imported, ram; later there were woodburning heaters of hot water, indoor sanitary plumbing, and for light, gas pressure lamps and candles. The exterior was composed of nearly one million bricks burnt locally, and the roof of flat, rectangular tiles, also manufactured of local ingredients. It had an imposing, Italianate caste, which was enhanced when the rows of cypresses planted on either side of the ascending drive grew tall and stately with time.

From the library's balcony Gore-Browne could capture an imposing view sweeping over the lake to the hills on the distant Mpika road. As Governor Storrs cried, it was all so "Pre-Raphaelite." For him, and for many later visitors, it was "just like spending a jolly weekend in a big country house at home."[26] Gore-Browne had at last created a seat suitable for the squire of Shiwa. The house, the roads, the bridges, and even the landing strip recalled and justified his Hentyesque dreams of decades before. The estate now possessed class sufficient to stand as a monument to the Gore-Brownes and Locke-Kings, and to the values for which the two clans stood.

These structural achievements paralleled and enhanced Gore-Browne's growing esteem as a pioneer of ability and wisdom. By the early 1930s he was recognized as a man of sense and sensibility, especially with regard to the "native question."

In the early years Gore-Browne stirred little from his tasks at Shiwa, but administrators important in the northern part of the Protectorate welcomed his views. Bunker Willis, the experienced provincial commissioner with headquarters in Kasama, was a frequent guest, as were E. G. H. Goodall and Harold Francis Cartmel-Robinson, his successors. The district commissioners and their assistants came from Mpika (William Hill, Harold Watmore, Thomas Fox-Pitt, and W. Vernon Brelsford), and Chinsali (Edward Munday, William Stubbs, John Peacock, and S. R. Denny). The acting governor, Claude Hatherley Dobree—"a dear old chap, but about as easy to talk to as a thoroughly agreeable oyster"—paid

26. Gore-Browne to Ethel Locke-King, 19 May 1932; 14 October 1933. Gore-Browne's ideas for his manor house were influenced by his reading in 1929 of John Buchan's *A Lodge in the Wilderness* (London, 1906). This didactic novel was set in an imaginary guest house (1918 edition, pp. 17–19, 112–113), set in equally exciting grounds, in the Kenyan highlands.

a state visit in 1930,[27] the Anglican bishop of Northern Rhodesia had come two years before, and once every two years or so when he passed through Livingstone by train Gore-Browne had detailed discussions with the leaders of what was still a small and, insofar as whites were concerned, very thinly settled country. But in terms of influencing the future of the country, he conscientiously did his own thing, and for the most part kept his opinions to himself and a small circle of locally resident admirers. In 1930, however, Willis asked him to attend a special conference in Kasama on the future education of Africans in the Northern Province. In addition to Geoffrey C. Latham, the Protectorate's director of native education, Willis, and other officials, the conferees were all missionaries. Gore-Browne was the only settler; as such, one of his roles was to arbitrate between the contending Roman Catholic and Protestant factions. This function was especially important after the conference divided into two sections to discuss purely instructional and purely linguistic matters, especially a new Cibemba orthography.

Ultimately Gore-Browne managed to make one side scrap petty preferences for clarity, and the other grammatical niceties for simplicity. Nevertheless, the controversy was never really stilled. A year later the Catholics and Protestants still tiresomely took opposite sides on, as Gore-Browne wrote, "how to divide up words as well as souls."[28]

Gore-Browne made one suggestion at the conference which the missionaries all shouted down. Wouldn't their work be assisted by African participation?, he asked. "It was amusing," Gore-Browne noted wryly, "to see how these good missionaries all with one accord and with a unanimity we hardly attained about anything else, shouted down the proposal." Later, when Gore-Browne summed up the activities of his section, he attempted to warn the assembled missionaries and officials of the dangers of paternalism. Often the result of what Gore-Browne still credited as well-intentioned benevolence was that Africans dug their toes in or said "Thank you for nothing." Indirect rule was the new philosophy of British colonial governance; Gore-Browne pointed out that in Northern Rhodesia the chiefs were not doing too badly and the way to advance Africans "was surely to make use of [their] own rulers & get them interested . . . [and] to get them to do things themselves for themselves." Most people, he reminded the conferees, preferred self-government, indifferent or no, to good government by aliens.

27. Gore-Browne to Ethel Locke-King, 27 July 1930. Dobree had been in the territory's Treasury since 1911.
28. Gore-Browne to Ethel Locke-King, 12 June 1932.

It would be a mistake to assume, however, that these prescient platitudes connoted what by more modern standards—or even by the standards of the anti-colonial lobby in contemporary Britain— were liberal sentiments. Certainly after ten years at Shiwa Gore-Browne has lost none of his humanitarian instincts. He was even more revolted than before by missionaries and commissioners who treated Africans as objects, or whose curling tones of voice demeaned those to whom whites still had a sacred duty. Occasionally he still ordered Africans whipped, or struck them himself, but the offender had always been disrespectful, or had been thought to have intruded on Lorna's privacy. His attitude was still feudal. For the most part, he knew and respected Africans as people and warm individuals, and accorded to them the same courtesies that he would have expected for himself, with the exception that he was their employer, or their superior by achievement and class ascription. He still eschewed the behavior and hostility toward Africans of his fellow white settlers, longing for conversation, just once, with a "real gent" of either sex—someone with what he called good breeding. (One poor physician, "a little fellow," was, alas, considered not remotely "a gent". He was "keen & sensible," but he sucked his teeth at meals.[29])

Yet Gore-Browne's experiences at Shiwa, and the suggestion at Kasama bore them out, had forced him to reconsider his earlier presumptions about the ease and propriety of playing patriarch and lord of the manor to "savages" slowly being uplifted by Western civilization. It wasn't so much that Africans were ungrateful, more that they needed him less. He was no longer the sole source of employment. Nor did rather old fashioned ideas about loyalty and deference in exchange for a blanket at Christmas seem to agree with Africans. Unlike others, however, he gradually recognized the changes, and was aware that he could not cling to the ways of a Rhodesia which was changing with urbanization, the extension of roads, and even the arrival at Mpika of transcontinental airplanes. "I used to have ideas of conferring patriarchal benefits on the Bantu & so on," he confessed in 1930, "but that's I'm afraid all moonshine. . . . The natives [don't] want to be patriarched."[30]

Even so, Gore-Browne could hardly discard his paternal instincts. He felt a responsibility for the welfare of Africans on the estate and, by extension, for Bemba and others beyond its borders. For someone like Gore-Browne, the sense of obligation was all, especially when his position made it possible to help Africans and to alleviate their distress. Thus, when the worldwide economic crisis

29. Gore-Browne to Ethel Locke-King, 20 February 1932.
30. Gore-Browne to Ethel Locke-King, 14 June 1930.

brought grief to Northern Rhodesia, and Africans in their thousands were turned away from the mines and the towns, Gore-Browne characteristically sought solutions of his own. Africans could in theory return to their farms and somehow subsist without inputs of cash. But, Gore-Browne realized long before the government, if there were no employment, how were Africans to pay their yearly head tax of ten shillings? At the time, he was worried about his own finances, his return on securities having fallen and expenses grown. For his aunt he listed all of the economic reasons why it was imprudent to return home in 1933 with Lorna and the children. "And with all the desperate unemployment and distress out here just now," he added, "I simply can't knock off all but the barest necessary work . . . and refuse to help these people who do look to us as their only standby. . . . When the time for their tax paying comes along, we shall simply have to take on more than one would like to under the present circumstances, and do what one can towards helping them out."

A few months later he devised an ingenious scheme to clearcut patches of scrub forest and replant trees which eventually could provide valuable timber. His motivation was primarily benevolent; he wanted "to give work to these unfortunate unemployed natives, who are being harried for their 10/- tax and at the same time refused work all over the country." "My idea," he continued, "is that there are literally millions of acres of 'bush' all over this territory . . . and ninety-five percent . . . of the trees are perfectly useless." Stumping and ploughing would be expensive, and the soils were anyway so poor that crops could not be grown profitably without expensive fertilizing. But if crops could not be grown or sold, timber might be. So what Gore-Browne proposed to do, by way of homegrown afforestation, was to use the Bemba *citimene* method of fertilizing the soil with the ashes of cut trees and then to plant *Eucalyptus saligna* and some *Cypressus lusitanica*. The main consideration in this endeavor was African welfare. But, he agreed, "it would be nice to leave some thousands of acres of useful forest behind one, where once there had been nothing but rubbish."[31]

Locally, Gore-Browne was capable of implementing a scale of reafforestation commensurate with the apparent human need for cash. But, having become both more aware of the problems of Northern Rhodesia as a whole and confident of his own ability to cope with crises of national dimension, in the 1930s he slowly sought out opportunities to offer concrete advice to the colony's administration. Thus, when Storrs dined at Shiwa in late 1933 Gore-Browne systematically offered remedies to cure the country's

31. Gore-Browne to Ethel Locke-King, 24 June 1933; 2 September 1933.

economic malaise. Goodall, accompanying Storrs, thought these ideas of such immediate importance that he urged Gore-Browne to stay up all that night setting them out in the form of an official memorandum. Gore-Browne urged the governor not simply to remit or reduce the tax since Africans expected and, if they could only find the funds, were prepared to pay. Moreover, Africans were not hungry or destitute, and there were plenty of men available for work. "But they are in rags, and they are penniless," he said. For two years there had been virtually no work for northeastern Rhodesians in the Congo, Southern Rhodesia, Tanganyika, or on the Copperbelt. The government had reduced appropriations for employment on the bomas. The road he would soon build to Mpika would help, but not enough. "It would be an act of weakness, which at best would be impolitic and at worst . . . dangerous," he said, "to remit the tax . . . or . . . to collect it from a few and not from others; to reduce it would be useless; while to insist on payment . . . and to imprison defaulters, would be so grossly unjust that nothing but African inertia and respect for authority would prevent the consequences being disastrous."

Gore-Browne had not read the works of John Maynard Keynes, nor from his letters is it apparent that he knew of the new economic theories. He appreciated, however, that taxes would remain unpaid until coin was somehow injected into the countryside. It was essential to restimulate its circulation, and only artificial measures would suffice. "I submit as my main suggestion," he said, "that public works should be started to enable the natives to earn money with which to pay their tax." He recommended that only permanent works of public utility, preferably involving the least charge for future maintenance, be undertaken; that projects be selected which would entail the minimum expenditure on tools, materials, and white supervision; and that Africans be paid in cash, and not simply be allowed to work off tax obligations. Otherwise it would look as if their labor were being forced. Gore-Browne recommended four kinds of projects which would satisfy his criteria of labor intensity and also assist the development of Northern Rhodesia; airfields, roads, reafforestation, and sanitary drains.[32]

Under another, more interested governor, Sir Hubert Young, a version of this scheme was later implemented, roads and bridges were constructed and a string of airstrips hacked out of woodlands. Storrs was bored in Rhodesia, however, and during his brief incumbency the Gore-Browne memorandum simply made the rounds of official desks in Livingstone. The secretary for native affairs wrote a long analysis which probably contributed sig-

32. Gore-Browne to Sir Ronald Storrs, 12 October 1933.

nificantly to its temporary shelving. He damned some of the proposals with faint praise, disputed some inessential premises, and then went on to indicate why nothing should or could be done. As a natural Parkinsonian, James Moffat Thomson, the secretary, reminded the governor that something similar had been tried before, after the war, and that the results had not been satisfactory. Moreover in remote districts the construction of roads "would serve very little purpose as there would be little traffic to make use of them." Primarily, however, the disadvantage of "schemes to provide work for unemployed natives" is that they entail expenditures which can ill be spared on tools, materials, and supervision. Thomson feared that Africans with cash who were able to pay their taxes would retain their savings and seek employment on the roads in order to keep their funds "for domestic or other purposes. Again, once such employment is provided by Government the people may in future rely upon similar assistance and neglect to earn money on their own initiative as at present while the urge to be thrifty in times of prosperity . . . might disappear." Anyway, said Moffat Thomson, "all schemes of this nature are liable to unforeseen repercussions." His solution was to send surplus labor to South Africa.[33]

How Gore-Browne would have reviled this expression of the official colonial mind in action. Fortunately, in northeastern Rhodesia he was no longer harrassed by the narrow interpretation of regulations or the rivalry of ambitious administrators. His age, longevity of settlement, and accumulated knowledge by 1933 had given him senior status. By 1933, too, he had gained the ear of governors. As Lorna put it, "eminences realize that they can make use of him, at last."[34] Gore-Browne could thus put forward ideas about all manner of major and minor questions concerning the development of Northern Rhodesia and the welfare of Africans. His diffidence had become a posture of the past. "I shall soon begin to think," he wrote after Young began to implement his tax relief schemes, that "I run this bit of the country from behind the scenes." Then he cautioned Dame Ethel: "Please don't repeat that sentence to anyone, "nor let it appear in my published life. . . ."[35]

Gore-Browne was clearly more relaxed about Africans than other whites, settler and official, in Northern Rhodesia. For the times, he was liberal, but he still regarded Africans as limited by their training, and therefore their horizons, from thinking "big"

33. 1/9/17, Volume 5, Memorandum by James Moffat Thomson to Storrs, 15 November 1933, Lusaka archives.

34. Lorna to Ethel Locke-King, 14 October 1933.

35. Gore-Browne to Ethel Locke-King, 28 November 1934. In 1934 Gore-Browne was only jesting about a biography.

and imaginatively about the future. He gave only limited responsibility to Africans on his own estate and still subscribed to a modified version of the white man's burden premise of African administration. Certainly in the early 1930s he was incapable of allowing himself to think as radically—and such mild radicalism—as his aunt, with her far off experience of Egypt under the Condominium.

In 1930 the Labour Government had been briefly in power in Britain, and Lord Passfield had decided publicly to make fully lucid the new directions of policy which he believed to be appropriate for Britain's African colonies, and which he had already enunciated in private directives to his governors and other officials. His *Memorandum on Native Policy in East Africa* reaffirmed the doctrine of trusteeship and paramountcy of African interests that had been enunciated, but in and for different circumstances, by the Duke of Devonshire in 1923. The new *Memorandum* made it clear that in any conflicts with the interests of whites or Asians, the rights of Africans should and would prevail. This, the declared policy for Kenya, was extended by Passfield to Northern Rhodesia and Nyasaland. Immediate steps, he said, were to be taken to "ensure strict conformity" to his directives. African development was henceforth expected to be the keystone of colonial policy.[36]

"I don't see," Gore-Browne commented at the time, "that the present home government by saying three times over in five paragraphs 'The interests of the African Natives must be paramount' . . . helps things. . . ." Nor did he think it made more soluble the difficult question of how blacks and whites should or could live together in the future. Obviously the Southern African method, of declaring that under no circumstances would the white man ever give way to the black over anything, was wrong, and unworkable. On the other hand, the Passfield proposals might make the object of colonial governments the independence of Africans. This trend Gore-Browne did not deprecate if, he said, "you really do think it possible that Bantu can, within an appreciate [sic] time, run their own show entirely." Then the more experienced whites would devote themselves for a generation or so to "set the black man's feet on the path of progress and prosperity . . . and then clear out." But he had his doubts and, anyway, if that were the case, the government should say so loudly and not simultaneously encourage settlers to make their homes in Rhodesia. Most of all, he felt that it was very unwise for the Labour government to have issued a *Memorandum* which was bound to impel settlers to fight for their very existence, and viciously criticize the ungrateful colonial gov-

36. Passfield's *Memorandum* was Cmd. 3573 (1930). For the earlier declaration of the Duke of Devonshire, see *Indians in Kenya,* Cmd. 1922 (1923).

ernment. Already, he told his aunt, there were meetings of settlers all over the Protectorate to protest against Passfield, "talk a lot of rubbish," and promote amalgamation with Southern Rhodesia. Gore-Browne went to no meetings, but he could not believe that his aunt really felt that "settlers should be prepared, eventually, to live according to the law of the land as administered by the Bantu."[37] Was self-determination really a relevant concept, he wondered? Was self-government right for India or Egypt? Yet the kinds of unnecessary discrimination visited upon Africans by settlers, officials, and missionaries gave him "a queer feeling of understanding of national congresses and all the other sort of idiocies that rise up against their benefactors."[38]

Gore-Browne was still groping toward some arrangement which would provide equitably for whites as well as Africans. He insisted that Africans be dealt with humanely and with justice, that they be offered the tools with which to progress, and that the magic of Western medicine, sanitation, and so on be made freely available. He favored no color bar, and South African racial mores always remained anathema. But he was then pragmatic, and believed that whites had and would always have a substantial role to play in the Protectorate. Settlers and miners were all participating in its growth; all deserved to continue to give, and to take, too.

Soon after Sir Hubert Young arrived in Northern Rhodesia to assume control of the country he came with his wife and a retinue of officials to inspect Gore-Browne's Mpika road and to visit Shiwa. Although Gore-Browne later described the governor as the "oddest mixture of modesty and bluster," the state occasion went very well. Best of all Young and Gore-Browne were in full agreement about the future of Northern Rhodesia. "He has identically my own idea," Gore-Browne wrote. "Up here, Abercorn and Fort Jameson European enclaves, all the rest a native territory; the 'settled area' on the railway, purely European, living for and by the mines; the far west and Barotseland native again; the whole to be administered from Lusaka, but given a very wide measure of local independence."[39]

Expanding on this same theme, a few months later he told the members of the African Circle in London that the only ultimate hope for Africa lay, "not in segregation or dyarchy, not in repression by a dominant race, nor even in some form of benevolent white

37. Gore-Browne to Ethel Locke-King, 26 August 1930; 6 June 1930; Ethel Locke-King to Gore-Browne, 23 July 1930. For the meetings, etc., see Rotberg, *Nationalism*, 102–104.
38. Gore-Browne to Ethel Locke-King, 15 February 1931.
39. Gore-Browne to Ethel Locke-King, 5 November 1934.

autocracy, though this last was the tradition in which my own generation was brought up, but in co-operation between the white and the black races, slowly and patiently achieved." His opposition to the Passfield doctrine, and to notions of Trusteeship, was based upon its fundamental premise: that eventually the trustees would step aside and hand over the inheritance in its entirety to their wards. How was this goal to be achieved? If, Gore-Browne argued, most Britons believed that "eventually" meant a time which could not readily be foreseen or dated, then trusteeship was a hypocritical, hence misleading, notion. It cheated Africans. Moreover, it split in two the white community in a place like Northern Rhodesia, pitting the officials—the "natural protectors of the Natives"—against the settlers who, by implication, were the exploiters. Gore-Browne wanted to substitute Partnership for Trusteeship. "I feel that this is a possible ideal for the future and moreover, that it is capable of being applied, little by little, in the present."

What Gore-Browne envisaged was a Partnership akin to that enunciated by Sir Stamford Raffles (he had recently been reading a biography) for Singapore in the early nineteenth century. "By Partnership I intend that all sections of the community according to their powers should share in Government." Local settlers would thus join the official white administrative class in governing African colonies and protectorates; a "generous measure" of local self-government would be substituted for the usual centralized system. As a start, provincial councils would be created on which appointed officials, non-officials, and Africans would sit. In the rural areas—places like northeastern Rhodesia and Shiwa—whites would have a diminished and Africans an enhanced role. Details would have to be worked out with care, he told the circle, but "without some system involving immediate co-operation, and based on the ideal of ultimate partnership between white and black, I find it difficult," he warned, "to conceive of any stable foundation for the future."[40]

Gore-Browne had begun to articulate opinions on African and related questions and to hold to them more firmly than ever before. After fifteen years in a remote section of Northern Rhodesia he "knew how to deal with" rural Africans. He had been disabused of romantic notions of African abilities. They were less responsive to modern ideas than he had anticipated. He had failed to instill initiative or to transfer any large fraction of his accumulated Western sense of loyalty and charity. But he counseled patience more than

40. Stewart Gore-Browne, "The Relations of Black and White in Tropical Africa," *Journal of the Royal African Society*, XXXIV (1935), 378–386. The address was delivered on 20 May 1935. The biography was Reginald Coupland, *Raffles: 1781–1826* (London, 1926).

despair. And he still believed personally in continuing to bear witness at Shiwa to a set of well-intentioned, if never too rigorously defined, ideals. These had not altered in outline since the days on the Boundary Commission. Nor had his fundamental sense of noblesse oblige been eroded by a decade among the Bemba. Doing positive good as he defined it for and with the Bemba, by developing Shiwa and setting certain kinds of colonial standards on one estate—where some hundreds of people could be kept busy and content—were sufficient goals. As he wrote to Brooklands after his fiftieth birthday, "at a time when most men are thinking of shelves, to have all this [Shiwa's development] opening out before one, is so wonderful that one lacks the words to say." It was better than searching for "some big gesture" and failing to find it.[41] Although, in a road-building context, he once exclaimed, "Oh, I'd like to be a governor for a bit," he was really content to the "big bwana" of the northeast.[42]

As much as he enjoyed the attention of distinguished administrators and Africanists, he still proclaimed no desire to spread the gospel as he saw it farther afield. Northern Rhodesia was his home, and he saw much in its governance and management which could be enhanced, but he was essentially content to do what little he could to improve conditions in and around Shiwa. Furthermore, he was still only intermittently informed about the situation of the remainder of the farflung colony. Certainly he was little involved in settler politics, having hardly anything in common with the whites on the line-of-rail or their elected representatives to the Legislative Council. He was thrown into contact with a few settlers in Kasama and Abercorn, and the truckers and traders who passed through Shiwa, but for them he had little time. He and Lorna felt even less in common with most missionaries. "My word," he wrote in desperation after relating yet another encounter with fractious, back-biting, jealous Presbyterians, "if you did want to write a sneering and cynical book, you'd just have to describe life on a Mission Station. . . . Anger, hatred, malice, and all uncharitableness, and oh such silliness."[43]

When Stewart and Lorna attended social functions or were feted by either the mission or the settler communities, they learned to grit their teeth. "How glad," Gore-Browne said more than once of Kasama, "one is not to live here. Eight households, not necessarily very congenial to each other, having to do everything, everyday,

41. Gore-Browne to Ethel Locke-King, 30 November 1933; 19 March 1933.
42. Gore-Browne to Ethel Locke-King, 16 September 1934.
43. Gore-Browne to Ethel Locke-King, 27 February 1932.

together—the men do a little mild office work . . . the women I suppose order dinner. They don't garden because there's no water . . . and they don't read (there was a library once, but white ants are eating the books). They play golf, and they play tennis, and they sit in each others' houses & talk about 1) each other, 2) the badness of a) native servants, b) the government, 3) the roads. They aren't vicious, and they're extraordinarily kind, but oh my word they are dull and they are aimless. Its no longer pioneering and 'bearing the white man's burden,' but its certainly not civilisation. It's the sort of life that, one would think, slowly enervated mind and body."[44] It was not a life for which Gore-Browne had much sympathy or patience. His community, and his life, was of a rather different, more self-contained (and yet expansive) kind.

Lorna, or the marriage to Lorna, had made much of this life—the role he had begun to play in the white orbit of Northern Rhodesia, the promise of Shiwa as an agricultural venture, and his sense of personal self-esteem and fulfillment—realizable. She had helped to bring a greater sense of tranquillity-within-adversity to Shiwa. With Lorna, Gore-Browne could share the tribulations, the false hopes, and the misplaced trusts of Shiwa, the inefficiencies and incompetencies of Northern Rhodesia, and the occasional happy prospects. He could also share his plans, the beauties of clear days in the wet season and the first moments of spring in August, and the solitary pleasures of his treasured hot springs. She could join him in paternally contributing to the uplift of local Africans. She was intrepid, not knowing what "being afraid" was, and, as one of the Kasama matrons said without intended sarcasm, Lorna was "vary originale," a trait Stewart much admired. From the first, Lorna thus joined Stewart in all his endeavors and pleasures, learning even to share his ribald witticisms (when there were no missionaries about to be shocked).

Every Saturday they habitually both wrote separate long letters to Dame Ethel, Lorna's more disjointed and self-deprecating, Stewart's in the same vein as before. Together they shared Ethel's weekly letters to Shiwa, and worried about her problems with the aerodrome and the farm, with her many relations and her widely connected, socially conscious, life. They worried for her safety when she flew across the Mediterranean to Alexandria, and then shared her thrills as she joined a lone pilot in a single engine biplane across the desert to Khartoum in 1931. (Had they crashed, Ethel said, it would have been only a fifty-mile walk to the railway line.) Ethel acted as their factor and chandler, too, so business was always well mixed with pleasure. This was an era permitting of long affec-

44. Gore-Browne to Ethel Locke-King, 22 March 1930.

tionate dialogues, with commentaries on the books they had all read, on the minutiae of running the two estates, rarely on the affairs of the world, the whole always being conveyed with an assured air that somehow made time stand still. Into this exclusive domain Lorna entered, and was allowed to partake on almost equal terms. But, given the quality of the original relationship, Stewart's marriage to Lorna never resulted in the tempering or falling off of a correspondence that had a rhythm and a meaning all its own.

"I don't know why Lorn married me," was Stewart's constant refrain, "but I thank the Lord daily & hourly that she did."[45] On the first anniversary of their marriage he told Ethel that he supposed other people had had wives as good, "but I can't believe it, and its a never-ending wonder to me that she should care for me. As I've said before I trust that I may never take that and her for granted."[46] By about this time Lorna had come to feel at home not only with Stewart, for that came early and easily, but with Shiwa. Gore-Browne was pleased at the extent to which his young wife had taken charge. She had quickly become responsible for overseeing the production of the good food of which he was so fond, and of making arrangements for the interminable guests. To his amazement and pleasure, she was never "fussed" by the bewildering quantity or eccentric quality of the guests who arrived in the middle of the night, just before dinner, or said they were coming and never arrived. (The worst example of this last unpardonable behavior was the "dirty little squirt of a Dundee doctor," Sir James Crawford Maxwell, the governor of Northern Rhodesia, who called off a stop at the eleventh hour, after "Lorna had slaved.")[47]

How the visitors tried Gore-Browne. "We had rather a lurid week," he wrote. "There was the missionary wave which swept over us. . . . You'd have just loved that. All Monday & Tuesday morning Lorn got the guest house ready . . . filling it with beds & commodes, and making it all topping. It really is a sweat, for it's close on a mile away & the gear has to be carried over & then all fixed up, & everything like soap & candles & towels & matches & baths thought of by L. . . . The first missionary car arrived containing such people as you only meet in books or on the stage—a youth with bent shoulders, big spectacles, & unshorn chin driving, a parson whom you couldn't caricature if you tried (really & truly he said

45. Gore-Browne to Ethel Locke-King, 20 October 1928.

46. Gore-Browne to Ethel Locke-King, 26 July 1928.

47. Gore-Browne to Ethel Locke-King, 16 July 1928. Much later Maxwell actually arrived and Gore-Browne found him "extremely shrewd & pretty obstinate." He "didn't put on any airs" and had "quite a lot of dignity of his own." Gore-Browne to Ethel Locke-King, 7 May 1932.

'Pray do not rise' when I got up when he came into the room) . . ."
The next day was "delirious". "L & I went early to the Kiln, & got
back to find hungry mishes on the verandah. Breakfast was all to
hell & Gone." Some of the missionaries went. Then Aaron came
running to say a child had put its eye out on a stake and Gore-
Browne hurried to the dispensary . . . "Then 2 out of the 3 carts
carrying the essential firewood to the kiln broke down . . . then
Lorn discovered that all the mealies in a 10,000 Lb bin had started to
foment [sic] & they'd got all to be got out; then at last the Moffats
left; then we'd our first puncture in the Morris . . . then in the dark
coming from the kiln we ran out of petrol."[48]

The visitors came weekend after weekend, announced and unannounced, and even sometimes during the working week. "I never
see Lorn alone these days," he complained in 1931.[49] During August 1932, they had guests for twelve consecutive days, "The majority of whom had to have for one reason or another hours of exclusive attention." On one of the days five separate parties converged,
only one of whom, a "perfectly charming" ornithologist from
Uganda (whose knowledge particularly excited Lorna), proved "of
any value."[50] Only occasionally were the Gore-Brownes blessed
with passersby of their "own kind," whether colonial officials or
others of education, broad horizons, good taste, and sensitivity.
These people enlivened their days, but Gore-Browne's praise was
reserved for a very few—especially for Audrey Richards, a thirty-
one-year-old anthropologist from Cambridge (later the distinguished Smuts Reader there), who took up residence, and began a
close friendship with Lorna, in 1930–31. She gained the confidence
of the Bemba, and, initially to the Gore-Brownes' mutual admiration, studied Bemba traditional life in nearly all of its ramifications.

Later, as the splendor of the Gore-Brownes' hospitality and their
mansion, their conviviality, and their stature grew, the number and
variety of visitors increased. The majority came by road. But the
availability of a private landing ground made possible the sudden
arrival of persons the Gore-Brownes liked best and found more
interesting—aviators and passengers of adventuresome disposition. Martin and Osa Johnson, the American big-game photog-
raphers, even landed on the lake in their seaplane.[51] Both Lorna
and Stewart particularly enjoyed the frequent stopovers of Charles
Cochran-Patrick and a team of men doing the first aerial photo-
mapping of the Rhodesian-Tanganyikan air corridor. Cochran-

---

48. Gore-Browne to Ethel Locke-King, 11 August 1928.
49. Gore-Browne to Ethel Locke-King, 28 February 1931.
50. Gore-Browne to Ethel Locke-King, 13 August 1932.
51. Osa Johnson, *I Married Adventure* (New York, 1940), 348–349.

Patrick even took Stewart and Lorna on separate sorties, and
Stewart on one occasion took two days away from his chores to fly
continuously up to Lake Tanganyika and down to Serenje with
Cochran-Patrick and the crew. "It almost makes me wish I was
twenty-five," he told his aunt, "and free to get onto a job like
that."[52] In late 1932, the existence of a landing ground, albeit temporary, even encouraged the arrival by air of Dame Ethel in all of
her sixty-eight years. She spent a month, and then flew gleefully
northwards in a Gypsy Moth to Kenya. All of Gore-Browne's
painstaking efforts and careful opportunism had, he felt, been
thoroughly rewarded.

Now and again, when the tide of visitors temporarily receded,
Lorna and Stewart relaxed alone. In the winter, especially, but during other times of the year, too, after the main work of the day was
finished, they could be together. "We bathe, and then feed by the
fire in the library as the dining room is too cold, and then she gets
out her work and mends while I sit in the arm chair and read aloud,"
often Hardy, or Rose Macaulay, or a biography of Napoleon or
Bismarck. "It's all very dignified and very quiet, rather like a Dutch
picture, and as if the earth were standing still."[53] Lorna and Stewart
were scarcely ever apart during the first year or so of marriage. "I
can hardly remember when I wasn't married to Lorn," he crowed to
his aunt after a year. "We've hardly been separated since we were
engaged, and I had to check her for saying we'd only slept apart 3
nights since that date. It's true but it doesn't sound quite as it
should."[54] Lorna—the irreverent young woman, as he called
her—even invented games to play. A particular pleasure was the
game of imitating the presumed habits of other couples in bed. "I
can't give you details, but you can imagine. . . ."[55] (Ethel suggested
a few more whose behavior they should try to fantasy.) As far as
their many intertwined letters testify, life together was equally zestful and rewarding for both. Each was managing to give to the other
what had for so long been wanting.

Lorna's first daughter was delivered in England in 1929. Her
name, chosen only weeks after conception, was Lorna Katherine,
known as Mark from the formula "Lorna, Mark III." When the
enlarged family finally returned to Shiwa in late 1929, the rhythm of

52. Gore-Browne to Ethel Locke-King, 24 June 1933.
53. Gore-Browne to Ethel Locke-King, 7 July 1928. For bathing they still used
water heated in a bucket and poured into a tiny tub. Only later, at Kasakalabwe
first, and later in their new house at the end of 1929, were there proper tubs, with
hot and cold running water. "Such luxury," as Gore-Browne often remarked.
54. Gore-Browne to Ethel Locke-King, 21 September 1928.
55. Gore-Browne to Ethel Locke-King, 19 May 1928.

Shiwa resumed. However, caring for an infant subtly altered—as it always does—ongoing relationships between the parents. This altering of rhythms became much more pronounced in 1931, after the birth in England of Xenia Angela, the Gore-Browne's second child.

If initially little reflected on the surface of their lives or even in the predominant quality of their interaction, Lorna became irritable and anxious. Yet both Stewart and she at first attributed her new unhappiness to apparent physical complaints. From a few months after Angela's birth, Lorna had suffered from frequent bouts of indigestion, flatulence, and a feeling of being bloated after eating. Yet she even assumed heavier and heavier burdens on the estate. She supervised brick and tile making almost exclusively, ran the dairy herd and dairy, during a time of potential famine toured the estate encouraging the villagers to plant security patches of sweet potatoes (they would be immune from locust infestation), and really contributed more to the development of Shiwa than Stewart had ever anticipated. After the cattle and oxen began sickening with trypanosomiasis in 1933, she single-mindedly inoculated fifty-eight cows and one bull in one morning, and then carried on until she completed jabbing the whole herd.

When Lorna was fit, she worked frantically, ceaselessly, only complaining about minor chores with the children, and then feeling guilty about their neglect. There were still comparatively lengthy periods when Stewart and Lorna both thought her physical ailments relieved, and any clouds in their serene life together consequently dissipated. "All the time," Gore-Browne wrote after celebrating their fifth anniversary, "I go on marvelling at my own good luck that came so unexpectedly and so undeservedly—and, very much in all serious earnest, thanking the Lord for Lorn. I used to fear sometimes that the time would come when I'd take her for granted, and cease to continue to be surprised at, and grateful for, my good fortune, but I don't think that will happen." A year later, Stewart again reiterated the warmth of his love. "Could a man have more to be thankful for than I have?" he asked rhetorically. "And Lorn says she hasn't regretted it." A few months before Lorna had written of "my good man, for whom, even after six years I am grateful, in fact beginning to be more so I think."[56]

Already, however, Lorna had begun to test her wings and unwittingly, ambivalently, to prepare herself for flight. She was twenty-five, attractive, zestful, but because of the intermittent physical discomfort, perhaps fearful of the loss of her youth and, now that the attractions of a substitute father had ebbed, concerned to realize her potential and esteem before it should be too late. In Northern

56. Gore-Browne to Ethel Locke-King, 24 July 1932, 22 July 1933; Lorna to Ethel, 5 March 1933.

Rhodesia there were few opportunities to gain an independence and match Stewart's creative confidence with a self-sustained stature of her own.

Although he later rued his generosity, Stewart realized that he could not hope to deny Lorna opportunities to be herself, alone. He had not intended to coop her up at Shiwa, saddle her with children, and appropriate the final flower of her youth. Hence when Richards returned to Northern Rhodesia in 1933 to continue her anthropological researches, it seemed natural that she and Lorna should resume their earlier friendship, that Lorna should spend occasional days with her, accompany her on safari, spend a week or so with her in a village sixteen miles from Shiwa, and then join her in 1933 for a month on Chilubi island in distant Lake Bangweulu. "I think," said Gore-Browne during the early part of the revived relationship, "it will really do her [Lorna] all the good in the world to be right away from the household and such like for a while. It freshens one up, and (as you always say) one is also so very glad to get home again when the time comes."[57] Richards came a little closer to the correct analysis when she wrote with guilt to Stewart: "I feel a brute sometimes, having descended on you with new interests & pursuits to seduce Lorna with! But . . . Lorna seems brighter & better today. . . . There is a great peace over the place now."[58]

Gore-Browne legitimately feared Richards' influence, but could not bring himself to act callously upon his suspicions. "Audrey is a queer person," he told Ethel. "I can't say I like her much, but I'm truly glad that Lorn should, & there's no doubt how much she likes Lorn. I do admire Audrey's power of concentrating, and of getting down to her work, but I think I leave it at that." Gore-Browne distrusted scientists and intellectuals (Richards was both), and anyone remotely like Bertrand Russell. They—he lumped together intellectuals, pacifists and "high souled folk"—lived in an unreal world and were too obsessively cocksure. "They haven't the guts to be ruthless, or even practical, all they can do is to appeal to a sort of League of Nations sense of reasonableness all round, which is just the one thing that doesn't wash in this rotten world." Richards learned that Stewart had been saying that she was a woman who preferred "porridge to sex."[59] And, as Richards took Lorna away from him for longer and longer periods, Stewart began more openly voicing his disquiet.

If nothing else, Richards, the slightly older woman, gave Lorna

57. Gore-Browne to Ethel Locke-King, 12 March 1933.
58. Richards to Gore-Browne, undated but c. 9–11 November 1933.
59. Gore-Browne to Ethel Locke-King, 12 March 1933; Richards to Lorna, 2 May 1933; Gore-Browne to Ethel Locke-King, 30 November 1933; Gore-Browne to Ethel Locke-King, 10 November 1933.

the opportunity to glimpse her life and her future from the outside. Lorna grew less in awe of her man, though the reverence in speech and prose never faltered. Unfortunately, she was enchantingly happy with Richards, savoring the companionship, the experience of doing scientific work of a meaningful sort, and—presumably— freedom from the "shackles" of Shiwa. If only Stewart could be happy, too, then she would be content, with horizons undimmed. But Stewart could not really share or fully exult in her new life. "This other ploy," she wrote, " . . . is certainly dangerously fascinating & when at it, one does not want to leave it, & its hard to think of anything else. . . . Audrey never fusses . . . & is able to laugh & laugh when things go just a little wrong." From Bangweulu she wrote that in some ways it would have been better never to have felt this "form of joy" for the more she knew it the wilder she wanted more, "& then it's no joke going back to the other life, & no joke for the others. But it will come all right again."[60] And during her long expeditions away from home, Lorna was rarely troubled by indigestion or other physical complaints.

Disasters never take the form in which they are anticipated. In late 1933, after Lorna had returned from Bangweulu, she and Stewart were as effectively affectionate and as close as ever before. Neither Richards' influence, nor the guilt of neglect, had soured Lorna or made Stewart vengefully jealous. Lorna directed her energies into the work of the estate, and Christmas preparations and entertainment. All seemed well. But her old complaints returned. She had developed adhesions. By February they were in England for consultation and a regimen of special diets. After an operation the surgeons thought that she was cured. Instead of returning to Shiwa, however, she decided to recuperate in England, taking a year-long agricultural course at Cambridge while Stewart returned to work on the Mpika road and the children followed a new nanny around the English countryside.

Up at Cambridge Lorna was not altogether well, but she lived her new student persona to the full, dining with her colleagues and teachers, beating her wings wildly and gleefully in the circle of Africanists, anthropologists (Richards was at the London School of Economics), archaeologists and soil scientists, and becoming deeply involved with a prominent young couple of eccentric demeanor. Some of her friends were homosexuals, she wrote in one of her long and expressive letters to Stewart, "My beloved" or "My beauty man," and some were not. Anyway, she said, "homosexual-

60. Lorna to Ethel Locke-King, 26 August 1933, 2 September 1933, 27 November 1933.

ity be damned—or perhaps that is the reason I think he [a teacher of drama] is the sort of person you would delight in (I don't mean this sarcastically or because you are one at heart)."[61]

Although regularly distracted from her studies by friends and would-be suitors, Lorna attended lectures and laboratory sessions, and threw herself into the agricultural disciplines. Gore-Browne was not overly worried about the married man with whom she spent much of her time; Lorna regularly reassured him that they enjoyed a relationship which could not impair their own.

Gore-Browne returned to England in January 1935. Lorna realized, suddenly, that she didn't really want to see him, that Cambridge and her new life meant too much, that perhaps they should never have married. She was ambivalent, guilty, troubled, and worried. Moreover, the arrival of Stewart saw the return of the familiar complaints. Finally, in March, she became so distended that a London physician prescribed a rigorous fortnightly starvation cure. A gland which was supposedly causing retention of fluids was the presumed malefactor, but as physicians finally began saying in April, the underlying causes were mental. Finally Lorna saw a psychiatrist who may have had analytical training, then another nonanalytical psychiatrist with whom she intended to consult until such time as she could return to Shiwa and the children, and to Stewart.

Gore-Browne had grown more and more distraught as the realities of Cambridge, which were difficult enough, gave way to the nightmares of potentially irreversible illness. Even Ethel's strength and presence could not console him. Yet, without solution, or more than the hopes of Lorna sooner or later resuming her place at Shiwa—and what would she be like there?—he had to go back. There was work to do, an estate to manage, roads to improve, and a life to justify. Already Northern Rhodesia had been convulsed by riots on the Copperbelt (caused partially by the government's failure to follow Gore-Browne's earlier admonitions about tax rates and tax collections), and had stepped more fully into the future than anyone there then realized. Moreover, a legislative council election had been announced for September, and, inexplicably, unexpectedly, flatteringly, he—the lone laird of Shiwa, the aristocrat, the idiosyncratic farmer—had been asked to stand, and by a rankle of white miners and railway workers.

No summons could so effectively have focused his mind at a time of profound despondency. The northern electoral district encompassed the whites of Kasama, Abercorn, and all of northeastern Rhodesia. But its basis was Broken Hill (now Kabwe), where five-

61. Lorna to Stewart, 7 August 1934.

sixths of the electors (exclusively white) resided. Most won lead and zinc from the local mine or drove and fired the engines of Rhodesia Railways. The electors, fewer than 600, were a tough lot. But for eight years they had been represented by Gerald Chad Norris, a sane but still settler-oriented metallurgist (the superintendent of the zinc plant at the mine.) Having become a farmer, he was leaving the council for personal reasons, and wanted to be replaced by someone with "a real stake in the territory." He was anxious lest the seat "fall to any old carpet bagger." In July the Broken Hill Political Association met, with Norris in the chair. A secret ballot overwhelmingly was cast in Gore-Browne's favor. Would he stand? A few weeks before, H. C. Donald C. Mackenzie-Kennedy, Northern Rhodesia's chief secretary, had written privately to Gore-Browne from Canterbury, where he was on leave. He had heard that the Broken Hill electors might want Gore-Browne to stand. "I am convinced it is your duty," he wrote, so as to bring into public life "an impartial and nonpolitical element . . . Our constitution does not permit of an opposition or of the formation of absurd 'parties' such as the one which disfigured the last Council and was largely responsible for my ticking off that ridiculous old man [Leopold S.] Moore [the leader of the white unofficials]". Then he assured Gore-Browne that he need not fear holding racial ideas too advanced for the Council. "I think you would be surprised to know the number of settlers who are changing their views as to the place of the African in our polity. You have only to watch the astute L. F. M[oore] to appreciate that. In any case, what most of the fellows want is a lead from a man whom they respect and you can ignore the ambitious wouldbe parliamentarians who will misrepresent the views of anyone but themselves." "Your duty," Mackenzie-Kennedy emphasized, "is clear."[62]

For someone previously so aloof from settlerdom and the problems of life on the railway line, it was an unusual invitation. He knew no one in Broken Hill. Yet Gore-Browne was flattered, pleased, and excited. He pondered the summons for a week and then agreed with Mackenzie-Kennedy that he ought to respond favorably to such an unexpected call of duty. Accordingly, he rushed home to embrace the heavensent opportunity to make something different and unjaded, if controversial and difficult, of his recently shattered life. The circumstances of his release from emotional bondage could not have been more fortuitous. However, the call was not without its attendant risks. He would have to win

62. Chad Norris to Gore-Browne, 3 July 1935; Mackenzie-Kennedy to Gore-Browne, 12 June 1935.

the support of Broken Hill and then overcome the challenge of Arthur Davison, a local resident and railwayman. Dare a fiftyish, balding, ex-colonel with a monocled eye, a manor house, advanced views on the "African problem," and an unusual reputation, not to say a young and then confused wife, seek election from—of all places—Broken Hill? Did he possess sufficient intuitive political sense to campaign effectively, and to win?

VI
Politics in a
Changing Society

A REMARKABLE career in politics began for Gore-Browne with a cleverly articulated, no-nonsense campaign in Broken Hill. At first he was nervous and apprehensive. Only during the war had he needed to sway men in groups, and then he could usually claim the assistance of rank. The electors in Northern Rhodesia were hardly soldiers, and many miners and railway workers—the majority of the electorate—instinctively distrusted and sought reasons to confirm their prejudices against the class of which the lofty sounding colonel was an archetypal representative. To win them over Gore-Browne consciously had to put himself and his beliefs on the line—to subject himself in a new way to the evaluation of others, especially others not of his class. "The election is rather cursed," Gore-Browne told his aunt. "I've to speak & canvas & do all these horrors when all I want is to be hid for a bit . . . in my own home. . . . [Moreover] I've a feeling it will all be wasted, & slightly shame making too."[1]

Pleasing the racist, fascist-leaning whites of Broken Hill was a tricky task for an inexperienced political campaigner. The railway and mining union branches in the town had only recently been rejuvenated, largely because of the energies and skill of Roy Welensky, a weighty prizefighter turned engine driver. The railway union was already pledged to support Davison, but Welensky and his cohorts most of all wanted someone to represent them who would stand up to the governor and the other "officials" in the fledgling Northern Rhodesian Legislative Council. They were particularly in favor of amalgamation—the joining of Southern Rhodesia and Northern Rhodesia in a unitary state under white control—in order to end colonial rule and remove the specter of potential black influence in the Protectorate's future.

Lord Passfield's *Memorandum of Native Policy in East Africa* had

1. Gore-Browne to Ethel Locke-King, 17 August 1935.

made it absolutely clear that African interests were to prevail in Northern Rhodesia should they conflict with those of the whites.[2] A year later, reacting to the fevered outrage of Northern Rhodesia's small and scattered white population (13,000 in 1931), Passfield indicated that Britain was not prepared to agree to amalgamation —the settler solution. Moreover, he declared that in Northern Rhodesia "problems of native development are in a stage which makes it inevitable that His Majesty's Government should hesitate to let them pass even partially out of their responsibility."[3] Even though the Labour government in which Passfield served was soon ousted from power, whites in Northern Rhodesia understood how completely their own futures as members of a tiny frontier ruling class were mortgaged by such imperial reluctance. They therefore clamored throughout the early 1930s for home rule or for some form of closer association with self-governing white Southern Rhodesia.

Leopold Moore, the crusty druggist from Livingstone who led the eight settler representatives in the Legislative Council, spoke for his constituents when he explained that whites had not come to Northern Rhodesia "solely and even mainly to raise the native in the scale of civilization. Our main object," he said, "is to survive ourselves, to improve our conditions if we can, and . . . to raise a family and perpetuate our race."[4] By 1933, moreover, it was clear that self-government was an economic impossibility. Northern Rhodesia's copper industry had been hard hit by the slump in world commodity prices and the Protectorate could not support itself without help. Yet in that year, Moore led the settler representatives of the Legislative Council in a vote in favor of amalgamation with Southern Rhodesia. (The white government of Southern Rhodesia and the settlers of Nyasaland welcomed and endorsed the proposal.) Thereafter, in all three territories, but especially in Northern Rhodesia, the issue of amalgamation remained popular, and even received some discreet local official support from the governor of Nyasaland. After the Copperbelt riots of May, 1935, such sentiment strengthened. But the Colonial Office in 1935 was as vigorously opposed to limiting its own control as it had been five years before.[5]

2. See above, 156–158; S 1/913/30: Passfield to governors, 20 May 1930, Zomba archives.

3. Sec/Ea/9: Passfield to Maxwell, 1 July 1931. Passfield's statement was read to both houses of Parliament the next day.

4. Moore, in Legislative Council, 29 May 1933, quoted in J. W. Davidson, *The Northern Rhodesian Legislative Council* (London, 1948), 94. See also Harry Franklin, *The Flag-Wagger* (London, 1974), 95.

5. For a fuller discussion, see Rotberg, *Nationalism,* 104–107. For the riots, see *ibid.,* 161–167.

Thus, by trumpeting "amalgamation" and espousing bigotry, and also by minimizing his aloofness (he hated to see his name stuck on trees, in capitals on the marquees of movie theatres, etc.), emphasizing his wit and clearheadedness, and by seeming strong and purposeful, Gore-Browne could maximize his chances of winning.

He could strive to satisfy the last three criteria. But he was no bigot, and amalgamation, in the naked form in which it was always discussed on the hustings, seemed absolutely wrong. At his first meeting with the electors in Broken Hill Gore-Browne felt that his supporters had unwittingly bought a "pig in a poke." He felt awkward and stiff explaining his views to listeners. The labor element seemed unrelievedly hostile. Most of all, much as he wanted to win, he could not bring himself to run "with the hounds & shout . . . 'Amalgamation'." Gore-Browne tried "to talk sense & keep honest" in the face of the popular outcry for what he believed was impossible to achieve and a not truly satisfying solution. "It's abundantly clear," he wrote toward the end of the campaign, "that anyone would not stand a ghost of a chance of election who turned down the idea. It put me in a fix. . . . I don't believe in it, for it means party politics, & government by not very competent settlers; I've therefore said 'all right, with proper safeguards, have your Amalgamation if you can get it. If you send me to Parliament and say I'm to vote for it . . . I will, but the point is you'll NEVER get it, so now let's think of something else!'"[6]

Gore-Browne walked a political tight-rope. He said what he believed, but articulated liberal views carefully. In this endeavor he was evidently successful. His candidacy gained rather than lost credibility as the campaign gathered momentum. Most significantly of all, he found that he could resurrect his wartime ability to move men with oratory. He was able once again to "get hold of a crowd of people"—that "queer thing that comes now & again." At a critical early meeting at the Railway Club in Broken Hill Gore-Browne knew that the key to success was winning Welensky (still pledged to Davison) to his side. They had talked before the meeting, but without Gore-Browne satisfying either Welensky or the other union critics. The meeting itself went well, however. "You should have felt those Broken Hill people rise to my hand," he wrote afterwards, "half of them actively hostile when I began, all of them doubtful, and I was attacking their own panacea too."[7]

Gore-Browne's speech evidently convinced Welensky and others that he could win, and would represent them skillfully. During Gore-Browne's peroration Welensky caught his eye, laughed, and

6. Gore-Browne to Ethel Locke-King, 26 August 1935.
7. Gore-Browne to Ethel Locke-King, 30 September 1935.

dramatically tore up a list of questions.[8] As a result, exulted Gore-Browne, "the women have formed a committee to work for me, and to drive cars; the parsons have had me to lunch & opened their hearts; and *so far* I've got the thing I'm told at my feet. . . ."[9]

The magnetism of Gore-Browne's appeal is hard to recapture four decades later, but its quintessence may have been caught in the reflection of an anonymous elector. " 'It comes down to this,' " the elector told Gore-Browne: " 'Are we justified in voting for a man we like and admire, but whose views we disagree with, against a man we dislike & distrust, but who's out for what we want'?"[10] Clearly Gore-Browne seemed plausible. His candor, openness, intelligence, and articulateness compensated to some extent for his views and his background. Equally decisive may have been the contrast with his opponent, for Davison was a "wrong'un." To Gore-Browne he seemed ordinary and not very intelligent. Most of all, although the railway union maintained its official support of Davison, Gore-Browne almost everywhere heard tales about his lack of character. With so questionable a reputation, he proved poor competition for someone publicly so unsullied as Gore-Browne.

The friendship with Welensky obviously did Gore-Browne's campaign no harm. Moreover, though an unexpected coalition of opposites, from the beginning it was no mere marriage of convenience. They both took to each other instantly, beginning in Broken Hill in August and September 1935 a warm relationship which lasted—despite later political divergences—until Gore-Browne's death in 1967. Welensky, Gore-Browne wrote immediately after their second meeting, "I really and truly like and respect . . . for he has a slow, winning, smile, and a shy confidence which is very attractive, and I'm sure he likes me." Welensky, the lowborn, rough-hewn, disadvantaged laborer, may have been attracted to Gore-Browne as part of his life-long compensatory striving to overcome early inferiority. "You're every bit as much an aristocrat as the governor, probably more," Welensky told Gore-Browne later. He learned from Gore-Browne, accepted his paternal advice, and, when he felt sufficiently tutored, went off on his own politically.[11]

8. Gore-Browne to Ethel Locke-King, 24 August 1935. Cf. the slightly different account, source unclear, in Don Taylor, *The Rhodesian: The Life of Sir Roy Welensky* (London, 1955), 42.

9. Gore-Browne to Ethel Locke-King, 24 August 1935.

10. Quoted in Gore-Browne to Ethel Locke-King, 26 August 1935.

11. Gore-Browne to Ethel Locke-King, 15 September 1935, 29 December 1935. Roy Welensky, *Welensky's 4000 Days: The Life and Death of the Federation of Rhodesia and Nyasaland* (London, 1964), 28.

Gore-Browne's campaign met with equal success in Kasama and Abercorn, at the other end of his vast constituency. The white coffee planters, missionaries, and administrators who voted there were apprehensive about their future and looked to their candidate and "neighbor" for security and reassurance. Gore-Browne's political skill was in appreciating the mood of those whites and in articulating his own view of the solution in a way which provided balm without promising a panacea. "Our salvation really lies within ourselves," Gore-Browne wrote of the whites. "We must pull ourselves together and think of the country rather than individuals, & above all face the native question unselfishly." Moreover, "being ignored by officialdom" & given no share whatever in running the country" made it harder to espouse or sell such a policy to settlers. Gore-Browne struck a particularly responsive chord in his white audiences when he spoke of the need for cooperation and partnership between settlers and officials and blacks and whites.[12]

It was at a surprisingly well-attended public meeting in Abercorn that Gore-Browne most fully articulated a political philosophy which, however embryonic, had grown during the campaign. He acknowledged the "utter weariness" which white settlers felt after years of living under what he called a working model of a miniature dictatorship. Yet amalgamation, the popular solution, was not for him. It means self-government and "Party-Government which I personally regard as something of an evil, certainly in a young country like ours." He promised to vote for amalgamation, "always provided that proper safeguards are included. . . . The main reason why I cannot share the present enthusiasm for wholehog amalgamation, is that I am as sure as I am of anything in this world, that we have not an earthly chance of getting it." Gore-Browne assumed that the elected members of the Legislative Council would all vote for amalgamation, send a deputation to wait on the colonial secretary, and then be rebuffed. What then? "Are we going to continue to 'blow off steam under adequate supervision' . . . or is there any likely alternative?" We simply want, he felt, "an effective voice in the management of our own affairs."

It was difficult successfully to govern a country as large as Northern Rhodesia. Communications were primitive. The only satisfactory solution, he told his electors, was "to scrap the highly centralised system of government . . . and to substitute a generous measure of self-government under which all [he did not mean to include black] sections of the community are entitled to share, with full power to deal with local interests, labour, police, education,

12. Gore-Browne to Ethel Locke-King, 9 September 1935.

roads, health, local taxation, but responsible to a supreme Federal Government controlling the 'reserved' departments of Defence, Posts and Telegraphs, Customs, Surveys, and, as important as any from our point of view up here, Research." This Federal government—in outline remarkably like the one which was eventually created in 1953 over Gore-Browne's opposition—would embrace both of the Rhodesias and Nyasaland. Economy and efficiency would be achieved. "This is the solution I put forward for our present troubles," Gore-Browne concluded to cheers. "Let us by all means try for Amalgamation, amalgamation with proper safeguards, but when that is refused, as refused it certainly will be, then let us concentrate on Local Self-Government, coupled with Federation, and I think we shall find we have not come off so badly after all."[13]

In the northern centers and back again in Broken Hill for the last week of the short (month long) campaign, there were dances to attend, committees to greet, interviews to give, addresses to women's groups, and public meetings at which to perform. By the end he was "dead weary"—tired even of seeing the black and yellow rosettes worn by his supporters, and fed up with having to speak carefully and to calculate. In the end, however, it was worth it, for on 16 September the voters cast 253 ballots for Gore-Browne and only 112 for Davison. Welensky was present when the ballots were counted, Gore-Browne wrote. When the result was announced he "just beamed."[14] The monocle now sat in the eye of a victorious politician.

Gore-Browne was at last where he had always wanted to be—near the center of power, "in the know," and with a definite role to play both on behalf of his not very numerous actual constituents and innumerable franchiseless blacks (his role in this respect was self-appointed, but welcomed), and also as a presumed representative of sane and enlightened imperialism. It was a combination of responsibilities for which Gore-Browne had been unknowingly but effectively preparing himself for a long time. He could be altruistic and paternal without giving offence, he could make proposals without seeming forward or pompous, and he could offer advice to the governor and other officials routinely. The exercise of power in his case depended far more upon informal contacts than upon argument in the Legislative Council or in committee. Indeed, since

13. Gore-Browne, address to a meeting at Abercorn, 6 September 1935, reported in the *Bulawayo Chronicle* (9 September 1935), 5.
14. Gore-Browne to Ethel Locke-King, 15 September 1935. At this stage Gore-Browne routinely spelled his friend's name Walensky or Wallensky.

the Council met only two or three times a year, for several weeks each, Gore-Browne was as active outside the chamber as within.

Because he, alone of the settler representatives, was interested in African welfare, Gore-Browne quickly found himself the only non-administrator on the Native Industrial Labor Advisory Board, the only non-administrative invitee to the twice-yearly meetings of provincial commissioners, and a welcome guest in Government House, Lusaka. Being elected had catapulted Gore-Browne from a position of rural eminence and respect, but limited overall influence, to a position where he had unquestioned and significant impact on virtually all policies affecting Africans and whites, and the future of Northern Rhodesia generally. The government recognized him as a potential ally among the cantankerous settlers; the settlers heard his views and knew that he alone could persuade the administration and the Colonial Office to heed their grievances. For Gore-Browne these new responsibilities were demanding, absorbing, and sobering. But he relished them and enjoyed his new and expanding role excessively. At last he was truly "somebody", his father's and his grandfather's equal, and worthy of his aunt's continued love.

In and out of the Legislative Council Gore-Browne wasted no time in staking out a series of issues on which he intended to provide guidance and leadership. Many were summarized in an extraordinarily long and broad-ranging legislative maiden speech in December, 1935. His fellow elected members had been informed and given their approval to his general line, and the governor knew a few days before approximately what he expected to discuss, but the full speech proved—Gore-Browne managed to say "all the things" he had longed to say for years—a sensation throughout the Rhodesias. It combined a proposal for the partial devolution of power to whites with a scathing attack upon the government's failure to fulfill its responsibilities to Africans. "The European portion of this country is seriously, and almost dangerously, disturbed by the present state of affairs," Gore-Browne began to the approbation of his fellow representatives. There was no point pretending that they had real power. Thus many legitimate grievances could be avoided if settlers were "given some share in the executive work of the country." As one way, Gore-Browne suggested reviving the practice of letting whites be justices of the peace, especially in outlying areas like his own, with limited but measurable responsibility for trying petty cases and maintaining law and order. Certainly "playing at parliament", in the present manner, had more entertainment than legislative value. Therefore, he told the startled chamber and the press, "we Elected Members have decided, solemnly and seriously, after due consideration, that, if the Constitution is not eventually altered in the sense in which we desire . . . by giving more power to the unofficial element . . . we shall collectively resign . . . because we do honestly feel that we are wasting time."

Trusteeship was at fault. Gore-Browne believed that the doctrine of trusteeship gave the government its major excuse for refusing to share power with whites. Trusteeship was thought, he said, to be predicated upon "the theory that responsibility for the native races must remain in official hands." But what, he asked pointedly, had the government ever done for Africans? Of what benefit was trusteeship? He accused the government of neglecting its responsibilities for the physical and material well-being of its wards. Famines every few years, a total failure to study and improve the nutrition of Africans (Lorna's favorite interest), and lack of attention to agricultural development all testified to the government's inability to carry out its responsibilities as a trustee. Moreover, he asked, "can we look with any satisfaction, or any pride, or anything but a feeling of considerable shame, on the record as far as our medical activities towards the natives are concerned?" The African hospital in Abercorn had formerly been a prison and even the new Lusaka hospital was squalid. "In this enlightened country," he reminded the legislators, we still adopt "the medieval practice of putting lunatics in prison, and . . . chaining them up." Overall there has been in the past "no considered policy for doing anything for the medical welfare of natives." Again and again the training of orderlies has been recommended, but nothing had ever been done.

Gore-Browne turned to the education of Africans. "I know we spend £25,000 on native education, but, after all, it is the natives' own money." After twelve years of colonial rule the education of Africans was still virtually entirely in the hands of missionaries— not "a suitable state of affairs." Most of all, Gore-Browne later in the session advocated separating the then combined departments of white and African education; neither he nor his colleagues wanted the attention and money devoted to one to suffer by being linked with the other. (They all felt that European education had been neglected; Gore-Browne was also worried about Africans.) A paternalist attuned to the times, Gore-Browne favored more technical or industrial education for Africans, but not the training of Africans for jobs held by whites in the settled areas of the Protectorate. "There is immense scope for the native as a workman in his own part of the country. . . . [but] we should not train a native for any job which does not exist."[15]

Northern Rhodesia was then in the process, however ambiva-

15. Northern Rhodesia, *Legislative Council Debates,* 25 (2–4 December 1935), 99–101, 149–151, 158.

lently, of introducing greater measures of indirect rule. Gore-Browne correctly saw, however, that in these matters the provincial administration was often hypocritical, always hesitant, and never effective. Lip service had been paid to ideals, but nothing very much of practical relevance had been done.[16] Gore-Browne believed that rural Africans were capable of doing much more for themselves under the guidance of an enlightened and expanded provincial administration. He urged the government to devote more of its scarce funds to improving rural life, surprising the officials by saying "with absolute certainty that, not only are the Hon. Members on my side of the House entirely in sympathy with . . . a well considered, thought-out proposal, even if it involves the expenditure of money, for improving native administration . . . but . . . that the feeling in the country . . . will be behind them." Gore-Browne urged the government to decentralize, to encourage provincial autonomy, and to give whites a greater influence in all decisions.

Since trusteeship had proved, he said, "a snare and a delusion—a snare for the native and a delusion for the unfortunate official who is carrying it out," and since it had been demonstrated in practice to amount to nothing more than "humbug," it should be scrapped. Particularly wrong was the implicit assumption of the doctrine of trusteeship that whites were eventually to withdraw and hand over Northern Rhodesia to Africans. "I for one, if it is a case of handing Shiwa Ngandu to Chitimukulu, would see red in every sense of the word. If we are not . . . then the doctrine is mere humbug, and I do not think we ought to base our policy on humbug." Trusteeship was thus unworkable. In its place Gore-Browne suggested a solution which, had it then been capable of adoption in any real sense, might have altered the future of the Protectorate. He proposed "regarding the native as a partner . . . a potential partner, but still a partner, and I think all our main principles should be laid down with that end in view." After all, he concluded "partnership is an ideal which we can advocate for the whole country, for the whole world—partnership between all sections of the community, and eventual partnership with what [another member] has called our black fellowcountrymen."[17]

As Gore-Browne told his aunt, "honestly I felt I'd never spoken worse in my life . . . however . . . old Moore the Bolshevik chemist . . . said it was the best maiden speech he'd ever heard. Sir

16. For a discussion of indirect rule in Northern Rhodesia, see Rotberg, *Nationalism,* 50–51.

17. Quoted in Northern Rhodesia, *Debates,* 25 (2 December 1935), cc. 195–209. For his recollections of this speech, see Gore-Browne, "Legislative Council in Northern Rhodesia Twenty Years Ago," *Northern Rhodesia Journal,* II, 4 (1954), 41.

Hubert was nice." The speech certainly "shook them", as the local newspapers made clear in reporting the debate.[18] Moore later took the, for him, unusual step of writing in praise about the speech and the session generally: "You have been a much greater help to me than it is possible for you to realise . . . We have made more progress than most of us can appreciate and *I know* . . . that it was entirely due to your hearty cooperation. I also feel that when my call comes there will be someone to carry on; I have never felt so before."[19] Colonel Arthur Stephenson, the comparatively liberal member for Ndola, seconded Gore-Browne's speech and was equally supportive. Most of all, Young, the pompous governor, reported to the colonial secretary that Gore-Browne "appeared sincerely moved with indignation that the non-native population of the territory should not be trusted to be fair to the natives, and honestly anxious that the elected members should be given more responsibility." Gore-Browne, said Young, was a new member "whose personality and knowledge of the world have placed him at once in a commanding position among his colleagues . . ."[20]

Gore-Browne could not have made a more auspicious beginning in terms of parliamentary impact and his effect upon public opinion. But would his (for the era) liberal sentiments have any real effect upon either governmental policy or settler attitudes? Could he bring about a renaissance in African affairs? Could he alter the direction of Northern Rhodesian life in any small degree?

Bettering the lives of rural Africans was Gore-Browne's overriding priority. Thus, by way of buttressing his maiden speech with a concrete call to action, he sent Young a memorandum early in January 1936. Since the work of so many departments of the government affected African development, and since the hands of the chief secretary were already fully occupied, another official—a director of native development—should be appointed to coordinate all organizations the policies of which were primarily concerned with African activities, sponsor research, and give policy guidance. He should be a member of the Executive Council so as to be able to deal on equal terms with the heads of departments. In particular, the director would give guidance and support to the provincial administration, and especially to the district officers who would be responsible for implementing programs of African development. Gore-Browne recognized that district officers were not then able to

18. Gore-Browne to Ethel Locke-King, 4 December 1935; *Bulawayo Chronicle* (3 December 1935), 7.

19. L. F. Moore to Gore-Browne, 24 December 1935, Gore-Browne papers.

20. S 1/7/35: Young to MacDonald, 15 January 1936, Zomba archives.

give African matters more than marginal attention. Although Africans should be their "first care . . . it is obvious that a single handed official who has to cope with his monthly returns, accounts, tax-collection, judicial work, maintenance of roads and bridges . . . cannot have much time over for constructive Native work." Gore-Browne thus urged the abolition of one-man stations, an increase in district staff, and continuity of officials in language areas in order to encourage a "contented and prosperous Native population."

The government was, Gore-Browne declared, out of touch with Africans. District officials should not be shifted frequently from station to station, making it difficult for them to learn local languages and gain the confidence of the surrounding populations. Transfers to bomas on the line-of-rail should no longer be regarded as promotions. Most of all, making provinces self-contained units would, Gore-Browne felt, encourage healthy continuity. Under his scheme each provincial headquarters team would comprise the heads of the agricultural, educational, medical, veterinary, and public works services, and, he hoped, a government anthropologist.

Despite his distrust of Audrey Richards, Gore-Browne followed Lord Lugard in believing that by learning more about African practices governments could ease the transition between traditional and modern life. Moreover, since "the object of all Development is to fit the Native to Govern himself, within the frame work of a composite state, [and since] The Stages by which this end is to be reached [must be] the result of carefully thought out policy . . . carried out by the Provincial Administration, the advice of experts in the shape of anthropologists . . . should have . . . an important part to play in the practical application of the policy." In addition to this overriding concern, he expected that his proposed reforms would also enable the government, at a local level, to improve agricultural practices and supplies, construct and maintain hospitals and train orderlies, educate Africans more efficiently, and pay close attention to problems connected with migratory African labor and the conditions under which Africans worked in the urban areas. Gore-Browne also bemoaned the absence of any department dealing with labor relations.[21]

No Northern Rhodesian—certainly none so esteemed as Gore-Browne—had ever publicly criticized the government's record on African affairs and then offered constructive remedies. In that sense, the message of his parliamentary debut and subsequent memorandum was long overdue. Equally, because the government of the

21. "Native Development," memorandum by Gore-Browne submitted to Governor Young in early January, 1936.

Protectorate was as yet unable and unwilling to think creatively as far as African enhancement was concerned, Gore-Browne's homily was in advance of the times. The government's main cry remained "economy", and during the 1930s there was no easier way to discourage projects than to dwell upon their costs. Yet Young and Charles Dundas, the chief secretary, were intrigued sufficiently by the implications of the Gore-Browne proposal to bring it before a regular meeting of provincial commissioners and other executives chaired by the governor in 1936. Gore-Browne was also invited, and thereafter, as the "unofficial" most intimately concerned with African matters, attended these meetings by right.

The provincial commissioners gave Gore-Browne's ideas a favorable reception although the implementation of many of his specific suggestions was denied on the grounds of expense. The conference decided that a director of native development was too costly an innovation and that, anyway, the "right man" was unavailable. The governor promised, however, to establish an anthropological institute. Surprisingly, too, the governor and his aides accepted the notion that new councils should come into being to coordinate governmental activities at the provincial level. But they were unwilling to support Gore-Browne's recommendation that the council should include representatives of the white settlers (not Africans) in each province. "Settlers," Gore-Browne argued, "had the impression that questions of public interest and importance were hidden from them." Later Gore-Browne was to make similar, equally valid, pleas on behalf of disenfranchised or neglected Africans.

More readily conceded by the commissioners were Gore-Browne's important points about administrative continuity. The conference thus drew up a set of rules to regulate the postings of district commissioners so as to maximize their knowledge of local affairs. Yet, despite Gore-Browne, they affirmed the superiority of the coveted locations along the line-of-rail and evinced no concrete enthusiasm for "native affairs," rural development, or any of the other decentralizing schemes so close to Gore-Browne's ideas about what was best for the modernization of the majority of the people of Northern Rhodesia. As a group, administrators in Northern Rhodesia, like their counterparts in the other East and Central African territories, were too close to settlers and hence as yet unready for the Africanization of direction and interest which Gore-Browne, for all his own natural attachments to the white way of life, was far-sighted enough to promote. C. R. Lockhart, the Protectorate's treasurer, typified the predominant attitude of the administration when he reacted to Gore-Browne's enthusiasm for African agriculture. "No considerable economic crops could be found," he concluded a long response. Moreover, he doubted if anyone could invent any. Products of the soil would remain unimportant: "Natives would have to rely chiefly on wages for wealth and in framing our policies we should recognize this."[22]

Despite the skepticism of men like Lockhart and the temporizing and hesitancy that is common in all bureaucracies, the results of Gore-Browne's several African-oriented initiatives began to be realized sooner than he anticipated. He had Young's ear, if not his friendship, his words carried weight with Dundas, and, when it heard them, with the distant Colonial Office. Equally, Gore-Browne's suggestions were modest, incremental, and conflicted with no special interest other than the status quo. During the later 1930s he also had ample opportunities to remind, prod, and persuade reluctant nay-sayers in Lusaka.

In late 1936 the first provincial council convened, appropriately in Kasama. It "was excellent value," Gore-Browne said, especially "as it's supposed to be my own child."[23] Other provinces held council meetings during the following year, and, by 1939, all had regular yearly or twice-yearly sessions. During the war, too, because of Gore-Browne's prodding these councils evolved into a forum for blacks as well as whites.

Gore-Browne could claim partial credit for the establishment of the Rhodes-Livingstone Institute, which was formed in 1937 to begin undertaking anthropological research throughout the Protectorate. The same year saw an even more far-reaching development, the formation of a Native Development Board in response (though in committee form) to the major thrust of Gore-Browne's concern. It provided an organizational means of focusing attention on African needs and a lobby for helpful appropriations. After the first meeting Gore-Browne termed the board the "best thing I've struck yet for the job in all these years."[24] Two years later, even Gore-Browne's notion of a director of native development was realized with the re-creation of the position of secretary for native affairs (a similar title had existed in the 1920s); one person was again responsible for the administration of Africans. Even so, Gore-Browne

22. All in the Report of the Meeting of Provincial Commissioners, March 1936, mimeo.; Gore-Browne to Lorna, 17 March 1936; Gore-Browne to Ethel Locke-King, 23 March 1936.

23. Gore-Browne to Ethel Locke-King, 12 September 1936.

24. Gore-Browne to Ethel Locke-King, 28 March 1938. Richard Brown, "Anthropology and Colonial Rule: The Case of Godfrey Wilson and the Rhodes-Livingstone Institute, Northern Rhodesia," in Talal Asad (ed.), *Anthropology and the Colonial Encounter* (London, 1973), 178–180, gives Gore-Browne no credit for inspiring Young to promote the idea of an institute, but his role is evident from family and official correspondence.

continued to have cause for complaint; musical chairs was still the game in the districts, taxes were too high for villagers, and indigenous agricultural uplift remained neglected. Further, the problems which Gore-Browne foresaw disturbing the tenor of labor relations on the mines and elsewhere received no attention until another dramatic strike convulsed the country in 1940.

Although for the first three years of his parliamentary life Gore-Browne assiduously attended to the needs of his white constituents, holding frequent meetings with them in Broken Hill, Kasama, and Abercorn, and genuinely seeking redress for their grievances in Lusaka, he primarily interested himself in larger, protectorate-wide issues like the welfare of Africans and constitutional reform. Into the legislative council debates he injected a hitherto rarely heard concern for the country's silent majority, for farsightedness and planning, on their as well as everyone else's behalf, and for abstractions like modernization, justice, and efficiency. In the debates he publicized problems previously masked and suggested solutions rarely advanced. But the Council was an advisory body; Gore-Browne's influence and impact was exercised more effectively behind the scenes—in committees, in conferences, in government house, and, when the occasion arose, in London's halls of influence.

He was a good committee man—patient, dedicated, full of common sense, always aware of the larger issues, and capable of devising workable solutions to knotty conundrums. Most of all, he had the knack for expressing moral outrage without seeming sanctimonious. These attributes Gore-Browne employed with success on the Native Industrial Labor Advisory Board, the Native Education Advisory Board, the Native Development Board, and the Northern Province Council, in the meeting of the provincial commissioners, and as the only non-administrative member of a number of special investigatory commissions. (During his first year of public life he spent 168 days away from Shiwa on public business.) In late 1936, for example, he helped chair a committee on African nutrition which publicized dietary deficiences earlier than other African territories. It recommended urgent professional study of how protein and caloric intakes could be enhanced.

The welfare of Africans was uppermost in his mind when he agreed to serve on a special task force to examine the conditions under which Northern Rhodesian migrants labored on the newly opened Lupa goldfields in southwestern Tanganyika. With Ronald Bush, the Chinsali district commissioner, he motored to Lupa via Mbeya in November 1936. About 25,000 Africans (10,000 of whom were Northern Rhodesians) and 1,000 whites were panning gold from streams (or blowing and washing if the equipment were available) scattered over 1,400 square miles of otherwise barren land;

comparatively few Africans and whites as yet worked underground. Housing and medical conditions were abominable. Workers lived "in utter squalor," Gore-Browne reported, "in grass shelters, in holes in the ground, under rocks. Water is very scarce, and all these alluvial workers are perpetually moving about." Africans were dying from lack of medical attention, from scurvy, and from starvation. There was a "total absence of sanitation." To make matters worse, many never received their pay, and claims were outstanding for months at a time. Moreover, said Gore-Browne, "our government does nothing to help them cover the 300 or 1000 miles they walk from their homes to get here."[25] In their report, which Gore-Browne wrote in December, the investigators recommended the establishment of rest camps twenty miles apart (preferably near mission stations) along the main roads leading to Lupa within Northern Rhodesia, making food and lemon or lime juice (from Shiwa?) available to the migrants, officially warning Africans of the squalid conditions in the gold fields, informing Africans of their rights as laborers, eliminating the taxation of workers in both Tanganyika and Northern Rhodesia, stationing a Northern Rhodesian administrator at Chunya, in the gold fields, to look after Northern Rhodesian laborers, establishing a postal service capable of maintaining communications between the miners and their homes, and, if possible, organizing a government-run recruiting service to encourage only healthy Africans to go to the mines.[26]

Although the gold of Lupa proved less abundant than was initially thought and the numbers attracted there would in any event have diminished, the report by Gore-Browne and Bush had the intended cautionary effect. The government of Northern Rhodesia saw the sense of nearly all of its specific suggestions, bar organizing a recruiting service and establishing a chain of camps. At Gore-Browne's urging, too, Northern Rhodesia put pressure upon Tanganyika (inquiries by the Permanent Mandates Commission and a caustic report for Nyasaland by the Reverend W. P. Young pro-

25. Gore-Browne to Ethel Locke-King, 28 November 1936. A year later, C. McMahon, the Tanganyikan Provincial Commissioner responsible for the goldfields, rationalized the still deplorable arrangements in and around Lupa: "Whilst the conditions of employment leave much room for improvement in many ways, labourers live a free and easy life and the element of a gamble appeals to them. The ration may not always be suitable but is adequate and complaints in this respect are few. The accommodation leaves much to be desired but in some cases their quarters are no worse than those occupied by their employers." Tanganyika Territory, *Annual Reports of the Provincial Commissioners on Native Administration for the Year 1937* (Dar es Salaam, 1938), 64.

26. Sec/Lab/103, report and diary of the Gore-Browne and Bush visit to the Lupa Gold Fields, 18 December 1936, mimeo.

vided additional support) to improve the quality of life in the gold fields and to ensure minimum levels of sustenance. Dundas, then acting as Northern Rhodesia's governor, initially wondered—reflecting a mentality that an outraged Gore-Browne called "beyond my comprehension"—whether it wasn't counterproductive to urge improvements on Tanganyika "as then our people will not be tempted to stay so long away."[27] But Gore-Browne, his compassion evident and aroused, proved persuasive. The Tanganyikan government, too, took heed of its critics and in 1937 posted a labor officer to the gold fields and established the Lupa Control Board in order to try to eliminate wage problems and alleviate other misfortunes.

Within Northern Rhodesia proper, Gore-Browne's indignation was similarly aroused, and his practical sense affronted, by the ways in which the government taxed Africans. The Copperbelt riots of 1935 highlighted African grievances, some of which concerned levels of taxation in the rural areas. In the Legislative Council he spoke vigorously in favor of exempting Africans without the means to pay; he understood better than many of his colleagues that taxes were still one of the critical sources of tension in Northern Rhodesia during the depressed 1930s. Males over eighteen paid between seven shillings sixpence and fifteen shillings a year depending upon where they worked (the Copperbelt naturally having the highest rate, the so-called labor-supplying areas the lowest). The total collected in 1936 was £211,709. None went into the coffers of the native authorities. At meetings of provincial commissioners Gore-Browne promoted rearrangements in official methods of taxing Africans, and often urged Young to act. Finally, after extensive discussions in 1937 by the provincial commissioners and the Legislative Council, Young decided to appoint a small committee to review the conditions of African taxation and to suggest new ways of arranging the collection and justification of African taxes. Any proposed reductions were to be suggested within a comprehensive financial framework. Along with Gore-Browne, Young appointed Lockhart, still the financial secretary, and T. F. Sandford, the senior provincial commissioner.

Starting from Shiwa Ngandu in January, 1938, and concluding a month later, the committee interviewed about 100 whites and 90 Africans in the course of their traverse of the territory by road, rail, and air. They visited almost every boma, covering 3,500 miles in the process, and nearly exhausted themselves. "It's queer what a fatiguing business it is asking the same questions of witnesses over & over again," Gore-Browne remembered. Some interviews lasted

27. Gore-Browne to Ethel Locke-King, 27 December 1936.

two hours, others far less, depending on the status of the person. But the quality of replies did not necessarily depend on the status. Bishop May gave evidence well; John Gaunt, then a district commissioner, spoke poorly. Yeta III, paramount chief of the Lozi, concentrated on his own personal interests "masked by an attractive smile which could switch over into a look of blank incomprehension when he didn't want to answer a question." Others of the chiefs, especially the old ones, were "pathetically bad (how could they be other?)." Gore-Browne was amazed by his fellows—with the "stupid selfishness they display." A "zealous education officer wanted a provision inserted in the tax regulations the effect of which would have been to enforce his own particular view of education at the expense of a community (Dutch Reformed Church) he disliked. A (French) missionary wanted the whole tax system directed in a carefully thought out gradation against polygamy."

The committee's final report was hammered out in Lusaka, Gore-Browne managing by his own lights to influence "a fairly good share . . . I got some fundamental principles shoved in which I hope may have a wider sphere of influence than Northern Rhodesia alone."[28] He and his colleagues believed that there were grave objections to introducing any system "which purports to assess taxation in accordance with individual capacity to pay and fails to do so to a degree which is bound to be apparent to many of those concerned. If the African is to be educated to appreciate the equity of a tax [this passage is pure Gore-Browne] assessed according to means, it appears to us that the Government must be prepared to satisfy the demand for such a tax, when aroused, on a scale which has some claim to accuracy and completeness. A scheme which missed wage-earners in part and non-wage-earners entirely would not . . . be worth introducing. . . ." Thus the committee set forth three principles: that the tax should be understood and capable of being accepted; be of such amount as could be found without undue hardship; and be simple and economical to collect and enforce. A poll tax (the then method) satisfied the first and third principles. "The natives of Northern Rhodesia have [no] objection to the principle of a poll tax or any desire to see it replaced." But, and again Gore-Browne's voice can be heard, "they object strongly to a hut tax with its necessary accompaniment of a tax on plural wives." The committee acknowledged that the pressure of taxation compelled many Africans to leave their villages; yet most would leave anyway. Therefore the committee decided that it was no hardship to tax Africans according to the wage levels of the area in which they resided (or to which they had migrated). Together the members of the

28. Gore-Browne to Ethel Locke-King, 18 January 1938.

committee approved labor in lieu of taxation in the rural areas despite this arrangement's potential abuse by unscrupulous or thoughtless district commissioners, and, at Gore-Browne's insistence, provided for partial exemption of elderly (over fifty-five was Gore-Browne's intent) or infirm persons, or those whose wages were lower than the prevailing mean in the relevant district. The committee also decreased the rate of taxation by a shilling a year in some of the more remote districts and raised it marginally in several of the industrial or white farming districts. In a departure from previous practice it also suggested that a fixed proportion—one-sixth—of the tax should be payable to the new native treasuries (aside from Barotseland, which by treaty received thirty percent of all tax payments). To have given a greater percentage of the funds to the native treasuries would, they thought, take funds away from centrally provided services (like native education) already running at a loss. Finally, in the matter of collection, the committee recommended that in the rural areas taxes should more and more be obtained by the African clerks of each boma or by the native authorities acting as agents of the central government.. Nevertheless, it was expected that the authorities would not be ready before 1940 to undertake this task with efficiency.[29]

Gore-Browne naturally welcomed opportunities like the taxation report which could directly reshape governmental policies. From the suggestions in the report numerous Africans could benefit individually and the whole country presumably could derive profit from the resultant improved relations between the government and the governed. That was Gore-Browne's model. He was the member for the northern electoral district, and in that capacity acknowledged priorities frequently different than his own. Nevertheless, as far as African rights were concerned, Gore-Browne rarely hesitated. He felt paternally responsible for airing and, if possible, remedying grievances even if the black constituents concerned represented no voters and no immediate power, and even though collectively they lacked an articulate voice.

An extension of his long, instinctive concern for the welfare of the people in and around Shiwa, this legislative role was self-appointed and at first exercised without more than occasional consultation with Africans, especially with those who had begun to live permanently in the towns as a part of the new Westernized technocratic class, had organized local protopolitical groups, and already started to make representations to the authorities about their treatment by a colonial, color–conscious society. Thus Gore-Browne at first focused upon the evident needs of rural Africans, only gradu-

29. Northern Rhodesia, *Report on Native Taxation* (Lusaka, 1938), 5–11.

ally, because of his interest in the fate of migratory mine labor, appreciating the long-term significance of urbanization and industrial development for black/white relations.

As a legislator speaking for Africans, Gore-Browne rarely postured. He was constructive, alerting the government to inequities or deleterious consequences of regulations and enactments, and advocating commonsensical reforms which were capable of helping Africans without enormous cost or major shifts in policy. Hardly ever did he propose panaceas or radical revamping of established programs. He was content for the most part with incremental achievements and with righting small scale but real wrongs. Over and over again, he demanded hospitals and dispensaries for Africans, by 1938 encouraging the government to inaugurate a scheme of building small rural medical facilities and training African orderlies to staff them. He urged the establishment of centrally located markets in the rural areas in order to promote better nutrition and minimize the likelihood of famine by ensuring steady supplies.[30] Debating a bill in 1938 which detailed arrangements for the sale of (white-grown) tobacco by auction, Gore-Browne unsuccessfully urged the government to permit Africans to sell their homegrown tobacco there, too. During a major and prolonged discussion of African development in 1937, he criticized the Department of Agriculture and its director for not giving African agriculture a "fair deal." (It looked after white farmers as well.) Nothing was being done to eliminate erosion or discourage deforestation. Nyasaland was trying to reeducate Africans to use the soil well. Why couldn't Northern Rhodesia do the same? Gore-Browne even recommended the application of "a certain amount of coercion" along lines pioneered by officials in the Belgian Congo. "We ought to be prepared to face," he suggested, "a certain amount of . . . slave driving, when the driving is for the good of the slaves."[31] Moreover, he told the council, spending money on Africans would bring rewards for whites as well as blacks. Anything which contributed to the regeneration of indigenous farming would, he promised, contribute to the stabilization of rural life and hence to the peaceful development of all Rhodesians.

Appealing in the same manner to white self-interest, Gore-Browne insisted throughout his first four or five years on the council that the welfare of blacks and whites was inextricably tied together. "A prosperous black man means a prosperous white man

30. For some of the history of markets, see Robert I. Rotberg, "Rural Rhodesian Markets," in Paul J. Bohannan and George Dalton (eds.), *Markets in Africa* (Evanston, 1962), 581–600.

31. Gore-Browne in *Debates*, 29 (November 1937), 208–209.

and *vice versa.*" For him the "native problem" was "not an ethical one, still less a sentimental one."[32] It was economic. Under this rubric Gore-Browne advocated the kinds of policies which could assist African advancement. Educating Africans was obviously of utmost importance even if doing so might ultimately mean competition between blacks and whites for semi-skilled positions. (He wanted whites to be given better schooling to obviate such a clash.) The aim of African education should be, he said in a 1939 debate, to provide a broad base of literate persons, not a very highly educated class of specialists who denigrated manual labor.[33] Long before either were possible, Gore-Browne also urged that schooling for Africans be free (in 1964 still not universal) and compulsory (in 1976 still a goal). He even suggested (without drawing any support) that Africans be appointed to the local education committees and the African Education Board established as a result of a 1939 ordinance.

For a white, his advocacy of African participation was heretical, going well beyond the appreciation of other elected members. As early as 1936 he urged the Council to consider the "question of ultimate native representation and immediate native consultation." Citing his own recent experiences addressing educated Africans in Lusaka, he told the members how intelligent the questions asked had been and how nearly everyone had agreed that chiefs could not speak for urbanized Africans: "They do not know what we are thinking, they do not know anything about it," he had been told. Evenhandedly, in the same debate he favored strengthening the writ of traditional rural leadership: he wanted more scope to be given to indigenous courts (then in their infancy under Northern Rhodesia's recently introduced practice of indirect rule), applauded the provision of councils of elders to help chiefs run the new native authorities ("anybody who knows . . . anything about natives realises that a chief was never meant to be an autocrat and never was"), and, to the consternation of reluctant district officers, supported the establishment of native authority treasuries. "I do not see," he pointed out in his most rational manner, "how native self-government can possibly be a working concern unless natives are given some control over their money."[34] Unlike most administrators, Gore-Browne actually believed in the devolution of responsibility and some power to the rural African aristocracy. Earlier than many, he believed that Africans deserved an opportunity to demonstrate their capabilities, to cease being wards in every respect,

32. Ibid., 207.
33. Gore-Browne in *Debates,* 33 (25 May 1939), 45–47.
34. Quoted in *Debates,* 26 (5 May 1936), 36. For official attitudes toward the implementation of indirect rule, see Rotberg, *Nationalism,* 50.

and to control at least a small segment of their own lives. How else could rural Africans begin to prepare themselves for greater and greater opportunities, even for the home rule that Gore-Browne thought must and should someday come?

To some extent as a result of his growing exposure to groups like the Lusaka Africans, and to urban realities generally, Gore-Browne more and more drew attention in the council to the concerns of town-dwelling, "modern" Africans. In 1938 and 1939 he sought to exempt educated Africans from the "pass" legislation which plagued them and constantly reminded them of the inferiority of their color. From his membership on the Native Industrial Labor Advisory Board, Gore-Browne had become aware of African complaints and potential sources of indigenous dissatisfaction. Thus he wanted both municipalities and the mining companies to provide suitable permanent housing for their employees. Such housing would make it possible for the mines to rely less and less on migratory labor and more and more on the kind of stabilized labor force that Gore-Browne (and others) believed would contribute to tranquil labor relations in the growing towns.

For some of the same reasons, and also because he had always abhorred the mistreatment of blacks by whites, Gore-Browne courted unpopularity by publicly condemning instances of injustice. Why, he asked in 1938, should an African who had thrown a stone at a white man's automobile be sentenced to seven years in prison when whites typically received mere two-year sentences for murdering Africans?[35] By the beginning of World War II Gore-Browne had come to appreciate how harmful a rigid color bar was to the growth of trust between black and white in Northern Rhodesia. Earlier than many he knew that without trust the atmosphere of Northern Rhodesia would be poisoned, and a potentially harmonious future destroyed by the same cancer that had eaten into South Africa and Southern Rhodesia.

Before World War II Gore-Browne had begun listening increasingly to Africans. Although the government viewed such activities with hostility, Gore-Browne felt that the joining together for mutual benefit of educated Africans was hardly a development which should or could be prevented. "Obviously," he wrote, "the line is to keep, or to try to keep, the thing on a reasonable and healthy basis." He spoke to one group of the pressing political issues of the day. "I tried," he reported, revealing as much about his own attitudes as his reception, "to cut out all the missionary & official

35. *Debates,* 31 (13 December 1938), 125–128. Moreover, Mwape, the offender, had been declared insane by a physician, a plea the presiding magistrate had rejected.

humbug, & I admitted at once that white men were here for their own good & that they meant to stay, but I said that white and black prosperity was interdependent, & I tried to explain my idea of partnership as the ideal. . . . They were most polite, very interested, & highly intelligent. They asked many questions, all good ones— and evidently they are very scared at the possibility of Amalgamation with S. Rhodesia with its cry of Rhodesia for the English.[36] Indeed, voluntary associations throughout the Protectorate had spoken out for several years against the notion of amalgamation. Despite active governmental hostility, the more aware had managed to communicate their concern to others, and, even if Gore-Browne were only latterly aware of African fears for their political future, the associations both on the line-of-rail and in the rural areas had consistently said "no" to amalgamation with Southern Rhodesia.[37] During 1937, 1938, and 1939, by which time Gore-Browne was meeting often with urban Africans (the educated class as well as those who mined copper underground), the cries of African apprehension grew ever louder and more unmistakable. They served to reinforce his own antipathy to any merger.

Gore-Browne and most educated Africans knew that amalgamation of almost any practical application would intensify white pretensions to hegemony in Northern Rhodesia, alter the balance of power between blacks (and the Colonial Office) and local whites, and consequently redirect the predominant thrust of race relations in what was still a Protectorate. Gore-Browne appreciated the dangers as much as he understood the enthusiasm for it of his fellow white settlers and many middle-ranking administrators. They had for long wanted to achieve the kind of power and assurances of future control in Northern Rhodesia for which their numbers were otherwise too insignificant. By 1935 the large-scale working of copper had made a merger economically reasonable and attractive, especially to their southern neighbor, Moore was incensed with the Colonial Office because it had moved Northern Rhodesia's capital from Livingstone to Lusaka, the riot at Roan Antelope mine had frightened whites, and, without rating the many possible explanations, in retrospect it simply was a popular solution for which the time appeared truly ripe. The territory-wide election at which Gore-Browne was first returned demonstrated, too, that the white electorate supported amalgamation. In October 1935 Moore therefore wrote to Godfrey Martin Huggins (much later Lord Malvern), the prime minister of Southern Rhodesia, proposing an accelerated mutual agitation for amalgamation. He said that Britain might turn

36. Gore-Browne to Ethel Locke-King, 28 March 1936.
37. See Rotberg, *Nationalism*, 131–132.

Northern Rhodesia over to the League of Nations, presumably as a mandate. Huggins replied warmly, indicating that he and his main colleagues all wanted a merger and were prepared to do battle with Britain to get their way. Ultimately, he would have to put the issue before the white voters of Southern Rhodesia. He therefore suggested that Moore should let it be known that the Northern Rhodesians were thinking of joining the Union of South Africa. "If by some means," he said, "it could get about that you are considering joining the Union . . . there would be an overwhelming vote here in favour of joining you to prevent what would be regarded here as a disaster."[38] Moore and Huggins also set in motion the train of events which were a few months later to lead to the first of several momentous constitutional conferences at the Victoria Falls.

Their actions, and the possibility that the conference would lead to a confrontation with the Colonial and Dominion Offices and potential embarrassments for persons like Gore-Browne who were openly distrustful of amalgamation, led in Northern Rhodesia to tactical meetings among the elected members which shaped major portions of Gore-Browne's (already quoted) maiden speech. He cleverly began espousing constitutional advance as an alternative to amalgamation, a tactic with which Young agreed. This suggestion, Young wrote to his superiors favorably of Gore-Browne, "would give the elected members something to fall back upon when, as [Gore-Browne] hoped, amalgamation had been turned down either by Southern Rhodesia or by the Imperial government, or preferably by both." Young was, in any event, at this stage no supporter of a merger. "I am doubtful," he wrote presciently, "whether it would be prudent to hand over the reins of government in advance to what may turn out eventually to be the less important of the two countries."[39] He and Gore-Browne thus became willing collaborators on this as on so many other significant issues.

Following the initial weeks of parliamentary maneuvering, Gore-Browne articulated a rational approach to what would be the overriding public issue of his entire political career. "I'm not looking forward to [the Victoria Falls conference]," he wrote, "but its got to be got on with, and the amalgamation issue cleared if we are to do any thing. I've got a difficult role to play. I've promised to give amalgamation its chance, though I've gone on saying its a waste of time as C. O. won't allow it even if S. Rhodesia wants it. So I mustn't try and bust the conference even if I could. But what I must

38. S 1/7/35: Huggins to Moore, 6 November 1935, Zomba archives. See also Lewis Gann and Michael Gelfand, *Huggins of Rhodesia: The Man and His Country* (London, 1964), 115–119.

39. S 1/7/35, Young to MacDonald, 15 January 1936, Zomba archives.

do is to work all out to get people to stick to the point, and arrive at a definite conclusion whether or no amalgamation is possible in so far as the European populations are concerned. If the conference fails then we can go on to something else, which is what I want; if it should succeed then the line is to ask the C. O. (through Sir Hubert) if they will give us Amalgamation now (which of course they won't) or at some *definite* future time, say in 10 or 15 years, or when the white population of N. R. reaches 20,000, or what you will, so long as it's definite. After which, equally, we can get on with some plan for the immediate present. The one thing I dread is some indeterminate waffle & form of words, which leaves things as they are. Indeed I've said I'll resign if that happens."[40]

The conference, attended by all seven elected members of the Northern Rhodesian Legislative Council and thirty representatives of the several Southern Rhodesian political parties, did come to a definite conclusion. Those attending decided that amalgamation under the constitution of partially self-governing Southern Rhodesia—a complete merger—was "in the best interests of all the inhabitants of both colonies."[41] Such a southern takeover of the north would bring the northerners within the self-governing orbit of the south and would, the delegates declared, permit Britain to give dominion status to the new, larger, entity. The Southern Rhodesian Labour Party had in fact made its support for amalgamation contingent upon a resolution in favor of "complete self-government" for the new entity. It was this proviso, wrote Gore-Browne, who had spoken persuasively against it at the meeting, which "enabled the Home Government to turn down the resolution out of hand. . . ."[42] The delegates also foresaw a legislative assembly composed partly of elected and partly of nominated members, three of whom would represent the interests of Africans. Both joining entities would maintain their separate laws until the new government of a united "Rhodesia" ruled otherwise. The capital and high court would be in Salisbury.

Even before the conclusions of the conference could have been considered seriously in London, Gore-Browne was busy at Shiwa drafting a new constitutional proposal. "I think it's important to be prepared with [an alternative] scheme," Gore-Browne said, "and I don't fancy any of my colleagues have so much as given a thought to it."[43] Nor would they, for unlike Gore-Browne, their minds were focused wholly on freeing themselves from the "yoke" of

40. Gore-Browne to Ethel Locke-King, 29 December 1935.
41. Sec/Ea/9, undated report of the conference.
42. Gore-Browne, "Legislative Council," 42; Sec/Ea/9, undated report.
43. Gore-Browne to Ethel Locke-King, 10 January 1936.

British rule. But Gore-Browne, who wanted the Colonial Office to remain in charge and was confident that it would, believed that some devolution of authority was warranted, especially if settler prerogatives could thereby be improved and African rights not be infringed upon. This first scheme for constitutional reform (many would follow through the 1940s and 1950s) was intended to accomplish these objectives even though Moore, to whom he showed it before submitting it to the governor, was unpersuaded. If amalgamation were "washed out" completely, and if the unofficials could really count on a cooperative governor then, and only then, would the Gore-Browne reforms make sense, he said.[44]

The memorandum which Gore-Browne submitted to Young in May proposed a decentralized and popular form of government, still under British control, with an unofficial majority in the Legislative Council balanced by the veto of the reigning governor. "The ideal form of government," Gore-Browne wrote, "should provide for the efficient representation of all the . . . various European interests [and] for the representation of [the] . . . in the main completely uncivilized . . . natives . . . not forgetting the fact that while the Europeans can speak for themselves, the natives are and will remain for a long time totally inarticulate as regards anything beyond purely local affairs." Therefore, and because efficiency could be equated with decentralization and because if a government is to be popular "it must give the people governed some share in the management of their own affairs," Gore-Browne proposed a whole set of new provincial arrangements. "Autocracy, however benevolent," he said, "will in time defeat its own ends."[45] Thus, Gore-Browne suggested carving up Northern Rhodesia into two "white" provinces; one, the mining province, would include Broken Hill and the Copperbelt; the other, the farming province, would include the remaining European settlements on either side of the railway line. The remainder of the country would, according to the plan, be divided into a northeastern native province and a Barotse or northwestern native province. Overall would reign the governor, his executive council consisting in addition to the chief secretary, the treasurer, the attorney general, the proposed director of native development, the director of medical services, a representative of the "white" provinces, and a representative of "native" provinces, both the last named being elected members of the Legislative Council. The unofficial members of that body would include

44. Moore to Gore-Browne, 18 February 1936. Moore wrote that his appreciation of the Gore-Browne proposal was handicapped by "ossification of the cerebrum; normal unadaptability."

45. Sec/Misc/10: Gore-Browne memorandum, May 1936, Lusaka archives.

three from the mining province, two from the farming province, one representing the whites in the northeastern province, another delegated by the mine managers, one (presumably nominated) for Africans, and another four nominated by the governor. The council would also include the five official members of the executive council.

The official reaction to Gore-Browne's proposal was mixed. An unsigned minute on the memorandum, probably contributed by Eric Dutton, then the chief secretary, was acid: "As regards the people managing their own affairs, those who argue thus invariably include in their own affairs the affairs of the natives who outnumber them by 100:1 and who, when they accepted the protection of the British Crown, had no idea that they might find themselves governed by a handful of European immigrants: not all of British nationality or stock." Moreover, Dutton thought that Gore-Browne's quadripartite division of the territory was impractical and "peculiar."[46]

Young, whom Gore-Browne felt feared the ire of the elected members, wanted to offer some concession to the settler craving for constitutional advance, especially after the colonial secretary had—as Gore-Browne had earlier presumed—definitively denied amalgamation in August. Moreover, in conveying this refusal officially to the Legislative Council, Young tactlessly, in Gore-Browne's words, said "Now that's over. Get on with your work, and be good boys, & don't waste any more time." But the elected members were "bound to do something," and Gore-Browne, after being "held up" by what he called "billowing oceans of stupidity" on the part of his fellow representatives, finally managed to persuade them not to resign without attempting to try to bring about some constitutional advance in lieu of amalgamation.

"The present position," Young telegraphed excitedly to the Colonial Office a few days after the session had opened, "is that the elected members have committed themselves through Colonel Gore-Browne to collective resignation if the constitution is not eventually altered in such a way as to give them more power."[47] Their proposals, which followed the line foreshadowed in Gore-Browne's memorandum to Young earlier in the year, and which Young endorsed ("some concession would be politic") and forwarded to London, were for giving the unofficials parity with the

46. Sec/Misc/10: Minute by Dutton (?), 18 May 1936.

47. Gore-Browne to Ethel Locke-King, 15 November 1936, 31 October 1936; Sec/Misc/10: Young to Ormsby-Gore, 14 October 1936. The official proposal from the elected members was drafted by Gore-Browne and contained in a long letter from Gore-Browne and the others to Young of 22 October 1936.

officials in the council, the governor to exercise a casting vote (an effective veto), including a new nominated member to represent Africans among the unofficials, recognizing as right and not privilege the sitting of unofficial members (preeminently Gore-Browne) on advisory boards, and consultation between the governor and the elected members between sessions of the council. Gore-Browne had also urged his colleagues to demand two seats on the Executive Council, but Moore and others were uninterested.

Except for Stephenson, the other liberal elected member of the council, his colleagues were also unimpressed with Gore-Browne's ingenious attempt to restructure Northern Rhodesia geographically and politically in order to make possible a federation of Central Africa. In a long presentation to the council in late 1936, Gore-Browne built upon two premises: most of Northern Rhodesia was peopled by "uncivilised natives" who surrounded the 10,000 whites living along the line-of-rail; whites had a responsibility to develop the territory to the benefit of everyone—"the only policy that we should really make up our minds to is the one of accepting the native as a partner: a potential partner if you will, and a junior partner for as far ahead as we can look, but I say we must accept him as a partner, with all that implies. . . ." It followed that Northern Rhodesia should be divided in four, as Gore-Browne had earlier indicated to Young. In the two white provinces the interests of settlers should prevail, in the other two, "native interests must be paramount." Gore-Browne did not want Africans to be "held back" in the white provinces, nor whites hindered in the black provinces, but each group would subordinate itself in the other's province.

As useful as these alterations might be for the Protectorate alone, they also served an ultimate purpose. Gore-Browne saw no other way of moving forward toward a federation with Nyasaland and the other Rhodesia. The mining and farming provinces (the entire line-of-rail) would be linked to Southern Rhodesia, northeastern Rhodesia—the black province—would be tied to Nyasaland, and the northwestern province would be raised in status to a kind of demi-state. The seat of the whole would be Lusaka so that its expensive new buildings could be put to some constructive use. Governmentally, the federation would be of the weak kind, with decisions of the tripartite authority having to be ratified by the Southern Rhodesian government (for application to all whites) and the Colonial Office (on behalf of Africans). Gore-Browne did not feel it possible (or practical) to ask Southern Rhodesia to part with any of her self-governing powers.

By no other means, Gore-Browne told the Council, could Central Africa be brought together harmoniously and productively. "I do submit," he said, "that this proposal should satisfy the people. It unites the white population with their brethren across the Zambezi. It concentrates all the railways, all the mines, the bulk of the farmers . . . and . . . it meets the . . . Imperial Government's objection as regards the control of the natives."[48] Stephenson applauded it as a more moderate proposition than the complete self-government of the two Rhodesias, and the major newspapers in Central and South Africa carried full accounts with banner headlines. Huggins liked it, but saw a number of practical flaws. (He still preferred a pure union of the two territories.)[49] Prime Minister Jan Christiaan Smuts of South Africa was intrigued, and spoke at length with Gore-Browne some months later in Capetown. Lord Kennet, who as Sir Hilton Young had led an investigation of closer union in 1927/28, volunteered support. Even the Broken Hill Political Association, the white heart of Gore-Browne's constituency, backed him, Welensky moving a motion of total support (admittedly more in personal terms) which carried unanimously.

The opponents were even more active. The *Bulawayo Chronicle* and the *Livingstone Mail* carried abusive letters from whites who remained wildly pro-amalgamationist. Moore, leading the other unofficials, bar Stephenson, attacked the scheme because it relegated amalgamation to an indefinite future, could cost the taxpayers more, and implied segregation. "We can't all think alike," Moore wrote privately to Gore-Browne. "I don't see why you should wish me to think as you do when you simply cannot think as I do. The dividing line is: . . . you are quite reconciled to remaining under Colonial Office control and direction indefinitely, and . . . I want the Territory identified with those who prefer local self-government. How can two such divergent points of view be reconciled?" Obviously they could not. Moore was putting their differences exactly: Gore-Browne was an imperial figure; his colleagues were settlers out for their own rewards. A later shaft (they were corresponding at least weekly during 1936 and 1937) sharpened the original distinction: "You," said Moore, "are a little inclined to let your care of and sympathy for the Natives obscure the main issue: the survival of white colonization in Central Africa. . . . We have got to . . . pursue the shortest route we can find to self-government."[50]

48. *Debates,* 27 (29 October 1936), 123–127. This address was reprinted as "The Federated States of Rhodesia," *Journal of the Royal African Society,* XXXVI (1937), 2–7.

49. Huggins to Gore-Browne, 19 November 1936; Gore-Browne to Kennet, 20 December 1936.

50. *Livingstone Mail,* 11 and 18 November 1936; Moore to Gore-Browne, 9 November 1936, 15 February 1937. Moore in *Debates* (1936), 128.

The coffee planters of Abercorn were even more aggressive. Under the Gore-Browne partition, they would be placed (like Shiwa Ngandu) in an African province. Naturally, these whites were vexed and, at a public meeting in Abercorn, several of his former friends voiced their criticisms harshly. One even attempted to move a motion of no confidence, Lorna apparently preventing that outcome by jumping up and saying that they might castigate Gore-Browne, but how could they do without him? Tempers subsided a little, although Gore-Browne, much bruised, made it clear that if Abercorn were not such a small part of his whole constituency he would certainly resign, and at once. Ultimately, after the meeting ended and Gore-Browne had exchanged numerous letters with the leaders of the Abercorn Planters and Settlers Association, it was agreed that Gore-Browne would make it known that the whites of that area were totally opposed to partition and in favor of Gore-Browne's efforts to obtain increased powers for provincial councils, representation on the Executive Council, and parity of representation on the Legislative Council. They might even consider a federal scheme which did not involve cutting them off from the whites on the line-of-rail.[51]

Partnership and federation were concepts and distinctions ahead of their appointed hour. In other, less scrupulous, hands they would be resurrected and employed against the interests of Africans. In 1937, however, Moore and most of the elected members chose to continue to concentrate on the chimera of amalgamation while Gore-Browne assiduously chased meaningful constitutional concessions. The imperial political climate was helpful. Moreover, his quest was fortuitously blessed by the unexpected intervention of an American divorcée. Gore-Browne wished he had not lived to see the day when our King "did this thing." "It is the worst thing that has happened in all my life." Even his servants were moved by their chief's distress: "So he has cast us all aside," Mulemfwe said, "for a thing that is worth nothing at all."[52] Given his background, Gore-Browne's reaction of revulsion was not unexpected.

Yet, tragedy though he may have felt it to be for Britain and the empire, King Edward VIII's defection and abdication brought unexpected consequences in its wake for Gore-Browne's conception of Northern Rhodesia. King George VI would be crowned in mid-1937. Gore-Browne, Moore, and Young would represent their Protectorate and, unexpectedly, obtain a perfect opportunity to lobby

51. Gore-Browne to Ethel Locke-King, 27 January 1937; C. R. B. Draper to Gore-Browne, 15 February 1937; Gore-Browne to C. R. B. Draper, 11 February 1937.
52. Gore-Browne to Ethel, 27 December 1936.

on behalf of its political needs. Nothing could have more suited Gore-Browne's temperament and need for change. Through friends and connections he could manage to meet the high and mighty and, if luck were with him, engage their interest in his pet programs. Whatever happened, he would be sure to establish rapport with those who guided the destiny of Northern Rhodesia from afar. And he would have time with Ethel, and for a wide range of commercial and family obligations.

Only Lorna resisted the temptations of a journey to the coronation. He very much wanted her to accompany him home, with the children, together to experience the ceremonies and fêtes he so loved and the balls and large social gatherings he so detested. But she thought it wiser for him to take the children to friends in Capetown, herself remaining at Shiwa. The estate was entering a potentially very prosperous stage. Lime oil was fetching increasing prices (nineteen shillings a pound in early 1937), although there were fears of competition from Madagascar and a possibility that his own limes were being afflicted by the fatal die-back disease, and neroli looked more promising than ever before. The estate's gross income in 1936 was a record high of £1,500. Lorna also had a number of projects with which she was intimately concerned: Shiwa was being made an official experimental agricultural station so that she would have a raison d'etre; she was involved with two University of Cambridge students in an examination of the fishing potential of Lake Shiwa and Lake Bangweulu; she was still investigating the nutritional needs of the Bemba; and she was interested in helping C. G. Trapnell, the territory's new ecologist, examine the soils of northeastern Rhodesia.

Most of all, Lorna's health always improved when she and Gore-Browne were apart. After psychological treatment in Britain, she had returned willingly, and with changed overt attitudes to Shiwa, in early 1936. Yet, soon after she had returned in good health, the "blowups", which were the main symptom of her mysterious complaint, began recurring. She was abed as often as she was up, the attacks coming whether or not she were tired, and seemingly independent of any obvious repetitive psychological variable. Although Lorna often criticized Shiwa Ngandu—in Gore-Browne's mind an instructive oasis of high class civilization in the midst of a receptive rural universe—labelling it a destructive and illegitimate intrusion into the indigenous way of life, she and her husband quarrelled less than they remained affectionate without the same intensity of warmth as before her illness. Gore-Browne knew the causes were psychosomatic, yet neither he nor she could fathom them, and so they remained baffled, and gradually learned to live comparatively separate lives. Lorna enjoyed travelling and working on her own, or with other, younger, companions, and for the most part found her physical complications lessened by absences—which grew more frequent as time went on—from Shiwa. During one desperate period Gore-Browne tried analyzing the problem. "It all hinges," he felt, "on a need to contradict me in everything . . . in spite of the fact that she now says she is fond of me for the first time in her life." For himself he counselled patience, yet it didn't "make it easier to run the place when one feels all one does is disapproved of by one's partner." And, he wrote at a particularly low point, "the years are slipping away, and they should be such happy ones. . . ."[53]

Shiwa endured despite their own vicissitudes and the increasing press of Gore-Browne's political commitments. Until 1940 there was substantially little change in the pace of life there. The production of lime and neroli oil expanded steadily under Savill's oversight until the onset of war, despite disease in some of the older trees, the price for lime remaining high until it fell to eleven shillings a pound in mid-1939. During this same period there was a welcome sudden demand by Yardley and other large perfume houses for oil of *Eucalyptus citriodora,* the hope of the 1920s, but interest faded as unexpectedly as it had come. Gore-Browne tried fumigating his oranges to eliminate scale disease, and built a new irrigation flume to provide year-round water to all of the trees. In some of his rare periods away from politics he also turned to his favorite occupation—construction. In 1938 he built a two-arch bridge and supervised the addition of an imposing tower onto the main Shiwa block. "I like designing and building better than anything," he reminded Ethel, "and when I'm at it . . . I feel I'm actually constructing & creating, however humbly. . . . I can't get over the wonder that a quite useless anthill should turn, by the agency of several hundred men working together intelligently into bricks, which other men put together, so that something springs up which a few weeks ago was only a thought."[54] At long last Gore-Browne also managed to realize an earlier dream of an African primary boarding school on the estate when, with government and missionary cooperation, the Timba school was opened late in 1938.

Gore-Browne continued to cling to the grand romantic vision of his seigneurial role. In 1937 he saw the film version of James Hilton's *Lost Horizon,* "about a wonderful colony of ageless people . . . living in peace and perfection completely cut off from the world, a sort of super Shiwa."[55] Unhappily, Shiwa had almost from the start been in a self-propelled mainstream. The guests—

53. Gore-Browne to Ethel Locke-King, 23 August 1936, 5 August 1936.
54. Gore-Browne to Ethel Locke-King, 5 November 1938.
55. Gore-Browne to Lorna, 9 May 1937.

governors, other dignitaries, wandering missionaries, and the like—arrived in increasing number to sample the cuisine, culture, and boundless hospitality of Shiwa Ngandu. Some, like Eileen Bigland, the British publisher's editor, came to view the curiosity of Gore-Browne's wilderness creation and to write books. Hers (*The Lake of the Royal Crocodiles* [London 1939]) particularly offended Gore-Browne. They had liked her and looked after her royally, and had given her critical introductions to close friends in the Northern Province and on the Copperbelt. Yet she had—ungraciously they thought—produced a gently mocking, chatty book which Gore-Browne felt "vulgarized" Shiwa and unfairly—if by indirection—satirized African and white friends and retainers. Nevertheless, it still contains the very best period descriptions of the physical scenery of the estate, and of the awesome impact of Shiwa on a "sophisticated" traveller who had already crossed the Soviet Union and traversed much of Europe.

There was one other major disillusionment in the private life of Shiwa. Unlike most settlers in the Rhodesias, the Gore-Brownes trusted their servants and had long assumed that their trust was reasonably reciprocated. There had been instances of peculation and other lapses, but given the size and complexity of the household and the estate, those instances were rare. In late 1937, however, Lorna uncovered a major and widespread conspiracy among the servants of the household. They had managed to obtain duplicate keys to the liquor cellar, which was protected by two separately locked doors, and, for months, had been tippling behind closed doors late at night, and sometimes during the day, and had even begun selling bottles of spirits to villagers on the estate. Drink worth several hundred pounds sterling had disappeared by the time an African detective summoned from Lusaka quietly obtained evidence of the extent of the alcoholic ring. With a very heavy heart Gore-Browne agreed to prosecute and, after a trial in Chinsali, some of Shiwa's longest serving retainers were sentenced to substantial terms in prison.

Off the estate, Gore-Browne was trying much and triumphing often. For him the late 1930s saw many political accomplishments, none more personally satisfying than those ensured by traipsing the corridors of power and influence during 1937. Together with Moore, Huggins, and Young, but more successfully than they, Gore-Browne urged the cause of white constitutional advance with W. G. A. Ormsby-Gore (later Lord Harlech), the colonial secretary, and Malcolm MacDonald, the dominions secretary. Margery Perham greeted him in Oxford with, "So you're plotting against the natives of N. Rhodesia. . . ," but his own reported response was fair: "I'm one of those poor asses," he told her, "who see both sides of a question and so I'm suspect in Rhodesia as a negrophil and

in England as a settler."[56] Moreover, Gore-Browne was still confident that local whites, guided gently by the Colonial Office from
afar, could administer an African colony without damaging the in-
alienable rights of the indigenous inhabitants. He did not then fully
share the fears of someone like Perham, the Oxford don who had
known settlers in Kenya, or Lucy Mair, of the London School of
Economics, whom Gore-Browne called a "pure negrophil." And
he believed in Huggins' intentions. He was autocratic by temperament, and much less roughly cast than most of the other Central
African politicians with whom Gore-Browne was customarily in
contact. Huggins was "entirely intimate & indiscreet. . . . I do like
the fellow."[57] Gore-Browne also found Moore much more pliable
in England than in Northern Rhodesia, perhaps because personally
he was overwhelmed by the proceedings. Gore-Browne managed
to persuade him to think of schemes other than amalgamation to
present to the authorities during their scheduled group interviews.

Most important of all, he was able to arrange a long private talk
with Ormsby-Gore. They were of the same class, and Gore-
Browne's charm enabled them immediately to confide in one
another. Ormsby-Gore told Gore-Browne in confidence that the
principle of the Rhodesias and Nyasaland forming a single unit as a
counterpoise to the "alien" Union of South Africa had been accepted, but that any arrangement which smacked of immediate
amalgamation or even federation was premature because to do so
would subordinate Northern to Southern Rhodesia. "Local self
government both for blacks and whites is the line Ormsby-Gore
warmly endorsed (It struck me it wd. be up to me to try and make
this a reality and it won't be easy). And he said he agreed with me
about Partnership being the ideal rather than trusteeship. He doesn't
want natives to have Western political ideas forced upon them, and
deprecates anything like a . . . common franchise." Three times he
said "Well you & I are going to agree about everything." "One
knows," Gore-Browne told his wife, "when one clicks."[58] (Elspeth
Huxley, back from Kenya and, with her husband, a frequent lun-
cheon companion, thought that Ormsby-Gore was ineffectual and
would do nothing.)

Later, at the first of several formal conferences at the Colonial
Office with Ormsby-Gore, Young, and Moore, Gore-Browne followed a long, emotional tirade by Moore (demanding constitutional reform if amalgamation were refused) with his own plea for

56. Gore-Browne to Lorna, 9 May 1937.
57. Gore-Browne to Lorna, 17 May 1937.
58. Gore-Browne to Lorna, 15 April 1937. Gore-Browne also told Ormsby-
Gore about the fracas in Abercorn, "and he roared with laughter."

local self-government because settlers and unofficials were discontented and Africans were losing faith in whites. ("Hubert," said Gore-Browne, "also gave tongue, like a sucking dove.") Moore (on Gore-Browne's urging) put forth requests for unofficial representation on the Northern Rhodesian Executive Council, Legislative Council parity, provincial councils with real powers, and the restriction of the governor's veto (this was a new point) to "reserved" subjects only. The outcome was appropriately bureaucratic: Ormsby-Gore promised to respond in due course.

The next week Gore-Browne was summoned to another, more crucial, conference, this time as the sole settler representative (Moore had returned home) of Northern Rhodesia. Ormsby-Gore was joined by MacDonald, and Young by Harold Kittermaster, governor of Nyasaland, and Huggins, in addition to a flock of Dominions and Colonial Office staff. MacDonald startled Huggins and Gore-Browne by reporting that the Cabinet had a few days before decided that the 1931 prohibition against the amalgamation of the Rhodesias no longer applied. Huggins welcomed this fresh initiative, saying that it might help prevent the Union from swallowing up Southern Rhodesia and that if the territories failed to unite soon they would never do so. He also reported that South African racial policy was personally repugnant and that Southern Rhodesians were becoming much more liberal in their own racial views. "Very skillfully," reported Gore-Browne, he "indicated that if closer union was refused the party in S. Rhodesia who wanted to join S. Africa wd. be immensely strengthened and before very long would get their way." Speaking for himself, Gore-Browne told the meeting that the uniting of technical services like posts, customs, research, and defence, was obvious. "I was however doubtful of complete amalgamation till we had got a clearer native policy outlined. I thought that Black & White relationship was the most vital & most baffling problem of the day, & one the solution of which one wd. gladly make one's life work if one could. My own scheme was to amalgamate the white areas, & keep the others out. . . ." After everyone spoke several more times, MacDonald summed up, saying that His Majesty's Government were committed to nothing and that he, personally, was still skeptical about the benevolent drift of Southern Rhodesian African policy. Possibly a commission would be sent out from London to study and recommend a permanent solution. MacDonald later informed Gore-Browne that he was about to tell Huggins that neither amalgamation nor federation were possible, only an inquiry.[59]

Had anything been achieved? For weeks it appeared that neither

59. Gore-Browne to Lorna, 21 and 31 May 1937, 7 July 1937.

Ormsby-Gore nor MacDonald would or could yield, and Gore-Browne visited his family's Scottish haunts with Ethel, saw all his living relatives, lectured on "Native Education" to the University of London Institute of Education, on colonial administration at Oxford, and on the future of the Rhodesias to the Royal Institute of International Affairs. He held earnest discussions with Lord Hailey, Perham, Francis Scott, Margaret Read, Dougald Malcolm, Reginald Coupland, E. S. Joelson, Sir Robert Williams and others concerned with the future of Africa. He talked to editors and academics, lunched with civil servants on leave, and everywhere enjoyed a rich diet of prominence until, forsaking a visit to Leningrad and Moscow with Ethel, he took the new flying boat back to Shiwa via Marseilles, Khartoum, and Entebbe (he had never seen such a beautiful, well-organized, and prosperous African state as Uganda).[60]

Gore-Browne remained convinced that Britain would simply allow the "whole thing . . . to slide" and Southern Rhodesia would therefore be forced into an unhappy union with South Africa. "I think a chance is being missed of having a go at a good constructive attempt to design a Black and White Federated State that will work."[61] Huggins, in private letters to Gore-Browne, was equally gloomy. This view was finally confirmed in October, when Young and his entourage descended upon Shiwa for the kind of sumptuous houseparty for which the Gore-Brownes had become justly famous. There Gore-Browne learned that Ormsby-Gore had quietly sanctioned the internal reforms which the elected members had demanded late the previous year. Of particular relevance to Gore-Browne, the colonial secretary had agreed to permit the governor to appoint one unofficial to represent the interests of Africans.

This aspect of their instructions Gore-Browne discussed at length with his fellow elected members during the November session of the Legislative Council. Moore was opposed to asking the governor to appoint Gore-Browne to the position, for which he was ideally suited, on tactical grounds. Doing so would mean the election by Broken Hill of a member of the Labour Party. The others favored the idea because he was the obvious person and the alternative (on Nyasa lines) would be a missionary who would more than likely "be useless" on any but African matters. (Coincidentally, from Capetown where he was vacationing, Welensky wrote to Gore-Browne asking to be permitted to sponsor Gore-Browne for reelection. It meant that he'd probably be returned unopposed.) In reality the discussion was of little account. Gore-Browne's distaste for political maneuvering, his experiences in Abercorn, and a deep-

60. He lunched with Evelyn Waugh, a "rumbird."
61. Gore-Browne to Ethel Locke-King, 11 September 1937.

seated disinclination to campaign once again, made it clear, even if the honor of representing "native interests" were not what he had always wanted, that he would accept the nomination if it were offered. "I do genuinely feel that the one thing I've a 'call' to is to take a hand in the settlement of black & white problems, and that I've no business to reject this opportunity which may never recur."[62] A further consideration was that by not taking such an appointment he would deliberately forfeit the many prerogatives he had been accorded since 1935 as the one unofficial member who had a right to be consulted on matters affecting Africans. Young agreed, and promised to appoint him when the time came. The next question was whether or not he should immediately resign, but the Broken Hill Political Association and the governor were both content that he should remain an elected member until after the next general election (set for mid-1938), giving Gore-Browne ample time to persuade and then groom Welensky as his successor.

As Gore-Browne had feared, the British government burked the big question. Instead of deciding against Huggins and Moore, and thus antagonizing the colonial whites, Ormsby-Gore and MacDonald appointed a royal commission with a mandate sufficiently circumscribed to discourage the rapid amalgamationists. "The terms of reference," Huggins growled, "were so worded that no report on amalgamation could be made."[63] Chaired by Viscount Bledisloe, a former governor-general of New Zealand, the commission was asked to discover "whether any . . . closer co-operation or association between Southern Rhodesia, Northern Rhodesia and Nyasaland is desirable and feasible, with due regard to the interests of all the inhabitants, irrespective of race . . . and to the special responsibility of Our Government . . . for the interests of the Native inhabitants."[64] It spent three months in Central Africa interviewing whites, who asked for that racial security which only amalgamation could ensure, and Africans, who unanimously condemned Southern Rhodesian racial attitudes and policies. Gore-Browne tried to persuade the elected members to give evidence in concert, but only Stephenson supported his initiative, the others persisting in "amalgamation or else." The commissioners, said Moore, were "a body of yesmen and will report in the sense that the Government wishes them to . . . I am satisfied that their report will favour procrastination, delay and a little compromise—it could hardly be otherwise. . . . It seems to me that the Commission, especially the noble Chairman, have been toadied out of all sense of

62. Gore-Browne to Ethel Locke-King, 20 November 1937.
63. Huggins to Gore-Browne, 30 August 1937.
64. *Rhodesia-Nyasaland Royal Commission Report*, Cmd. 5949 (1939), 4.

proportion."[65] Nevertheless, both the Broken Hill and the Abercorn political groups asked Gore-Browne to speak for them, so when the commission came in all of its multitudinous splendor to Shiwa (Gore-Browne had everything orchestrated neatly, with many chiefs waiting, numerous women singing, dozens of men dancing, and so on, a total of 500 retainers regaling commissioners after their airplanes had landed near the lake) he could offer it his own personal views as well as those of his rather differently-minded constituents.

The European population of Broken Hill and Abercorn, he told the commission, wanted immediate amalgamation with Southern Rhodesia under its existing, quasi-self-governing constitution. Such an amalgamation would "give the European population the right to share in the choice of government under which it would live. . . . Together [both Rhodesias] would form a powerful economic unit . . . [and it] . . . should result in increased administrative efficiency." If Amalgamation were not possible, the Broken Hill constituents favored partition, with the line of rail being annexed to Southern Rhodesia. If both of the above schemes were deemed impracticable, the settlers wanted the amalgamation for all three countries of technical services—posts, defence, European education, prisons, police, agriculture, etc. They suggested a federal advisory council chaired by the governor of Southern Rhodesia and the upgrading of the provincial councils of Northern Rhodesia. Most controversial was a final proposal—even more clearly than the other influenced by Gore-Browne—that a Native Development Board be appointed for the three countries, and "native policy . . . be brought into line as far as possible."[66]

For himself, Gore-Browne could not "conscientiously support a policy which would put one and a half million natives under a popularly elected Rhodesian Parliament." In Southern Rhodesia "the accepted policy is to keep the native down, and it is difficult to imagine any circumstances arising which are likely to modify this policy and to bring it into line with our more enlightened one. . . . I certainly do not feel" Gore-Browne continued in words that could equally well have served him in 1950 and 1951, "that any Imperial Veto would accomplish this once control had been surrendered." For these reasons—because he recognized how anxious the white settlers had become and because he despaired of satisfying either blacks or whites with the status quo—Gore-Browne advanced his pet alternative (together with carefully printed maps) of partition. He admitted that to do so would apply Southern Rhodesian antagonism toward Africans living on the line-of-rail, but that objec-

65. Moore to Gore-Browne, 4 and 5 August 1938.
66. Memorandum by Gore-Browne, 4 June 1938.

tion was for him outweighed by the advantage of creating two African states "where natives will be free to live their own lives in their own way, under their own institutions. Material prosperity is not everything, and I would be prepared to risk a slower rate of progress [said the paternalist] in return for greater individual freedom."

If the commission should deprecate his scheme, then he would fall back on a division of Northern Rhodesia into four large provinces, two African and two white, with deficit-ridden Nyasaland possibly being combined with one of the African provinces. Or the whole could be tied into some federal arrangement (Lorna always accused him of not thinking through his plans to the final contingency) similar to that advanced by him on behalf of the white settlers. With regard to Northern Rhodesia alone, one of the commissioners having privately told him that partition and federation were unacceptable, Gore-Browne boldly elaborated his newest reform—a Legislative Council which would have a bare unofficial majority (nine to eight) presided over by an appointed chairman or speaker (not the governor) and a small Executive Council including three civil servants and two unofficials.[67]

Gore-Browne testified before the Commission in his own library the day after a formidable dinner for thirty-four (planned and supervised by a radiant Lorna) in the old Shiwa style. He was cross-examined for two hours and couldn't "complain that [he] hadn't a full, patient, exhaustive, and exhausting hearing." The climax of the commission's visit, however, was a dance (to a concertina and a drum played with "that feeling & rhythm . . . only Africans can quite manage") in the big hall of the mansion, with servants and "sophisticated natives" joining in as well as the commissioners, their servants, their pilots, and so on. "The whole thing [was] as seemly, and as natural, & as fine an object lesson of how black people & white people can live reasonably side by side, as anyone could well wish to see. . . . I do think it was a good show."[68]

No show could have been better. But as personally pleased with Gore-Browne (Bledisloe had been a lineal successor to his grandfather in New Zealand, and esteemed the memory) and as impressed with his sincerity as the commissioners must have been, they had heard damning complaints from Africans and had seen for themselves the quality of most of the Central African whites. (Huggins had viewed the Gore-Browne proposals skeptically, too. "The strongest point in favour of your scheme in its entirety", he wrote privately, " is the probability that it would prove unworkable, and

67. Gore-Browne to Bledisloe, 4 August 1938.
68. Gore-Browne to Ethel Locke-King, 15 August 1938.

then no alternative to amalgamation would remain open."[69] He saw more practical difficulties in the actual implementation of the Gore-Browne ideas than there would be with amalgamation.) The commission's final report was labored and, consciously, an inconclusive compromise. The Central African territories, the commissioners suggested, would probably "become more closely interdependent in all their activities." Their identity of interest would sooner or later lead them into political unity. Nevertheless, they reported that Africans in the protectorate overwhelmingly opposed any withdrawal of the crown's customary oversight, and that their fears were well founded upon an appreciation of the restrictive racial policies of the south. The color bar was an insurmountable obstacle to immediate or medium-term unity. Therefore, the commission could recommend amalgamation between Nyasaland and Northern Rhodesia (a modification of the Gore-Browne scheme) only, and the establishment of some kind of inter-territorial council to coordinate governmental services without any executive authority (something close to one of Gore-Browne's concerns).

Huggins said that he had asked for a loaf, and had been given a "crumb."[70] Gore-Browne was even more depressed. The commission had "funked" the issue by declaring amalgamation good in principle but impossible because of Southern Rhodesian attitudes toward Africans. "No number of councils, and no number of years spent in discussion or investigation will ever make the white settler in either S. Rhodesia or the Union abandon his privileged position. . . . all that part of the report seems to me just the expression of pious hopes, and not worth the paper it's written on."[71]

The commission had, however, endorsed Gore-Browne's scheme for an unofficial majority on the Legislative Council and unofficials in the Executive Council. So Gore-Browne had, in fact, won a major endorsement of his long-standing proposals of constitutional reform. Moore, however, had resigned in a huff to express his disapproval of the report, thus opening up a whole range of interesting political possibilities even though he was bound to be reelected to the council in the ensuing by-election. Moore, whom Gore-Browne had found increasingly garrulous and irascible in his later years, had already succeeded in alienating his fellow elected members and Gore-Browne, technically—though now a nominee —became the senior unofficial.

To make his position clearer, if much more annoying to Moore, Gore-Browne, still a reluctant politician, in 1939 was elected leader

69. Huggins to Gore-Browne, 6 January 1938.
70. Cmd. 5949, 214, 252. *Bulawayo Chronicle,* 25 November 1948.
71. Gore-Browne to Ethel Locke-King, 25 March 1939.

of the white representatives in the council, with the faithful Welensky his prime follower. Moore, outraged and impotent, used his newspaper to mount a full-scale, sneering attack on Gore-Browne and the other elected members, what a rueful Gore-Browne called a "violent storm in a tiny tea-cup, but . . . it damages any influence the unofficials may have. . . . and it doesn't do . . . [the] nasty old man . . . any good."[72]

As the shadows of war lengthened perceptibly in Europe, Gore-Browne climbed unexpectedly to the height of local political power. The Bledisloe Commission had endorsed some of his most significant reforms, he and Welensky had replaced Moore, and, in place of Young, there was Sir John Alexander Maybin, a quiet, co-operative governor with whom Gore-Browne had close rapport. Ormsby-Gore, when appointing Maybin governor, commended him as a Scot who had a good record in Nigeria, where he had been the chief secretary after coming from Ceylon. "Incidentally he is a very keen sportsman and has spent most of his leave trying to catch salmon in Scotland, and I cannot imagine a man who would fit into your requirements better." Gore-Browne was content with this kind of assessment. "I don't picture him setting the Thames on fire, but should anyone else chance to do so I feel confident he'd prevent the conflagration spreading to the city of London."[73] Together they could advance sensible policies in Northern Rhodesia and prepare wisely for the war which must soon come and conceivably involve them (the threat of a German reconquest of Tanganyika was still present).

Gore-Browne thought that he would try to wear the mantle of his Uncle Wilfred, the Bishop of Kimberley and Kuruman, and "be the fellow who speaks for natives but is trusted by white people too." He had ideas and energy and, as he had exclaimed the year before when turning 55, "just when many people are thinking of retiring . . . I've a new life of fresh opportunities in every direction. . . . It's too good to be true."[74] On the very brink of war he flew home to collect little Lorna, deposited by her mother in school there the year before, and, after meetings with MacDonald, Bledisloe, and Huggins to discuss the eventual implications of the royal commission's recommendations, Gore-Browne sailed home a few days after the German invasion of Belgium and France. He sailed home to lead the legislature, to sit on the Executive Council, and, in short, to help run Northern Rhodesia. His old dream of being a Lugard-like proconsul had, in fact, come true.

72. Gore-Browne to Ethel Locke-King, 4 July 1939.
73. Ormsby-Gore to Gore-Browne, 1 June 1938; Gore-Browne to Ethel, 4 July 1939.
74. Gore-Browne to Ethel Locke-King, 24 May 1939, 28 March 1938.

VII
Realizing the Dreams
of Boyhood

THE WAR, and contingent circumstances—not least his good relations with the governors of Northern Rhodesia—provided ample opportunity for Gore-Browne to lead his adopted country in time of crisis. The government consulted him on all important issues and implemented no legislation affecting Africans without his approval. With Welensky's assistance, he dominated the proceedings of the Legislative Council and pushed vigorously (and achieved) notable social reforms as well as advances in the constitutional prerogatives of the elected members. For the governors he was a troubleshooter and confidant. Indeed, before long the laird of remote Shiwa found himself spending virtually all of his days, bar a few short, hurriedly snatched holidays, in hated Lusaka. He built a house there and, for much of the duration of the war, left the estate and the now suddenly prospering business of essential oils in the hands of managers. Although Gore-Browne turned sixty in mid-conflict, the guns of war once again propelled him to a peak of power and prominence. It was the period of his prime.

Gore-Browne's closeness to Governor Maybin permitted him a range of activity and policy involvement unprecedented for a settler, even a legislator, in British colonial Africa. As leader of the unofficials in the Legislative Council, and, from late 1939, a de facto member of the Executive Council, he would naturally have needed to work closely with any governor, especially in war time. But Gore-Browne's relationships with Maybin transcended the requirements of ordinary business. Maybin was a confirmed bachelor ("no amount of putting wedding cake under his pillow ever shewed him his future wife," Gore-Browne said, repeating Maybin's own aphorism), which made it easy and natural for Gore-Browne to "put up" (Lorna and Stewart were together during the war only very infrequently) at Government House whenever official needs required his presence in Lusaka.

210

Young had only occasionally confided in Gore-Browne and sought his assistance. With Maybin, however, there sprung up a feisty mutual respect. Only two months after the outbreak of war Gore-Browne was already feeling comfortable in and around Government House. "I think Maybin does truly like my presence," he wrote. "We spend many hours walking up and down together, and discussing pretty well everything that turns up—and sometimes we break off into History or Literature (never art or music or travel)." A few months later, after the legislature had sat and they had together endured a number of sessions of the Executive Council, Gore-Browne felt even more comfortable with Maybin. "He seems to rely on me a lot," Gore-Browne confessed, "& I have the position I've always wanted of trusted confidant. . . . When work allows the Governor and I go for long walks in the evening, and discuss every subject under the sun."[1] On two early occasions the governor felt duty bound to offer Gore-Browne substantive positions, first in the Information Department and subsequently as a commandant of African battalions, but, when pressed, the governor declared that he would much prefer Gore-Browne to serve his country by remaining in Lusaka and at Government House.

Maybin could rely upon Gore-Browne's energy, discretion, and good sense. Although the leader of the unofficials should have been a natural adversary, Maybin trusted Gore-Browne. They were intellectually and temperamentally compatible, humane, and gently pro-African in instinct and action. Opposite in stated roles, they shared goals and believed in the same methods of attaining those goals. The governing of Northern Rhodesia in a time of war, when copper and soldiers were urgently needed in order to support the Allied effort, proved a surer, easier task because of their easy cooperation. Each could count on the other's understanding of difficult decisions or positions. Most of all Maybin knew that Gore-Browne would, if asked, assume any responsibility and discharge it appropriately, and with imagination.

By mid-1940 Gore-Browne had resigned himself to "whole time work with the Governor"[2]—to infrequent oversight of Shiwa, to no more than glimpses of his more and more remote wife, who at first remained at Shiwa, and his daughters at school in Johannesburg, and to almost constant travelling around the country on official business. In addition to the Legislative and Executive Council rôles, Maybin appointed Gore-Browne commissioner for civil defence and member of a small manpower committee. The committee was responsible until mid-1941 for what Gore-Browne called the

1. Gore-Browne to Ethel Locke-King, 2 November 1939; 28 January 1940.
2. Gore-Browne to Ethel Locke-King, 12 July 1940.

"queer business" of forbidding Northern Rhodesian whites from enlisting in the armed forces. By legislative action, it could conscript men and property, and enforce mobilization for the home front. The efforts of most male whites were deemed more valuable mining copper, zinc, or lead for the Allied cause, or driving the locomotives which hauled coal from Southern Rhodesia to fuel the mine smelters, than fighting. During much of 1940 Gore-Browne therefore found himself interviewing men on the Copperbelt or in Broken Hill or Livingstone who wanted to fight, but whose requests he almost uniformly was forced to deny. Since he himself had also hoped to join up, possibly with the East African command in Nairobi, but had specifically been forbidden by Maybin to do so, Gore-Browne could empathize with the fervor of other keen whites while being unable to sanction their mobility.

Gore-Browne had no great liking for the predominantly South African white population of the Copperbelt. He found the men difficult. Their attitude for the most part was epitomized by "Tell me what to do and I'll do it, only remember I won't do anything I don't want to—and I won't take orders from anyone." It was this kind of unreasonableness during war time which tried Gore-Browne's rather short patience but, as he remarked accurately, "The Lord gave me the gift of being fairly good at getting on with people . . . and at times like this it comes in useful."[3]

The tasks of civil defence commissioner were, in retrospect, less real, but at the beginning of the war the old fear of a German attack on eastern and central Africa remained, together with the vision of an Italian sweep southwards from Somalia. During 1940 Gore-Browne therefore bustled around the country designating air raid shelters, appointing local preparation and disaster committees, and publicizing the potential dangers. There was the safety of miners to consider, plans to prepare for the government offices in Lusaka, and innumerable visits to outlying and conceivably vulnerable schools and mission stations. On one journey southwards along the railway line towards Livingstone, Gore-Browne dealt drolly with the security of the Choma Girls' School. "With the help of a sensible school-mistress we chose an inner corridor where they'd be quite reasonably secure in the 1,000,000 to 1 event of bombs being dropped."[4]

Gore-Browne carried out his jobs earnestly, usually managing to combine the necessary peregrinations of a civil defence commissioner with manpower investigations and interviews, sittings of the

3. Gore-Browne to Ethel Locke-King, 23 August 1940. Gore-Browne particularly disliked adjudicating the rights of conscientious objectors.
4. Gore-Browne to Ethel Locke-King, 3 November 1940.

Native Labour Board, and his meetings with urban Africans as their representative. By early 1941, however it had become clear that Africa would not be threatened by the Germans, or the Italians, contained as they had been in Somalia (largely by African troops), and Gore-Browne could thus consider that responsibility discharged. He urged the Legislative Council to relax anti-air raid precautions and, although remaining commissioner for some months longer, turned to other tasks.

The manpower committee had also completed its interviews, miners and engine drivers having settled down and copper production having increased, so Gore-Browne, proud of having helped to "stave off a nasty situation," persuaded Maybin that it was time to dissolve the committee and release him, personally, for more strictly administrative activities. The governor thus appointed a director of manpower and gave the job, which Gore-Browne insisted should now be largely propagandistic, to Welensky. "We must get it across to all these people who are held back from the war," Gore-Browne told Welensky, ". . . that they are not sheltering, and that they are doing their duty just as much [here Gore-Browne tried to persuade himself as much as others] as if they were in the army."[5]

Gore-Browne had simultaneously discharged one difficult and one routine, but at first sensitive, responsibility to widespread satisfaction. Of greater significance to Maybin and Northern Rhodesia, he had contributed intelligently in the Executive Council; in its committee on estimates, the budget priority setting body; in its discussions on drafting price control and manpower regulations; in its examination of official policy toward such diverse and contentious subjects as African land tenure and African education; and had helped to steady the otherwise bitterly divided Legislative Council. Naturally, harboring as he did a deep-rooted distrust of pure democracy, especially in war time, he felt more at home in the Executive Council, where his speeches were made in private and could reflect personal decisions uncontaminated by the opinion of constituents or other political determinants. The government, for its part, had no need to conceal motives or otherwise play the cat-and-mouse game to which it resorted in the legislative chamber. "I find myself ever so much happier in that [Executive Council] atmosphere than in the other," Gore-Browne told his aunt. (Gore-Browne contrasted his own pleasure with that of Moore, "the old beast", who preferred being destructive in the Legislative Council.

5. Gore-Browne, in *Debates*, 40 (7 July 1941), 12. The appointment of Welensky was in fact made by W. M. Logan, the acting governor and sometime chief secretary.

For him taking responsibility was "quite foreign", despite much bombast. He was "little or no use," being unwilling to read briefs.[6])

Gore-Browne had been elected chairman of the unofficial members of the Legislative Council in 1939 (for the duration of the session which lasted until 1941) despite the vitriolic opposition of Moore and Captain A. A. Smith, the member for Nkana (Kitwe). With Welensky as an effective and devoted ally, he sought to guide the council along a path of constructive criticism tempered by the realities of wartime but alert (more so than civil servants) to the kinds of changes which could enhance Northern Rhodesian life afterwards. There were times when he despaired of guiding such a motley crew—the cantankerous and "gaga" Moore, an "utter swine"; Smith, representing the bigots of the Copperbelt; T. S. Page, a narrow-minded farmer from Fort Jameson who was tiresome ("with him it's mainly vanity coupled with obstinacy"); and Major H. K. McKee, from the Midlands Constituency, who always had to "think how any proposal affects himself and his prospects."

Gore-Browne often felt the impotence and futility of his increasingly uncongenial role. He wearied of it all, especially of parliamentary arrangements which combined the evils of democracy with bureaucracy. He was already questioning, too, how effective such arrangements could be if the elected representatives spoke only for a tiny white population and, except for himself, the voice of the black majority continued unheard. As legislators, Gore-Browne said, "we waste an infinity of time and we accomplish very little good."[7] In his exasperation he often contemplated resignation, but Welensky's firm support and Maybin's needs, as well as his own knowledge that the legislature would be more of a trial if he abandoned the chairmanship, always mattered more than the exasperation of the sessions. In 1941, too, a new legislature was due to be elected, and Gore-Browne felt that he ought to hang on in the hope that its composition would improve.

The major policy differences between the elected members (including Welensky) and Gore-Browne reflected their divergent perspectives on Africans, race relations, and the color bar. To his colleagues' discomfort, Gore-Browne more and more defended African interests in the chamber and used his leadership position in order to promote their point of view. In these endeavors he could always count on Maybin's support and appreciation. Likewise, neither Maybin nor his subordinates could afford to contemplate legislation or administrative actions affecting Africans without in-

6. Gore-Browne to Ethel Locke-King, 2 November 1939, 25 February 1940.

7. Gore-Browne to Ethel Locke-King, 15 September 1940; to Lorna, 16 March 1941; to Ethel Locke-King, 23 March 1941.

volving Gore-Browne from the inception of their thinking and planning. Furthermore, he was always informed immediately of potential crises affecting Africans, particularly after his dramatic intervention on the Copperbelt in 1940.

With wartime requirements, the economics of copper production had turned sharply in Northern Rhodesia's favor. Its mines could now extract and export the precious metal to London for about £27 a ton. There each ton fetched about £43. Since 1929 the total revenues of the Protectorate, 70 percent of which were directly attributable to copper, had increased fourfold.

Although white workers had shared significantly in the prosperity of times, African wages had remained at their 1935 levels. Africans, although they drove trucks, blasted, or shovelled—the hard, dirty jobs on which copper production depended—earned less in a month or two than whites, who exerted themselves comparatively little, earned in a day. No matter how adept, they could never hope to advance upwards in work classification to occupy positions held by whites. Although they labored overtime and on Sunday, Africans only received straight time while whites earned time-and-a-half pay. Everywhere Africans met discrimination. Whites abused them verbally and physically. One worker, for example, complained that a white "boss" had "called him a monkey and had further stated that all natives were monkeys and had to have their tails removed at the hospital on recruitment and that the native police were only fit to superintend the removal of excrement from European houses."[8] In large, African miners knew themselves to be underpaid, poorly housed and fed, generally exploited, and in every respect underprivileged compared to the whites under whom they worked.

The white miners precipitated confrontation with Africans by striking themselves. Displeased with their rates of pay and conditions of service, they left the Mufulira and Nkana (and Mindolo) mines (but not Roan and Nchanga) in late March 1940. Production ceased for ten days, after which the government abruptly intervened and persuaded the copper companies to boost the average wages of the white employees by about five percent. They also granted a number of other concessions, including one that increased overtime earnings and another which gave the white union a closed shop.

The existence of widespread African tensions (they were not permitted unions) had become apparent even before the successful

8. Sec/Lab/58: Quoted in H. F. Cartmel-Robinson to the Chief Secretary, 19 November 1940, Lusaka archives. Much of the discussion of the background to the strike of 1940 follows that in Rotberg, *Nationalism*, 168–176.

conclusion of the white strike. At Nchanga, a few days after the whites walked out at Mufulira, the wife of an African miner argued violently with an African *capitão* responsible for issuing rations from the company's grain store (the copper firms still fed their black employees). The *capitão* assaulted the woman and, in order to put her more firmly in "her place," the white assistant compound manager handcuffed and flogged the woman and her husband in public for "causing a disturbance." This was not an unusual workaday experience for blacks in colonial Rhodesia, but, for once, Africans vented their anger publicly. "Which cause us to be angry is this," several later reported. "We came here to work from home with our wives . . . Now we saw that the . . . capitao was beating a woman and took her to the compound manager's office, the capitao then made a statement to the European who listened to him, but the woman was never asked to make a statement, but she was merely being beaten without her statement [and] she was handcuffed. The husband came and was instantly handcuffed, then the compound manager . . . started beating them with a sjambok without reasons. . . . Seeing this, we were very, very angry. We said these people despise us and also our wives, then see these Europeans the meal they give us . . . does not fill our stomach, yet they make us suffer for it."[9]

The African employees at Nchanga went on strike, demanding that the management alter its method of distributing rations. They also urged the local district commissioner to set an example by publicly flogging a white man and wife. "Now before we go to work, a European must handcuff his wife and be beaten, both the European lady and her husband together. If you refuse to do this, then do to us things you like. We have finished. We are all Africans."[10] The strikers stayed out for two days, stoned several policemen, broke the arm of a white police officer, and threatened the white compound staff until the district commissioner promised to prosecute the assistant compound manager (he later spent fourteen days in jail) and compel the company to reform its food distribution arrangements. Then they trooped back to work.

Gore-Browne was busy distilling limes and orange blossom, as well as making a fireplace, at Shiwa. Only after the white and Nchanga strikes had both been settled, however, did he receive a much delayed letter from Government House asking him to hold himself in readiness in case Africans became violent. Then his presence would be desired on the Copperbelt in order to "keep the

9. Sec/Lab/132: Elders from Abercorn and Isoka to the District Commissioner, Nchanga, 23 March 1940.

10. Ibid., letter of 22 March 1940 to the District Commissioner, Nchanga.

peace." Meanwhile the African employees of the Nkana and Mufulira mines had been watching the progress of their friends at
Nchanga and the whites on their own mines. There was talk among
Africans of a massive walkout if the white mineworkers' union
obtained its demands.

Even before the conclusion of the white strike, a notice appeared
in the Nkana compound counselling a demonstration of strength.
"My friends, listen to me my fellow workers. I say to you, are our
grievances many in number? . . . The Europeans left their work
without any trouble falling upon them. Cannot a slave, too, speak
to the master? . . . So if the Europeans receive an increase by leaving
their work then we should cease working too. . . . If you fail in this
you are only women. You have defiled your mothers. . . . They
are only human beings like ourselves."[11]

Governor Maybin, who had hurried to the Copperbelt, urged the
mining companies to give their 15,000 African employees a
monthly pay increase equal in percentage value to that obtained by
the 1,700 whites. But the companies offered only a wartime cost-
of-living increase that would add seven percent or two shillings
sixpence to the average African monthly take-home pay. The companies refused to alter overtime arrangements or to resolve any of
the other African grievances. At Roan and Nchanga, where the
whites had not gone on strike, Africans accepted these terms without much opposition. At Mufulira and Nkana-Mindolo, however,
Africans derisively rejected the proffered increase. "We asked for
[more] money," a miner explained, "because we saw Europeans
. . . who do not work very hard asking [and getting] . . . an in-
crement." Another coolly explained that at a time when "our King
George VI is in the trouble of war, we were surprised to see the
Europeans refuse their work. We know the Europeans are responsible people and we have seen what they have done. Today they came
back to their work very happy and we know they have got what
they wanted by refusing to work. We want more money too, and if
we do not get it, we too will refuse to work."[12]

Ad hoc representatives of the miners asked that they receive five,
ten, or twenty times their average daily wage of about ninepence.
They argued that incompetent whites received enormous sums
while they did all the work, "a line of reasoning," Gore-Browne
later admitted, "which had more than a little truth in it." But,

11. Sec/Lab/136: Diary entries of 24 March 1940.
. 12. Ibid., letter from Kwafya Kombe, May, 1940; speech at Nkana quoted in
A. T. Williams, "Report on the Strike of African Employees at Rhokana Corpora-
tion, Limited, at Nkana and Mindolo . . ." in *Confidential Reports . . . Concerning the
Copperbelt Disturbances. . . .* (Lusaka, 1940), 127.

Gore-Browne also explained, meeting such demands would have added about £1 million to the companies' annual outlay on wages, which they could ill afford. "Apart from that," he also said, "there are precious few Africans in this country to whom £180 a year wouldn't be a quite deadly gift."[13] The crux of their demands was advancement. They objected to "the low class and unexperienced Europeans who are put over them underground." The feeling was that Africans were "doing the Europeans' work and not receiving fair treatment from the Europeans that they have put over them." They offered to demonstrate that Africans could produce more copper than whites on a comparable ore face during the same shift.[14]

Two days after the end of the white strike, Africans downed tools at Mufulira and Nkana. The more militant strikers managed to prevent their less determined colleagues from reporting for work and to call out the non-mine laborers in Kitwe. They forced the mine manager to close down the smelter at Nkana and refused even to discuss their grievances until he and his counterpart at Mufulira raised their wages. At the very end of March, at a mass meeting on the Mufulira football field, Africans demanded ten shillings a day and described how they did all the work for which the Europeans were paid. (The average African wage was about twenty shillings a *month.*) The district commissioner noted: "Graphic description of the European ganger at work. His abuse of his natives and his laziness and inefficiency. Parables used." As Gore-Browne told the colonial secretary, the strike was against the color bar and raised a host of delicate issues.[15]

The situation was turning nasty. The governor summoned Gore-Browne. "You can imagine I hurried but it's 500 miles of truly awful road—at the end of an abnormally wet rainy season." At Nkana he found 8,000 Africans on strike, a solid organization, and "the whole place" terrorized. Only four African hotel employees had dared report for work. There were only fifty police available on each mine, together with a company each of the African regiment which had been raised since the outbreak of war. The white defense force (which had been Gore-Browne's idea in 1939) was patrolling the townships, and Southern Rhodesian troops were on their way. At Mufulira about 7,000 Africans had begun to sleep out on the football field because they preferred to "die sitting down

13. Gore-Browne to Ethel Locke-King, 11 April 1940.

14. Sec/Lab/139: William F. Stubbs, minute of 5 April 1940; Sec/Lab/137: Report of meetings of 27–28 March 1940.

15. Stubbs, "Report in Diary Form on Native Strike at Mufulira," *Confidential Reports,* 33. Gore-Browne to Malcolm MacDonald, 8 April 1940. The headline in the *Bulawayo Chronicle* (24 May 1940) read: "Astounding Demand for 10/- a Day."

and offering no resistance." The whites worried about an African mass attack on their homes. The mine managers worried about sabotage to expensive plant.

Early on the morning following his arrival on the Copperbelt, Gore-Browne went down to the Nkana mine shaft and then to the compound. "There was no trouble, and there were no men going back to work. The compound was an extraordinary sight. Thousands of men wandering about, apparently quite orderly." Thomas Sandford, the secretary of native affairs, A. T. Williams, the local district commissioner, and Gore-Browne all tried unsuccessfully to persuade the men who gathered around them in large numbers to return to work. "Colonel Gore-Browne," Williams reported, "was anxious to find out if negotiations were possible. I was convinced myself that negotiations were no longer possible as the mob in control had no intention of allowing any arguments to be offered or heard. The strike had changed . . . into a minor revolution." Nevertheless, after breakfast Gore-Browne and company and government officials all met on the football field with about 2,000 Africans. For two hours Sandford and Gore-Browne attempted to respond to the grievances shouted out by individual strikers. But their efforts were poorly received, and when Gore-Browne said that he would personally undertake to obtain better compensation for their injuries a wildly applauded heckler bellowed "Whatever you get for us it will be less than the white man gets. Has not a black man blood in his veins too? In any case we don't want to hear about compensation . . . We want 5/- a day." When one African volunteered that three shillings a day might be sufficient, he was hounded out of the crowd. The crowd was determined to press its case and was very unwilling to listen to what Gore-Browne called Sandford's "not very suitable reasoning." He was "the worst person imaginable to deal with an unreasonable mob. I felt myself veering over to their side when he explained that the fundamental laws of economics forbade the copper companies to disburse more in wages than the selling price . . . warranted—so true, but so inappropriate." As Gore-Browne commented, the crowd was "not violent but . . . certainly not polite, and it would surprise people who only know the Government employee or house-boy to see what a tough crowd of Bantu, fired by long-felt grievance, really can be like."[16]

Still, had Nkana's compound manager not followed these com-

16. Gore-Browne to Ethel Locke-King, 11 April 1940, 30 April 1940; Williams, *Confidential Reports*, 139–140; Stubbs, ibid., 35. For motives, see also Ian Henderson, "Early African Leadership: The Copperbelt Disturbances of 1935 and 1940," *Journal of Southern African Studies*, II (1975), 90–94.

paratively conciliatory efforts with a threatening harangue, the strikers' militancy might not have erupted into violence. He told them that the mining companies had no intention of increasing their pay offer, that they would cease issuing meat and relish at once, and end the supply of maize meal in two days. This news the strikers received in sullen silence. However, later in the day, Gore-Browne having gone off to Mufulira, the strikers stuffed their identity certificates into three large metal drums and carried them to the compound manager's office. Only by turning in his certificate could an employee be removed officially from the company's books. It was a calculated show of defiance.

"I've not conveyed the atmosphere of tension," Gore-Browne recalled. "Telephone calls ceaselessly, conferences, reports, anxious people asking if there was any news, soldiers . . . a sort of active-service-and-things-not-going-right atmosphere." The whites remained fearful, and in Mufulira where no Africans were reporting for work on the mine or in the town, even the night-soil workers and house-boys being absent, Gore-Browne marveled at the "masterly manner" in which Africans ran their stoppage. The "old idea that natives can't combine" was, he said, completely exploded. He also noted how whites on the Copperbelt found it particularly "tiresome" that 7,000 or 8,000 "niggers whom you despise and hate and fear have the whip hand over you, the more so I imagine if you can't in your own heart help realizing that it's you who've put them up to doing it by your own strike first."[17]

Gore-Browne feared trouble at Mufulira, especially because the situation in the Nkana compound seemed so quiet when he looked in there before dinner at the end of his first full day on the Copperbelt. The next morning, Nkana being still calm and orderly, Sandford and Gore-Browne again motored the thirty-eight miles to Mufulira. They were due back at noon in order to fly to Lusaka for a hurriedly called conference with the governor, who had returned there. As they reached the airfield, however, messages summoned them urgently to the Nkana compound. A few hours before, the strikers, provoked by police patrols and the visible arrival of military reinforcements, and antagonized by the paying of wages at the compound office to men who might have been strikebreakers, had gone beserk. After about fifty men had lined up to receive wages, a large crowd poured out of the football enclosure and raced menacingly toward the compound office. The waiting troops tried to head them off and the police held others who were moving on the office

17. Gore-Browne to Ethel Locke-King, 30 April 1940. Also, running accounts taken by Rowland Hudson and W. M. Logan by telephone from Sandford and others, 30 March, 1 April, 2 April 1940.

from a different direction. The strikers then began to stone the offices, the troops, and the police. Retaliating, the police hurled tear-gas bombs, which only infuriated the crowd. From among its mass came a profusion of bottles, iron bars, bricks, and stones, which forced the police and soldiers to retreat toward, on, and into the compound office. Inside, the noise of falling missiles and shattered glass created a monumental confusion. Finally, after about a half-hour of bitter confrontation, soldiers and a police officer opened fire on the surging mass.

The strikers went mad. They bit the barbed wire with their teeth, charged the soldiers, silenced a machine gun with a well-placed brick, and knocked out the sergeant commanding another machine gun. But the army managed to kill thirteen of the charging Africans and wound sixty-nine, four of whom subsequently died. In turn, the rioters injured twenty African soldiers. "The place," wrote Gore-Browne of his first impressions after driving rapidly from the airfield, "was just a shambles—bandaged and wounded soldiers, broken glass everywhere, shattered doors and windows, huge stones lying about everywhere, white-faced Europeans, and stolid African soldiers standing and sitting about with their rifles in their hands, cartridge cases everywhere, and blood—outside the barbed wire a sullen, angry mob, cursing, cursing, cursing, and shaking their fists."

Sandford and Gore-Browne ate lunch and then walked back to the compound office, where the rioters were still shouting abuse at the frightened whites and Africans inside what had become a fortress. Gore-Browne and a government official plunged into the crowd, where several asked him to go back and persuade the soldiers to put down their rifles so that the attackers and defenders could fight to the finish, "man-to-man." A car driven by an unpopular missionary arrived, and the strikers tried to obstruct its passage. Gore-Browne's companion feared another rush and a determined attempt to silence the second machine gun. He urged Gore-Browne to turn back. But at that point several Bemba walked up to Gore-Browne and asked him to come view the dead. "You can guess I didn't want to, but I went," said Gore-Browne. In the middle of the crowd was a temporary mortuary, from which whites had thus far been excluded. His guides shouted for the Africans to clear a path for "the Chitimukulu". They wanted him to see what the whites had done to the people, and for Gore-Browne the blankets were stripped off and the ghastly damage exposed, individual by individual. Then he was taken to see the wounded.

On the third day Sandford flew to Lusaka for an Executive Council meeting and Gore-Browne and Henry Mulenga, his African driver, went into the compound. There had been some further stoning of mine property and the burning of the huts of mine policemen in the night, and Gore-Browne found every single man armed with lengths of iron, bits of gaspipe, sledge hammers, long knives, and bottles. Several told him that he would be killed if he didn't turn around and leave. These threats, Gore-Browne remembered, "had the effect of making one feel that one would do anything but go back. I said to one man, 'Are you going to kill me?' and he smiled, took off his hat, and put his . . . horrible looking length of piping, into my hand." Yet the crowd was growing thicker and everyone else was armed. Men with spears arrived. Then there was a discussion and, afterwards, an ultimatum from one of the obvious leaders. "No one," he said, "is to pester the chief . . . anywhere he likes he can go." So for two hours, with an escort of three Africans, Gore-Browne toured the compound, greeting Africans and discussing major and minor complaints. Most of all, Gore-Browne was told that he should keep the soldiers and police out of the compound. Then there would be no trouble.

This information—the sense of the mood of the compound—proved invaluable later in the morning when the provincial commissioner, mine general manager, army commandant, police commissioner, and other white officials met to discuss further action. The police commissioner and the military leaders wanted to enter the compound, arrest the ringleaders, and disarm everyone. Gore-Browne argued persuasively, however, that he alone of the whites had been inside, and that it would be criminal folly to send troops into the compound. He promised that there would be no further disturbances if the strikers were not again provoked.

Gore-Browne's instinct, as well as his courage and ability to "get on" with Africans, prevented almost certain carnage. Instead, as he had predicted, with the military withdrawn the strikers soon began to bury their dead peacefully. Neither at Nkana nor at Mufulira were there further outbursts of violence. Two days later the miners even began to troop back to work without receiving any concessions whatsoever—bar the promise of some kind of inquiry. "I think," Gore-Browne mused, "that was the day of my life most worth living for . . . I'd never believed I'd any hold over these people, except that here at Shiwa my own employees were reasonably content . . . and here was this strange business of walking in unarmed amongst an angry throng . . . It's what one dreamt of as a boy, but thought didn't happen in real life, certainly not to elderly gentlemen . . ."[18]

This, more than any other experience, may have given Gore-Browne credibility with both Africans and official whites, espe-

18. Gore-Browne to Ethel Locke-King, 30 April 1940.

cially Governor Maybin. It also sensitized him to the realities of urban African life, to the prevalent despair and potential misery, and to the case for urgent social reform. His subsequent service as a local assessor with the British commission of inquiry into the strike and riots served further to heighten his awareness of the ways in which the color bar prevented African progress. He went underground in the mines for the first time, talked more than ever before to mining officials, white workers, and Africans and helped Sir John Forster and his Commission take and interpret evidence.[19] He came away feeling very "Bolshevik." "The pettiness and narrowmindedness of the managers . . . is quite unbelievable," he wrote. "The General Manager of Roan & Mufulira mines for instance refused to allow the Trade Union a telephone merely out of petty spite!"[20]

Gore-Browne agreed substantially with the commission's rec-ommendations and helped persuade Maybin to try to see that they were implemented at once. The commission urged the companies to increase African wages by five shillings a month, freely issue protective clothing for underground use, pay overtime rates identi-cal in percentage terms to those enjoyed by whites, periodically revise the cost-of-living bonus, provide a more satisfying diet, build new, more adequate houses (Gore-Browne was scandalized by the standard of shelter erected by the companies), and devise some form of industrial conciliation machinery. Most important of all, the commission recognized that the key to resolving industrial discon-tent was the breaking of the color bar and the fostering of equal opportunity and job advancement. In a delicately phrased way, the commission suggested that steps be taken thus to satisfy African aspirations. But neither the report nor Gore-Browne could per-suade Maybin and the companies that the moment was appropriate to risk antagonizing white miners. Copper was needed too urgently for the Allied war effort. Thus Maybin and the mine managers hoped that Africans would be content with material rewards and other promises. But Gore-Browne and a few other sensitive whites knew that discontent would fester until such future time as the color bar could be breached. It was to remain one of his foremost and continuing concerns.

For Gore-Browne a color bar made no sense in a modern-izing Northern Rhodesia. Although he at first refused to advo-

19. The commissioners said that they were greatly indebted to Gore-Browne for his assistance in "Bringing out every fact and argument which could tell in jus-tification of the action taken by the African workers." *Report of the Commission Appointed to Inquire into the Disturbances in the Copperbelt, Northern Rhodesia* (Lusaka, 1940), 3.

20. Gore-Browne to Ethel Locke-King, 4 June 1940.

cate absolute political or social equality, he believed that Africans should be allowed to rise up the employment ladder as far and as rapidly as they could. He stressed equity for blacks for its own sake—because Africans deserved to be treated justly and humanely as a matter of right—and because the economic health of white Northern Rhodesia depended and would increasingly depend upon black prosperity and satisfaction. In this respect, as in so many others, Gore-Browne was more prescient than his settler contemporaries. The training and experiences of his earlier years, his close acquaintance with rural Rhodesia, and his more recent awareness of the ills of African urban life made him so and also gave his pro-African interventions in the Legislative Council greater authority. Certainly the government and the distant Colonial Office listened, and Africans applauded silently even if most whites thought his deep concern for blacks misplaced, if not irrelevant. Throughout the war years and well into the late 1940s, his was the only voice raised loudly in Northern Rhodesia on behalf of, first, African rights and, later (but still earlier than others) African aspirations. That it was raised at all—that African grievances were aired articulately— proved significant in terms of preparing colonial minds for postwar indigenous expressions of their own discontent. Certainly Gore-Browne's role as a constructive public scold contributed to the long-term legitimizing of African interests, even if his efforts did not necessarily or always accomplish the immediate amelioration of specific problems.

When he drew attention to abuses, Gore-Browne characteristically set each within a more generalized framework of long-term concern for the future of Northern Rhodesia. "We Europeans must make up our minds whether this country is to be based upon a colour bar or not," he warned in mid-war. "Everybody knows my own view, everybody knows that I am not asking for social or political equality between Africans and Europeans, but I do feel that so long as there is an artificial restriction, as indeed there is in this country, on the black man rising as far as he is able to rise in the scale of industry, we are asking for trouble and heading for ultimate disaster. I have said again and again, that in this country I regard the white man's interests and the black man's as irrevocably interlocked. I am quite sure that the black man does not threaten the white man in industry or . . . anywhere else; the white man, if he is worth it, will be able to keep his end up, without the assistance of an arbitrary colour line."[21]

The color bar, Gore-Browne said on a subsequent occasion, is an "unnatural thing" dependent for its existence upon fear. It was

21. Gore-Browne in *Debates,* 44 (9 December 1942), 101.

economically unsound and morally indefensible. As an alternative
he again (recalling the mid-1930s) urged whites to make Africans
their partners. Africans were essential to the development of the
country, he argued, and should be accepted as junior partners. Most
of all, he wanted his fellow whites to recognize their "common
humanity" with Africans. Comparing relations between black and
white in Northern Rhodesia to relations between the lower and
upper classes in England in the early nineteenth century, he approv-
ingly quoted Lord Rosebery's anodyne words: "We have in our
generation . . . to effect that union of classes without which power
is a phantom and freedom a farce. . . . We are all privileged . . . to
restore or create harmony between man and man, to look not for
the differences which chance or necessity has placed between class
and class but for the common sympathies which underlie and con-
nect all humanity."[22]

Gore-Browne usually espoused causes less utopian. As early as
1941, for example, he began decrying the standard of housing provided for urban Africans. He was shocked and scandalized by the
conditions of squalor which workers, especially those who were
employed by the Rhodesia Railways, were forced to endure. A year
later, the railways having done nothing, he urged special legislation
to compel improvements. At Mufulira, he reminded the Council,
"human beings are living in places where one would not confine an
animal in whose well-being one took an interest." Luanshya was
worst of all. "There the houses are wattle and daub . . . nearly all of
them full of holes, and many almost falling down. The roofs are also
in holes, and the rain pours in."[23] As late as 1944 an official commission confirmed Gore-Browne's tales of "miserable" housing on the
railways and in ordinary urban (but municipally owned) "locations", all of which fell short of minimum requirements.

At the end of 1945, nothing whatsoever having been done,
Gore-Browne returned to the battlements with weary memories of
earlier debates. He reminded the government (which bitterly resented being told) that it owned locations where the houses were
literally awash with water during the rainy season; that most locations lacked running water or more than the most primitive sanitary
facilities; that most housed children and parents together in a single
room; and that several had been condemned in the 1930s and were
still being used to house official employees. None had sinned more
openly and defiantly, however, than Rhodesia Railways, a private
firm headquartered in Bulawayo. Gore-Browne continued his

22. Gore-Browne in *Debates*, 45 (27 May 1943), 71–74; 46 (23 November
1943), 27.
23. Gore-Browne in *Debates*, 44 (1 December 1942), 48–49.

legislative onslaught by describing the filth and wanton disregard of essential civilities in the railway compounds. "The worst thing," he made clear, "is that so far from resulting in any uplift in social conditions or rise in standard of living—high sounding words we use about our intentions towards the African—we are actually compelling him to live under far worse conditions than obtain in his own villages."[24]

As the member representing African interests Gore-Browne was tireless in attempting to make the cross of color easier to bear. His causes ranged from rest camps for travelling Africans to compulsory education. He demanded to know why, in terms of percentages, Africans received so much less than whites of their wages under workmen's compensation, why the railways could not provide better coaches and more amenities (like waiting rooms) for fare-paying Africans, why only whites qualified under the country's minimum wage legislation, why postal facilities for Africans were so inadequate, why Africans were prevented from purchasing War Saving Certificates, and so on. None of the answers he received proved satisfactory or in any way exculpatory. Yet, eventually, he was delighted to congratulate the railways on constructing a waiting room for Africans at Lusaka. "I should like to tell Council," he said at the very end of 1945, "that one of my gramophone records is not only withdrawn from circulation, but the mould has now been broken and hon. Members will hear no more of it. . . . That waiting room [at Lusaka] has been built . . . and it is extremely satisfactory. . . . That does not mean [however] that the Railways deserve very great gratitude. . . . It is incredible that all these years we should have had these miserable people lying out in the rain and cold waiting for the midnight train."[25]

Despite the paucity of such concrete achievement, Gore-Browne's public advocacy was tireless. On several occasions, for example, he described the extent to which Africans were everywhere in the country systematically discriminated against by white shopkeepers. He deplored the white-administered physical and verbal abuse which they endured when traveling on the trains. Debate after debate was larded with detail—with case by case recitations culled from official records and/or his own personal encounters. During every sitting he reported sentiment gathered from meetings with African organizations throughout the country. No other white was in as good a position to appreciate the kinds of antagonism which would later serve to legitimize wholesale disaffection. Thanks to Gore-Browne, the African case was presented

24. Gore-Browne in *Debates*, 52 (18 December 1945), 401.
25. Gore-Browne in *Debates*, 52 (20 December 1945), 535.

long before there were Africans in the Legislative Council and long before other whites would do more than mildly yawn at yet another airing of African anxieties.

In private, too, Gore-Browne lobbied on behalf of specific individuals as well as for general causes. He personally obtained pensions for deserving Africans and made sure, in repeated correspondence, that the annuities were, in fact, paid. In 1943 it took about seven letters and many telephone calls to ensure that an African soldier who had lost a leg in the Somali campaign received a proper artificial limb rather than a wooden peg. He tried to help a young mulatto obtain funds for school fees from his real father, an administrative officer, who resided in England; intervened on behalf of Isaac Muwamba, a prominent African clerk who wanted to send his son to school in South Africa; and urged the Director of African Education to provide special opportunities for Harry Nkumbula, then at the Chalimbana Teacher Training School and later, thanks to Gore-Browne, a student at Makerere College and the London School of Economics.

Gore-Browne could do nothing, however, for a Nyasa physician named Hastings Banda. In early 1945, Banda and Gore-Browne having been in correspondence, Gore-Browne asked his friend John Haslam, the Director of Medical Services in Northern Rhodesia, if Banda, a qualified venereologist then practicing in North Shields, England, could not be employed in Northern Rhodesia. Gore-Browne had just returned from a tour of the Namwala district, where syphilis and gonorrhea were rife. He envisaged Banda leading a campaign against venereal disease. If Banda were prepared to leave his lucrative British practice Gore-Browne thought that there would be only one problem. "There has been some trouble . . . between him and the Nyasaland Government due possibly to misunderstandings on both sides [regarding the salary scale on which he would be put]. . . . Banda told me himself that he was anxious to work amongst his own race, but he was quite clear that it would be wrong on his part to accept a position at a lower salary than that to which equally well qualified Europeans would be entitled. He felt that if he did accept the £200 a year which . . . the Nyasaland Government offered him, he would be prejudicing the case of future African doctors. It is a point of view with which I must confess I myself have a good deal of sympathy."

Haslam did, too, but still temporized. "There is much that attracts me about the proposal," he wrote. "I myself have a good deal of sympathy with his view that, since he holds a qualification entitling him to be registered as a medical practitioner . . . anywhere in the Empire, it would be wrong for him to accept a lower salary than is paid to British members of the Colonial Medical Service." West

Africans were, however, employed at lower rates than British physicians in their own colonies, said Haslam, and thus he doubted whether the colonial secretary would want to create a precedent which could "embarrass him elsewhere." Furthermore he suspected that persons like Banda should really be encouraged to enter private practice for Africans, neatly sidestepping the critical question of access to government-run hospital and laboratory facilities, which could well be denied to black doctors and their patients.[26] Banda moved his practice to London, to Ghana, and eventually to Nyasaland (now Malawi), where he became president.

Gore-Browne represented an otherwise muted constituency. For example, after a heated airing of indigenous complaints during a visit to Livingstone, he vainly sought to persuade the government to give passports to Africans. "The introduction of this practice," replied the chief secretary, "would be open to objection." If they held passports they might think that they could avoid the registration (pass) laws and labor regulations of Southern Rhodesia. There would be even greater umbrage taken by the South African authorities, where there were standing orders against the issuance of passports to Africans (except for those going overseas). In Nyasaland an exception was recently made, the chief secretary admitted, for a clerk who had completed over 30 years of service, and presumably thought that he could avoid harassment in South Africa and Southern Rhodesia by showing a proper passport rather than identity papers. Even so, the chief secretary concluded, departures from the general rule would not be made again.[27]

Although the leader of the unofficials and conscious always of white sensibilities, Gore-Browne never feared raising and condemning the kinds of inequities which most settlers took for granted and which, for them, justified much of the Northern Rhodesian way of life. For example, during a particularly virulent council debate in 1943 he castigated a system of justice which punished Africans severely for minor crimes against whites although whites received insignificant punishment for offenses against Africans. A white man kicked an African almost to death and was fined £25. An insane African was jailed seven years for throwing a stone near a white civil servant. A white woman tortured her servant and was fined £10.[28] These were outrages, and but examples, he said. The mere act of drawing attention to such matters may

26. Gore-Browne to Haslam, 11 February 1945; Haslam to Gore-Browne, 16 February 1945. See also Rotberg, *Nationalism,* 189, 197; Philip Short, *Banda* (London, 1974), 47–49.

27. Tucker to Gore-Browne, 14 October 1943.

28. Gore-Browne in *Debates,* 45 (2 June 1943), 141–143.

conceivably have helped to curb judicial excesses even if doing so could not have ensured the kinds of fair treatment to which Gore-Browne believed Africans were entitled, and which they received so rarely in Central Africa.

Usually Gore-Browne was more constructive, not to say didactic, in the council. More so than others, he concerned himself about the momentous changes which would certainly occur as a result of the war. Would Northern Rhodesia prepare itself for the challenge? Was its government alive to the varied responsibilities and opportunities which were bound to follow an allied victory based upon pious public compacts and platitudinous public utterances (like the Atlantic Charter)? Gore-Browne had clear and workable recommendations based on a keen perception of colonial reality and indigenous ferment within and without the territory's borders. In the wake of signal victories at Stalingrad and in the Egyptian and Libyan deserts, Gore-Browne reminded his colleagues that they all talked about "a better world based on some general ideas of better conditions." But, he said, "the idea that we ourselves should make sacrifices does not come into the picture. To take one instance, are we really prepared to include the black man in any of our plans for this New Order? I think not. And yet how can we, if we are honest with ourselves, regard Africans . . . as forming anything but the proletariat, the workers on whom in the long run our society is built up? And if so how can we deny them their share of the good things to come even if it involves sacrifice on our part, as indeed it must? . . . By and large the underdog here is the black man, and he must not be left out of any scheme for the improvement of life in this country."

"The main thing," he pronounced, ". . . . is to provide equality of opportunity for all."[29] Very early, from the beginning of hostilities, Gore-Browne was in favor of compulsory education for Africans. Reluctantly, he also agreed that it should be provided free, a reform which ultimately became possible only after the independence of Zambia. He supported the opening of secondary schools for Africans (before 1941 there were almost no opportunities in the Protectorate for Africans who wished to progress beyond the primary grades [plus a post-primary teacher-training course]), and was delighted to learn that secondary school leavers would be absorbed by the government and local employers. "If we can help the Africans to take the places that are open to them in the social life of this country so much the better." Jealousy between African and European education "would be disastrous for us all." By the end of the war, alone of prominent whites, he had also become a formida-

29. Gore-Browne in *Debates,* 44 (30 November 1942), 15.

ble proponent of university education for Africans. His thoughts were radical for the time and place. "We have all agreed that it is much more than desirable, it is our duty, to educate the African, and now it is only a question of how much we can afford . . . and . . . how far the African himself is ready to go." Gore-Browne believed that Northern Rhodesia should offer university education to twenty to fifty carefully chosen Africans "because we shall need them, in fact we do need them already." Exceptional Africans might even be sent to Oxford or Cambridge, a privilege Gore-Browne had himself foregone. "I feel our one hope for enabling the African to take his share in the development of the country is to have a very considerable body of well-educated and well-trained Africans capable of taking the lead amongst their own people."[30] As a personal gesture Gore-Browne had begun assisting a few Africans financially and was tireless in trying (and sometimes succeeding) to obtain governmental support for upwardly mobile Africans.

Much of Gore-Browne's progressiveness was influenced by his personal experience of the Union of South Africa and his fear that, if he and his contemporaries were not thoughtful in anticipating problems, the racial cancer of the south would spread relentlessly northwards. In 1945 he and Governor Sir John Waddington represented Northern Rhodesia at a large conference in Capetown on the future air policies of all of British East, Central, and South Africa. In fact Smuts had summoned the conference in order to discuss wider issues. "Obviously," said Gore-Browne afterwards, "we in southern Africa are not ready for political unity (racial & native questions make that impossible) but the more we get together and agree (or at the worst agree to differ) about common problems, the better."

Gore-Browne welcomed such a good opportunity to meet the leaders of much of English-speaking Africa, to compare notes about the problems of the post-war world and, not least, to renew his acquaintanceship with South Africa's supposed solutions to these problems. One old friend was minister of native affairs, the governor-general was a friend of a friend, and he had known Smuts, if only briefly. Through their good offices Gore-Browne talked with the whites who represented Africans in the South African parliament,[31] investigated the shocking slum conditions on the Windemere flats near Capetown, and listened to reports of the

30. *Ibid.,* (11 December 1942), 165–166; *Debates,* 49 (7 February 1945), 274; *Debates,* 52 (12 December 1945), 236–237.

31. Brookes, Senator Edgar, one of the representatives of Africans, knew so much about him by reputation that Gore-Browne was moved to comment: "I suppose where so many are blind, having one eye counts more than, in one's knowledge of real worth, one realises."

good as well as the bad side of South Africa. He was excited that the Union had managed to institute an old-age pension scheme for its indigenous working population and, at a time when Northern Rhodesians were squabbling over the location of a junior secondary school, marvelled at the acceptance of Africans in South Africa's major universities. He appreciated the paradoxes and much of the bittersweet condition of black South African life. But it was also impossible to overlook the "terrible racial antagonism, which we at present," wrote Gore-Browne, "haven't got (though we soon shall get it if colour-bar in Industry continues in the way we allow it to in N.R. today)." For Gore-Browne, South Africa was a "white 'civilization', if you can call it that, just as determined as ever to entrench itself in privileges which are just about as justifiable as those claimed by Divine Right for the upper classes in England in the days of my and your youth and earlier."[32]

Because of this experience and his close acquaintance with the 1940 strike, Gore-Browne was heretical about the urban employment of African labor in Northern Rhodesia. He attempted to include Africans in the categories of workers covered by minimum wage legislation. He sponsored a bill to provide pensions to African employees, and was fierce in his pursuit of those companies which refused to acknowledge their obligations to maimed or injured workers. After serving on an official committee to investigate the extent and prevention of silicosis in underground miners, he fought energetically in the legislature to entrench the obligation of full compensation for Africans thus afflicted. The Chamber of Mines (on behalf of the companies) naturally argued against such new requirements and even balked at returning silicotic miners to their original homes. Gore-Browne was outraged. To do otherwise, he said, was plainly immoral, a view which prevailed during a subsequent division of the council. In a private letter written after taking evidence at Mufulira and discussing the problems of silicosis with the mine management, he recalled how he had "seen Red, in every sense, as they refused to be ordinarily decent towards their diseased employees, especially native ones, grudging them the price of the journey home to die."[33]

Despite his background, Gore-Browne's mind was sufficiently supple to see the dangers for Africans in the advocacy by the European Mineworkers Union of equal pay for equal work. This was more than a slogan. Gore-Browne knew that theoretically equal pay made sense. But he also perceived that equal pay for equal work could well serve to curtail African employment and, probably, most possibilities of promotion to more responsible positions.

32. Gore-Browne to Ethel Locke-King, 29 March 1945.
33. Gore-Browne to Ethel Locke-King, 26 March 1945.

Gore-Browne realized, too, that African grievances were innumerable and growing as a result of the ferment of war-time and the cognate agitation of the white union. He was therefore among the first to urge that Africans be permitted to form trade unions (which they were only in 1948). "The African is very conscious to-day of grievances," he said in 1945. Some were ill-founded, but Africans were becoming conscious of the economic power that they could wield in Northern Rhodesia. "We have got to recognize that and to think how to handle the situation it gives rise to."[34] Gore-Browne's solution was unionization so that the privilege of bargaining (long withheld from Africans) could be extended with the help of a Labour Department oriented toward the problems of black labor, not white-run trade unions and their narrow aspirations.

As if to prove his argument, blacks walked off their railway jobs a few months after the end of the war. Beginning in Southern Rhodesia, the strike action spread to the north, where Gore-Browne and the government worried that the mines would have to shut down (and then they would flood and not be able to reopen for years) for want of coal hauled from Wankie on the railway line in Southern Rhodesia. Then, in sympathy, Africans at the Broken Hill mine downed shovels and paralyzed lead and zinc production. "The men have got ample grounds for striking," wrote Gore-Browne. "No one has attended to their grievances for years and they are not allowed to have unions to voice these grievances. The conditions under which they live and work . . . are damnable. Two families with children in one room ten feet by ten feet—average wage 28/-per month with cost of living trebled since the outbreak of war. And so on."

The ensuing crisis enabled Gore-Browne to act directly on their behalf. "You can imagine the meetings of Executive Council, the private talks between H. E., Cartmel-Robinson [the chief secretary], Welensky, and myself, the rumours, and the secret cables to the Colonial Office, the plans and the counter plans." Gore-Browne drove to Broken Hill from Lusaka and attempted to pacify the strikers. "It was blessed," he reported afterwards, "to feel the way the black men all trusted me." The railwaymen agreed to return to work and the miners followed suit a day later. A group of miners from Southern Rhodesia were even told by the strikers that they were waiting "for someone called Brown to come & tell them what to do".[35] Once again, too, the governor made Gore-Browne a member of a commission of inquiry (headed by Justice [later Sir]

34. Gore-Browne in *Debates,* 52 (20 December 1945), 541.
35. Gore-Browne to Ethel Locke-King, 11 November 1945. Gore-Browne's account of deplorable conditions was supported by the Northern Rhodesian Labour Commissioner, memorandum of 28 November 1945 in Sec/Lab/144.

Robert Tredgold of Southern Rhodesia) to assess grievances and make recommendations for avoiding future conflict between blacks and the railways.

As the commission visited the various compounds along the line, convening meetings of Africans and interviewing the firm's officers, Gore-Browne grew more and more furious. "It makes one savage to realise what the Africans have to put up with in the way of housing and conditions generally. . . . It just makes one sick & furious. The Company is making millions, largely out of the African traffic, & pretends it can't do other or better. They deserve to be smashed."[36] The report, which was tendered before Christmas, 1945, did not go that far. In fact, Gore-Browne had to be satisfied with fewer reforms than he thought justified. Tredgold, who knew the Southern Rhodesian situation, could agree to Africans being given only so much. Nevertheless, Gore-Browne felt that he had tempered the harsh edge of injustice—that he had done what was right, necessary, and overdue.

Gore-Browne's role in settling the 1945 strikes, and his various other activities on behalf of Africans, had since 1941 been made possible only because of his healthy grip on the elected legislators, and, even more, his solid relationship with Sir Eubule John Waddington, Maybin's successor as governor. At the moment of Maybin's sudden death in 1941, however, Gore-Browne had greatly feared the end of his own commanding place in the affairs of Northern Rhodesia. On a Monday in early April, Maybin, who had recently undergone a tonsillectomy and had been feeling generally unwell, and Gore-Browne, who had motored that day from Shiwa to Lusaka, entertained a group of Royal Air Force officers, and Major (later Sir) Ferdinand Cavendish-Bentinck of Kenya, who had recently been in Cairo and in Delhi for meetings. On Tuesday morning Maybin convened an Executive Council meeting. "Sir John was considerably better in health than for some time," Gore-Browne remembered, "& we'd a bit of private talk" about Shiwa and refugee problems. After lunch Gore-Browne took the slow luggage train to Broken Hill and stayed with a cousin by marriage. About midnight the light in Gore-Browne's bedroom was switched on by Welensky. "Can you hear some bad news?" he asked. "Sir John is dead [of a heart attack], I've just had a telegram telling me to tell you." It was with a "sore, sore, heart" that Gore-Browne buried "the little man" the next day. "Luck for him maybe, but not for us," was Gore-Browne's rueful epitaph.[37]

36. Gore-Browne to Ethel Locke-King, 4 December 1945. The evidence submitted to the commission is contained in Sec/Lab/80, 81, 144, Lusaka archives. Tredgold's *The Rhodesia That Was My Life* (London, 1968) does not mention this period.

37. Gore-Browne to Ethel Locke-King, 10 April 1941, 20 April 1941. Maybin was fifty-two.

Shared esteem, genuine rapport, and the intangibles of relationships between partners in the pursuit of a commonweal provided
the basis of Gore-Browne's generativity as a public figure. The
personality of Maybin's successor—especially his congeniality and
receptivity—therefore mattered more to him and implied a greater
impact on his conduct of unofficial parliamentary business than it
might have in almost any other contemporary African colony.
Waddington, who was to remain Northern Rhodesia's chief executive until 1947, was thus a key factor in determining much of the
tone of Gore-Browne's participation in public life. A tall, ungainly
man who had been educated at Dulwich College [School] and Oxford, where he studied mathematics, Waddington had already
served as colonial secretary in Bermuda and British Guiana and as
governor of Barbados. He came well recommended to his new,
more lofty position. Late in 1941, after Waddington had been in
Lusaka nearly two months, Gore-Browne cautiously gave his endorsement. "He is certainly out to be friendly, & approachable, and
moreover I think he'll be good at making up his mind and giving
decisions which is badly needed just now . . . [but] it's . . . too
early to size [him] up."[38]

It took six months to satisfy Gore-Browne, but by then he was
comfortable in his praise of both Waddington and his wife. Waddington had none of Maybin's charm nor background of interest in
"life and simple culture." He could not match Maybin's grasp of
detail and untiring energy. But he was "all there" and entirely
unformal. He was remarkably kind and friendly. "He's also willing
to trust one, and to confide in one." Colorless he was, but one
couldn't help saying that he was nice. Lady Waddington was even
more impressive. "Completely charming, rather shy and unassum-
ing and very much a gent," was Gore-Browne's summing-up.[39]
Together with Lorna he had enjoyed a number of pleasant visits to
Government House (no longer was it his temporary abode) and, by
mid-1942, it was clear that Waddington was fully prepared to welcome Gore-Browne's continued participation in significant and unexpected ways in the governance of the territory.

If anything, under Waddington Gore-Browne's responsibilities
grew multitudinous and all-encompassing. So much did they involve him, in fact, that he was compelled for the balance of the war
to create a permanent residence in Lusaka and leave the daily management of Shiwa to an Austrian Jewish refugee and, later, a retired
works supervisor, during years when lime oil, at thirty shillings a
pound, was grossing as much as £6,000 annually, orange blossom

38. Gore-Browne to Ethel Locke-King, 21 December 1941.
39. Gore-Browne to Ethel Locke-King, 20 June 1942.

was being produced in profusion and converted easily into equally profitable neroli (both were sold in South Africa as well as Britain), and there seemed the chance (which never materialized) that oils from indigenous plants grown at Shiwa would be needed for the production of copper. The Shiwa estate thus made money (about £1,400 in 1941, £20,000 gross over six years) for the first sustained period in its history. It could no longer be derided contemptuously as an uneconomic plaything.

These were the same years, too, when Lorna and Stewart, though they wrote to each other lovingly, grew more and more estranged. Sight of each other grew more and more infrequent, largely but not exclusively because of his hectic public life and her preference for being at Shiwa when he was in Lusaka, and vice versa. For many months, too, Lorna lived in Johannesburg in order to be closer to the two children, who were at school there, and so that she might take courses in biology at the University of Witwatersrand. Upon her return—for the last nineteen months of the war—Lorna worked in the government pathology laboratory in Lusaka, but such proximity brought her no closer emotionally to Gore-Browne.

Except for vacation visits from his children and infrequent snatched days at Shiwa, the second half of the war proved a personally lonely period for someone still in the prime of political life. With Waddington's encouragement, he threw himself into administrative as well as legislative tasks with unreduced energy. After the defeat of the Italians in Somalia and the liberation of Ethiopia the Allies were faced with the problem of disposing of both prisoners of war and civilians resident there who had to be interned. Even before Waddington took office Northern Rhodesia was told to receive 2,500 (the country's white population was then still only 14,000) women and children almost immediately and Logan, the acting governor, gave the "truly appalling job" of organizing their reception, care, and housing to Gore-Browne. An entirely new town would have to be built to accommodate this inflow, there being no spare camps or housing suitable for such an addition. Within forty-eight hours of first hearing of the possibility, and being told that making preparations for the influx took priority over any other government work, Gore-Browne concocted a complete set of plans which took account of the need to ensure adequate supplies of water, food, and medicine, a salubrious climate, and the logistics of moving persons and providing beds, blankets, nets, cutlery, and so on for such a comparatively large number. Assuming the availability of shipping on Lake Tanganyika, he proposed building the necessary camp or town near Abercorn. In 1941, however, no one arrived, and Gore-Browne's scheme languished. A few weeks

later he was told that Italian prisoners of war would be coming to
Northern Rhodesia instead, and that he would be put in charge of
that similar but still somewhat different organizational problem.
But no prisoners came.

In early 1942 Northern Rhodesia was abruptly told by the East
African High Command to expect 1,500 Italian men and women
internees being deported from Eritrea. A camp along the banks of
the Kafue River, where malaria was rife, but where there was existing accommodation for about 500, was hurriedly erected and put
under the overall command of Gore-Browne, now styled Director
of War Evacuees and Refugees (at £1,000 a year). Under his authority the acutely difficult task of locating sufficient blankets, mosquito
nets, suppliers of provisions, and so on was begun. Gore-Browne's
qualities of coordination and persuasion were fully stretched and
sorely tried, too, for coping with a lack of building materials, with
bureaucrats in the Lusaka secretariat who cut his requests for
equipment ridiculously, and with the hiring of camp commandants
and assistants all took the kinds of patience and good humor which
were then in short supply. Small accomplishments became signal
achievements—obtaining equipment with which to provide the
Kafue camp with electric light and the establishment of a vegetable
garden represented the triumph of perseverence. Yet, despite all of
his efforts, which included flights to Nairobi and Salisbury for the
purpose of tying his own plans closely to those of the East African
Command (his new friend Sir Philip Mitchell was in charge) and
Rhodesia, this second buildup and many false alarms later produced
no Italians.

As a substitute for the Italians, Northern Rhodesia became a
haven for Polish refugees. Gore-Browne was responsible from 1942
to 1944 for their welfare. The first 500, who were of middle-class
background and from cities, were initially accommodated in hotels
and boarding-houses in Fort Jameson and along the southern line-
of-rail. They were full of requests—for better shelter, better sustenance, schooling for their children, and so on. Gore-Browne was
thus forced to mediate endless disputes between local whites and the
newcomers and among different factions within the Polish community. It was a thankless and wearing task. "Did I tell you," he
asked his aunt, "of the hunger strike at one of the hotels because
they only had one egg apiece for breakfast on top of porridge, and
liver & bacon? And the honour of Poland is impugned almost
hourly. Their class consciousness is something one has to see to
believe, and the anti-semitism that splits their own ranks is something one would not credit." He bemoaned the petty jealousies and
the constant bickerings, not appreciating that—partially because in
the council he had stressed Northern Rhodesia's moral obligation to

take in more Poles, no matter how bothersome and burdensome—
their intensity and frequency was about to increase to unimaginable
proportions.[40]

By the end of 1943 Gore-Browne had welcomed nearly 3,500
more Poles, some from rural peasant stock, to special camps which
he had established in Abercorn, Lusaka, and Bwana Mkubwa. Making allowance for their refugee status, and their dislike of living off
charity in a foreign country, Gore-Browne still found the Poles, as
people in a predicament, impossible. 'They get free issues of clothing from Red X and if they think their neighbour's issue is better
than their own they will tear up their own clothes or throw them at
the donor's head." He even had to cope with a riot, with attempted
murders, and with a "regular gang of Apaches" which preyed on
their own folk. He broke it up by sending the troublemakers to
Southern Rhodesia and Kenya. At the camp near Lusaka he had to
contend with a different kind of problem: the Lusaka Women's
Institute, led by the wife of a Methodist minister, worried that the
Polish peasant women housed there were providing clandestine
services for the white officers and enlisted men of the two military
battalions stationed nearby. Gore-Browne could not condone pros-
titution, but he preferred regular liaisons between frustrated whites
to the troubles which might follow miscegenation.[41]

Gore-Browne was delighted to be relieved of his evacuee responsibilities in mid-1944. By then the factions had, to use his term,
"settled in," and his directorship had become more routine and
tedious than challenging. He also had a number of other projects to
oversee and complete, and several constitutional alterations to
promote and implement. Among his quasi-executive priorities was
the vexing question of land rights for Africans. For many years
beginning during Sir Hubert Young's governorship, Gore-Browne
had complained bitterly about Northern Rhodesia's failure to make
more land available to Africans and to reform indigenous notions of
usufruct. In the 1920s reserves had been created for Africans in the
Eastern and Northern Provinces and along the line-of-rail, but assessments in the late 1930s by critical outsiders demonstrated that
the segregated areas were grossly inadequate and overcrowded.
The territory needed to expand the existing reserves, create new
ones, and find ways of satisfying the legitimate aspirations of land-

40. Gore-Browne to Ethel Locke-King, 28 July 1942; Gore-Browne in *Debates,*
43 (14 September 1942), 12.

41. Gore-Browne to Ethel Locke-King, 23 October 1943. Gore-Browne summarized his experiences in 1947, when the government promulgated legislation to
force the Poles to be removed to a friendly country. Gore-Browne in *Debates,* 56 (3
February 1947), cc. 519–521.

hungry Africans. During 1942 and 1943 Gore-Browne had thus been pleased at Waddington's request to serve as a member of a small investigatory commission. Its task was to decide which of the areas in the territory not already alienated to whites should be set aside as crown land or constituted as native trust land, i.e. land to be held in perpetuity for the sole and exclusive use of Africans (whether held in common or by individual lessees).[42] This was a new concept in Northern Rhodesia; it granted a larger swath of the territory (but not necessarily its most arable soils) to Africans without merely extending the reserves. It was a flexible policy tool which could conceivably limit any large-scale post-war annexation of African-farmed lands by whites.

The task of the commission, chaired by Launcelot W. G. Eccles and assisted by C. Gordon James and Gore-Browne, was to visit and take evidence from whites and Africans in all of the territory's districts (it travelled 7,000 miles), to describe the physical features and ecological variables in each, to establish the current state of the reserves and the ways in which the reserves were being farmed, and then to divide the remaining land into the two available categories. (Once again—decades after the initial experience—Gore-Browne was engaged in establishing boundaries in Northern Rhodesia.) This it did painstakingly, its results being embodied in an Order-in-Council in 1946. Its final report, clearly influenced by Gore-Browne's special expertise and interests, also offered some general guidelines—all of which were ultimately accepted by the colonial secretary. Chopping rural land into islands of white and black settlement (as in South Africa) was, it said, foolish. Therefore the commission recommended large homogeneous blocks only, and rejected the segregationist notion that there should be buffer zones between white and black farmholdings. The commission further made it clear that without adequate demonstration of modern methods "no amount of land which can be set aside will be permanently sufficient for the needs of the African population." The members urged the governor to permit Africans to continue occupying crown lands until those areas might someday be required for white settlement. Finally, at Gore-Browne's insistence, they went beyond their strict terms of reference to request an investigation into African methods of land tenure. It was currently difficult for educated Africans or successful peasant farmers to establish in-

---

42. Under certain circumstances even native trust land could be alienated to whites "where such alienation [was] for the benefit of the natives," or for the purpose of establishing townships, running railways, and opening mines. See Northern Rhodesia, General Notice No. 416 of 1942 (Gore-Browne had a hand in writing this order).

dividual rights or the kind of security which was conducive to the maximum utilization of available resources. "One of the most difficult problems which we shall have to solve," said the report, "is that of the agriculturally progressive Africans who not unnaturally resent being placed too rigidly under the jurisdiction of a petty chief who may be much their inferior in intellect. To graft them on to village life will not be easy . . . but . . . it is far better not to segregate the progressive farmer and thereby deprive the tribe of his knowledge and influence."[43]

In 1945, after Gore-Browne had exerted pressure in the Legislative Council for the implementation of the full report of the land commission, Waddington took note of its final recommendation and asked a committee, chaired by Gore-Browne and including Eccles and John Moffat, a district officer, specifically to investigate the future of indigenous land tenure. For almost two and a half months, including twelve straight days on tour by air, the committee interviewed numerous Africans individually and in groups and the leading whites of each of the major districts in the territory. Gore-Browne also brought his own strong, unconventional views to the task. For a white, he was in close touch with the needs and views of modern-thinking Africans. On their behalf, and because of his own paternal attempt to foster change, he was also an advocate of those improvements which would permit progressive Africans to till the soil to the limits of their ability and/or capital. The report of his committee therefore began firmly with an unusually explicit, and, for the time, usefully didactic definition of existing methods of usufruct. "Native land tenure . . . can be described as communal ownership by the tribe vested in the Chief, coupled with an intensely individual system of land usage." Although the government thought that villages were integral to the traditional system of land use, in fact current villages—any collection of ten or more taxpayers living close together under a headman—were white constructs forced upon Africans for administrative convenience. Africans preferred to live as family units: the report recommended that "existing instructions which impose a minimum of ten taxpayers before a unit can be registered should be abolished."

Gore-Browne and his colleagues urged the adoption of a new parish council tier of local authority, composed of several or many villages connected by clan ties and run not by the chiefs but by a

43. Northern Rhodesia, *Report of the Land Commission* (Lusaka, 1945), 3–5; G. H. Hall, secretary of state for the colonies, to Waddington; 27 December 1945. The resultant Northern Rhodesia (Native Trust Land) Order-in-Council of 1946 limited the amount of trust land which could be alienated to whites, provided lessee arrangements for Africans, and mandated compensation if mining operations ever displaced African farmers.

council of "progressive" Africans. The village system, in their view, offered no incentive for Africans to improve their living conditions and generally deterred development in the rural areas. Under the parish system individuals would be registered as belonging to an area, not merely a village, and could thus build and farm anywhere within a comparatively large zone. The committee also envisaged the formation within parishes of community centers, central markets, schools, recreation halls, etc. Although family settlements might still move within parishes (most Northern Rhodesians exhausted soils every few years and then moved their fields and villages), parishes would provide those nodules of permanence which had for so long been lacking in rural areas and which could provide an underpinning for real development. Gore-Browne's committee also proposed that parish councils "be the bottom rung of the ladder which leads ultimately to a seat on the Legislative Council" for Africans. Additionally, the committee recommended that blocks of land be set aside near the Copperbelt and other urban industrial areas for advanced Africans who wished to enter the cash economy as farmers totally devoid of communal tenure or rural parish arrangements. The committee also saw that its parish scheme could only be implemented by a corps of African surveyors, and proposed the establishment of a school for that purpose, a recommendation which the governor promptly endorsed. He also abolished the "ten taxpayer" rule and in principle accepted both the parish proposals and, at first to a limited extent, the urban leasehold scheme.[44]

Although the reforms proposed by Gore-Browne were ultimately never implemented in full, the discussions which they engendered, and their direction of public attention to the problems of African tenure, encouraged enterprising Africans to invest their energies and savings in the production of cash crops and helped, during the immediate post-war years, to reassure Africans worried about the further expropriation of their lands for incoming whites. This was particularly an anxiety of the Tonga, who had for many years grown maize near the railway in the Southern Province and now found themselves lacking acreage on which to keep expanding. Gore-Browne was able to build upon his committee's report by making public Tonga fears and, in 1946, by obtaining official recognition of their complaints.

The ideas of his constituents and his own awareness of the implications for the colonies of wartime promises and activity had given

44. Northern Rhodesia, *Report of the Native Land Tenure Committee* (Lusaka, 1945); Waddington to the colonial secretary, 23 January 1946. Gore-Browne's ideas drew to some extent upon Lord Hailey's confidential *Native Land Tenure in Africa,* a report printed for the Colonial Office in March, 1945.

Gore-Browne's ideas an increasingly radical cast. His genius, and the secret of his long-term hold on the affections of Africans, rested upon a flexibility of mind that was unappreciated by most of his parliamentary colleagues. For all his strength of character and moral certitude, even dogmatism, Gore-Browne was never content to be guided by fixed opinions and the status quo. He was a political evolutionist capable of recognizing and even moving slightly ahead of rapidly altering circumstances. Hence, during the war, he began espousing the cause of indigenous political participation at all levels and, before many Africans (or any whites) were striving for it, strongly advocated the election by Africans of their Legislative Council representatives. These were departures from past practice even though the actual pace of change proposed by Gore-Browne was, by the experience of subsequent decades, modest.

Gore-Browne believed that he represented Africans energetically and effectively at the national level, and felt that even though he played sometimes seemingly contradictory roles in addition to his legislative one as their representative, they trusted him still. Yet he had the sense of perspective to know that no single individual, especially no white, could hope to represent all shades of indigenous opinion. It was physically impossible for anyone to visit every part of the country regularly, and it was thus impossible for a single nominated member representing Africans to voice the concerns of all of Northern Rhodesia's 1.5 million black inhabitants equally. Gore-Browne addressed large meetings of Africans wherever his other war-time business took him, and he was thus particularly well-acquainted with a range of urban problems. But despite endless exuberance, even he could not assimilate and articulate them all. "I hope that sooner or later," he wrote in mid-war, "I'll be able to accomplish something that will last, on their behalf."[45]

For these several reasons, Gore-Browne in 1942 proposed a method of greatly increasing indigenous political participation which was new to East and Central Africa but similar to an institution existing (in very different circumstances) in South Africa. In Northern Rhodesia the only organs of African opinion in any way representative were the Urban Advisory Councils which had been established on the Copperbelt in 1938. Their members were drawn (as nominees) from the educated as well as the traditional (tribal elder) class, and were meant to serve as a collective safety valve. Gore-Browne urged that similar councils be established in all the towns of the territory, a principle which the government promptly accepted. Addressing the Legislative Council, Gore-Browne at the same time suggested the creation of councils in each of the provinces, the membership of each to be drawn by election both from

45. Gore-Browne to Ethel Locke-King, 28 July 1942.

the ranks of chiefs and other traditional leaders and from their middleclass counterparts (teachers, evangelists, and so on). Election, albeit indirectly, by the existing native authorities and native advisory councils in each province, was the most radical aspect of this motion. Nevertheless the whole was introduced with the support of all of the elected members.

Gore-Browne told the startled official members that the major principle behind his motion was "that of giving representation which really will be representation to Africans in a country like this." He warned the government not to delay accepting this principle for it was important to anticipate African requirements and demands. He reminded his listeners of reluctant concessions in Ireland and India. "If the British empire ever does fall—which Heaven forbid—surely the words 'They acted too late' would be fittingly engraved on its tombstone." He admitted that there were two methods by which Africans could exercise greater political responsibility. They could be given the franchise, subject to certain property and educational qualification, or they could share some form of communal representation in a subordinate, advisory, and indirectly elected assembly. Gore-Browne was advocating a version of the second form. He assured his colleagues that Africans were not yet ready in 1942 to sit beside them on the parliamentary benches, but they could assuredly speak for the majority of Northern Rhodesians in regional bodies. "For a long time," he said, "any representative of native interests sitting in this legislature will have to be a white man, but eventually I envisage that it will be to everyone's benefit to have an African speaking for Africans. I know a good many of the more advanced Africans . . . I have a great respect for them, and I often consult them, but I cannot picture any of them sitting in this council yet with advantage either to themselves and their compatriots or to us. But the day will come."[46]

The government reluctantly accepted the Gore-Browne proposal even though nearly everyone thought the need for African representation premature and the likelihood of listening to Africans in the Legislative Council beyond comprehension. The provincial (at first regional) councils, of which there were initially six, began their annual meetings in 1943. By creating them and giving their members a measure of verbal freedom, the government believed that it was providing an alternative sufficiently meaningful to satisfy the political passions of refractory Africans for years, if not decades.

46. Gore-Browne in *Debates,* 43 (17 September 1942), 74–77. Gore-Browne's ideas regarding the need for indigenous representation began to take their mature shape at least as early as 1940. They may have been influenced by Audrey Richards and Governor Maybin. Gore-Browne to Richards, 9 November 1940.

Educated Africans, many of whom had earlier led the country's politicized welfare associations, joined chiefs and other traditional personalities on the councils. Provincial commissioners presided, and the secretary for native affairs, district commissioners, and Gore-Browne attended. According to the official pronouncements read at the first meetings of each of the councils, the government expected members to inform Gore-Browne of those matters to which Africans thought he should pay attention. A provincial commissioner suggested that the councils had been devised in order that the representatives of the various native authorities could hear what younger and more educated people were thinking.[47] The government made it clear, however, that it would regard the deliberations of these councils as merely advisory. They would perform no statutory or administrative functions, and would remain a forum for the expression of feelings and grievances only.

Thanks to Gore-Browne, Africans openly used the new councils to criticize the policies of the government and the machinery of the color bar. They complained about white proprietors who refused to permit Africans to enter their stores. They demanded that the government should outlaw the common white use of the word "boy" to describe mature Africans. At the first meeting of one of the Northern Province councils, Headman Chitulika asked when Africans "will stop smelling in the nostrils of Europeans?" At a Western Provincial Council meeting, a prominent African schoolteacher denounced a leading white trade unionist for using pejorative sobriquets to describe Africans in public. Another speaker in the same council summed up the feelings of his fellow councillors: "We have seen that there is only one great thing and that is the colour bar." In the various councils members also spoke deprecatingly of laws curtailing indigenous land use, of the need for schools and hospitals, of divorce legislation, of the registration of African marriages, trade unions for Africans, overcrowding in the buses and trains, and of a host of communal dissatisfactions. They all regularly spoke with one refrain, too, against amalgamation with Southern Rhodesia, and most went to the trouble of voting annually against its implementation in any form.[48]

Participating in the work of the councils gave Gore-Browne greater confidence in his more radical instincts and helped to ad-

47. Sec/Nat/103: Minutes of the Northern Province (Northern Areas) Regional Council, 22 May 1944, Lusaka archives.

48. Sec/Nat/103: Minutes of the first meeting of the Northern Province (Central Areas) Regional Council, 19 May 1944; Sec/Nat/102: Minutes of the fourth meeting of the Western Province Regional Council, 8 October 1945; ibid., Minutes of the Sixth Meeting, 9–10 July 1947.

vance his own thinking on the question of African political participation. After joining the first of the Copperbelt assemblies Gore-Browne wrote home enthusiastically. "The whole thing was a triumphant justification of what I've always urged in season & out . . . that the African is ready for political institutions, & that it's not only silly but dangerous to drive his legitimate aspirations in that direction underground."[49] In the year which elapsed after his introduction of regional councils, he also began to revise his views on the pace of indigenous political development. He believed that Africans could and should elect their own representatives to the Legislative Council, even though "for some time to come" such representatives would be whites. "Even there," he said, "the good showing made recently by the African members of the African Education Advisory Board leads one to think that the time when Africans can usefully sit in Legislative Council may not be so very remote." As an interim step, he urged the chief secretary gradually to introduce the principle of election in place of nomination, and initially to permit the regional councils to select their representative to the Legislative Council from a list of nominees. But after a time he wanted to see outright (albeit still indirect) electoral choice.[50]

After another year had gone by he advocated placing Africans on some kind of voting roll because then elected members would have to take their interests into account. "I cannot bring myself," he declared, "to do anything so repugnant to my sense of justice as to deny a man who is adequately qualified the right to vote, merely on account of the colour of his skin."[51]

Gore-Browne managed to attend the meetings of nearly all of the regional councils during their first few years. He did his best, too, to prevent provincial commissioners from dominating the sessions, and to see that even the more subservient councillors were encouraged to speak forthrightly. After an early Copperbelt meeting he told his aunt that he hoped to see his experiment evolve quickly into a "real council, *not* just a lot of Africans asking for things while the Europeans present think out reasons for refusing the requests. That is a legacy from ancient meetings, which we need to grow away from."[52] Subsequently he complimented those provincial commissioners who refrained from playing schoolmaster during the meetings of the various councils. He was particularly pleased that the

49. Gore-Browne to Ethel Locke-King, 1 January 1944.

50. Gore-Browne to the Chief Secretary (George Beresford Stooke), 28 July 1943.

51. Gore-Browne in *Debates*, 48 (9 August 1944), 92, 96–97. Gore-Browne had said much the same thing at a meeting of provincial commissioners in 1942. Sec/Nat/75.

52. Gore-Browne to Ethel Locke-King, 22 July 1944.

councils managed to combine chiefs and intellectuals successfully for, in West Africa, the serious cleavage between the old black regime and the newly emergent one endangered stability and, Gore-Browne believed, any gradual devolution of authority.

For Gore-Browne the provincial councils became but a first step toward full-scale African representation. (His ideas progressed rapidly.) He pushed the government to take the logical next step and, before the end of 1945, form a territorial council with a membership selected (by the Africans themselves) from the provincial councils. Later, he hoped, such a national council could send a representative to sit in the Legislative Council. (After all, he remarked, in Kenya an African had just joined that colony's legislature.) The territory-wide council would, Gore-Browne felt, provide a good test of the extent to which there were Northern Rhodesian Africans "capable of expressing the point of view of their fellow Africans rather than a sectarian or personal one, and . . . whether there are Africans here of the mental calibre to sit in Legislative Council. . . . I do believe . . . that there are Africans in this country who are much nearer being ready to sit in this Council than the general public, or even officials, believe. . . . On the other hand, I realise that it would be a fatal mistake to start too soon." In the interim Gore-Browne now strongly favored permitting Africans to select a white representative through elections held at the provincial council level. More tersely, he wrote privately, whites needed to "keep just ahead of native demands" if they wished to avoid serious racial confrontation and potential violence.[53]

As Gore-Browne had proposed, an African Representative Council was duly inaugurated in 1946, the steady deterioration in race relations in Northern Rhodesia and the quickening pace of Central African politics having hastened the decision. Drawing its membership from the six provincial councils and Barotseland only—six of the twenty-nine members coming from an urban area—this new council quickly justified all of Gore-Browne's hopes. Its members spoke forthrightly on the issues which concerned them—the return of alienated land, increased educational opportunities, obtaining the freedom to purchase European-made whiskey and brandy, and so on. They condemned miscegenation and tabled awkward motions, one of which favored having the council elect its own Legislative Council representatives.[54] They, too, condemned the notion that Northern Rhodesia should be joined with Southern Rhodesia in any kind of union. For them that was still the overriding issue.

53. Gore-Browne in *Debates,* 49 (18 January 1945), 137–139; Gore-Browne to Ethel Locke-King, 17 April 1945.
54. For a fuller account, see Rotberg, *Nationalism,* 207–209.

Amalgamation was still, although initially pushed into the background by World War II, the issue around which Northern Rhodesian politics revolved throughout the 1940s. As both the leader of the unofficials and the representative of Africans, Gore-Browne's part in debating and resolving it remained no less complicated than it had been in the 1930s. As Maybin and Waddington's confidant, however, he was able to exert considerably more influence than ever before and, by his suggestions to them and to the Colonial Office, his dealings with Southern Rhodesia, and his guidance of the elected members, was able to promote policies capable of forwarding interterritorial cooperation without, he calculated, injuring Africans. At least that was the general intent of his often contorted political maneuverings during the 1940s. Specifically, Gore-Browne saw the wisdom of combining constitutional advance locally with encouragement of the kinds of regular, quasi-political trans-territorial consultations which, given a liberalization of Southern Rhodesian attitudes toward blacks, could bring about some closer union or federation in Central Africa. Only by going into such a combination with strengthened institutions of its own could the future of Northern Rhodesia, Gore-Browne's prime object, be safeguarded. Furthermore, Gore-Browne still believed that he could moderate the agitation for amalgamation by increasing the scope of white power in the Legislative Council.

In 1941, shortly before Maybin's death, Gore-Browne and Welensky took the initiative by preparing detailed constitutional proposals. Their assumptions were three fold—that although responsible government (the complete control of local policy by elected members) would be the ideal arrangement, it could not be achieved in wartime; that responsible government could best be brought about by amalgamation with Southern Rhodesia; and that constitutional improvements short of responsible government (a "half-way house") should not be delayed until after the war. Gore-Browne and Welensky recommended a legislative council with a healthy unofficial majority, an executive council with greater, cabinet-like powers than the present advisory body of the same name, but with the retention of a slight official majority, and the reservation of financial matters and all legislation affecting Africans to the governor.[55] A few months later, as a subordinate and interim suggestion, Gore-Browne urged the establishment of a war cabinet (on the British model) to expedite decision-making during the conflict. He asked if government by committee, especially by a committee of civil servants (the usual colonial

55. Gore-Browne (on behalf of the unofficials) to Maybin, 19 and 22 March 1941. See also Gore-Browne in *Debates,* 46 (30 November 1943), 159–163.

mechanism), was "anything but a danger in time of war." Civil servants were trained to be right, irrespective of the time it took to reach decisions. But during war-time he said, the reflexes of the military were required. Decisions had to be made quickly, and hopefully correctly. What was to be avoided was the civil service's "fatal insistence of never making a mistake."[56] He therefore proposed another coordinating committee composed of the governor, the chief secretary, the financial secretary, and two unofficials—Welensky and himself.

Although a war cabinet, with more limited decision-making abilities than Gore-Browne had wanted, was established in mid-1942 (Welensky and Gore-Browne joining the three leading officials), the Colonial Office rejected all thought of more far-reaching constitutional alterations until 1944. During the spring of that year Gore-Browne joined Waddington, Huggins, Andrew Cohen (then in charge of Northern Rhodesia for the Colonial Office), Sir Cosmo Parkinson of the Dominions Office, and Colonel Oliver Stanley, the secretary of state for the colonies, in London for detailed discussions on the future of Central Africa. Gore-Browne took that opportunity to promote his constitutional suggestions of 1941 as well as to articulate his own and African views against amalgamation and yet in favor of some measure of interterritorial coordination. His major point, which he put forcefully and successfully to Cohen and Stanley, was that the Colonial Office must settle Northern Rhodesia's own political future before meaningful steps could be taken in the direction of larger groupings.

The constitution which emerged from these talks, and a flurry of cables back and forth to Lusaka during August and September, 1944, drew heavily upon the Gore-Browne-Welensky initiative three years before. Beginning in late 1945, the unofficial members of the Legislative Council were to constitute a majority, their numbers being increased by the addition of two new members to help Gore-Browne represent Africans. Gore-Browne regretted that those new legislators (he was responsible for suggesting the names of Dr. Charles Fisher, his nephew by marriage, and Anglican Bishop Robert Selby Taylor) were to be nominated, not elected. The governor would have reserve powers to safeguard African and financial concerns, and the unofficial membership of the Executive Council would be expanded slightly.

These were significant increments to settler power, albeit some whites felt that the specific safeguarding of African rights negated

56. Gore-Browne in *Debates,* 40 (7 July 1941), 12–13; 41 (9 December 1941), 18; Gore-Browne to Ethel Locke-King, 20 July 1941.

any achievement of an unofficial majority. Even more important in the broader context of white aspirations was the simultaneous announcement by Stanley explicitly forbidding amalgamation and establishing a Central African Council. Stanley announced that he had concluded (as a result of the discussions in London) that "under existing conditions"—because of the incompatibility of the two Rhodesian policies toward Africans—amalgamation was not then practicable.[57] Waddington and Gore-Browne had made it clear that virtually every African in Northern Rhodesia was bitterly afraid of Southern Rhodesia's segregationist methods and wanted to remain under the protection of the crown. Africans also knew, Gore-Browne had said, that amalgamation would mean rule by those very whites who had been scheming for years to prevent the granting of equality of opportunity, or any other rights, to the indigenous majority of the territory.

Gore-Browne's posture on amalgamation was, in fact, more complex than it might have appeared in London. Although he acknowledged the accuracy of African observations and supported the vehemence of their antagonism, he also appreciated the economic benefits which might result from some closer association with Northern Rhodesia's neighbors. And, deep down, he hoped that Southern Rhodesia might be persuaded to alter its ways. As early as 1941 he enunciated a position—really a series of positions—which he maintained consistently during the war and up to the debate on federation in the late 1940s. Whites were for amalgamation and blacks against it, but everyone, he thought, could admit the advantage of big units over small ones. "The day of the small territorial units, comfortable as they were to live in . . . has passed," he declared. "Given sufficient local freedom," running a postal service, educating whites, defence, and so on could be discharged more expeditiously in a larger setting. Although blacks were right to cavil at Southern Rhodesia's restriction of rights in good land to Africans, and to question the ways in which Southern Rhodesian policies inhibited black prosperity, Gore-Browne still saw the wartime task of Northern Rhodesians as one of making their own little corner of Africa into "something which may some day prove to be an ideal state." Such a state should include Nyasaland and Southern Rhodesia as well, he declared, and be based on "ordinary decency, justice and freedom."[58]

Without links to Southern Rhodesia, Gore-Browne worried about the continued development of his own country after the war.

57. Stanley in Great Britain, *Parliamentary Debates,* 403 (18 October 1944), cc. 2366–2368.
58. Gore-Browne in *Debates,* 41 (9 December 1941), 19–22.

Surely, he and others assumed, there would then be a slump, and, isolated, Northern Rhodesia would stagnate. In 1942 he began talking, at first off-handedly and rather vaguely, of federation as a plausible solution. What he had in mind was a very loose linking of three or more Central and East African territories, the sharing of common services (already begun in East Africa), and continued internal autonomy in African matters. Two years later he proposed (both in London and in Lusaka), an immediate association of Northern Rhodesia with Nyasaland and southern Tanganyika as an alternative to amalgamation with Southern Rhodesia. Doing so would ensure the larger-sized unit which had become his obsession.

For these mixed reasons Gore-Browne enthusiastically supported the decision to transform the Interterritorial Conference, which in 1941 had begun to coordinate the military assistance efforts of Southern Rhodesia, Northern Rhodesia, and Nyasaland into a permanent organization with a secretariat and a broad-ranging mandate.[59] Huggins called the decision to create a Central African Council "nothing more than a sop" and agreed to it only under pressure. But Welensky realized that its formation at least left "the door slightly ajar towards amalgamation. If we can make a success of it," he said, "I believe it is a lead towards amalgamation." Gore-Browne, however, regarded the council as a more neutral experiment which would have the advantage of increasing the scale of Northern Rhodesia's thinking, and perhaps bring about multiterritorial cooperation in economically valuable spheres of activity. If properly handled, he said, "nothing but good should eventuate from this Council." Africans would, he thought, benefit as much as whites.[60]

Conferences between Waddington, Huggins, and Gore-Browne in early 1945, and cables back and forth to Stanley in London, settled the final organization and composition of the new council. An ad-

59. The Interterritorial Conference came into existence following periodic meetings by the governors of the three countries. Its handful of civil servants dealt upon behalf of the governors with transport and food supply problems caused by the war, with the distribution of refugees and internees, and with such tenuously related subjects as the secondary education of Africans, migratory labor, and the like. In 1942, however, Huggins used the conference to organize a settler discussion on the furtherance of amalgamation, which brought forth immediate criticism from London and official instructions that the conference secretariat could not be employed in such a manner. See 1a/355; 1a/356; 1a/358; 1a/359; 1a/360; 1a/444, all Zomba archives.

60. Huggins, quoted in A. J. Hanna, *The Story of the Rhodesias and Nyasaland* (London, 1960), 249. Welensky, in *Debates,* 49 (16 January 1945), 96; Gore-Browne in *Debates,* 49 (18 January 1945), 136.

visory body with no executive powers, it was originally responsible for coordinating the research activities, the medical, educational, and economic policies, and the transportation and communication systems of the three territories. Gore-Browne joined Waddington; Cartmel-Robinson, the chief secretary; and Welensky as a member of the Northern Rhodesian delegation. At the first session, in April 1945, Gore-Browne objected to the name of the council, since no Africans were represented and it was central in no policy-making sense. He also proposed the creation of the kind of common services which might encourage multiterritorial unity. Gore-Browne found the proceedings interesting, and complimented Waddington and Huggins on the way they ran their teams, but was critical of Admiral Sir Campbell Tait, the new governor of Southern Rhodesia, who presided ineptly, and the Nyasaland delegation—Governor Sir Edmund Richards, an "ill-mannered oaf," an acting chief secretary who was a non-entity; a fatuous and long-winded settler; and Malcolm Barrow, a truculent teaplanter.

The Nyasalanders were equally "futile" during the second meeting of the council in October 1945. The discussion centered around the advisability of establishing a jointly controlled air service, the damming of the Zambezi River at the Kariba Gorge and the consequent production of hydroelectricity, the development of an archives service, the hospitalization of mentally ill patients, the need for a customs union, the provision of a single currency for the three territories, soil conservation, educational facilities for Europeans, forming a central statistics board, African housing, the problems of tuberculosis, and many other items of mutual concern.[61]

The council for the most part thus concerned itself with a variety of technical problems affecting the economic and social development of the region. It advanced the cause of closer political association only indirectly, by demonstrating the advantages of cooperation across a range of activities. It brought the settler representatives of the three territories together twice a year and thus provided a natural forum for the sharing of amalgamationist sentiment. It performed many of the kinds of functions which Gore-Browne had long had in mind.

As Northern Rhodesia entered the postwar era Gore-Browne instinctively knew that major changes of all kinds were in store for his territory, and especially in the area of his main concern— relations between black and white. There would be an influx of white settlers, new white expectations of amalgamation or home rule, and intensified African tensions. His ordinarily heavy burden

61. Gore-Browne to Ethel Locke-King, 29 April, 11 November 1945; 1a/336, 1a/337, 1a/344, Zomba archives.

of leadership would grow more weighty. Not only was he the leader of an unofficial section of the Legislative Council which, for the first time, constituted a majority which it must exercise constructively. A delegate to the Central African council and the inter-territorial road and air councils, senior member for native interests, and a member of endless committees, he had also received a knighthood in the New Year's honors. As Sir Stewart, having actually earned a knighthood like his father and grandfather before him, both his standing and responsibilities were commensurately more inclusive. He had become Northern Rhodesia's, indeed Central Africa's, elder statesman without being able to shed the chores of office or relax his involvement in all of the locally important issues. (By this point, too, Gore-Browne and his wife had separated, so the kind of steady family support which he craved was totally absent.)

Of these issues, the one which would preoccupy Gore-Browne throughout the remainder of his parliamentary life was hardly new: was Northern Rhodesia to follow Southern Rhodesia and become a self-governing white colony or was the Colonial Office to continue to run it on behalf of Africans? (No one then considered the possibility of African self-government or independence). "I cannot believe that it is impossible to find some means to enable white people to stay on in this country and prosper, and at the same time to deny the black man no advance of which he is himself capable," Gore-Browne concluded a long debate in the Legislative Council. "That," he said, "is my confession of faith, and I would be prepared to devote my whole life to achieve that end." He went on: "I do not want to see the black man pushed ahead too fast. That has happened in too many of our colonies, *to his own detriment.* . . . But . . . I have too much faith in my own people and my own race to fear that if we allow the African all the advantages of which he is capable he is bound sooner or later to push us out of the country."[62]

Gore-Browne's confession of faith in no way obscured his gloomy recognition, which grew stronger after the war, that most whites would not make concessions willingly and would intensify their mistreatment of Africans if not checked. Stimulated by the grievances articulated by Tonga farmers, he brooded on the very basis of Northern Rhodesian, even colonial, race relations and, after being brushed off by Waddington, decided to make an electrifying speech in the Legislative Council. It won him the enmity of his fellow non-officials and the unstinting praise of Africans.

Welensky had recently told both the members of the Southern Rhodesian Labour Party and white railway workers there that "the African would judge the European by the way the Europeans be-

62. Gore-Browne in *Debates,* 51 (29 August 1945), 118.

haved towards him," and had made it clear to those hostile groups that he thought the course of prudence dictated befriending Africans. Gore-Browne alluded to these statements and then told the stunned legislators that relations between Africans and Europeans were steadily worsening. "What moves me to speak as I intend speaking now, is my firm conviction that in this country it is not too late to put things on a proper footing once again." Whites had "not done all [they] should have done for [their] African fellow-citizens," he said. As a result Africans distrusted whites.

There were six reasons for this distrust.

1) Africans were persuaded that whites had taken the best land in the country. Gore-Browne quoted the testimony of a Tonga farmer: "'To us native reserve means where the soil is poor and Crown land where it is rich. Our population has increased to the stage where we have no land because Europeans have taken the best from us.'"

2) Missionaries were seen to be working against African interests. Gore-Browne again quoted an African: "'Why colour bar? Did the Lord ever teach his disciples to use colour bar principles? . . . Some of the missionaries want to be looked upon as Government officials and not as the servants of the Lord.'"

3) District commissioners, the backbone of the administration, were out of touch with changing Northern Rhodesia.

4) The informal enforcement of the color bar vexed Africans. Gore-Browne saw no justification for the discrimination against Africans practiced in stores, post offices, railway stations, banks, and the like. In each long lines of Africans were kept waiting interminably until the last whites were served.

5) The economic color bar caused even more distress. It meant, said Gore-Browne, that because a man had a black skin he was not allowed to do skilled work, and the amount of any kind of work he could do was also limited.

6) The social color bar unwisely prevented whites from extending common courtesies toward Africans, and behaving toward them as if they were fellow humans. Gore-Browne said that if Africans happened to be in his own house at tea-time, they were naturally asked to stay and take tea. He suggested that other whites try to act more naturally toward Africans. "The solution," he said, referring to this and the other problems, "comes in appreciating the value of our common humanity. We English people are not cruel by nature. I think the worst that can be said of us is that we are inconsiderate and perhaps not very perceptive." But these were hardly strengths when "dealing with our friends. That is all I would ask . . . this recognition, as I have said . . . before, of our common humanity with the African."

Gore-Browne ended his critique on a note pitched appropriately high. "I have kept sentiment strictly out of anything I have said this morning because sentiment is a dangerous thing. . . . But I would . . . ask whether those men back from Burma, who marched past . . . the other day, I would ask whether they are stinking kaffirs? Sir, I have said all I need to say."[63]

These remarks signified the end of an era and marked, although few noticed, the outline of the black/white battleground throughout the next two decades. The other white legislators demanded and obtained a recall of the council for an unprecedented two-day debate solely to answer Gore-Browne and defend white prerogatives, justify the color bar, and declare that he had been crying "wolf." Africans, however, cheered loudly. At last someone had said very plainly that there were serious grounds for complaint. E. M. L. Mtepuka, the editor of the *African Weekly,* published in Salisbury, wrote ecstatically: "It certainly makes one think you've a black heart under a white skin!" Dauti Yamba, a leader of the newly formed Federation of African Welfare Societies of Northern Rhodesia, was full of compliments. "You left no stone unturned, and I humbly beg to say Well Done."[64]

63. Gore-Browne in *Debates,* 53 (6 April 1946), cc. 450–458.

64. Mtepuka to Gore-Browne, 1 May 1946; Yamba to Gore-Browne, 13 April 1946.

VIII
The Last Hurrah

THE ISSUE was fairly joined. With the end of the war, the wielding of political power in Britain by a Labour majority, and continued colonial domination being challenged everywhere in Asia and the Middle East, Northern Rhodesia could no longer presume the sufficiency of past policies and practices regarding settler prerogatives and indigenous rights. Gore-Browne saw more clearly than anyone else, and much more perceptively than he himself had only a very few years before, that black political consciousnesses had been raised irreversibly. Whites would thus deny African aspirations only at the risk of prolonged confrontation. Equally, however, Gore-Browne understood the extent of white political deprivation. They had been kept waiting by commissions and conflict in Europe. In the post-war era whites would resume their self-righteous quest for hegemony—for a final, favorable settlement of the long battle to gain the upper hand over the Protectorate's black majority. How else could they—to echo Moore's phrases—control their destinies and counter the superiority of African numbers? But as much as whites schemed, so newly aroused Africans would agitate, each side pleading with Whitehall and Downing Street for attention, absolution, and support.

Gore-Browne knew not where it would end. But he saw the prevailing predicament in its fullest ramifications and devoted his penultimate political energies to resolving the Northern Rhodesian version of what turned out to be a common colonial dilemma. It was too early for him to have glimpsed the possibility of a thoroughgoing black triumph without major bloodshed or the total breakdown of race relations. Instead, he worked assiduously throughout the last half of the 1940s for greater white and black cooperation, for the removal of the more offensive articulations of white supremacy (as expressed via the color bar), and—most of all—for improved political opportunities for Africans. Almost singlehandedly (among whites) he advocated the advancement of Africans in the political life of the country. Greater political participation would, he believed, help assuage realizations of black powerlessness. Moreover, the experience of speaking in provincial and national assemblies, no matter if they were merely advisory, would prepare Africans for greater and greater responsibility and—in the fullness of time—the sharing of power in the territorial legislature.

Gore-Browne envisaged the gradual devolution of responsibility and power to black representatives, the eventual incorporation of Africans into the national electorate, and, although he never fully sketched the end result or elaborated upon his own fantasies, a national parliament where black and white would work harmoniously for the common good. This multiracial solution was ahead of its time (no matter how naive it now appears) and—given Gore-Browne's tactics—unattainable. For he knew only too well how local whites would and could block any provision of new opportunities to blacks which did not couple such advances to white accretions of power. He therefore chose during the late 1940s to play a political game far more dangerous than he appreciated: he would promote black political growth within a context of simultaneous settler progress. This, to him, was a policy of realism. For he feared widening the gap of black/white enmity, saw no way of satisfying African aspirations without white cooperation, and could perceive a prosperous, stable future for Northern Rhodesia only under the banner of some honest, if paternal, multiracialism.

Gore-Browne's was a task Sisyphean in magnitude and, though neither he nor anyone else could have foreseen it, constrained by a remarkably inelastic and foreshortened framework of time. Thus, no matter how energetically and perceptively Gore-Browne sought to broaden the participation of Africans in national life and alleviate the disabilities with which they were stigmatized, the lag between advocacy and accomplishment was often too prolonged for his achievements on their behalf to have an impact as salutary, and politically and socially relevant, as he had hoped and expected. But to say so is to anticipate, for as much as Gore-Browne personally appreciated the growing African determination to be assertive, he could accomplish little without obtaining the cooperation of his fellow unofficial members of the Legislative Council, especially Welensky; of the governor and his staff; and, as before, of the Colonial Office (which had its own trans-colonial comparabilities and policies to consider). Furthermore, of this shifting group of persons, none, not even Cohen (now in charge of East and Central Africa for the Colonial Office and a member of the Fabian Society) were sufficiently prescient to appreciate the true velocity of change in colonial Africa.

Despite the startlingly pro-African outburst in early 1946 which had enraged his fellows, Gore-Browne remained the leader of the unofficials for a number of months longer—for a period sufficient for him to help guide Northern Rhodesia's constitutional negotiating team in London. As a way of forestalling renewed pressure for amalgamation by whites, and as a means of giving Africans reason to continue to believe in British benevolence, he sought to obtain a document capable of advancing and balancing the claims of both, but without eroding the ultimate safeguard of metropolitan oversight. In London from May to early September he consulted informally on numerous occasions with Cohen; with Arthur Creech Jones, then undersecretary of state and soon to be secretary for the colonies; Rita Hinden of the Fabian Society; Banda; Eliud Mathu, Kenya's first African legislative councillor; Margaret Read; Gervase and Elspeth Huxley; Colonel Stanley, the former colonial secretary; Brian Nkonde and Safeli Chileshe, two Northern Rhodesians studying in London as a result of Gore-Browne's exertions; James Davidson and Ronald Robinson, two young Cambridge dons interested in imperial problems; Cavendish-Bentinck, over from Kenya; Sir Alan Pim, who had issued a famous economic report on Northern Rhodesia in the late 1930s; Audrey Richards; and Margery Perham. He devoted time, too, to his many relatives and old friends and to Dame Ethel. Many of the consultations were either for the purpose of exchanging information about African problems (Banda was especially grateful and began a vigorous correspondence which continued into the late 1950s) or as a means of advancing his constitutional cause. Equally productive, although not until late August could he claim success, were the formal meetings with Waddington and Welensky, and with Cohen and other principals of the Colonial Office. Together an agreement was finally drafted giving Northern Rhodesia a form of what Gore-Browne, in his diary, called "modified self-government, including adequate African representation."[1]

In this context "adequate" representation for Africans turned out to be two. Of the four representatives of African interests, two would be selected by the fledgling African Representative Council and the two others, still white, would (over Gore-Browne's objections) continue to be nominated by the governor. In addition the number of elected members would be increased from eight to ten. Only nine officials would sit in the house, and a speaker, not the governor, would preside. Thus, even without the representatives of Africans, the elected whites would have a clear majority. (But Gore-Browne reasoned that the Africans and their white representatives could, if the elected whites tried to pass legislation inimical

1. Entry of 7 August 1946. The details of the negotiations are contained in Sec/Misc/72: Hall to Waddington, 30 July 1946, Lusaka archives. The account in L. H. Gann, *A History of Northern Rhodesia* (London, 1963), 395, is based upon partial information.

to blacks, vote with the officials against the elected members.) Of more importance to Welensky, the position of the elected members in the Executive Council was left in abeyance. None of these changes were to be implemented, however, until 1948 (the life of the eighth council being extended until then) after fresh council elections and the anticipated arrival of a new governor.

Despite these significant additions to white power, the rather modest concessions to blacks caused a striking outburst of white antagonism, especially on the Copperbelt. The leader of the racist opposition was J. F. Morris, the elected member for Luanshya, who ranted and raved even after Welensky, at a private meeting with the unofficials in October, declared that African representation was inevitable, that opposition by the European public would be harmful to the reputation of whites, and that it would exacerbate racial discord. In these as in so many other respects, Welensky still heeded Gore-Browne's advice and the force of his logic. Even later in the council, he followed Gore-Browne's lead when he could so easily have adopted the protective coloring of his constituents: "When we were in Great Britain," he told the assembly, "I expressed the opinion that it was premature to give direct representation to Africans. But once the Secretary of State . . . had made up his mind that this had to be done . . . I felt the best thing was to accept it. . . . Now the best thing we can do is not to let the Africans who come into this Council feel that we . . . are antagonistic to them. That would be a tragic error."[2]

Gore-Browne assumed full responsibility for pushing the African case. "I do not want to shelter behind the fact that it was . . . a Colonial Office decision," declared Gore-Browne in the midst of a forthright speech. "I put it as my own personal request, and I do not want in any way to back out from any responsibility. . . . My Colleague did not endorse it." For him, as for so many others, said Gore-Browne, African representation in 1947 or 1948 came too soon. Yet the rationale was clear. "We should be able," he continued, "to have the services of an African who can view problems with an African outlook, which obviously is different from our own. . . . The value of having an African to say how a thing strikes him as an African is very great." Gore-Browne believed that only a highly educated African, and one fully literate in English, could hope to take part in the debates. Even so, and even granting (which he did) that the majority of Africans were still "primitive," he was convinced that African representation was essential because of the matter which caused him "more apprehension and more anxiety than anything else in the world to-day. It is the fact that,

2. Welensky, in *Debates*, 56 (3 December 1946), c. 55.

not only in Africa but all the world over, the coloured races are
losing, and in many places have already lost, their trust for the European race." This state of affairs was not necessarily the fault of
whites. Moreover, Gore-Browne asserted (though he may not
really have believed it), Northern Rhodesia was still ahead in this
respect. "I do not think the African has lost trust in us yet, and if we
take time by the forelock, and do what we should do, we may put
race relations on a proper footing and keep them there, but there is
not much time to lose." Hence, Gore-Browne concluded his peroration, to deny Africans what had already been achieved in East
Africa "would be a mistake which would be interpreted by Africans
in this country as an attempt to frustrate and keep them down."[3]

During the same debate, and for many of the same reasons that
had influenced his decision to demand African representation,
Gore-Browne again urged action in other spheres to relieve equally
damaging African bitterness. Put differently, he had become an
advocate of modernization; how else could Africans play a responsive and responsible role in post-war Rhodesia? How else could the
Protectorate avoid the crisis of confidence—the breakdown of
good relations between black and white—which seemed about to
paralyze West Africa as it had Asia?

Foremost among his long list of categorical imperatives was educational advance. As a lone voice he had for many years publicly
promoted providing educational opportunities for Africans and
privately done what he could to propel likely scholars forward.
Nyasas as well as promising Northern Rhodesians obtained financial support from or through him, Harry Nkumbula's educational progression in the mid-1940s being due almost exclusively to
backing from Gore-Browne. By 1946 Gore-Browne was also a
member of a three-man committee to award government bursaries
(at first only two) for overseas study, the problem being initially to
obtain a quantity of nominees among whom to choose. But Gore-
Browne realized that no matter how effectively he and his influence
might expand opportunities for individuals, Northern Rhodesia
could not hope to modernize with any speed unless the government
altered its churlish attitude and provided its own post-primary
facilities on a broad scale.

Although many whites thought his arguments utopian, Gore-
Browne talked himself hoarse explaining why funds should be devoted to the apex of the territory's educational pyramid. Practically,
his premise ran, "in due course we are to associate Africans with us
in the Government . . . of this country." Therefore "we must do
our part by fitting them to take these jobs." Hitherto, he said,

3. Gore-Browne in *Debates,* 56 (4 December 1946), cc. 115–118.

whites had not been fair. They had said that Africans were not fit for responsible positions and yet firmly denied them the opportunity of making themselves fit for such posts.[4] He deplored the dilatory way in which the government was going about implementing a much earlier decision to develop the first stages of secondary education locally (what became the Munali Secondary School in Lusaka) and complained that quasi-university arrangements made by him in London (for diploma courses and so on at the Institute of Education) had been foolishly neglected. In short, knowing what Africans craved, and knowing how all his own proposals for increased political participation by Africans depended upon their gaining access to and benefiting from Western style education—the obvious key to success in the post-war colonies—he pushed the otherwise slow-moving bureaucratic machine and his reluctant colleagues to recognize the importance of educating Africans beyond the perfunctory stages which had for so long been accepted as adequate by missionaries and the officials who supervised Native Education in Northern Rhodesia. Gore-Browne had returned from Britain in 1946 via Makerere College, in Uganda, and knew the high levels of opportunity which, given the administrative will and the funds (available locally from copper surpluses), could be made available by any energetic and self-respecting colonial government.

There were other imperatives about which Gore-Browne reminded his fellow legislators. "Reminded" is apt, for many of the African grievances which he had been voicing in the council for years were, in the period after the war, still unassuaged. There was no hospital for the insane, so "lunatics" still had to be chained in country prisons. In Balovale, Gore-Browne reported, he had been asked to inspect the prison and had there seen "an extraordinary thing—it must have been an optical illusion, but I saw one of these poor miserable lunatics there . . . It must have been an optical illusion because we have been assured so often in this Council . . . that lunatics aren't put in prison in Northern Rhodesia. . . . And he had been there for seven years."[5] The conditions of travel for Africans on the overland buses and the railways remained shocking. Seats were unavailable, sanitary arrangements were lacking, and blacks continued to be treated like cattle being taken to market. On the mines there was an obvious need, said Gore-Browne, to end a reliance on migrants and provide accommodations suitably conducive to a stabilized labor force. Even the companies would benefit, he argued. And, as a pendant to all of his concerns, he had persuaded everyone to begin referring officially (in legislation) to Africans,

4. Ibid., cc. 112–114.
5. Gore-Browne in *Debates,* 59 (27 November 1947), c. 206.

not "natives." It was more dignified, but the agreement was being honored in the breach. He urged his fellows on this, as on so many other counts, to appreciate how much they would depend in the postwar era on the confidence of Africans. Whites could no longer assume—and he spoke to the groans on the lips of his white colleagues—that Africans would necessarily remain cooperative.

The differences between the stance of Gore-Browne and that of the other whites became more sharply drawn when Welensky vigorously reactivated the settler quest for sovereignty in the guise of amalgamation. In part he was responding to the mood of his fellow white legislators and their constituents, nearly all of whom felt that they must assert themselves immediately, or watch the pendulum of power in Northern Rhodesia shift inexorably toward blacks. The granting of two council seats to blacks foreshadowed a serious erosion of white privilege. In 1938, Welensky pointed out, Gore-Browne was nominated to represent Africans. In less than a decade the council contained three such representatives, and in 1948 there would be four, of whom two would be Africans. It followed, said Welensky, that "by 1958 no European will sit in this Council . . . representing African interests, and possibly there will be an increase in the number of African representatives." Moreover, "by 1968, if the present policy continues, there will be an Elected African majority in this Chamber . . . . [and] . . . unless we bring about a change of Government, that will happen."

Welensky made it clear that as far as he was concerned, Africans would not be ready "for our form of government" for fifteen or twenty years. "I think it will be a tragedy if that should happen. . . . I say that for the next 50 or 100 years the African has an important part to play here, but he has to play that part as a junior partner, and I am prepared to accept him as such." (Many of Welensky's supporters would not have expressed themselves so positively.) Furthermore, he continued, "every African who recognises the complexity of our government must realise that he is not fit to step in as an equal partner."[6]

Only by amalgamating with Southern Rhodesia, Welensky concluded, could Northern Rhodesia avoid being transformed into a black man's country. White self-government was therefore essential, desired by all whites, and opposed, he thought, only by ill-informed, detribalized Africans and by those sincere persons (including his friend Gore-Browne) who, misguidedly, took the protestations of Africans at face value.

Since much of the debate in the Council had been anticipated in private by discussions among the unofficials, Gore-Browne's

6. Welensky, *Debates,* 56 (11 December 1946), c. 277–278.

public response emphasized not the arguments against amalgamation—those had been voiced too often to be fresh—but the
one issue of paramount salience. Articulate Africans were unanimously opposed to any loss of their rights and deserved—this
was the key point—to have their objections heard and weighed in
the balance. Moreover, he had extracted a promise in writing from
George Hall, the late secretary of state for the colonies, that he
"should not fail to consult the wishes . . . of the inhabitants of the
Territory in regard to any changes which might from time to time
be contemplated affecting the status of Northern Rhodesia."[7]

It was on this issue that Gore-Browne chose to resign his leadership of the elected members in the council. Unless he did so he felt
that he could not maintain the confidence of Africans or represent
their interests as effectively as he should. Equally, the other white
legislators could hardly be expected to continue to relish being led
and spoken for by someone so unsympathetic to their views.
Welensky had pressed this point before the council meeting and
Gore-Browne had agreed to resign providing that Welensky would
be elected in his stead. When this shift was assured, Gore-Browne
removed himself from the position he had filled so magisterially
(ambiguously, from the white point of view) since Moore's removal in 1939. To the public it seemed a dramatic resignation on a
point of principle. And so it was. But equally he was content to be
free of the task of holding the white legislators together. "It's a
relief," he wrote to his aunt after the maneuvering had taken place
and Welensky had acceded to power. "I make no bones about that,
to be quit of responsibility, and it was becoming increasingly
difficult to hold them (Roy is finding it a shocking task, and may not
succeed either, which would be bad all round), I also clear up my
position vis-à-vis the Africans. . . ."[8]

Although their personal friendship remained as firm as ever and
they continued to cooperate in a number of political ways, it was
symptomatic of the slowly gathering storm in Central Africa that
Gore-Browne and Welensky were now set on demonstrably divergent tacks. Welensky, the parvenu, could no longer afford to go
along with Gore-Browne's pragmatic handling of the "race" question. The pursuit of greater influence, which Welensky wanted,
depended upon the support of local whites and the use of that
support to win concessions from the Colonial Office. Gore-

7. Hall to Gore-Browne, 16 August 1946. Gore-Browne quoted the letter in full
in his council speech. *Debates,* 56 (11 December 1946), cc. 291. Two years later
Gore-Browne admitted that the letter had been full of empty phrases.

8. Gore-Browne to Ethel Locke-King, 8 December 1946. But see Don Taylor,
The Rhodesian: The Life of Sir Roy Welensky (London, 1955), 79.

Browne, by contrast, was freed of the constraints of leadership and could at last express the anxieties of Africans as fully and as un-abashedly as the times required. As a consequence (and partially, too, because disagreements between white and black were growing more dangerous), during 1947 he devoted more time and energy than ever before to the gathering of African opinion. In rural areas and along the line-of-rail he held meeting after meeting to report back to his far-flung constituents and to hear their impressions and complaints. He spent days with the Lozi court, with the chiefs and commoners of remote Fort Jameson, Lundazi, Kasempa, and Sol-wezi, and with workers in nearly every town on the Copperbelt. One gathering, at Luanshya, began at dusk and continued well past midnight as 1,200 to 1,500 persons made their feelings known.

Gore-Browne often thought of resigning entirely, and of devot-ing his remaining energies to Shiwa's problems, but whenever he wrote about this possibility he always admitted that as hopeless as he felt in the face of worsening race relations and white agitation for amalgamation, Africans did not seem to want him to cease speaking for them. "I'd gladly step aside, that is no less than the truth, but for the Black men. At every one of the 18 or 20 big meetings I've held," he wrote in late 1947, ". . . they've urged me to carry on. . . . I certainly have got their confidence in a way no one else in the country ever has." In 1948 blacks would take their seats beside him (presuming his own renomination) and "will want one more than ever before." These were immodest but accurate assessments of his own role, confirmed—if confirmation were needed—by articles of praise in the local African press and flattering personal letters from the African intelligentsia. "Sir Stewart," wrote Godwin Mbikusita, the first president of the Northern Rhodesian African Congress, "has been our beacon light since his nomination as our represen-tative. . . . He has been and is still a reliable interpreter "of African opinion and thought . . . [and] . . . it is the hope of every African . . . that the two Africans to be elected will be guided by him . . . as they will be the outcome of his untiring efforts."[9]

Africans had reason to trust Gore-Browne. Not only had he helped Africans individually and collectively to right wrongs, gain access to levels of preferment, and obtain British as well as local notice of their powerlessness, but over the years he had embodied their faith in the essential fairness of British rule. His was a paternal vision of a harmonious multiracial Northern Rhodesia, and one still believable by and capable of being shared by Africans. Indeed, by all Africans. For Gore-Browne resented any imputation by whites that

9. Gore-Browne to Ethel Locke-King, 23 November 1947; Mbikusita (later Godwin M. Lewanika) in *The African Weekly*, 31 December 1947.

he somehow spoke only on behalf of educated Africans. In fact he claimed to speak for Africans of all classes and stations, and was particularly proud of his regular visitations to Native Authorities and his rapport with the chiefly leaders of the country. But, especially after spending several weeks in the Sudan in 1946, and in the Sudan and West Africa on his way to and from a colonial airways conference in London in mid-1947, Gore-Browne was anxious—as he had been throughout his entire parliamentary career—to avoid creating an African elite which would be cut off from the Northern Rhodesian masses. "If there is one thing I am sure of," he said, "it is that all Africans will suffer irretrievable harm if a rift is allowed to grow up between the educated classes and other Africans."[10] Later, after traveling in the Gold Coast, he felt that he had found a colony where this danger had been avoided. The emergence of a broad ranging middle class, as in the Gold Coast, was exactly the model for a modernizing Rhodesia. In Kumasi, particularly, but also in Accra and elsewhere in the Gold Coast, he was struck with the refreshing absence of any color bar. "It's the spirit of the whole thing," he wrote, "and the way Africans and Europeans are working together, *not* just Europeans doing what they consider right for acquiescent Africans."[11] In Nigeria, he was equally pleased to see Africans doing all the skilled work, even on the railways, a policy which the trade unions refused to condone in the Rhodesias. However, continuing on to Léopoldville, the capital of the Belgian Congo, plummeted Gore-Browne and Mulenga back into the grip of the color bar. "Oh the dominant white men and white women are unattractive," he contrasted with his happier weeks in West Africa, "the former with tummies swelling their whitish trousers, the latter heavy breasted and sloppy. Even a Lyons Corner House crowd can give them many points. The black men look cowed & fugitive."[12]

The seeming contentment and progress of West Africa reinforced Gore-Browne's determination to create a viable multiracial society in Northern Rhodesia. Yet his method of realizing this vision in the short run proved excessively eccentric, and to Africans, traitorous. The context of Gore-Browne's unexpected initiative may, admittedly, have contributed to his faulty analysis of the politically possible: in early 1947 Welensky and Geoff Beckett, a nominated unofficial member from the southern region, resigned their positions on the Executive Council in order to establish a "constructive opposition" to the government and make it completely clear that white

10. Gore-Browne in *Debates,* 56 (12 February 1947), c. 876.
11. Gore-Browne to Ethel Locke-King, 5 July 1947.
12. Gore-Browne to Ethel Locke-King, 22 July 1947.

Gore-Browne and Henry Mulenga, 1964.

unofficials were determined to have amalgamation and end Colonial Office rule. Gore-Browne had stayed on as the only unofficial member of the Executive Council. This had made his role as a white spokesman for Africans even more lonely than before, but his situation was further confused in late 1947 when Welensky toyed with the offer of a wellpaying job in Southern Rhodesia (he almost accepted it) and by the likelihood that Gore-Browne would then have had to resume leading the unofficials. (Whenever Welensky fell ill, which happened fairly often, Gore-Browne led the unofficials at his request.) Or, as some commentators have suggested, did Gore-Browne in the last months of 1947 crave being boss again and hope to oust Welensky?[13] This is a conclusion unsubstantiated by any evidence, for Gore-Browne was enjoyably active again at Shiwa (where there were serious financial problems), and would hardly

13. Gann, *History,* 395.

have sought to scheme (given unattractive odds) against his close friend and, what was more significant, his protege. Rather, Gore-Browne thought that he saw how he could reconcile white and black, head off amalgamation, and ensure political progress under the new constitution. Overconfident, he counted on not being misunderstood by the blacks, with whom he still had boundless credibility. Overconfident, again, he assumed that the Colonial Office and their local representatives (a new governor was due in early 1948) would recognize the practicality of his proposals for an alteration in the established framework of home rule.

By this time Northern Rhodesia, having begun to welcome white immigrants, counted 25,000 whites and 1.8 million Africans as its population. Of the latter, most, said Gore-Browne, lived under "primitive conditions" and lacked "anything but very elementary education." More significantly, he described their condition as "politically immature" and "at present without leaders."[14] This was only partially correct, for by virtue of the increased opportunities for political participation which he had encouraged and seen inaugurated, most notably the African Representative Council, African leaders had emerged and had begun speaking loudly on behalf of their fellows. The men whom he had sent on to university were also beginning to return with new found importance and educationally conferred legitimacies. Most of all, in 1946 representatives of fourteen of Northern Rhodesia's African Welfare Societies had created a Federation of African Societies which was becoming an obvious focus of urban political activity. Under Dauti Yamba, a Luapula schoolteacher who became its first president, and Mbikusita, his successor, the federation was an obvious vehicle for the expression of indigenous grievances and for the mobilization of further discontent. Thanks to Gore-Browne, Africans were collectively not as voiceless as they had been. Immature they perhaps were by some standards, but—ironically—by 1948 Gore-Browne had provided sufficient outlets and respectability. Africans were far more sophisticated and politically aware than he appreciated. Too late, Gore-Browne—like so many other politicians—was to discover that he could no longer take the views of his constituents for granted.

The bombshell burst early in January 1948. Two days before the end of the fourth session of the eighth Legislative Council, during the "cross-country" debate on the supplementary estimates, Gore-Browne told the surprised officials that it was his task to conclude seven weeks of constitutional wrangling in the council (with much talk of amalgamation by Welensky and others). "There

14. Gore-Browne in *Debates,* 59 (12 January 1948), c. 829.

must be no room for doubt about what we mean or where we stand," he warned. The unofficials were—amazingly—united: "We are one and all convinced that government by bureaucracy, however enlightened and well-meaning, is no longer good enough for Northern Rhodesia, especially with the prospects for development which lie ahead." The days of unofficials being content with promises of "close cooperation" and informal guarantees (as were contained in the 1946 agreements scheduled to be implemented later that year) were over. "Their day is past." Therefore the unofficials wanted responsible government under a scheme which made allowance for the lack of white numbers and provided for adequate African representation. "If it did not . . . I, for one, would have had no share in sponsoring the plan." But—and this aspect caused widespread consternation outside—Gore-Browne refused to disclose the details of the plan until the arrival in late February of Sir Gilbert Rennie, the new governor (lately chief secretary in Kenya).

All that Gore-Browne would say publicly was rhetorically sound and politically catastrophic: "The essential thing is . . . that something must be done and done soon. We have, one and all, made that clear, and I cannot for one moment think that either [the acting governor, Rennie, or Creech Jones, the colonial secretary] . . . will be so ill-advised as to force us to adopt the only alternative open to us. That alternative . . . would be to use such powers as we already possess to paralyse . . . government. That would be a shocking thing to do—I use the adjective advisedly—and normally it would be quite indefensible. But once in a thousand times such tactics are justified, and if such a situation should arise we would none of us hesitate."[15]

The press was bound to seize upon the more inflammatory elements in Gore-Browne's speech and Africans—although Gore-Browne subsequently professed surprise that they should have—were equally certain to read the press accounts. Even more damaging, however, the local press (a twice weekly affair) coupled its report of the mysterious proposals to a gloss provided by the government. Replying for the officials the day after Gore-Browne had spoken, George E. Thornton, the financial secretary, said that the request for responsible government was both remarkable and far-reaching in its implications. Moreover, said Thornton, "unofficial Members have made it clear they regard [their proposals] as no more than the prelude to amalgamation with Southern Rhodesia."[16]

The actual proposals were both more and less frightening than

15. Ibid. (12 January 1948), cc. 817–831.
16. Thornton, in *Debates,* 59 (13 January 1948), c. 867.

Thornton and alarmed Africans imagined. Gore-Browne had certainly begun thinking about them during his months in Britain during 1947, but he also told his sister that he had been puzzling over the problem—"how to devise some workable form of self-government which could apply to a colony where a) there was only a limited number of Europeans, & b) a large number of mainly primitive natives"—for about ten years. During the summer of 1946 he had discussed his ideas with Cohen ("the best brain in the Colonial Office"') and Creech Jones. Cohen was "taken with it" and Creech Jones, he said, praised it for being ingenious, and did not condemn it.[17] There were further discussions with Creech Jones, Cohen, and many others during the summer months of 1947. It is not known if Gore-Browne talked about his scheme with Banda, who was then sharing a house in north London with Mrs. Margaret French, and whom Gore-Browne saw frequently, or with Nelson Nalumango, Chileshe, and the other Northern Rhodesians with whom he had ample contact in London. But the proposals were not committed to paper at least until December, 1947, by which time it was clear that Welensky had finally refused to be promoted to Southern Rhodesia. "Having him still with us means it's worthwhile putting up some plan for genuine constitutional advance," explained Gore-Browne. Furthermore, R. C. S. Stanley, the acting governor, had proved himself—from the local point of view—the epitome of Colonial Office foolishness. "Daily some fresh gaucherie sets us back . . ." commented Gore-Browne. A contributing factor may also have been Gore-Browne's impatience with old T. S. Page, the elected member for the northeastern precinct. Page persisted in demonstrating the futility of the position of elected members by nitpicking budgets which the unofficials could only accept or reject, and were never allowed to help prepare. Page's "final triumph," wrote Gore-Browne, "was when he criticized the waste of water in the central offices due to the automatic flushing of the urinals all night. One could hardly sink lower."[18]

In mid-December Gore-Browne had put his draft plan before Beckett and Welensky. "I think you will agree," he told them, "that the present situation is impossible. We have got an unofficial majority, but if we analyse it it only amounts to this. We can embarrass the Government . . . but . . . have no real power whatever over the

17. Gore-Browne to Sapphire, 1 March 1948. Although I corresponded with Creech Jones, who praised Gore-Browne, I was unable to ask him specifically about these points before he died. Cohen and I also had a long talk, mostly about the Central African Federation, and corresponded, but I did not ask him specifically about the 1948 imbroglio.

18. Gore-Browne to Ethel Locke-King, 13 December 1947.

executive, and the Government has only to go on delaying the implementation of our wishes over any particular matter till we are finally reduced to impotence." The new constitution provided for an unofficial majority but since the governor controlled the council and its agenda the personality of the governor determined to what extent unofficials could share power meaningfully. The elected side had come to occupy "an uncomfortably halfway house which may at any moment become completely uninhabitable." Gore-Browne's other assumptions were that amalgamation was impossible in the foreseeable future, that normal self-government was equally out of the question, that Parliament would not permit the domination of Africans by an elected settler majority, that adequate African representation would be required to ensure "fair-play" for Africans, and that because of the paucity of qualified local whites, officials would still have to play a role in government and the council. In short, Gore-Browne argued that his scheme was the only one which stood a chance of passing British scrutiny. It was the most practical compromise.[19]

The suggested new constitutional arrangements were deceptively simple. The Legislative Council would consist of ten elected whites, three whites representing Africans, two Africans chosen by the African Representative Council, one African selected by the paramount chief of Barotseland, and four officials. That is, the six representatives of Africans, joined by the officials, could frustrate any legislation desired by whites. The Executive Council would be transformed into a cabinet composed of three elected whites (their chairman, i.e. Welensky, would be chairman of the Executive Council), two other elected members, and one of the whites representing Africans. The last (Gore-Browne?) would be minister for African Affairs, the other members of the Executive Council also taking charge of portfolios. The ministers would be responsible to the legislature. The governor would retain the power of veto.[20]

Gore-Browne was genuinely surprised when Welensky, who had only reluctantly been persuaded that amalgamation could not win, and Beckett both accepted the scheme. He was even more astonished—or so he said—when the other unofficials (even the representatives of Africans) met in his house in Lusaka and approved the plan "without a murmur." Since it called for "considerable African representation" and was "so wildly favourable to the African" Gore-Browne had doubted its acceptability to the other

19. Gore-Browne to Welensky and Beckett, 15 December 1947.
20. Copy typed on Gore-Browne's typewriter and dated 15 December 1947. This is identical with later printed copies of the proposal, and reports in the press.

whites.[21] What had happened was that Welensky and the other whites, as Thornton had said, in fact probably envisaged the constitutional draft as a prelude to amalgamation even though Gore-Browne believed that his plan was "the only thing" that would save Africans *from* amalgamation, "or anyhow put them in such a position that when it does come they will be able to claim their own terms." He told an influential African journalist how important it was to entrench Africans firmly in the government so that they could then frustrate any imperial attempt (here he was prescient) to thrust amalgamation, or something similar, down African throats.[22]

Whatever the merit of Gore-Browne's explanations, the main damage was done long before the actual proposals were released to the public (with Rennie's arrival). All chance of discussing their suitability and dispassionately testing Gore-Browne's hypotheses in any serious way were lost during the tumult of the five intervening weeks. "Never [in] my wildest dreams," wrote Gore-Browne, "[did I imagine] as possible [that] Africans [would] read the announcement . . . in the newspapers and . . . without waiting to hear anything about the proposals, & without an inkling of what the plan was, assume . . . that Amalgamation . . . was what was intended . . . ."[23]

Africans believed themselves betrayed. They denounced "responsible government" as a sly scheme designed to deprive Africans of their rights as protected persons. The Kitwe African Society, one of the major African associations on the Copperbelt, held an extraordinary public meeting in early February. The 250 Africans in attendance decided that there was no difference between responsible government and amalgamation, and they reviled both equally. Gore-Browne was told to consult with Africans before so involving himself with anti-African ideas. Moreover, said the aroused yeomen of Kitwe, if Gore-Browne would not vote against responsible government he would have to cease representing Africans. Mbikusita, the Society's president and so recently a firm supporter of Gore-Browne, declared that the new proposals demonstrated that settlers were determined to deny Africans true partnership. Nkumbula cabled angrily from London. Nalumango,

21. Gore-Browne to Ethel Locke-King, 9 January and 13 January 1948; Gore-Browne to Sapphire, 1 March 1948.

22. Gore-Browne to Ethel Locke-King, 15 February 1948; Gore-Browne to E. M. Mtepuka, editor of *The African Weekly*, 20 February 1948.

23. Gore-Browne to Sapphire, 1 March 1948. Gore-Browne also admitted in the council how fully he had blundered psychologically. Gore-Browne in *Debates*, 61 (28 June 1948), 516.

in Livingstone, declared (in the Cibemba edition of *Mutende,* Northern Rhodesia's fortnightly African newsmagazine) that whites favored responsible government because they wanted "to take all the land from the chiefs in the same way Southern Rhodesia has done to its Africans." The Federation of African Societies and members of provincial councils all condemned the proposals. Ashton Musonda, of Chingola, spoke for many during a later meeting of the Western Provincial Council: "I am suspicious that the unofficial members will put the Africans in an envelope or a ditch. What I am afraid of is amalgamation."[24]

After the arrival of Rennie—"a dour little Scot, pleasant to meet, but obviously not going to give anything away"[25]—Gore-Browne tried to retrieve what had become a desperately uncomfortable situation. Quickly he held nine meetings with Africans from Livingstone to Chingola, some of which lasted for hours and all of which were heavily attended. Everywhere he was criticized, if politely. He managed to persuade only a small proportion of his critics that his plan had been well-intended and designed to benefit Africans. To Gore-Browne it was obvious that he had utterly lost their confidence. Given their general antipathy, and the fact that his term as a nominated member would run out in July, resignation was the only clear option. His position had become impossible. "The Africans have, for the time being, completely thrown me over- . . . and I've an absolute horror of staying on where I'm not wanted."[26]

After further clarifying (perhaps even shading or modifying) his views in the Legislative Council, however, Gore-Browne began to receive letters of support from Africans, and, though provincial councils passed resolutions against responsible government, not all condemned his own role as strenuously as they had earlier. (Welensky argued forcibly, too, against any precipitous resignation and even—in a private letter—urged Dame Ethel to restrain

· 24. *Mutende,* 12 February, 18 March 1948; Sec/Nat/354; Minutes of Kitwe meeting; Address of Welcome to the Secretary for Native Affairs, 10 May 1948; Minutes of the Seventh Meeting of the Western Provincial Council, 28–29 April 1948, Lusaka archives. Nkumbula's cable rankled, and not only because of Gore-Browne's consistent patronage. Shortly before Nkumbula had written to Gore-Browne agreeing "in principle" with self-government providing that drastic alterations in African policy preceded the inauguration of such a scheme. "The building up of parallel political and social institutions based on racial discrimination . . . are measures which cannot be defended any longer." Nevertheless, in the strongest terms he urged Gore-Browne not to resign. Nkumbula to Gore-Browne, 4 April 1948.

25. Gore-Browne to Ethel Locke-King, Easter Sunday, 1948.

26. Gore-Browne to Ethel Locke-King, 14 March 1948.

Gore-Browne from a distance.) When the Legislative Council resumed sitting in mid-March Gore-Browne said that he would "have no part in the acceptance of any proposals which do not guarantee the full rights of Africans." He reiterated his opposition to amalgamation. But he warned that the moment the home government saw an imperial advantage in amalgamation—for trade, for development, for chrome, for waterpower, for defence, or whatever—a pious formula would be devised and nothing Rhodesians could do would make a difference. ("Long before [1960]," he told the Fabians, "some specious formula for getting round the Colour Bar policy of S. Rhodesia will have been devised."[27]) "For the greater part of the time I have sat here representing Africans my main preoccupation has been to find some method by which the rights of Africans, or what I considered to be their rights . . . could be adequately safeguarded in the event of union between Northern and Southern Rhodesia." His plan provided that security, his colleagues accepted it, and "for a moment" it seemed that "we in this country might be going to show . . . to the Empire . . . how, thanks to the generosity of the dominant race, a constitution could be devised under which the rights of both races would be amply safeguarded." Yet Africans had "thrown it all away through ignorance. That is to my mind a tragedy of the highest order."[28]

At the very end of the session, answering a number of the officials who had spoken in the interim, he repeated his belief that his proposals would suitably protect Africans against the evils of amalgamation of both Rhodesias. Then he went on to say, as a way of further strengthening the position of the Africans of Northern Rhodesia, that the next stage in the Protectorate's political development should include union with Nyasaland. It would make economic sense, Northern Rhodesia being able to avoid its food deficits by drawing on the more prosperous agriculture of its neighbor. Finally—and here he may consciously have been attempting to submerge or at least diffuse the responsible government proposals—he carried union with Nyasaland to its logical extreme. If one country were created it would immediately be possible "to federate—I say federate—with Southern Rhodesia, and so bring into being that Central African State which seems to my mind to be essential for the welfare, and if the worst comes to the worst, possibly even for the very existence of the three territories."[29] Defending the three territories would be far easier.

Gore-Browne had been talking in this vein for many years, and

27. Gore-Browne to Marjorie Nicholson, 25 May 1948.
28. Gore-Browne in *Debates,* 60 (12 March 1948), cc. 130–135.
29. Ibid., cc. 438–441.

the word federate was not new to him. But the concept had hitherto had little impact, for its possibilities had seemed limited. Gore-Browne always imagined a weak federation, a confederation, sharing significant responsibilities but with real power (as far as Africans were concerned) reposing in the territories.

He elaborated privately. The previous week while attending a meeting of the Central African Council in Salisbury, he had decided that a Central African State *must* be created with a Federal Council to deal authoritatively with aviation, food supplies, research, transport, and, above all, defence. "God knows what wd. have happened at one period of the last war if the Japanese had got hold of Mozambique as looked likely." Under the Central African State the rights of blacks would be preserved, "and [their] fears allayed, & a Federal Council would deal with all the things which would be too difficult for the local parliaments. Its so simple a solution that it won't even be considered."[30]

Gore-Browne decided to let the African Representative Council, due to reconvene in early July, decide his fate. During April, May, and June the Kitwe Association again condemned him, the Lusaka African community expressed no confidence in him, Fort Jameson said that its people had "lost faith" in him, some of the provincial and urban advisory councillors kept up their attack, and, as he wrote home toward the end of the period, "far from dying down the flood of ill-informed vituperation increases daily." The attacks were not on federation or his Nyasa suggestions, but, as before, on the meaning of responsible government. More concretely, many Africans felt that he had behaved treacherously—that he had flung them "like felons into the gallows of self-government."[31]

During the first few days of the African Representative Council speakers echoed this theme. Chief Ikelenge said that his people felt that responsible government was for Europeans, not Africans." If we wanted this form of Government we would ask for it." J. Chipepa, from the Luapula area, said that his constituents were opposed because they were afraid of losing their rights, their freedom, "and many other things. We want to be ruled by the present Government, until we have grown up." Others spoke eloquently of their fears that land would be lost, that chiefs would be cast aside, that Africans were not ready to give up British oversight, and that somehow, if the local settlers favored it, Africans would be disadvantaged. "When we are further advanced, and when we are ready for it, we shall ask for it," said R. Kalepa, of Solwezi. A motion opposing responsible government was carried unanimously.

30. Gore-Browne to Ethel Locke-King, 13 April 1948.
31. Gore-Browne to Ethel Locke-King, 16 June 1948; Sec/Nat/96: Lusaka and other resolutions, 27 June 1948.

Gore-Browne said how sorry he was that the council was rejecting proposals for "a partnership" which had been made by whites.
He feared whites would now not attempt to join hands again with
Africans. "I am also sorry for myself that you should have thought
that I should have been capable of supporting proposals which were
harmful to Africans. I would have thought that you would never
have believed that I could lead you into amalgamation, which . . . I
have been against all these years. . . . I should not change suddenly
in one night." He would abide by their decision whether or not he
should continue. Many wanted him to recant, and to promise to
foreswear responsible government, but all that he would do was to
promise that he would make their opposition known everywhere
(he had already persuaded the governor to send two Africans with
Welensky, Beckett, and himself to present the proposals to Creech
Jones in London).[32] After all, he could not oppose a scheme which
he still believed would benefit Africans. But he did understand that
no Africans agreed with him, and that their opinions must be respected. "I do not want to see self-government forced upon
Africans against their will," he said.

Mateyo Kakumbi, from Serenje, moved a motion of confidence in Gore-Browne, and, after a number of surprisingly warm
speeches, the council, satisfied that he was still their friend, voted by
19–2, with 7 abstentions, that he should continue to represent them,
a decision which Rennie later formally endorsed.[33] For Gore-
Browne, it was a victory won on narrow grounds, and because of
the general respect and affection in which he had long been held. For
the Africans, it was a signal victory, the extent of which they could
not then have appreciated. The country's leading white politician
had been held to account.

The months of wrangling over responsible government had a
number of other, equally significant—if less obvious—results. The
debate itself, the collective flexing of their muscles which it sym-
bolized, and the emergence of a number of sharp-tongued spokes-
men for the masses, all indicated the degree to which Africans had
been politicized as never before. Unwittingly, Gore-Browne had
indicated the dangers inherent in trusting whites. His actions had
also brought back all of their old fears of being sold out, and of the
frailty of British "protection." Educated Northern Rhodesians had
learned (as had South Africans, Nigerians, and Nyasas before them)
the value of loud protest and, foremost, organization. In mid-1948,

32. The actual details of how the African delegation was chosen are contained in
Sec/Nat/97. The African Representative Council wanted to send three delegates
and thus match the white settler number. Rennie initially agreed, but then sent the
Secretary for Native Affairs in the place of an African.

33. *Proceedings of the Third Session of the First Council* (5–10 July 1948): Ikelenge, c.
36; Chipepa, c. 37; Kalepa, c. 43; Gore-Browne, cc. 47–48, 60–61, 67.

the leaders of the Federation of African Societies therefore transformed their association into the Northern Rhodesian African
Congress, the forerunner of the parties which ultimately obtained
self-government and independence for their country.

Gore-Browne's initiative, and the vociferous African opposition
which it had aroused, also altered the thrust of white politics. The
pursuit of amalgamation could not be continued, at least not directly, and anything which smacked of white self-government—as
had the Gore-Browne plans—was anathema. Gore-Browne may
have thought that three black seats (six including the whites) were
sufficient, but Africans had not. The delegation that went to the
Colonial Office in the summer of 1948 therefore learned that responsible government, as presented, was a non-starter. Creech
Jones, Cohen, and their assistants all wanted to continue with the
agreed-upon implementation of the 1946 alterations, which were
due to come into effect almost immediately. After many conferences, all that Creech Jones would concede to whites was four places
on the Executive Council (their number had never before been
agreed upon formally, and since 1947 Gore-Browne had sat alone),
one of which was allocated to a representative of Africans. This
would not constitute a majority, but it was agreed that the governor
would henceforth be obliged to regard the unanimous advice of the
unofficial members of this council as the advice of the entire council,
subject only to a complicated exercise of his power of veto. The
Colonial Office also refused to transform the council into a cabinet;
nevertheless, from 1949 two unofficials would exercise portfolio
responsibility (for agricultural, veterinary and analogous services,
and for health and local government). Gore-Browne's cryptic
comment on the result was confided to his diary: "The formula
seems to be to make a mule as much like a horse as possible."[34]

Biological impossibility or not, the constitutional alterations
were only the most specific (if really ephemeral) of the consequences of the agitation for responsible government. Gore-
Browne's diary for the summer of 1948 records the usual lengthy
visits with Banda and Nkumbula, with Creech Jones, Cohen, various members of Parliament, editors of *The Economist,* the head of
the Anti-Slavery and Aborigines Protection Society, and so on. It is

34. Gore-Browne, diary, 28 July 1948. The precise formula by which the governor would be obliged to take the advice of unofficial members of the Executive
Council was not devised until Creech Jones' visit to Northern Rhodesia in 1949.
"Like all these sort of things," Gore-Browne commented, it all depends on how its
actually worked. Our present Governor is not blessed with either superabundant
tact or sense of humour, and our Mr. Welensky is not an easy fellow to handle
either, so the omens are not too favourable." Gore-Browne to Norton, 22 April
1949.

also evident that a number of influential persons had taken note of Gore-Browne's espousal of amalgamation with Nyasaland and, critically, a Central African federation. The idea was not new, but the impasse over responsible government, and the distinct distaste of Africans for any of the old proposals, gave new glamour to the notion. Gore-Browne's stress on defence needs also resonated with official thinking in London. The existence of the cold war had only recently been acknowledged and fear of further martial adventures was widespread. Equally, Cohen and others had taken note of Smuts's smashing defeat in the May, 1948, general elections in South Africa. No one in the Colonial Office favored creeping Afrikanerdom and the tainting of Central Africa with the apartheid policies of the new government in the Union. Conceivably, linking Northern Rhodesia and Nyasaland with Southern Rhodesia could keep that last territory from sliding southwards into racial perdition.

Many of Gore-Browne's public and private arguments had, by this time, begun to influence Welensky. As early as May Welensky had taken a cue from Gore-Browne and started talking of federation as a possible solution. And the Southern Rhodesians had meanwhile organized a United Central Africa Association to make propaganda for some kind of alliance. In London, Gore-Browne and Welensky had several talks with Creech Jones about federation, and in subsequent private meetings, both Creech Jones and Colonel Stanley, the Tory shadow colonial secretary, made it clear to Welensky that amalgamation was out, but that some other arrangement, perhaps a federal one, might pass parliamentary muster.[35] It only took these hints from high British places to confirm Welensky's shrewd appreciation of the possible (of how a federation could resemble an amalgamation, which was not Gore-Browne's intention), and for him to persuade Huggins, still clinging relentlessly to amalgamation, of the advantages of Gore-Browne's ideas.

The willingness of Cohen, Creech Jones, Welensky, and Huggins was attributable largely to Gore-Browne. Thus, unwittingly and unexpectedly he contributed to what the Africans of the two northern protectorates came to regard as an unmitigated political disaster. But in 1948 these consequences could not be glimpsed clearly.

Paradoxically, although it was also not yet evident, Gore-Browne's influence on Northern Rhodesian and African affairs had been diminished appreciably by the battle over responsible government. The African Representative Council had backed him and Rennie had reappointed him for three years, but the emergent Con-

35. See Taylor, *Rhodesian,* 95–107; Garry Allighan, *The Welensky Story* (London, 1962), 154–157.

gress and proteges like Nkumbula continued to oppose his renomination. His credibility was diminished, none appreciating this more
fully than Gore-Browne. The middle of 1948 marked, not the end
of an illustrious political career, but the beginning of a denouement,
the ebbing away of influence (Rennie's indifference also contributed), and the symbolic as well as actual return (or was it a retreat?)
to the shores of Shiwa Ngandu.

Shiwa had long needed him. "What I do mind is that nothing will
ever, it seems, allow me to take hold of Shiwa, and till I do things
will go on going astray there. And if they go astray long enough it
means disaster. I can't feel that my value to the country, if any,
equals that."[36] (He was still Welensky's deputy, and although he
resigned from the standing finance committee, there were
fortnightly meetings of the Executive Council, budget committees,
his membership of the national development authority, administrative conferences, and his usual African responsibilities.) The
financial state of Shiwa was particularly worrying, lime oil having
been virtually unsaleable at any price since the end of the war. From
1940 to 1946 the annual average gross income from oil exports
approached £6,000. In 1947 the gross income fell to £3,600 and,
during the financial year that ended in March, 1948, to £264. (His
personal income from dividends and the government amounted to
nearly £4,000 in 1948 and £5,500 in 1950.) Yet the running costs of
the estate had, along with everything else, continued to grow. His
1947 and 1948 household expenses were over £5,000 each year, the
cost of keeping his elder daughter in university and his younger
daughter in private secondary school amounted to £1,000 a year,
and there were other large amounts spent on capital improvements
to the estate, such as a new truck and new cattle.

There were four main problems. The world market for essential
oils was now in oversupply, French and Bulgarian centers having
been reopened. Gore-Browne's limes had begun to produce far less,
qualitatively and quantitatively, than before. Many trees were
dying from collar rot and from die-back, a virus disease, which in
the 1950s eventually ended Shiwa's lime oil production entirely.
Casual labor was becoming scarce, which made the harvest of
orange blossom (for neroli oil) impossible, and production of that
commodity ceased in 1951. Finally, being so often absent from the
estate on governmental business, a condition which would not alter
appreciably until his final retirement from the Legislative Council,
Gore-Browne had to rely completely upon young hired managers
brought out on contract from Britain. Fortunately, his postwar
choices proved far more adept than those who had tried to run the

36. Gore-Browne to Ethel Locke-King, 10 September 1948.

estate in the 1930s and early 1940s, but none were a truly satisfactory substitute for his own intimate direction. Whether true or not, he believed that they spent unwisely and used African labor less efficiently than would he. Lorna Katherine and Angela, his daughters, could help him oversee the estate during their university and school vacations, but when neither he nor they were there, Shiwa lacked any familial guiding hand, Lady Gore-Browne having long been absent.

Her interests had lain elsewhere since the middle of the war. Although she stayed on in Lusaka after the end of the conflict, she and Sir Stewart publicly lived apart from about that time. She befriended others and maintained her position in the pathological laboratory until mid-1947, when she moved to London.

They were divorced in 1950 without contest or scandal. As Gore-Browne commented forlornly, "it regularizes things."[37] They would again be together on occasion, but the fantasies of the 1920s (or were they of 1906?) were incontrovertibly erased throughout the 1940s.

Many aspects of Gore-Browne's life were altering, if not with such obvious finality. The gradual diminution of his political influence coincided with the start of a bitter battle between black and white for hegemony in Central Africa. The centerpiece of the battle was a federal scheme which perverted his own. After 1949, it was clear that whites, Welensky foremost among them, were attempting to use his federal device to achieve the underlying goals of amalgamation.

The result of the Welensky-Huggins conversations in London had been a decision to convene a conference of elected legislators from the three territories at the Victoria Falls in early 1949. Gore-Browne refused to go as a delegate but attended as an observer, said little, and went away in disgust. Huggins and others openly expressed contempt for Africans and African opinion and made it clear that they intended to circumvent the force of African opposition by formulating a hypocritical proposal which the Colonial and Dominion Offices could sanction in good faith. Huggins spoke of a federation which approximated a Greater Southern Rhodesia and Welensky used federation as the code name for an independent dominion. In order to mollify African opinion, they proposed to affirm existing land rights and make the individual states responsible for African education and agriculture and for "native administration" generally. "I want to take the Africans all the way with us if we possibly can," said Welensky. "If they don't come it is just too bad but I want to be reasonable and if it is possible to bring them

37. Gore-Browne to Ethel Locke-King, 18 September 1950.

along with us I want to do so. It would help tremendously."[38] Even
so, the delegates planned to deny Africans effective representation
in the federal parliament. The total package, in fact, was offensive to
everything for which Gore-Browne had always stood. But all he
could do was caution Welensky, since the conference had no official
standing and issued no formal demands. Huggins and Welensky
expected, however, that the substance of their decisions (ninety
singlespaced foolscap pages) would subsequently serve as the basis
for the actual drafting of a federal constitution by committees of
experts.

From Gore-Browne's point of view, the conference had been
badly mishandled from start to finish. He had long advocated some
kind of larger grouping to discharge interterritorial responsibilities.
The utility of the Central African Council had demonstrated the
need for a more powerful coordinating body, and Gore-Browne,
like Cohen, was persuaded of the economic developmental and
strategic defense advantages of some kind of Central African state.
"Provided," he wrote, "African rights and African Land in the two
Protectorates were adequately guaranteed *by the Imperial Government,* and moreover provided enough money remained under the
sole control of these two local Governments to enable them to carry
out their African policy free of any fear of dictation by the Federal
Government, and finally provided there was adequate African representation in both the Federal houses, then I think a good case
could have been made out." But instead of discussing these matters
quietly and revealing some sort of definite plan for general discussion, whites had foolishly held a much-advertised conference, had
refused to invite Africans, even as observers, and had kept the actual
deliberations secret while publicizing only vague generalities and an
insulting speech by Huggins. "I would never be a party to putting
our Africans in any way under Southern Rhodesian Government,"
said Gore-Browne, "and speaking confidentially it was quite obvious from the trend of the discussions . . . that this was what was
envisaged by most of the members of the Conference." On the
crucial financial side, Gore-Browne pointed out much later that
Huggins first showed his hand by describing the position of the
Protectorates in the federation as county councils and proposing to
divide the federal revenues (most of which were bound to come
from copper) unfairly, eleven twelfths going to the federal side and
one twelfth being returned to the Protectorates.[39]

38. Report of a Conference of Delegates from Northern and Southern Rhodesia
and Nyasaland, 16–17 February 1949 (unpublished typescript), 35. For fuller details, see Rotberg, *Nationalism,* 220–223.

39. Gore-Browne to C. W. W. Greenidge, Secretary, Anti-Slavery Society, 21
April, 17 June 1949; Gore-Browne, interview with author, 28 July 1961. Cohen,
interview with author, 11 September 1963.

."Unless," wrote Gore-Browne to *The Economist,* "there is some under-current in Imperial politics of which personally I have no inkling, Huggins' tactless approach to the whole problem will have queered the pitch completely." Since it was as obvious to Africans (or soon would be) as it was to him that what had been agreed upon at the Victoria Falls was one huge amalgamation, with Southern Rhodesia in control, Africans could not accept it and he could hardly imagine the government at home forcing it down their throats.[40] Certainly, since Huggins' whole attitude was so anti-African and pro-Southern Rhodesian, and since Africans even before the conference had been thoroughly suspicious (in late 1948 the Northern Rhodesian Congress condemned federation since it was obviously amalgamation in disguise, and predicted that Welensky would bring "the miseries of civil war to Northern Rhodesia"),[41] there was no reason to assume that anything could be salvaged from the presumed wreckage of the federal framework.

Nevertheless, though he wrote to Banda as he had to Norton and Greenidge, Gore-Browne did not feel that he could immediately condemn publicly, and to Africans, an idea to which he was still attached until some actual proposals were offered for inspection. His role as a representative of African interests therefore initially remained ambiguous. With Henry Kasokolo and Nalumango, the African members of the Legislative Council, he toured the main urban centers of the Protectorate, holding long, well-attended meetings to explain the meaning of federation, and balancing the presumed advantages against the potential disadvantages. He described the details which were still lacking, and how the list of federal subjects, precise financial arrangements, and particulars about the composition of the federal assembly would all be required before Africans or anyone else could truly judge the utility of federalism in Central Africa. He urged Africans not to criticize before these facts were known—to hold their fire and be calm. And many did as he bid. Even so the dominant mood among Africans was that they were reasonably happy under the rule of the Colonial Office and saw no need—whatever the final shape of the scheme—to change. "So far," wrote Gore-Browne in late March, "they've . . . been remarkably restrained, but they are gradually beginning to break out into denunciation of what they call submission to Southern Rhodesia, and they are not so far wrong, as far as the present proposals go."[42]

40. Gore-Browne to Patricia Norton, *The Economist,* 1 March 1949.

41. Sec/Nat/353. Strictly Confidential Memorandum on the Federation, by Robinson Nabulyato (General Secretary), 28 December 1948.

42. Gore-Browne to Norton, 29 March 1949; Sec/Nat/117: Gore-Browne to Secretary for Native Affairs, 21 January 1949. Gore-Browne to Norton, 19 September 1950.

This point was equally obvious in London, too, where Banda, who had not hitherto been opposed to federation in principle, easily deduced from press reports that neither Huggins nor Welensky had changed, that they obviously meant to deprive Africans of their remaining rights, and to amalgamate under another name. "Africans would never get justice under the Federation," he wrote condemning it. The guarantees to Africans offered by Huggins and Welensky could not be taken as more than words, said Banda.

Africans could trust neither Welensky nor Huggins. "We know that were Federation to become a reality, Sir Godfrey . . . and . . . Welensky would be the two most powerful men. Sir Godfrey would be most certainly the Prime Minister and Mr. Welensky would be next. . . . And . . . neither of them is in favour of Africans' advancement. . . . They remain confirmed opponents of our progress." Only realistic African representation based upon a full franchise could guarantee Africans any say in a federal government. "Both Sir Godfrey and Mr. Welensky talk glibly of 'partnership'. . . . [but] they have a very queer way of proving their sincerity. . . . Have you ever heard of a business partnership in which one partner was not allowed in the board meeting or in the inner councils of the company?"[43] He promised to advise his people to do everything they could to oppose federation, even as he was still content to contemplate amalgamation between Nyasaland and Northern Rhodesia.

When Creech Jones visited Central Africa in April, 1949, to investigate the problem at first hand, Africans repeatedly spoke to him of their distrust of Southern Rhodesia and federation. Gore-Browne communicated his own and African dissatisfactions privately, but also urged the colonial secretary to try to concoct a plan which would transform the settler scheme into something more acceptable to liberal opinion. He again advocated quiet, private talks with the whites. To Creech Jones, however, it was clear that the slate had to be wiped clean. To Gore-Browne's consternation (for he feared the antagonizing of local whites unnecessarily) Creech Jones unilaterally assured Africans that nothing would be done by the British government without consulting them fully. "We shall honour the responsibilities we have entered into." He urged Africans not to be anxious, told one reporter that African interests would always prevail over white ones, and indicated that white settlement in Northern Rhodesia should be controlled. Banda was pleased. Whites were angry, he thought, not because Creech Jones had said any-

---

43. Banda to Gore-Browne, 2, 17 April 1949. These arguments were also contained in the anti-federal pamphlet which was later circulated in London over Banda and Nkumbula's names.

thing new, but because he had refused to reverse traditional British policy.[44]

Gore-Browne and Norton both thought that federation would "die on its feet." He was confident of this view toward the end of the year, when Welensky introduced a motion asking the imperial government to "take the lead" in establishing a federation. Had such a motion been introduced prior to the Victoria Falls conference, Gore-Browne reasoned, and been acted upon appropriately, a proper federal scheme (the whites had never released their own in full) might have emerged. "Now," he wrote, "it will only serve I fancy to confirm the collapse of the idea."[45]

During the debate Gore-Browne did what he could to make his prediction become reality. In no doubt about African opinion, with Banda berating him from afar, and with the loss of legitimacy in 1948 painfully fresh in his memory (the Congress had repeated its call for the substitution of black for the remaining white representatives in the legislature), Gore-Browne eloquently opposed Welensky's initiative. Divergence between the benevolent autocracy of Southern Rhodesia and the Colonial Office policy of associating Africans with the governments of the Protectorates as quickly as possible had, if anything, been accentuated by the federal arrangements discussed at the Victoria Falls. The suggested constitution expressly excluded African representation in the lower, policy-making house of the proposed federal parliament, and offered to guarantee Africans rights to land—about which they felt very strongly—through the federal parliament only. Thus Africans justifiably believed that the federation had been designed entirely for the benefit of whites. Africans wanted no part of such a federation. "We ourselves," said Gore-Browne on behalf of the three other representatives of Africans and himself, "are opposed to the proposals . . . on the grounds that to us they appear to be amalgamation under another name."[46] All four, together with J. F. Morris, the maverick elected white from Chingola, voted against the motion. The remaining elected whites all voted for it and, to African perplexity, the officials—acting on instructions—all abstained.

Gore-Browne never deviated from his expressed opposition to Federation. Neither his nor the mass of African opinion, however, proved sufficient to halt the pro-federal juggernaut. His prediction that the whole idea would collapse was overtaken by events and

44. Creech Jones, before the Eleventh Meeting of the Northern Rhodesian Central Provincial Council, 21 April 1949; *Bulawayo Chronicle,* 22 April 1949; Gore-Browne to Norton, 11 May 1949; Banda to Gore-Browne, 27 June 1949.

45. Gore-Browne to Norton, 19 September, 26 November 1949.

46. Gore-Browne in *Debates,* 66 (25 November 1949), c. 370.

superseded by his earlier, more accurate, prediction that, when it suited Britain, some pious formula would be contrived and a federation created despite any and all protests. No Northern Rhodesian could control the variables of prime concern to Britain. Because of Britain's economic worries and deteriorating international position, arguments advanced by the British South Africa Company and the mining companies in favor of rationalizing Central Africa's political and economic structure began to have greater appeal. Only some such larger entity, everyone agreed, would attract new developmental capital to Central Africa. Equally the financial houses and key officials in the Colonial Office came to view a federation as the only alternative to the gradual spread northwards of the Afrikaner racial policies which they so distrusted. The menace of Afrikanerdom to Northern Rhodesia could not, everyone agreed, be contained so long as the Colonial Office refused to limit immigration. Welensky and others feared that the tide of South Africans who were streaming to the Copperbelt to work on the mines would, before long, result in Afrikaner control of the Legislative Council. Gore-Browne was as exercised as any: He wrote of the "menace of infiltration" from South Africa and of what such infiltration would do to relations between blacks and whites if "sane folk" lost control of the legislature. Thus for economic and humanitarian, as well as strategic, reasons, men of influence finally decided to construct an ideological buffer state wherein multiracial partnership would offer an alternative to the extremes of black nationalism and white apartheid.[47]

In 1950 Welensky took this cue and extolled the virtues of partnership. "I hold out the hand of friendship for the African people," he said. But "until such time as his contribution is greater than it is to-day, he must take the role of the lesser partner." Africans were hardly excited by this definition of their rôle, and Gore-Browne issued a pointed warning that the "essence of the thing is that the relationship [should be] not the relation of master and servant, but the relation of sharing, sharing in the responsibilities of Government, sharing economic responsibilities and sharing in social responsibilities. If that policy is accepted, then no thinking African has anything left to complain about."[48]

But the policy and program outlined by Gore-Browne was never accepted, nor was more than the most cynical lip service paid to its spirit. His warnings were ignored, especially by those, overseas, who should have known better and for whom the concept of

---

47. For a fuller unfolding of the federal battle, see Rotberg, *Nationalism*, 227–252.

48. Welensky, *Debates*, 69 (19 June 1950), cc. 373–374; Gore-Browne (19 June 1950), c. 399. See also *Bulawayo Chronicle*, 13 April 1950.

partnership took on a surprisingly beguiling aura. At least they allowed themselves to be beguiled, to assume that white Rhodesians could voluntarily bring themselves to share real power with Africans. Equally there was a misguided feeling that there would be time sufficient to construct a multiracial state. Nearly all underestimated the cunning of Huggins, who threatened to end his colony's existing limited cooperation with the Protectorates through the Central African Council, and devalued the determination of Africans to have nothing to do with any scheme which purported to exchange British protection for settler domination. Cohen was among those who failed, for all his sympathy for Africans, to appreciate the depth of African dissatisfaction or to listen to Gore-Browne on the subject. The other considerations seemed paramount and, in late 1950, Cohen persuaded James Griffiths, who had replaced Creech Jones as colonial secretary, and Patrick Gordon-Walker, the secretary of state for commonwealth relations, to permit a committee of theoretically impartial Central African and British civil servants to consider and decide whether or not the Rhodesias and Nyasaland could feasibly and profitably federate.

This proved the coup de gráce, whatever assurances were then given that African opinion would be taken fully into account. The bureaucratic steamroller was relentlessly flattening any other than federal alternatives, in the process overriding protestations of once-influential voices like Gore-Browne's. Months before the announcement of the special study committee his appreciation of the dangerous drift of events and the increasing polarization of black and white attitudes had even led him desperately to offer the British government first a stalling option and then a solution dramatically different from federation. He had been driven to take these initiatives not solely because of the growing anti-African winner-take-all approach that had begun to infect the public pronouncements of Huggins, Welensky, and Central African whites, the complacency of the Colonial Office, nor his own loss of influence. More than others, he was alert to the rapid rise in African political consciousness. This was apparent in the towns (the president of the Congress had recently demanded "Africa for the Africans"), but Gore-Browne had been startled to view the sprouting of nationalism even in the countryside. "The striking thing," he wrote, is the intense 'political consciousness' which is now to be found everywhere in these far away country places."

He had been to Isoka and other Northern Province centers, but was particularly struck by the posture in nearby Chinsali, where men like Kenneth Kaunda, Robert Makasa, and Reuben Mulenga had recently invigorated the old welfare association. How amazed the early district commissioners would be, said Gore-Browne, "to

find the Chinsali villagers discussing increased African representation . . . & the Immigration Policy for the Territory."[49] More and
more they spoke of whites (although not of himself) with apprehension tinged with hostility. He understood intuitively that pursuing
the federal notion could only exaggerate their bitterness and accelerate the likelihood of unpleasant confrontation. Africans were
more aroused than one would have expected.

Gore-Browne first sought to defuse an increasingly parlous situation by demanding that the British government enunciate an un-
ambiguous statement of policy for its mixed-race colonies. He
wanted something which would assuage African anxieties and
dampen white enthusiasms, and at least remove the atmosphere of
uncertainty which was clouding race relations. He personally urged
Griffiths to do something, but Griffiths could promise nothing.
Hence, in order to give his plea public effect, Gore-Browne
employed what was to become a favorite, tactically useful
weapon—the carefully planted article or letter-to-the-editor in a
major British publication. When he could no longer affect events
locally, and when the fulcrum of power had anyway shifted to
Britain, it was obviously efficacious to appeal directly to public
opinion at home.

His request for a declaration of policy appeared in the *Manchester
Guardian*. "The colour question in Africa" was the world question
second in importance only to that of relations with Russia, he began. Disaster was likely and, in the long run, "the only thing that
[could] save the situation [was] the complete elimination of the test
of colour in all walks of life." But present problems could not wait
for this resolution. The only way by which serious trouble could be
avoided was by the clear statement of British policy, endorsed by
"moderate men of both parties in the House of Commons. . . . It
should be made quite clear that on the one hand, Europeans in the
colonies . . . will not be allowed to relegate the African to an inferior position merely because he is an African, and on the other
hand that Africans, merely because they are Africans, cannot expect
privileges and advancement that they have not earned. A genuine
partnership between the two races is the only possible goal." He
knew that such a statement would not satisfy the extremists on
either side. Indeed, he admitted, with his usual rhetorical flourish,
"it may be that it is already too late. It is not pleasant to contemplate
what the final result of racial animosity and mistrust in a continent
like Africa will be."[50]

The same day the *Guardian*'s lead editorial endorsed Gore-
Browne's plea and mused about the meaning of equality between

49. Gore-Browne to Ethel Locke-King, 24 August 1950.
50. "Black and White in Africa," *The Manchester Guardian*, 10 April 1950.

men. It subsequently printed a number of favorable letters, and Gore-Browne lobbied assiduously with Creech Jones and others when he was in London about the same time, but no matter how politicians in Britain shared Gore-Browne's worries, official responses were necessarily conspicuous by their absence. Gore-Browne had been right. It was, in fact, already too late, even had the British government had a policy to enunciate clearly.

Upon his return to Africa, this time via Portugal and Angola, Gore-Browne realized that the deterioration of race relations, based as it was on the drive toward closer union, could conceivably be arrested only by shifting attention toward a more radical proposition. "It may be that the problem of getting Africans and Europeans to work closely together," he wrote sadly, "is . . . too difficult of accomplishment and that one had better adopt the second best solution of keeping them as far apart as possible." To Banda, Gore-Browne said that although the ideal was still partnership, he was coming around to a view that he had held as long ago as 1919—that the difficulty of combining African and white government was so great that "there should be separate African and European areas in Africa, each with its own Government." (At first Banda tended to agree. "I would not be as strongly against the kind of partition you have described . . . as I am of either self-government or federation. I would welcome it, if in reality it means real partition and not a sham.")[51] Drawing upon his proposals of an earlier era, Gore-Browne wondered—again for the benefit of British public— whether partition, "an admittedly second-best solution," would not be appropriate. It could reduce "the points of contact between the two races as much as possible, frankly admitting that certain parts of those territories where Europeans are already established are to be European areas, others African." Two conditions were essential, that the African territories—Gore-Browne again envisaged a tripartite Northern Rhodesia, with separate northeastern and northwestern Rhodesias in black hands, and the whites (linked to Southern Rhodesia) in control of the line-of-rail—were guaranteed a portion of the income of the white areas, and that good land were available for Africans.[52] Optimally, northeastern Rhodesia would be amalgamated with Nyasaland. "The essence of my . . . proposal," Gore-Browne explained, "Is that the African protectorates should be purely African. They would probably contain a certain number of European settlers who are there already, over and above

51. Gore-Browne to Norton, 23 June 1950; Gore-Browne to Banda, 30 July 1950. Gore-Browne had put forth the same proposition in 1936, see above 194–195. Banda to Gore-Browne, 23 October 1950.

52. Gore-Browne, "Partition in Africa," *Manchester Guardian*, 25 August 1950. The *Guardian* again endorsed Gore-Browne's ideas editorially.

the officials helping to administer the protectorates. The settlers if they didn't like it would have to get out. . . . One would hope that before very long the African protectorates and the European colony would be federated, and eventually perhaps unified." That would happen when black and white problems had been satisfactorily resolved, which he still hoped would someday happen.[53]

Unfortunately partition smelled too much of segregation and apartheid, and was not really in the interests of a British government determined to create something meaningful and in its own long-term African interests. Creech Jones was blunt: "I don't much like the Partition Plan." Banda, too, having had an opportunity to examine the plan more closely and to discuss its implication with friends in Britain, was caustic. Africans, he pointed out, would be denied the full benefit of wealth derived from mining. "This would be . . . robbery." Africans would be foreigners in the white areas of what was recently their own country. "We could never trust Europeans in the African area." In fact, Banda said, "when closely studied, the plan seems a trap to entice us into a form of security, which is illusory." With the Colonial Office behind them, Africans at least could count upon "moral support". Later on the white territory might seek to take over the black ones. "Partnership," he concluded, "is the only thing that can win African's [sic] support."[54]

Neither trial balloon elicited African support or the kind of white backing that could have been decisive. In fact, after returning in late 1950 from a long visit (as an East African delegate to the Commonwealth Parliamentary Conference) to the haunts of his grandfather and the scenes of Dame Ethel's childhood in New Zealand, Tasmania, and Australia, Gore-Browne could not but appreciate that partition was an idea which belonged either to the future, or the distant past. Impressed by the extent to which the Maori had been integrated into New Zealand political life, he also logically had to resume his espousal of partnership, forlorn as he thought its chances of surviving the controversy over federation.[55]

Given the drive to amalgamation, Gore-Browne's voice of paternal rationality had become less and less relevant to the evolution of Northern Rhodesia. Not his public but his official public role had

53. Gore-Browne to Norton, 19 September 1950.

54. Creech Jones to Gore-Browne, 10 October 1950; Banda to Gore-Browne, 26 November 1950.

55. In New Zealand Gore-Browne was everywhere revered as the grandson of the early governor, no more effusively than in the small town of Gore, named after the family. In Tasmania, where an old friend was now governor, he slept in the very rooms once occupied by his ancestors. Nothing thrilled him more than this tangible physical association with his grandfather.

become less central as his actual interventions in assembly debate had—because of his more extensive travels and dissatisfaction with the drift of events—sharply declined. Since 1948 his vision and approach had not been those of the times, none being more conscious of this shift in sympathies than the man who had once so enjoyed riling the official bench with superbly paced, finely honed criticism, who had basked in African adulation, and who had been pleased to shape the future of his adopted country. The monocle was still firmly in place above the long straight nose and the wispy mustache, and the double-breasted blue suits were as tight and stiff as ever, but it had become less enjoyable to sprinkle speeches with witty Latin and Greek phrases that were understood only by a few of the officials, and somehow no longer worthwhile to share his observations on the state of the world with power-hungry whites and with Africans, one of whom even appeared drunk in the Council chamber.

Although Gore-Browne decided to retire from his legislative responsibilities early in 1950, both Rennie and Welensky urged him to do nothing so rash until later in the year. By then it had become apparent to him that he was "no longer of use to Africans." He had become "sick and tired" of being attacked by both blacks and whites, often for the same utterances but from different sides. He hardly enjoyed being the object of "ceaseless suspicion the whole time." Northern Rhodesian Africans still hounded him, no matter how politely, the attacks of the Congress particularly rankling. Banda, too, laid it on rather thickly, castigating him for associating so closely with Welensky (a dart that other Africans also threw). "I would not be fair," said Banda, "if I hid the fact . . . that there is now a growing number of Africans in Northern Rhodesia who think that you are not . . . serving their interest but those of the Europeans. . . . It would be silly for anyone . . . to pretend that you enjoy the confidence of the Africans . . . as much as you did five years ago." No longer did the politically conscious "take your good intention for granted. You have to prove it to them."[56]

These were home truths which could only have widened Gore-Browne's wounds. Nor did the situation change during his long visit to New Zealand. After his return even Welensky failed to give support. "I don't know what you intend to do," he wrote lamely, "though if you make up your mind that the time has come for you to settle down at Shiwa I will understand it."[57] That may have been the final straw, for almost immediately Gore-Browne told his aunt that he was determined to resign. "I can't influence either African or

56. Gore-Browne to Banda, 30 July 1950; Banda to Gore-Browne, 13 July 1950.
57. Welensky to Gore-Browne, 27 December 1950.

European opinion any longer, and I'm just a lay figure in the councils of both. Welensky would tell you I'm away too much . . . & maybe he's right." Moreover, Shiwa needed his full-time attention. In late January he wrote formally to Rennie and Welensky, informing them that he did not wish to be considered for renomination after his term expired in late February. He believed that he had ceased "pulling his weight," the existing constitution, with elected members serving as ministers, yet responsible to the "opposition," only making his own role more difficult. Most of all, he could not see how to overcome the territory's "terrible racial distrust." He could not agree with the Africans who were increasingly following the Northern Rhodesian African Congress line of "Africa for the Africans". Nor could he accept the white cry for hegemony. "I could no longer represent the vocal Africans . . . with any honesty, nor could I work as previously with the Europeans who had also kicked over the traces . . . nor do I think the temporising Government here is worth supporting," he told Norton. "Anyway the day of Europeans representing Africans is over in countries like this. Its a pity for one can do a lot for them they can't do for themselves, but there it is."[58]

Gore-Browne was not then ready to abandon the multiracial premises of his entire political career. He espoused verities that the whites who had flooded into Northern Rhodesia after the war thought radical and the newly aroused Africans thought timid. Had he not retired from his legislative position he would have become increasingly uncomfortable and isolated as the pious formula was contrived by civil servants, and as the coming to power in Britain of a Conservative government enabled the Federation to be brought into being over vociferous African protests. There was violence, as he had predicted, and the further politicizing of an African middle-class which believed that it had been betrayed. Long before this drama was played out in full, however, Gore-Browne had retired, his ears ringing with speeches and letters of praise delivered and written by blacks and whites who appreciated what he had been trying to do for sixteen legislative years.[59]

58. Gore-Browne to Ethel Locke-King, 1 January, 5 February, 9 March 1951; Gore-Browne to Rennie, 25 January 1951; Gore-Browne to Welensky, 25 January 1951; Gore-Browne to Norton, 12 March 1951.

59. The one vocal exception to this paean of praise was a letter to a local newspaper from John Edward (Chirupula) Stephenson, whose arrival in Northern Rhodesia had preceded Gore-Browne's by more than a decade. He had lived far closer to the indigenous inhabitants of the country and had never managed to play much of a part in its political life. There was a certain natural antipathy between the two. When the Central African Post eulogized Gore-Browne upon his retirement, Stephenson raked over all the half-forgotten coals—that Robert Young, not

Yet Gore-Browne was abdicating a public position and moving to the sidelines (if that is a fair description of Shiwa) without either intending or expecting to refrain from continuing to exert an influence on local events. As much as he took a more active part in the running of the Shiwa Estate, Gore-Browne never relaxed his surveillance and commentary on public affairs. No longer could he claim public attention by speaking in the Legislative Council. Now, whatever he hoped to accomplish had to be done through other means, using other platforms, or by direct action. It was not to be the kind of placid retirement that others might have envisaged. Nor, though he did not yet know it, had he ended his political service to Northern Rhodesia.

Gore-Browne, had discovered Shiwa Ngandu, that the lake should still be called after Young, etc. Most of all, Stephenson blamed Gore-Browne for bringing to fruition "this mongrel Congress—a Frankenstein monster composed of Africans claiming . . . to be representative of the three score tribes comprising the Territory." In reply, Gore-Browne calmly agreed that either Young or Hector Croad had discovered his lake. As to the Congress, Gore-Browne took credit only for preventing the government from suppressing the Federation of Welfare Societies and for giving financial assistance to Yamba, its first president. He pointed out that the Congress did represent nearly all educated Africans. If, he said, Congress could "avoid the extravagances and exaggerations to which, like most similar young institutions, it is at present prone, it should prove an extremely valuable organisation." Stephenson, 11 February 1951; Gore-Browne, 2 March 1951, in *Central African Post*.

IX
The Triumph of
the Majority

As much as Gore-Browne henceforth was divorced from the direct exercise of political power, his return to Shiwa implied no lapse into obscurity. Even had he preferred an uninvolved, mellow enjoyment of retirement, advocates of one or another political persuasion would have continually turned to him for support and involvement; only a churlish curmudgeon could thus have refrained from participating in the complicated dialogues of an increasingly volatile Northern Rhodesia. It suited him temperamentally to become involved and to try to make his own a voice of rationality in the irrational context of imposed federalism.

Throughout the 1950s Gore-Browne grew more and more disenchanted with the supposed federal solution and the era of partnership which had been its prime justification. Formerly he had sought to protect African interests, interposing his own influence between colonial conceptions and African anxieties. Increasingly, however, he followed where he would previously have led. Africans were defining their own concerns and tactics and required his backing more than his guidance. Yet gradually, almost imperceptibly, he adapted his approach to these changing circumstances, emerging in the late 1950s and early 1960s as a wise multiracialist as well as black nationalism's most revered white collaborator.

Initially, however, Gore-Browne expended his energies upon Shiwa's, as much as Northern Rhodesia's, future. For him this was a partial return to the kind of life he had tried to lead before he entered politics. It meant resuming his oversight of Shiwa's affairs in a manner which had not been possible since the 1930s. Yet conditions had changed drastically. Northern Rhodesia was far more prosperous than before, and Shiwa was not as insulated as it had been from the resultant drastic increases in costs, especially of labor. The Shiwa estate consequently could no longer devote its resources to projects which demanded vast numbers of Africans. Equally, as expenses escalated, two disasters struck the citrus crops on which Gore-Browne had based the economy of the estate. Lime oil prices kept falling at a time when its production at Shiwa also fell markedly. After several years of consultation with local experts, South African investigators finally proved in 1954 that the limes were afflicted by the common, deadly die-back (*tristezia*) virus which, spread by aphis fly, killed the trees no matter how well they were fertilized, mulched, and otherwise nourished. For a time Gore-Browne harbored the hope that he could graft his limes onto the stock of rough lemons (which were supposedly immune to the virus), but physiologists in the Gold Coast, where die-back had earlier destroyed plantations of limes, effectively scotched that idea. Alternatives, like the production of neroli (from bigaradia oranges) or petit grain from the leaves of the same tree, were foreclosed by the scarcity of seasonally available labor and the relatively few trees which were still producing. Another possibility was *Eucalyptus citriodora,* the old standby, but Gore-Browne's costs of production and shipping were too high to make its sales to soap manufacturers (*citriodora* contained citronellal, which the soap process required) attractive.

In 1954 Gore-Browne therefore came reluctantly to the conclusion that he must close down the distillery which had provided Shiwa's rationale for so long. Instead of the pre-1948 average yield from limes of 3,000 pounds of oil, in 1954 Shiwa managed to produce a mere 120 pounds, the amounts having diminished steadily for six years. Looking at the figures from an income standpoint, in 1949 Shiwa had grossed £2,413 from lime oil and £670 from neroli. The comparable figures in 1951 were £731 and £110, in 1954 £250 and £90. In 1958 he considered trying geraniums again, and in 1963 *citriodora,* but each time the expected rewards promised to be too sparse for Gore-Browne to reopen the idle distillery, although small batches of all of these oils were processed from time to time. When the Southern Rhodesians began growing geraniums for their oil in the late 1950s, or Malawi shipped oil of the Nindi weed to London in 1967, Gore-Browne could but look on, and remember his long, so briefly successful, struggle to outwit nature.

As early as 1951 Shiwa's future had become a matter of serious concern. Since the end of the war the estate had been run by a British manager who was accustomed to a comparatively free hand and the relatively lavish expenditure of Gore-Browne's income. This approach was compatible with the steady production of a ton or more of lime oil, but as the yields fell the manager spent even more money in a desperate attempt to counter the at first mysterious failure of the limes to bear, and then to thrive at all. Only in 1951 did he and Gore-Browne begin to suspect that the cause was not in some way human. But it took several years to verify that suspicion, to explore options, and to decide on new methods of operation consonant with Gore-Browne's refusal simply to live grandly in his Italianate mansion without any economically sound agricultural pursuits to sanction Shiwa's existence. "Sometimes," he wrote, "I feel I'm an ass not to live very comfortably, as I could, on my own income without trying to make this place a going concern, for the rest of the years the Lord may intend me to have. But I think you, and Nunk too, would agree that would be unworthy, and that one would be even more an unprofitable servant."[1]

Two other considerations also shaped Shiwa for the remainder of Gore-Browne's life. In 1951 he was operated upon successfully first to relieve a double hernia and then, in London, because the surgeons had discovered a diseased gall bladder. Upon his return to Shiwa in August, 1951, he gave his daughter Lorna in marriage to Major John Harvey, late of the King's African Rifles, in a blazing ceremony hitherto unequalled at Shiwa. (The guests, including one hundred prominent whites from Lusaka and the Copperbelt and many more Africans, consumed 240 gallons of beer and 1,500 pounds of beef.) The Harveys initially lived in Luanshya, where he was employed by the Roan Antelope mine as a labor officer, but they returned to Shiwa in 1953. Although they had initiated the move partially in order to be able to help at Shiwa and look after Lorna's father, Gore-Browne welcomed their decision, gave Harvey a salary, and, later in 1953, ousted the manager so that Harvey would have a free hand to alter the basis of Shiwa's economy. Under Harvey's leadership Shiwa began selling timber, butter, and beef throughout the Northern Province of the territory. Capital formerly expended upon citrus crops throughout the 1950s was devoted to building up the Shiwa herd until its numbers exceeded 2000. The herd provided reasonable if unspectacular revenues for Shiwa until the time of Gore-Browne's death in 1967. At no time, however, did the estate support itself for, as clever as the Harveys were at reducing unnecessary expenditures (the permanent labor force, once over six hundred, fell below one hundred during the 1950s), two comfortable white households, their many African dependents, and a widespread infrastructure, not to mention the fabric of the mansion house and incessant guests, could hardly be supported by income derived from the sale of beef five hundred miles from Northern Rhodesia's center of consumption. (In the 1970s, when the Chinese-built railway traversed the Northern Province about fifty miles from Shiwa, the estate could raise chickens and battery hens for the increasing population at Mpika and Kasama.) Even Gore-

1. Gore-Browne to Ethel Locke-King, 1 July 1955.

Browne's personal income, which had always subsidized the estate to some degree or another, might have proved insufficient for the yields on his stocks and bonds could hardly match the inflation of the post-war world. However, as before, the Locke-King fortune gave timely assistance.

Despite a serious attack of dropsy in 1953 (Gore-Browne spent five months with her), Dame Ethel maintained a keen interest in the affairs of Shiwa until her death in 1956 (Gore-Browne was at her bedside), when she was ninety-two. Thereafter, of course, funds for the development and maintenance of Shiwa were readily available. Gore-Browne was the main legatee of the Locke-King estate; even after paying fifty-five percent death duties he realized at least £15,000 from her Weybridge house and about four times as much from her remaining real and personal property. (An old four-poster bed, a full-length portrait of Dame Ethel, and many other heirlooms, together with letters from him which she had so devotedly saved for more than sixty years, were sent to Shiwa.) In death as in life, Shiwa could not have been realized in its fullest sense without the steady, unflinching backing of the Locke-Kings.

With Dame Ethel's death the brightest lodestar disappeared from Gore-Browne's view. He had his daughter and son-in-law, and their children close at hand—his other daughter Angela having married Basil Bell, an ichthyologist, and moved to Kenya—but there were no substitutes for the kinds of bonds which he had shared with Dame Ethel. Lady Gore-Browne still maintained strong ties to Africa, but she lived in England.

Henry Mulenga accompanied him almost everywhere until his death, and shared many experiences, but Gore-Browne was happiest when Mrs. Violet Vincent Monro, his old friend and contemporary from Kilmarnock, came out to Shiwa. She attended the Harvey wedding in 1951 and then returned to make her home in a wing of the mansion at Shiwa from 1953 to 1955, and from 1959 to 1961. In 1962 she returned to Britain, dying there shortly thereafter.

Mrs. Monro, although she grew very deaf by the end of the 1950s, helped give Gore-Browne the steady support which he desired. She assisted his daughter Lorna in running the house and entertaining the stream of visitors which swelled rather than receded as the aura of Gore-Browne's reputation intensified and his home became an obligatory way station for overseas visitors as well as the usual panoply of local dignitaries.

Even more than before, Shiwa was regarded throughout the 1950s and 1960s as an outpost of civility, urbanity, and culture in the midst of a narrow-minded, parochially concerned Central Africa. No one within the three territories so epitomized the more noble and even-handed aspects of the imperial connection. No one had a library so large and catholic, a kitchen which (given the estate's remoteness from the usual shopping facilities) served such successful meals, a wine cellar so well-stocked (the port was always passed properly), and a guest list of such interest and multiracial variety. Shiwa was an oasis remarkable for its buildings, for its ambience, but most of all because it was presided over by a man who dispensed political and racial common sense with a patrician manner. It was the correctness of his background and bearing which drew many, the curiosity of his remote edifice that drew others, and, increasingly, his closeness to politicized Africans and his shrewd assessment of political necessities which transformed the nominally retired statesman into a venerated sage.

Sacha Carnegie, a distant relative and an established British writer, testified to the attractive ambience of Shiwa in the late 1950s. "Often while at Shiwa I had to pinch myself good and hard to make certain I really was in such a fantastic, such an idyllic spot. . . . Sitting in the warm magnificent library sipping sherry from a fine glass, cut off from the night by the rich folds of dark red curtains, it was not easy to realise that I was literally in the heart of Africa; that within a few hundred yards of the electric lamps, the gleaming ranks of books, the portraits on the walls and the dark lustre of the furniture, wild animals hunted and were hunted in the darkness. . . . Crocodiles moved in the waters of the lake and there we were, immaculate in dinner jackets ensconced on the most comfortable of sofas. . . . We dined by the pleasant light of candles in holders; large prints of a religious nature hung on the walls; the glass and the silver sparkled in the subdued fashion of perfect taste. We ate roasted harte-beest . . . drank most excellent wine."[2]

As a state of mind, Gore-Browne's retirement from politics had lasted only a year or two. Powerless to prevent the progress of the machinery of federation once the Tories were returned to power in 1951, he could mutter warnings privately while publicly reminding anyone who would pay attention that partition was the only scheme capable of preventing ultimate disaster. The idea that the British government would thrust federation down African throats seemed incredible. "I simply cannot see how the Government can force the present Federation proposals . . . on the Africans with any moral justifications whatever," he wrote to *The Economist,* "or without grave practical apprehension. The results, possibly not the immediate results, but the ultimate ones, will be disastrous."[3] At the same time, he was not yet prepared to condone either the rhetoric or the response of the local African National Congress. After John

2. Sacha Carnegie, *Red Dust of Africa* (London, 1959), 76–78.
3. Gore-Browne to Norton, 23 January 1953.

Moffat, his successor in the Legislative Council, had foolishly declared that Africans would accept the Federation if partnership ever
became more than useful propaganda, the Congress had immediately declared that it would never condone the Federation—
that Africans wanted "an African nation" not partnership. Gore-
Browne saw the reasonableness of their anger, and appreciated that
events in the Gold Coast and the Sudan were influencing African
aspirations. Nevertheless, for him it was "quite fantastic" that
Africans should in their "present state of development" fancy governing a country as industrialized as Northern Rhodesia. They were
not ready, but he acknowledged that nationalism was in the air, that
they had the "bit" between their teeth, and that they were justified
in reacting to the inflammatory statements of local white racists and
the continuance of the industrial color bar with flamboyant proposals of their own.[4]

When the Closer Association Conference was convened by Britain in 1952 in Livingstone, whites protested because the African
delegates were allocated quarters in a hostel used by white civil
servants. Those were the types of attitudes for which Gore-Browne
had no patience. Immediately afterwards he publicly recognized
that since neither blacks nor whites wanted any form of partnership,
self-government and some form of black rule, he said, "ought to
come." By early 1953, long before most other whites understood, it
had become clear to him that the threat of federation had permanently poisoned the atmosphere of race relations and pushed
Africans to the point where only the ouster of whites would prove
satisfactory. "It was sheer nonsense, born of wishful thinking, to
say that African resistance [to the Federation] is weakening," he
wrote at a time when the British government and its supporters
were persuading themselves that Africans would be better off
under, and come to appreciate the benefits of, the Federation.[5]

Despite his antipathy, Gore-Browne could at first counsel no
course but that of watching and waiting. During a visit to Lusaka
(he remained chairman of the trustees of the African War Memorial
Fund there throughout the 1950s) he spent several whole days with
the Congress and Nkumbula. At the time the Congress wanted to
demonstrate their last-ditch, implacable opposition to the federation idea by organizing boycotts, finding other ways in which to
thwart the whites peacefully, and—generally—to follow Gandhi
and Nkrumah by somehow promoting passive resistance. But, said

4. Gore-Browne to Ethel Locke-King, 20 November, 11 December 1951.
5. Gore-Browne to Patrick Monkhouse, 31 March 1952; Gore-Browne to Norton, 23 January 1953.

Gore-Browne wryly, "Nkumbula isn't Gandhi."[6] As he had predicted, the days of prayer which Congress promoted, and the with-
holding of African labor which it urged, proved modest protests
incapable of forestalling the Federation. It officially came into being
in August, 1953.

Gore-Browne had equally little patience with some of the ways
by which well-meaning whites and Africans attempted at this time
and subsequently to reconcile blacks to continued white domination. Like so many others, but even more vehemently, he deprecated the breakdown of race relations which was apparent by 1953
and promised to become more traumatic. Yet he, almost alone of
liberal whites in Northern Rhodesia, refused to grasp at straws.
When he was staying with Governor Rennie in 1953 in Lusaka he
found himself surrounded by proselytizers for Moral Rearmament,
the crypto-religious movement which was then based in Switzerland and which, for a variety of reasons, concentrated much of its
outreach upon settler Africa during the 1950s. Rennie thought that
he could not afford to miss any opportunities of ameliorating race
relations. Gore-Browne thus "got roped in for a couple of meetings." "I must say," he reported, "I thought it pretty fair tripe. The
set smile of gracious loving kindness on all their silly faces was very
annoying . . . the confessions were futile, no one admitted to a
good, rousing, sin." Most of all, at close quarters they were "crash-
ing bores."[7]

Gore-Browne reacted much the same to Colonel David Stirling
and his Capricorn Africa Society. Early in World War II, when
Stirling was in his twenties, he and a brother invented the Special
Air Service, a virtually freelance British military arm run by well-
born officers. It specialized in parachuting behind enemy lines and
attacking from unusual angles. Courageous to a fault, Stirling and
his special unit gained fame in the North African desert campaigns.
He was taken prisoner in Tunisia, escaped from the Germans, was
retaken by the Italians, and then spent the remainder of the war
incarcerated in a prison camp in Germany. After the war he consorted with Moral Rearmament and, in 1949, conceived the Capricorn Africa Society. It represented an attempt to forge an alliance
between responsive whites and "the right kind" of blacks. Stirling
believed that he could form a common front composed of superior
figures of both colors. They would comprise a leadership bloc ca-

6. Gore-Browne to Angela, 28 April 1953; Gore-Browne to Director, South
African Information Office, 21 June 1953. For an account of the maneuvers of the
Congress, see Rotberg, *Nationalism,* 250.

7. Gore-Browne to Angela, 28 April 1953; Gore-Browne to Ethel, 28 April
1953.

pable of saving eastern and central Africa from the hell-fires of left and right extremism. At the core of the Capricorn doctrine was the affirmation of a "common patriotism" which could bring about the rejection of the "barren doctrine of racial nationalism." Initially, however, Capricorn supported the Federation, and, to militant Africans, the word Capricornist thereafter was the epithet for a turncoat.

Stirling's romantic ideas and personal charisma attracted many whites and Africans in Kenya and the Rhodesias with whom Gore-Browne would normally have had much in common. Charles Fisher was Stirling's key disciple on the Copperbelt, for example. But the society was too much a "do-good" organization to appeal to Gore-Browne. He did not see how Stirling and his acolytes could reform the attitudes of blacks and whites. Moral Rearmament was trying to do precisely the same thing, without much success. Gore-Browne, after all, knew the quality of Rhodesian white self-interest, and appreciated the great gulf that separated the races as a result of federal rule. He also was skeptical about the kind of highly qualified franchise that Stirling was putting forward as an ideal. Under it the mass of Africans would be disenfranchised in the near term, and Gore-Browne was sufficiently a realist to know that none of the militants, and few Africans generally, would have patience with such a scheme. Nor did he think it valid. Gore-Browne also distrusted Stirling's authoritarian personality. The society was not meant to be an association of equals; rather decisions were taken by Stirling and then ratified by others. Usually his qualities of determination and charm managed to satisfy objectors who otherwise would have cavilled at such methods, but they could not have comforted Gore-Browne. For all of these reasons, Gore-Browne chose in 1956 to refuse Stirling's personal invitation to open a large Capricorn conference at Salima in Nyasaland. The conference, with delegates from Kenya, Tanganyika, the Rhodesias, and Nyasaland, was meant to launch Capricorn definitively and to inaugurate an era of multiracial harmony in Central Africa. But Gore-Browne, like Africans sympathetic to the aims of the congress movements, stayed away.

This was among the many politically wise choices which Gore-Browne made during the 1950s. As a subsequent account by his Kenyan friend Clarence Buxton, who attended, makes perfectly clear, Gore-Browne would have felt uncomfortable in the cloying climate of Salima. Buxton, warming to the Capricorn motto "Who dares, wins," joined forty-three other black and white delegates from Kenya, twenty from Northern Rhodesia, sixty from Southern Rhodesia, twelve from Nyasaland and twelve from Tanganyika, at the Salima Hotel on Lake Nyasa's shore. He commented on the racial harmony which prevailed throughout the five-day assembly, and on Stirling's dismay on the one occasion when he caught the Kenyan whites talking together without Africans and Asians. "The evenings were great," wrote Buxton, "not too much drinking— just enough to loosen tongues in grave and gay conviviality, with as always, a hotch potch of skin colours. There were no strains or stresses though talk was free and frank. Usually the 'fuhrer' as David was nicknamed could be seen giving someone a caning for ill-judged amendments during the day's debates, or a brain wash about future policy and activities but all interspersed with the amazing personal touch which has drawn so many diverse men and women to him in the Crusade for Capricorn Africa." Buxton praised Stirling's performance as chairman. "He won his way over everything without any breach of the rules and with the utmost good humour." There were minor revolts among the delegates, but he managed to obtain their assent to the Capricorn Contract, or constitution, with which Gore-Browne had earlier expressed fundamental disagreement.

Buxton hoped that the sense of the sanctimonious contract would soon sweep Africa. "I hope and believe . . . that the Movement is not too late to bring new hope in Africa."[8] But it was too far into the colonial twilight for the notion that responsibility should be "left to those people of all races who [were] qualified for it" to carry any weight. Although Capricorn as a romantic idea and a movement lingered in Kenya and Southern Rhodesia until about 1960, its high point was the Salima conference. Even Stirling eventually agreed, as Gore-Browne had immediately sensed, that Capricorn had been hopelessly utopian, "almost Walter Mitty. . . . We were a total failure."[9]

As far as Gore-Browne and most Africans were concerned, the Federation had, by 1956, proven a bust. Gore-Browne had all along been prepared to recant—retrospectively to disavow his earlier predictions of disaster—if Huggins' federal government had in fact implemented, or shown any signs of implementing, policies capable of promoting partnership in its generally understood sense. If

8. Clarence Buxton, "Capricorn Convention Salima: Some Personal Recollections for friends and relations only," 19–20 June 1956, unpub. typescript. See also Peter Gibbs, *Avalanche in Central Africa* (London, 1961), 88–91; Susan Wood, *A Fly in Amber* (London, 1964), 99–105. For an exposition of the Capricorn ideals, see J. H. Oldham, *New Hope in Africa* (London, 1955).

9. Quoted in Gavin Young, "Drinks at White's with the Colonel," *The Observer*, 25 August 1974. Stirling in 1974 organized "GB 75", or Great Britain, 1975, a secret "private army" to save Britain from imminent financial and moral disaster. See also F. B. Rea, "Rebirth of a Notion: Can Capricorn Rise from its Ashes?" *Central African Examiner*, II, 26 (23 May 1959), 14–15.

anything, however, Africans had lost ground, and whatever vestige of racial good feeling remained in 1953, had, Gore-Browne observed, been erased. "Federation . . . has not only done nothing towards bettering race relations, but has even made things worse by failing to do anything constructive and by seeming to be satisfied with platitudes about a vague partnership which Africans may be forgiven for writing off as hypocrisy." In 1954 he warned the editor of the *Northern News,* the Protectorate's main newspaper, that whites "must stop talking and do something to show not only that we care for the African's material needs . . . but that we regard him as a human being not so very unlike ourselves, and stop penalising him for having the black face with which the Lord provided him at birth." He criticized Huggins for having said in the federal parliament that blacks need never expect seats in railway dining cars, in the federal cabinet, and so on. In fact, he boiled with rage at the stupidity of all white politicians, territorial and federal. In a published article he urbanely indicated that nothing was being done to make partnership a reality. And without doing so, he warned, federation would fail. He suggested that Central African whites accept the full meaning of Cecil Rhodes' dictum that there should be "equal rights for all civilised men irrespective of race." He wanted Africans to be admitted to hotels, restaurants, and so on, and for all social and industrial color bars to be broken under the aegis of federation.[10] In a subsequent article in which he again advocated partition as a solution to racial discontent, he flatly urged, as the only alternative capable of assuring harmony in Northern Rhodesia, that whites immediately abolish the color bar. This would not, he said, mean equality, only decency.

A long journey of inspection throughout the Federation only confirmed, for Gore-Browne, the absence of any federal concern for Africans or indigenous uplift. Partnership, he said, was "humbug." From Shiwa to Lusaka; to Salisbury (where he was feted by Welensky, the governor-general of the federation, the governor of Southern Rhodesia, and so on; to Blantyre and Zomba; and then home via Lilongwe, Rumpi, and Fort Hill—a distance of about 2,000 miles—he saw no indications of "the 'Partnership' between races there is so much talk about. . . . Colour-bar seems just as strongly in evidence as ever."[11] Decent accommodation for

10. Gore-Browne to John Spicer, 6 September 1954; Gore-Browne, "Real Partnership the only Key to Riddle," *Bulawayo Chronicle,* 6 August 1954; Gore-Browne, "Partnership or Partition," *Northern News,* 21 December 1954. See also Gore-Browne, letter to the editor, *Manchester Guardian,* 20 December 1954.

11. Gore-Browne to Ethel Locke-King, 1 July 1955. For the comparable dissatisfaction of a contemporary observer, see Harry Franklin, *Unholy Wedlock: The Failure of the Central African Federation* (London, 1963), 97–120.

Mulenga, for instance, was everywhere impossible, and all of the old divisions remained. Economically, too, Gore-Browne saw renewed evidence that the federal arrangements were short-changing the northern territories and making medical and agricultural requirements more expensive. The decision to build the Kariba rather than the Kafue dam shattered any residual belief in the even-handed application of federal decisions. As Gore-Browne explained in the *Manchester Guardian* "Those of us who live in Central Africa know very well that partnership between white and black at the present time anyhow is at best a pious hope, at worst a disingenuous myth propagated for political purposes." Since one of the most urgent needs of the day was for whites to retain the confidence of Africans, "the sooner the partnership myth is dropped the better. It will be time enough to revive it when something has been done about the colour-bar. . . . Partnership between races is a fine ideal, fraternity is perhaps a finer one, but nothing is gained and much is lost by pretending that either the one or the other is being attempted when actually nothing of the sort is happening."[12]

Never one to refrain from offering constructive alternatives capable, in his own eyes at least, of averting racial conflict and attendant disaster, Gore-Browne sought throughout the 1950s to enhance the status of Africans without frightening whites. One scheme, which he urged white allies like Dr. Alexander Scott, of Lusaka, to promote, was the broadening of the franchise in Northern Rhodesia to include "British protected persons," for the most part Africans. (Since Northern Rhodesia was a protectorate, whites and some Asians were citizens of the United Kingdom and Colonies, although Africans were but protected persons; and the electorate was comprised of citizens only.) Doing so would constitute a gesture of goodwill capable of counterbalancing the "arrogance of the Europeans" which so endangered local race relations. Gore-Browne also discussed this proposal with Kaunda, from the Chinsali district, whom he had long known, and who was then the secretary-general of the congress. But the congress wanted more than gestures of goodwill and Scott, although a nominated pro-African member in the federal parliament, had an effective political following smaller even than Gore-Browne's own. Thus this suggestion, like Gore-Browne's occasional dusting off of the partition plan (he wrote

---

12. Gore-Browne to the editor of the *Manchester Guardian,* 6 February 1956. Gore-Browne contributed similar sentiments to *East Africa and Rhodesia.* Letter (5 January 1956). His private letters to F. Stephen Joelson, editor of the weekly, were even more critical of the absence of partnership in the Federation, 10 February, 16 March 1959.

about it with vigor as late as 1958) aroused no groundswell of popular support.

Nor could he and his old friend Welensky, deputy prime minister of the federal government until late 1956, and then prime minister (and a knight), agree to do more than to disagree about politics. Although they corresponded uninterruptedly and warmly throughout this period—indeed until Gore-Browne's death—the old political rapport was totally absent. Welensky would have derided the alarmist tone of Gore-Browne's prophecy for the future: in the wake of unrest in 1955 in formerly quiet and still remote Chinsali, Gore-Browne predicted that "for long years to come there is going to be a period when everything will be unstable and difficult. The European doesn't like having to give up any of the privileges he used to enjoy as a matter of course . . . and he frequently hasn't the sense to see that he'll have to give them up whether he likes or no before long."[13]

Gore-Browne was not the only Northern Rhodesian searching for alternatives to federation. The Congress, led by Nkumbula and Kaunda, was organizing boycotts of urban butcheries, encouraging antagonism to white authority in the rural areas, speaking out against the color bar, and putting its case before sympathetic British public opinion. It demonstrated whenever possible at home and patiently explained its case to visiting foreign journalists and politicians. It organized and raised funds, waiting not so patiently for chinks in the armor of white control to widen.[14] Virtually no whites resident in the territory were members of the Congress. Nor were there many in the mid-1950s, who, even privately, believed that the methods of the Congress were appropriate, or were likely to prove effective in altering or ending the Federation. Instead, a tiny band of liberal whites were themselves active in trying to promote a multiracial middle-way as a bridging solution to Northern Rhodesia's, if not Central Africa's, gulf between white and black antagonism.

Scott, Fisher, Moffat, and Harry Franklin, once Northern Rhodesia's director of information and later a nominated member of the Executive Council, constituted the core of the shifting alliance which espoused liberal values and consequently thought both the Federation and the Congress extreme. Individually and as a group they solicited Gore-Browne's support; he, after all, was the senior and most widely-known liberal white in the territory. Africans trusted Scott, but they trusted Gore-Browne more, and

13. Gore-Browne to Ethel Locke-King, 24 April 1955. For the Chinsali disturbances, see N/0001/2/15/4, Lusaka archives.

14. For detailed discussion, see Rotberg, *Nationalism,* 253–281.

the others hardly at all. Thus, Gore-Browne was at the center, even if he did not always fully share the practical aims of the convoluted liberal caucus which explored one political possibility after another in a vain attempt to stem the twin avalanches of minority racism and majority nationalism.

Gore-Browne looked favorably upon a return to public life almost from the moment the Federation became a reality. He wanted to exert an influence on behalf of sanity, fair play, and Africans. In late 1953 the Congress had asked him to accept nomination to the federal assembly on its behalf, as a representative once again of African interests, and he had cabled a warm agreement from Genoa (where he then was on his way back from London). The actual appointment was completely in the giving of the governor of Northern Rhodesia, however, and Rennie instead nominated Dr. John Haslam, Gore-Browne's old friend, and the former territorial director of medical services. In the same year N. O. Earl-Spurr, a military friend in Lusaka, asked him to help found a conservative party, which he refused to do, and, slightly afterwards, there was public speculation that Gore-Browne would join the newly-established Confederate Party, a right-wing, pro-partition coalition of whites in the three Central African territories. Newspapers supposed that since Lord Graham of Southern Rhodesia was a prime mover of the party, and knew Gore-Browne, that he and other titled friends would naturally (since the Confederates supported partition) persuade Gore-Browne to link their fortunes together. Their support of partition, however, was based on the practice of apartheid, and Gore-Browne, as much as he may have wanted renewed political action, gave no thought, even after a visit to Shiwa by Lord Graham, to lending his name to the Confederates. Instead, in 1954, he redoubled his efforts to obtain the Northern Rhodesian nomination to the federal assembly. With Haslam suffering from a stroke and unlikely to recover (he died in late 1955) he asked Moffat to indicate his own availability, as a federal or even as a territorial nominee, to the governor. This Moffat did, twice, but without arousing official enthusiasm.

Gore-Browne's formal involvement with the liberals began in late 1955. Scott took the initiative and, later, when Gore-Browne visited Lusaka, Scott, Franklin, and Gore-Browne had long talks about how multiracialism could best be promoted in Northern Rhodesia through the formation of a new political movement. Gore-Browne told the others how important it would be to obtain solid and credible African support—not the usual Uncle Toms who were pleasant but were regarded by other Africans as ineffectual—and actually to propose to do something concrete on behalf of Africans. He went so far as to urge formal cooperation with the

Congress. The usual liberal waffle (sometimes he called it "piffle") would not do. He warned Franklin to steer well clear of Capricorn, since sensible Africans would remember its pro-federal stance. He suggested, too, that the proposed new political party should not confine itself to Northern Rhodesia. He even spent some time revising Franklin's proposed draft of its constitution. There were clauses reflecting his own special urgencies—opposition to any form of color bar; the promotion of equality of opportunity without regard to race; the introduction of compulsory elementary education for all; the granting of an equitable system of parliamentary franchise to all races, "conferring the right to vote on all who are capable of exercising it"; the reorganization of local administration (with African participation); and emphasis upon the development of peasant farming, rural fisheries, and plantation forestry.[15]

The formation of a Liberal Party—its name began appearing on different draft constitutions—proved premature. Support proved limited among both whites and blacks, some of whom had shifted their energies from party politics, strictly defined, to the promotion of the Capricorn Society. In the aftermath of the Salima experience, many, including some of the erstwhile supporters of the proposed Liberal Party, persuaded themselves of the dawning of a new era of multiracial good feeling. They chose, for a time, exclusively to disseminate its message. By mid-1957, however, those among the liberals who had, like Gore-Browne, stood apart from Capricorn, as well as some of those who had joined, began rethinking the need for a multiracial party. Alan Lennox-Boyd, the secretary of state for the colonies, had earlier in the year declared to anxious black Northern Rhodesians that the Federation had come to stay. "It is good for you and you must accept it."[16] Welensky was making equally bombastic statements in Salisbury and, everywhere, the lip-service once so enthusiastically given to partnership had been effectively quenched. The Congress consequently had redoubled its verbal militancy and promised trouble to come. Equally, it was obvious to observers that Northern Rhodesia would have a territorial election in 1959, and a Federal election was expected even be-

15. Gore-Browne to Franklin, 25 November 1955, 12 March 1956; Gore-Browne to Moffat, 22 January 1956. Scott agreed with Gore-Browne's views on the need to cooperate with the Congress. "We shall have to work with them as we find them and try to influence them by our complete sincerity. We must try to see the world through African eyes. I can see the responsibility of a new party with democratic views. If it attracts Africans as it must then we cannot permit it to fail . . ." Scott to Gore-Browne, 14 November 1955. For Franklin's earlier sharp views of Gore-Browne, see Franklin, *The Flag-Wagger* (London, 1974), 152, 196.

16. Lennox-Boyd, address to a meeting of the Western Provincial Council, 4 January 1957, in N/0049/19/2, Lusaka archives.

fore, perhaps in 1958. For all of these reasons, the liberals, led again by Scott ("I do not think we can look for any liberal development from the present British government"[17])—and joined now by Stirling, Fisher, and the Reverend Merfyn Temple, a Methodist minister who was a local leader of the Capricorn Society—summoned Gore-Browne and Franklin to a planning meeting in Luanshya in late 1957. Declaring Welensky's United Federal Party reactionary, and promising to seek a more liberal franchise for blacks, they gave birth, informally, to the Constitution Party. (Its initial constitution resolved to establish a society "free from racial discrimination with a system of law based on a solemn contract between our peoples to acknowledge our human unity under God and our unity in one loyalty to the Crown." [Beside this clause in his draft copy Gore-Browne wrote: "What does this mean?"] Yet, following Capricorn practices, the constitution declared that the vote was not "a natural right, but a responsibility to be exercised for the common good.") Shortly thereafter Lawrence Katilungu, president of the African Mineworkers Union, Norman Hunt, a local architect and C. L. Patel, an Asian businessman, agreed to take positions of leadership on the Copperbelt. The young Reverend Colin Morris, a Methodist parson from Chingola; Denis Acheson, a young chemist working for Rhodesian Selection Trust; Henry Makulu, a respected Congregationalist minister; Safeli Chileshe, another of Gore-Browne's old proteges; Henry Thornicroft, a coloured leader; Wittington K. Sikalumbi, a member of the Congress; Frank Barton, a Lusaka journalist; and Hans Noak, a Lusaka architect, also gave support.[18] Monica Fisher reported great enthusiasm for the nascent party everywhere on the Copperbelt. It was determined, she wrote, to make the Federation work, to reject the notion of secession, and equally to refuse to condone methods which were illegal or extra-constitutional. The party did not believe in intimidation, riots, and boycotts. "One wonders," she asked, "whether Nkumbula may not soon join us?" He was, she said, "known as being more moderate than many of his associates" in the Congress.[19]

17. Scott to Gore-Browne, 19 March 1958.

18. Fisher complained that Morris was "trying to hitch us up with the socialists." Fisher to Gore-Browne, 3 February 1958.

19. Monica Fisher to Gore-Browne, 28 October 1957. A similar sentiment was expressed by Scott's wife. She reported that Nkumbula had promised not to oppose the Constitution Party. "Other Africans we hope will gain courage in time and join us. . . . The Party is alive and kicking and there seems to be no good reason why it should not go from strength to strength." Elnace [Grace] Scott to Gore-Browne, 21 November 1957. In the margin of the letter Gore-Browne noted: "Sent £20."

These were unrealistic sentiments that Gore-Browne could hardly share. He profoundly distrusted the links with Capricorn, which were bound to be misunderstood by Africans, feared Stirling's attempts to regiment the party as he had the Society, and—most of all—saw the party's espousal of a qualified franchise as the major barrier to effective African participation. Without such participation, he warned, the party—and any party led by whites—would accomplish nothing. Nor could he accept the likelihood of the imminent collapse of the Congress. He knew that the African militants were more determined and more able than most whites, even supposedly liberal whites, believed. He was beginning to suspect, too, that even the liberals could not bring themselves to share effective leadership of any new political movement with blacks.

. In appreciation of the seriousness of the times, and his own awareness of the profound changes in African attitudes towards whites, he had come to realize that nothing else would do—that the hour of Africans was coming and that whites, if they wanted to make a place for themselves in the future Northern Rhodesia, would have to assist rather than direct Africans. These sentiments, hardly ever expressed in full except perhaps to Scott, were profoundly radical for a white Northern Rhodesian. They were far too advanced for the framers of the Constitution Party, and, because Charles Fisher would not let Gore-Browne address the inaugural congress of the party in early 1958 unless he actually joined the party (Fisher thought that Gore-Browne's failure to affirm membership would damage the party in the eyes of Africans), Gore-Browne played no further part (Franklin also refused to join) in the progress of the Constitution Party, or its 1959 successor, the Central Africa Party.

It is not clear exactly when Gore-Browne began making a mental commitment to African nationalism. For at least ten years before 1957 he had appreciated and urged others to heed the rising political self-consciousness of the African elite. From the onset of the anti-Federation campaign he had understood its popularity with the masses. Almost alone among whites he had refused to underestimate the potential power of organized Africans. Sooner than most, too, he sensed that sharing real governmental responsibility with African leaders was essential if a catastrophe were to be averted. As Welensky once said, Gore-Browne was eminently adaptable. He was a realist. Most of all, he had no fear that his own way of life or the ways of life of his daughters and grandchildren would be affected adversely by African rule, as such. He had made his home in Northern Rhodesia, among Africans. Despite his advanced age and his enjoyment of many decades of happy paternalism, Gore-

Browne was confident that the values that mattered most to him could just as easily be ensured by an African as a white government. It was the quality of any rule, not the color of the rulers, which had always concerned him. Sometime toward the end of the 1950s, too, he became persuaded that his earlier assessment of African capabilities for self-government had been too pessimistic—that congressmen had shown considerable talent and that many of the new graduates of African or overseas universities were providing a cadre of potential national leaders. (Even if he still thought that the removal of British control and the realization of African independence was a distant possibility, so in the later 1950s did nearly everyone else, including most important Africans.) Further, many of the congress's more dynamic personalities were Bemba, several from the Chinsali district. Gore-Browne naturally felt more at one with his neighbors—with men with whom he could converse intimately in their own language. Nkumbula, too, although not a Bemba, was someone with whom he had once had close association. Yet it is not apparent that Gore-Browne would so completely have made the African nationalist cause his own in spirit, and then in actuality, had it not been for Kaunda, the son of a Nyasa Presbyterian preacher who had grown up at the Lubwa mission and whose mother Gore-Browne had known almost from the establishment of the Shiwa estate.

Gore-Browne and Kaunda were both in England in mid-1957, Kaunda spending six months under Labour Party auspices studying its organizational procedures, and learning about British politics generally. (He and Nkumbula had originally gone to London to demand a "one-man, one-vote" constitution for Northern Rhodesia). Gore-Browne was there to attend the fiftieth anniversary of the official opening of the Brooklands Race Track and to deal with the winding-up of the King and Locke-King estates. During a one-month period Gore-Browne and Kaunda were together at least ten times—for lunch or dinner alone or lunch with David Stirling or Thomas Fox-Pitt, then secretary of the Anti-Slavery Society. On at least one occasion Kaunda stayed the night "sleeping in the dining room" of the small flat which Gore-Browne used in London. They thus talked together at length about political matters, not for the first time but probably for the first time as equals whose aspirations were similar. By then Gore-Browne wanted to bring about the end of the Federation as much as did Kaunda. He and Kaunda both wished Africans to share more fully in the government, and both hoped that the British government would grant a significant increase in participation when the new constitutional arrangements were announced in the coming year. (Gore-Browne lunched with

Lennox-Boyd and specifically urged him to pay attention to Kaunda's requests.)

In early 1958 Governor Sir Arthur Benson (both Gore-Browne and Welensky unfailingly referred to him in their correspondence as B. B.—"Balmy Benson") announced the promulgation of constitutional arrangements which would take effect in 1959, after a territorial election for seats in the Legislative Council. According to the plan devised by Benson and Lennox-Boyd, whites and Africans were to vote separately, according to a series of complicated arrangements, for their representatives in the council. Despite the demand of the Congress for a universal franchise, Benson gave Africans only a minority of the available seats. To accept the proposals of the Congress, he said, would invite whites to "paralyse" the government. "Are you implying," Kaunda responded, "that for our demands to be met we have got to be in a position to paralyse the Government?"[20] Nkumbula burned the White Paper that embodied Benson's proposed constitution and Kaunda and others released counter arguments in a so-called "Black Paper." During this period—at the onset of Zambian winter—Gore-Browne was in Lusaka for meetings. Together with Mulenga, he took Kaunda to dinner at the new international hotel which had recently opened in the capital and discussed political maneuverings late into the night. As trivial as it may now seem, for a leading white to dine ostentatiously with a leader of the militant Congress was certain—and was designed—to raise eyebrows. Gore-Browne in no way feared being associated with such an anathema.

Kaunda probably discussed his growing estrangement from Nkumbula cursorily, if at all, for he was about to go off to India for a few months and their mutual disagreements had not yet come to the point of crisis. Younger congressmen had grown increasingly disenchanted with Nkumbula's lack of leadership. He had behaved dishonorably in London and discredited the Congress. Then, while Kaunda was in India, Nkumbula attempted to purge the Congress of those branch leaders whose loyalty to himself seemed suspect. Simon Kapwepwe, the Bemba treasurer of the Congress, demanded a stricter accounting of Nkumbula's use of its funds. Finally, despite his public opposition to the Benson constitution, Nkumbula decided to run a slate of candidates in the 1959 elections. At a special party congress in October, 1958, Nkumbula urged the delegates to accept Benson's scheme, and to give him greater per-

20. Quoted in Kenneth Kaunda, *Zambia Shall Be Free* (New York, 1962), 87. For the constitution, see *Proposals for Constitutional Change in Northern Rhodesia* (Lusaka, 28 March 1958); *Proposals for Constitutional Changes,* Cmd. 530 (1958).

sonal powers to run the Congress as he saw fit. Opponents criticized Nkumbula's authoritarianism and his oft-displayed hedonism. A majority of the delegates, many of whom Nkumbula had personally chosen, endorsed their leader's demands. But many of the more militant congressmen, led by the Bemba contingent, walked out of the conference and immediately formed the Zambia African National Congress, with Kaunda as president. (Zambia was a contraction of Zambezia, the earlier name for the general area of Northern Rhodesia.) The old Congress promised to contest the 1959 election; the new group urged Africans to boycott the balloting.[21] Gore-Browne was in no way involved and, if asked, would not have backed a boycott, but he understood the discontent with Nkumbula's leadership. He trusted Kaunda's abilities as the leader of what, at first, was considered by nearly all observers as a potentially insignificant breakaway movement.

A few months before, Banda had returned home to Nyasaland to assume the leadership of its congress movement. Gore-Browne had known of his intentions as early as any outsider, for their lengthy correspondence had resumed in the mid-1950s. Rejecting Britain after the imposition of federation, Banda had emigrated to the Gold Coast and begun practicing medicine in Kumasi. "It is a real joy to me to be able to help in the work here," he wrote, "even though for a few years only. I have the satisfaction of knowing that at last, I am doing medical work, where my services are really needed." He agreed with Gore-Browne that spiritual rather than material things counted most, and therefore felt in a good position to appreciate what the British had done for Africans. Yet there were a few Britons who besmirched their nation's image. As Gore-Browne had said, "arrogance and lack of human understanding spoil everything." He went on to be personal. "No, Sir Stewart, we do not want to get rid of you. Certainly, for myself, I have no intention of getting rid of Europeans. What we want is that Europeans should now recognise the fact that we, too, are human beings and should be treated as such." Banda explained that far from being a "trouble maker," he was far more conservative than other Africans. "Without my influence," he boasted, "most of the boys from Nyasaland and Northern Rhodesia would have returned home convinced communists. I did my best to guide them along what I thought were safe lines."

"No, Sir Stewart, you have not lived in vain," Banda closed a long letter. "Africans . . . may . . . have their disagreements with you . . . but most of them . . . greatly appreciate what you have done for our people. I do not think your work is entirely finished

21. For more detail, see Rotberg, *Nationalism,* 291.

yet. We shall see." In 1957 Banda revealed his imminent return home. He coupled that with an announcement that he still supported Gore-Browne's partition scheme. "Whatever the other two territories may do in 1960," he promised, "we in Nyasaland intend to secede, if possible, with part of Northern Rhodesia. . . . They will have to reoccupy Nyasaland to keep us in the Federation." Banda promised to come to Shiwa when he had returned to Nyasaland. He had purchased land near Fort Hill, in northern Nyasaland, where he intended to grow coffee privately while becoming more active politically in the south. Isoka, north of Shiwa in Northern Rhodesia, could, he supposed be the capital of the state.[22]

After Banda's return to Nyasaland in mid-1958 and his assumption of the presidency of the Nyasaland African Congress, he had no time for coffee farming or for visits to Shiwa Ngandu. Instead, he was absorbed in winning the political kingdom for Nyasas in a way paralleled only to a more limited extent by Kaunda and his much less well-organized new party. At the end of 1958 Banda and Kaunda were together in Accra, for the All-African People's Conference. Upon their return both, in their respective spheres, launched an aggressive verbal attack upon the various forces responsible for betraying and oppressing Africans. "To Hell with Federation," Banda shouted. Kaunda refused to rest until he had removed the union jack from Northern Rhodesia, "whatever the consequences.'" In Northern Rhodesia the Zambia African National Congress exhorted urban and rural dwellers to stay away from the polls in March, 1959. The Nyasaland African Congress meanwhile sponsored a campaign of disobedience in the towns and the rural areas. It held unauthorized meetings, defied agricultural regulations, obstructed airfields, blocked roads, stoned whites, and burned buildings. The Zambia Congress held illegal meetings and was blamed for occasional outbursts of arson. Leaders of both groups had met together secretly and whites presumed that they had conspired.

Amid an atmosphere of rapidly deteriorating security—although Gore-Browne noticed nothing amiss at Shiwa—the governments of all three Central African territories, in concert with Welensky's federal government, banned their three militant congresses (only Nkumbula and his followers were exempt) and, by mid-March, nearly all of the leading Nyasa, Southern Rhodesian and Northern Rhodesian blacks were in jail or detention. "I don't know whether you will believe me," Welensky wrote to Gore-Browne of Nyasa-

22. Banda to Gore-Browne, 18 July 1955, 27 November 1957, 16 January 1958. If Banda in fact purchased the land, it escaped the attention of most contemporary observers.

land, "but I want to tell you that this hasn't been the normal political disturbance. This has been an insurrection. I don't know to what extent Banda is concerned in it from a political angle. I myself think that he has been used by some people who are a lot more evil than he is."[23]

Kaunda and Banda both emerged from prison in 1960 stronger politically than before. In African eyes, Kaunda now had more legitimate claims on the leadership of the local nationalist movement than Nkumbula, who had been elected to the Legislative Council in 1959. Becoming president of the United National Independence Party (the successor to the Zambia African National Congress) Kaunda thereafter concentrated—as Banda did with expectations of more rapid success in Nyasaland—on winning the kinds of concessions from the British government which would result in the destruction of the Federation and the inauguration of a black government in Northern Rhodesia. Gore-Browne's posture was supportive. As before, it was clearer to him than to whites of Welensky's stamp that the victory in 1959 had been pyrrhic—the winds of change had blown and Britain no longer had either the justification or the will to resist the tide of black nationalism which was sweeping southwards from Ghana, Nigeria, and the Congo. Moreover, Gore-Browne knew that most Africans—the African common man and his friends—wanted change and supported Kaunda wholeheartedly. So did he.

As Northern Rhodesia's elder statesman, Gore-Browne came into his own in the 1960s. As part of its long promised reassessment of the Federation, the British government had appointed a prestigious multiracial, multinational commission (named after Lord Monckton of Brenchley, its chairman) to tour Central Africa, sample opinion, examine assumptions, and make recommendations. Half of the commission, led by vice-chairman Sir Donald MacGillivray, even made a journey to Shiwa especially to take Gore-Browne's evidence (as well as the evidence of his staff and others) in the manner of all previous royal commissions. Earlier in the year Gore-Browne had privately noted that Northern Rhodesia must be prepared to "go black." Meeting in his library, Gore-Browne told the commissioners that he favored majority rule and the secession by Northern Rhodesia from the Federation. That was what Northern Rhodesian Africans wanted and any delay in acceding to their

23. Welensky to Gore-Browne, 8 March 1959. Curiously, Welensky was then of the opinion that Nkumbula was more dangerous than "our friend K. K." His security reports pointed to Nkumbula and company being thugs and the Zambia Congress being "great believers in democracy." But "Balmy Benson" had in fact thought the reverse. For the details of this period, the arrests, and so on, see Rotberg, *Nationalism,* 292–302.

wishes could well mean revolution. "My own clear convictions are," he wrote afterwards to MacGillivray, "that African opposition to Federation is now so strong that it would be disastrous to force it on them any longer . . . that at any cost the Franchise must be sufficiently liberalised to give Africans a *genuine* share in the government of the country, and that this must happen immediately."[24]

Kaunda's credibility was suspect as far as most Central African and many official British whites were concerned. Gore-Browne acted consistently to counter that suspicion. Since black rule was coming and should come, it was important that it should arrive under the best possible auspices. Gore-Browne had no doubt that Kaunda was to be trusted to lead Northern Rhodesia to self-government and beyond. Indeed, for him there was no other conceivable choice. He told Temple, who had asked him to write a foreword to a book that Kaunda and Morris were putting together, that he had admired Kaunda for a long time. "I hope and pray, that he may be strong enough to stand up to lesser men in his entourage if and when they advocate any policy which falls short, either morally or practically, of what his own high principles and common sense tell him is right."

The book, produced by Temple's United Society for Christian Literature in Lusaka, was an attempt to make Kaunda and Kaunda's views known more widely. Temple also hoped to persuade local whites that the Protectorate was soon bound to experience a black government and that it was wise to begin focusing not on whether or not black government was appropriate, but on what kind of government Kaunda's team would provide. Gore-Browne was given no opportunity to read *Black Government?* before it appeared, and his foreword said so. His message was therefore relatively simple: Northern Rhodesia would experience a genuine crisis if a broad franchise were not granted to Africans. "Those of us who know Mr. Kaunda," he concluded, "feel sure that we can trust him. He is certainly not a careerist nor a would-be dictator, still less a terrorist."[25]

Throughout the remainder of 1960 Gore-Browne aligned himself firmly on the side of UNIP. He and Harvey permitted local organizers to hold meetings on the estate and in the dance hall near his own home. (At the time of the visit of the Monckton Commission UNIP workers had erected a number of anti-federal signs,

24. Diary entries, 24 January, 8–9 March 1960. Gore-Browne, "Note for Monckton Commission," 8 March 1960. Gore-Browne to MacGillivray, 25 March 1960.

25. Gore-Browne, Foreword, dated 29 April 1960, to Colin Morris and Kenneth Kaunda, *Black Government?* (Lusaka, 1960).

including one that said "Settlers are Bloodsuckers." But Gore-Browne had been told that the sign did not refer to him.) Although both were a little nervous, there were no incidents and Gore-Browne was often impressed with the dancing and the speeches and the controlled cries of "Freedom." He also received provincial UNIP leaders like Andrew Mutemba and John Malama Sokoni on numerous occasions, and always allowed himself to be generous. He supplied fuel and petty cash, bus tickets to Lusaka, and, according to a cancelled check that still remains, £50 drawn to Kaunda. In between visits from Sir Evelyn Hone, the new governor of Northern Rhodesia, and Lord Hailey, then eighty-nine and on tour, as well as other luminaries, he himself turned seventy-seven, and watched the Queen Mother officially open the Kariba Dam and establish Kitwe as a city. He kept up his usual furious correspondence with Temple, Kaunda, Moffat, and Welensky about matters local, and with editors and liberals in Britain about conditions federal.

Intermittently, at Shiwa or in Lusaka, there were long conversations with Kaunda about what Gore-Browne should do to promote majority rule. In September, immediately after the party's national conference, Kaunda wrote at length to Gore-Browne. Ian Macleod, the British secretary of state for the colonies, had asked him to bring the country under control. During a subsequent period of comparative calm Macleod promised to make significant constitutional concessions. Kaunda had since ensured calm, and wondered how long Macleod would take. Kaunda asked whether his own followers would wait. Most of all he urged Gore-Browne to write to Macleod and Sir Alec Douglas-Home and advise them to act quickly. This Gore-Browne did immediately, having in the interim personally informed Duncan Sandys, secretary of state for commonwealth relations and a visitor to Lusaka, of his high regard for Kaunda. If Macleod failed adequately to back Kaunda, Gore-Browne wrote, an extremist might gain power. Gore-Browne repeated the same sentiments to Hone, and also suggested himself as a member of the delegation to any new constitutional talks in London. Hone and Macleod both replied promptly saying that they knew the accuracy of Gore-Browne's comments. Further, by the time of Macleod's reply, the British government had moved ahead, promising constitutional talks in early 1961.[26]

The *African Mail,* Lusaka's new pro-African weekly which had been established by Richard Hall, in mid-1960 openly urged

26. Kaunda to Gore-Browne, 8 September 1960; Gore-Browne to Macleod, 19 September 1960; Gore-Browne to Hone, 18 September 1960; Hone to Gore-Browne, 24 September 1960; Macleod to Gore-Browne, 3 October 1960.

Gore-Browne to return to politics. His statesmanship was needed. A few months later Moffat, a member of the Central Africa Party who had been elected to the Northern Rhodesian Legislative Council in 1959, asked Gore-Browne to join him and the remaining members of the hardy band of liberals of the mid-1950s (Scott had recently died) in forming a new United Liberal front—what subsequently emerged as the Liberal Party—to bring about that still hoped-for reconciliation between black and white. Yet, for all of the old reasons, Gore-Browne had to refuse. Additionally, he and Kaunda had agreed that he could be more useful "by keeping in the background and remaining available for top-level discussion."[27] He would lose influence with official Britons if he joined UNIP openly. But this did not prevent Gore-Browne from asking Kaunda that he should be allotted a proper constituency when new elections were held. "I am only too pleased to know [say] that the Central Committee of the United National Independence Party," the welcome reply read, "know too well the much you have done to advance the African not only politically but socially and economically too so that when the battle is over it would be an automatic act to hook you on to the line of any outstanding member of the Party."[28]

As the battle for control of Central Africa built up to a final crescendo, with the old claims of white privilege competing for attention with the new demands of black power, Gore-Browne's contribution became more and more valuable. Banda had wisely predicted that his moment would again come. Almost eighty, Gore-Browne's was widely accepted as the voice of sanity and wisdom. Respective secretaries of state had heeded his advice and the Monckton Commission, when it finally reported in late 1960, had issued recommendations consonant with (even if not necessarily influenced by) Gore-Browne's own views. It had suggested a rapid transition to majority rule in Northern Rhodesia and Nyasaland, had implicitly condoned the secession of those territories and, hence, the breakup of the Federation.[29]

Even before the publication of the Report, Macleod had made it clear that Nyasaland would move forward rapidly to black rule under Banda's auspices, an election being scheduled for mid-1961. Control of Northern Rhodesia therefore became decisive. Whomsoever controlled Northern Rhodesia would control Central Africa. Welensky and his followers could not afford to lose, or the Federation would recede into Southern Rhodesia and perhaps, in

---

27. Gore-Browne to Moffat, 17 September 1960.
28. Sokoni to Gore-Browne, 30 November 1960.
29. *Report of the Advisory Commission on the Review of the Constitution of Rhodesia and Nyasaland*, Cmnd. 1148 (1960), 43, 98–99.

the long, run, its demise might even herald black rule there. Kaunda, similarly, could ill afford any slowing of the momentum. If he and his supporters faltered, the resolve of Britain might weaken, and white control be maintained for years to come. Moreover, his brand of moderate but firm leadership, with its appearance of gentleness to outsiders, might well be superseded by something more emotional and flamboyant.

Two men for whom Gore-Browne had great personal respect, and with whom there were close bonds of friendship, were locked in combat. The clashes began in earnest in late 1960, in London, when Welensky tried with modest success to sabotage the federal review, and simultaneous territorial constitutional, conferences which had been convened under British direction. Yet when the Northern Rhodesian discussions resumed in early 1961 they resulted in an ingenious but somewhat complicated compromise which favored an electoral victory by UNIP, but gave the balance of power (between Welensky's whites and UNIP) to Moffat's Liberal Party.[30] This was a solution which did not especially please Kaunda, but it was one which he could abide. Welensky, on the other hand, rightly saw this constitution as his epitaph.

From the announcement of this constitutional alteration in February, 1961, Welensky behaved like the prizefighter he once was; trying to recover from a knockdown in order to win on points at the final bell, he hit out wildly but strongly. He threatened to declare the Federation's independence, to battle any British troops which tried to prevent him, to stop sharing Kariba power with Northern Rhodesia, to sponsor white unrest and strikes, and generally to make Macleod's life, and that of the Conservative Party, miserable. In fact, Macleod's February announcement had left the door of reconsideration slightly ajar, so Kaunda and others naturally feared the kinds of new compromises which might be reached between Welensky's emissaries in London and the harassed British government. These were thus months of particular tension in Northern Rhodesia. Whites were as alarmed as Welensky, blacks as worried and also as flushed with temporary success as Kaunda.

It was precisely the moment for Gore-Browne to make a symbolically critical contribution to the triumph of nationalism. In March Kaunda visited Shiwa and made it obvious that tangible evidence of support would be helpful in the struggle against Welensky. Gore-Browne was willing. After mulling Kaunda's request over in his own mind for several days, he wrote unequivocally that he would

30. For details of these and the other intricate maneuvers of 1960 to 1962, see David Mulford, *Zambia: The Politics of Independence 1957–1964* (London, 1967), 174–210.

do whatever Kaunda thought could best help UNIP and the country, "which so sorely needs help from all decent people, black or white." A few weeks later he drove to Lusaka and had long talks with Temple and Hall, both of whom urged Gore-Browne to declare for UNIP. Kaunda did too. "Decided," reads Gore-Browne's diary, "to throw in my lot with his." Immediately, Gore-Browne therefore announced that he had become a member of UNIP. "I think the time has come," he wrote in a letter published in the *African Mail,* "when I may conceivably be of some use and I propose to offer my services to Mr. Kaunda as a member of his party. As I have already said . . . I am convinced that he can be trusted, and that his abhorrence of violence is certainly sincere. I believe too that he will do everything in his power to tighten up discipline in his party. Otherwise he cannot possibly hope to succeed."[31] In the magazine *African Life* (run by Sikota Wina, a UNIP leader), he further explained that he had joined UNIP because the United Federal Party still practised a paternalistic partnership which was "bogus." He could not disagree with the principles of the Liberal Party, but he believed that Northern Rhodesia had reached a stage when it could only be run by "the pick of a combined Black and White party, and not merely be a mixed party under white leadership."[32]

Newspapers throughout southern Africa headlined the sensational news. A former leader of the settlers in the Legislative Council had joined UNIP and wholeheartedly espoused black rule. Kaunda, who had flown to New York to testify before the Committee of Decolonization of the United Nations, wrote how wonderful it had been to read of Gore-Browne's decision to become a party member. He promised to make good use of Gore-Browne's "vast knowledge and experience." "I am," he said, "fully conscious of the task I have to face—one of *discipline.* It is a very delicate matter. . . . My policy must prove correct, i.e. that it pays to be non-violent in these matters. The way independence came to the Congo and the way its affairs have been conducted do sandwich me. . . . The Nyasaland upheaval . . . [does] not make a non-violent struggle . . . an easy method because those who would rather see other methods used will say one is too slow. . . . If [the talks with Macleod] should break down—God help us—I don't know what might follow."[33]

As symbolically significant as Gore-Browne's membership in UNIP may have been in southern Africa, where its propaganda

31. Gore-Browne to Kaunda, 11 March 1961; diary, 29 March 1961; letter to *African Mail,* 2 April 1961.

32. Front page story, *African Life,* 15 May 1961.

33. Kaunda to Gore-Browne, 28 April 1961.

value was profound, it little influenced the intricate game of bluster
and counter-bluster which Welensky and Macleod were playing in
London and Salisbury. Perhaps because members of the British
cabinet wanted Welensky's party to obtain a favorable result in the
Southern Rhodesian constitutional referendum, which had been
scheduled for July (the new constitution gave fifteen of sixty-five
seats to Africans), and equally because of the pressure Welensky had
exerted on reactionary Tories, Macleod in June amended the previously published Northern Rhodesian constitution to meet most of
the settler objections. He altered the crucial provisions that had been
expected to provide UNIP with a number of the important "multiracial" seats in the Legislative Council. Instead, he suggested an
exceedingly complicated formula which devalued African votes for
those seats and permitted white electors to exercise a virtual veto
over prospective African candidates.

Angry, and believing themselves doublecrossed by Britain,
Kaunda and his followers held their annual party conference only a
few weeks later at Mulungushi, near what is now Kabwe. Gore-
Browne was there, sitting on the main platform behind Kaunda. He
even gave a short speech and was interviewed by the press and
television. Never before had UNIP so prominently featured a
white. Immediately after the conference Gore-Browne was pressed
into service to plead with Hone, in Lusaka, that the latest constitutional design was unfair and unworkable. What Gore-Browne did
not know was that the UNIP leadership at Mulungushi had also
decided forcibly to make the British government recant. Throughout the remainder of July, August, and September, Africans in the
Northern and Luapula provinces blocked roads, destroyed bridges,
stoned cars, burnt down schools and dispensaries, and generally
demonstrated their displeasure violently. Even the Shiwa estate was
not immune, although Gore-Browne was never threatened directly. (Lord Hailey wrote anxiously about Gore-Browne's safety.
"I can think of no one more innocent than yourself of the [alleged]
crimes of colonialism."[34]) The Timba School was razed by fire,
the Mpandala bridge cut and burnt, the Manshya drift demolished,
and a local store looted. At once Gore-Browne's manor house was
completely cut off by road from the remainder of the country. Even
Shiwa's post office radio transmitter went dead. He mobilized the
home guard, Mulenga slept in the main house, and Gore-Browne
put a loaded revolver beside his bed. To add insult, Gore-Browne
received a "saucy and silly" letter from the local branch of UNIP.
But then the army began to patrol the roads in the Northern Province, Gore-Browne's own men and the Public Works Department

34. Hailey to Gore-Browne, 1 September 1961.

rebuilt the bridges, and, after many urgent requests by Gore-Browne, the Timba school was reopened. Gore-Browne was appalled by the entire experience but he was prepared—like Temple and others—to blame the violence on irresponsible elements in UNIP whom Kaunda had been unable to control.[35]

Whatever, or whoever, had really precipitated the unrest, such resolution and determination forced Macleod's hand. In mid-September, after consultations with Kaunda in London, he promised to reconsider the constitutional proposals afresh if violence ceased. By October Kaunda's appeal to this affect had been heard and manifestations of rural discontent died away as suddenly as they had first erupted.

Once more Northern Rhodesia was forced to endure a period of months during which all sides—the battling participants now included the Liberals, who had been given a critical stake in the Protectorate's future—urged the British government to issue yet another constitution, this time more favorable to their own interests. Reginald Maudling replaced Macleod and visited Lusaka to receive local opinion himself. This included a meeting in Government House with Kaunda, Gore-Browne, and other UNIP members, consultations with Moffat and the Liberals, and representation from Welensky and his lieutenants. At last, in early 1962, the ultimate compromise was struck. The constitutional provisions of June would remain with but one single concession to UNIP. The percentage of racial crossvoting required for the crucial "multiracial seats" would be lowered to give UNIP a better chance of winning a clear majority in the elections which were scheduled for late 1962. Minor though it may have looked, this was an important shift in the direction of the dismemberment of the Federation, and UNIP was at least pleased, if not overjoyed, to have won the year-long struggle for supposed parity of electoral opportunity. The final stage on the road to majority rule could at last begin.

As a highly visible member of UNIP, Gore-Browne was intimately involved. Although Welensky had announced that "the Federation is mine and I am prepared to fight to keep it," Kaunda and his cohorts were equally determined. Boosted in spirit by their new constitutional leverage and the knowledge that Britain understood that the spontaneous disturbances of the previous year could always reoccur, they still had organizational and financial handicaps to overcome. These needs, as well as the international visibility and legitimacy which could not but prove advantageous electorally and

35. Gore-Browne was shaken by the gruesome murder of a white woman by blacks on the Copperbelt and, at the end of the year, by UNIP publications which referred to those responsible as heroes.

financially, were high on Kaunda's list of priorities in preparation
for the electoral campaign which would commence in the African
spring. Gore-Browne was the centerpiece of one of these efforts, a
highly publicized journey to the United Nations in April with
Kaunda and T. L. Desai, an Asian adherent of the party. Although
Gore-Browne and Desai had to pay their own ways, both had been
nominated by the UNIP Central Committee. A telegram announc-
ing this decision arrived at Shiwa on 5 April and Gore-Browne was
airborne to the United States for the first time five days later. En
route, they all addressed a large public gathering in London—to
much applause—and Gore-Browne, staying as years before in the
Army and Navy Club, lost his lower dentures down a bulbous bath
drain there.

In New York, Gore-Browne, Kaunda, and Desai were all lion-
ized by Americans interested in African affairs. They addressed the
UN's Special Committee on Decolonization, Gore-Browne tes-
tifying when Kaunda began weeping as he told the committee of the
shooting of his people under British rule. They also attended a
celebration in Town Hall of Africa Freedom Day, Kaunda in his
purple toga being the principal speaker, and both addressed a meeting sponsored by the African-American Institute.

Gore-Browne's message in London (where there were more public meetings on the return journey, including private ones with
R. A. Butler, now the minister responsible for Central Africa, the
Duke of Devonshire, and the editors of the *New Statesman* and the
Guardian), in New York, and a few days later in Cambridge, Massachusetts, where he and Kaunda together, and then Gore-Browne
alone, spent the Easter weekend addressing faculty and students on
several different occasions, was simple and direct. Northern
Rhodesia would and should become a black country. The sooner
this transition came about the more peaceful life would be there. He
did not yet believe in a completely universal franchise, preferring
some kind of educational qualification, but he was content to agree
to disagree with UNIP on this one issue since his faith in Kaunda as
the best possible leader was unlimited. Although interviews with
journalists in all three cities tired him (he was nearly seventy-nine),
and his enjoyment of the rich and ample American food was hindered by the missing dentures (potato chips, he confessed afterwards, were an impossibility—and American university dining
rooms seemed to serve nothing else), his spirits were buoyed by the
evident enthusiasm for African advancement of the Americans he
met. Years later he also pleasurably recalled a visit to nearby Concord, where with his monocle clasped in place and his double-
breasted pinstripe suit tightly buttoned, he carefully examined the
"rude bridge" immortalized by Ralph Waldo Emerson as the scene

Gore-Browne at Harvard University, 1962.

of an opening battle in the American War of Independence against his own mother country.[36]

By the time of Gore-Browne's return home in late July, final preparations were being made for Northern Rhodesia's first truly multiracial election. The British government had constructed one of the most absurdly complicated regulations ever used anywhere. Whites, Asians, and some Africans—depending upon their literacy and income qualifications—would vote for fifteen upper-roll (basically white) representatives in single-member constituencies. All others, if they earned at least £120 a year and could complete the registration application unaided, would choose fifteen lower-roll (black) members, again in single-member constitutencies. Both groups (34,000 registered on the upper and 92,000 on the lower roll) would next vote together on a "national" roll, selecting fourteen more representatives in seven double-member constituencies. In four of these constituencies voters had to cast ballots for one African and one white. But successful candidates (as a result of the Maudling clarification) could only be elected if they managed to obtain at least ten percent of the votes cast by members of each roll (or race) and at least twenty percent of all those cast on one of the two rolls. Asians would vote separately for the forty-fifth legislative seat.

Before the election Kaunda, ever optimistic, persuaded himself that whites would be sufficiently realistic to vote in reasonable numbers for members of his own party. In the weeks before the polls opened in late October, he therefore attempted to bring white and black together in order to make the difficult constitution work. In speeches to white and mixed audiences, he patiently tried to eliminate the fears of whites that African self-government would mean "another Congo." He explained candidly that he could promise whites a secure future only if his party were to receive white electoral support. Everywhere he wooed whites assiduously. For the national and several of the upper roll seats he and UNIP even put forward a carefully selected group of whites. Their number included a Methodist minister, a well-known lawyer, a businessman, and Gore-Browne.

Gore-Browne stood for UNIP in the Chambeshi constituency. A national seat, it was also one of the four completely biracial ones. For a near octogenarian, this was a strenuous assignment. It meant campaigning for six weeks from Kitwe on the Copperbelt to Isoka near Tanzania. In order to win he would have to do the impossible—to attract sufficient white voters (ten percent of those registered) to match his presumed support from Africans. As

36. Emerson, "Concord Hymn," 1836.

Gore-Browne noted when Kaunda gave him the nomination, it was "a pretty top job but I suppose suits me." Immediately he drove to Kitwe, established himself in the main hotel there, and began meeting with white miners and their African counterparts. The main burden of his addresses was that no "intelligent inhabitant" of the territory should imagine that a white minority could continue to rule or the Federation continue to exist. Since a black government was bound to prevail, "it is surely only common-sense that the change should come now, when it is still possible to bring it about peaceably, and while both races are willing to cooperate in affording each other the assistance needed to overcome the many difficulties and dangers with which we are likely to be faced during the next few years." This was a lucid statement of his point-of-view, but one which only a few of the whites in his constituency were then prepared to accept. As he noted, "the required 10 per cent may prove my undoing."[37]

From late September until the end of October, Gore-Browne moved tirelessly throughout his vast constituency. From Kitwe he returned briefly to Shiwa (where he found Joshua Nkomo, fleeing from Rhodesian security forces, enroute to Tanzania) to hold a meeting on the estate. Then he put his case to a large assembly on the Chinsali football field, repeated the performance near the Isoka boma, returned to Shiwa, campaigned in Mpika and Serenje on the same day, and then drove all the next day to Mufulira on the Copperbelt, where he spoke before a crowd estimated at 4,000. After several more days trying to obtain white support on the Copperbelt, including a joint meeting with Kaunda and Aaron Milner at the Mindolo Ecumenical Center in Kitwe, he returned to Shiwa with Milner, only to leave the next day for Mpika and meetings with chiefs (Milner was standing in a lower roll constituency) in the Mpika area. A few days later he returned to Isoka, continuing on, after another meeting, to campaign in Nakonde, a village on the Tanzania border. There UNIP's regional secretary made all this travelling seem worthwhile by introducing him pleasantly: "He helped us when we had nothing, and he helps us still when we are powerful."[38] From Nakonde it was necessary for Gore-Browne and Mulenga to drive back all the way to Kitwe in order to address the local Lion's Club. The next day he shared a platform with Kaunda in the Hindu Hall in Luanshya. This was followed by a major meeting with whites in Kitwe, where both Kaunda and

37. Diary, 15 September 1962, 19 September 1962; Election Address, 20 September 1962. His opponents included Robert Moffat (Liberal Party), John Mitchell (UFP), and Sykes Ndilila (ANC). The full results are in David Mulford, *The Northern Rhodesia General Election, 1962* (Nairobi, 1964), 158–159.

38. Quoted in Diary, 15 October 1962.

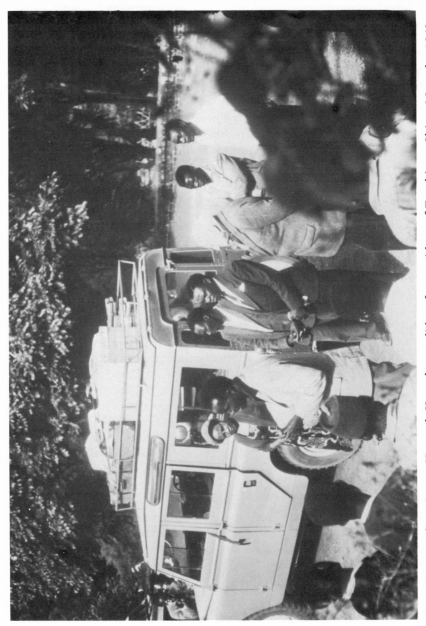

Gore-Browne listening to Kenneth Kaunda, candidate for president of Zambia, at Shiwa Ngandu, 1962.

Gore-Browne were severely heckled. One of the offenders, a young white, shouted at Gore-Browne: "You'll soon be dead!", to which Gore-Browne replied, "Thank you for your courtesy."[39]

Gore-Browne took his case to the leaders of the expectedly hostile European Mineworkers Union, to a group of African ministers, to a group of white contractors, and to rural white missionaries. Until the eve of the election he was as active as a man of his age and experience could have hoped to be. But it was all to no avail. Throughout the rural areas Africans and whites voted overwhelmingly for Gore-Browne and UNIP. On the Copperbelt Africans did the same. But urban whites voted with equal determination for Welensky's UFP. The African percentage for Gore-Browne was 93.4 (11,264 votes). But Gore-Browne received only fifty-five or 1.25 percent of the white vote cast. Thus his deposit was forfeited and the seat frustrated. That is, according to the electoral rules, since neither side obtained a multiracial percentage high enough to win, it would have to be contested again.

In the election as a whole, ninety percent of those registered had cast ballots. More than 60,000 persons had voted for UNIP, 17,000 for Nkumbula's Congress, 21,000 for the UFP, and 1,500 for the Liberal Party. As a result UNIP had obtained 12 lower-roll places (Nkumbula and his followers won the other three), the Asian seat, and one on the upper roll. The UFP won thirteen upper-roll seats and, with the help of the Congress, two national seats in constituencies also taken by the Congress. In all of the other national areas Kaunda's candidates received impressive African majorities but, as in the Chambeshi constituency, failed to obtain white votes in sufficient number to win.

The frustrated seats were contested in December. Again Gore-Browne was often on the road trying to elicit white support anywhere it could be found. In the middle of one of those hectic weeks he returned home in order to preside over the kind of impressive bipartisan dinner for which Shiwa had long been famous. In addition to American researchers and a cousin by marriage who was collecting butterflies, there were two staunch supporters of Welensky—a Federal minister and a successful Northern Rhodesian UFP candidate. Then five UNIP candidates and provincial officials arrived. Gore-Browne guided the proceedings with serene equanimity except when one of the UFP visitors proved unnecessarily offensive to the Africans.

On the eve of the second polling Gore-Browne went down to Kitwe for more addresses to large meetings. "If only African voters

39. Quoted in the *Northern News* (19 October 1962).

were concerned I would be safe enough," he wrote. But whites were involved and the final results, although an improvement over those of October, were still not good enough. Africans gave Gore-Browne 10,567 votes, whites 101. Thus he obtained 94.3 percent of the African vote and 2.6 percent of the white vote. The seat was again frustrated. Overall, the electors had managed in both elections to fill only thirty-seven of the forty-five places. Gore-Browne properly blamed the "peculiar rules of the constitution under which we live and which was imposed on us by the British government."[40]

Although Kaunda eventually persuaded Nkumbula, despite the antagonism between themselves and their parties, to form a coalition of convenience, Gore-Browne could share only vicariously in UNIP's accession to power. Creech Jones, and presumably Gore-Browne, hoped that Northern Rhodesia's resulting transitional black government would need the assistance of well-respected whites, and that Gore-Browne would consequently be asked to serve his adopted country once more.[41] But Gore-Browne's age and the need of both the governor and Kaunda to satisfy the African parties meant no place for Gore-Browne.

Although he continued to hope for a return to the legislative assembly, this time with Africans, Gore-Browne had come to the end of his long, unstinting devotion to political service in Northern Rhodesia. After the British government in 1963 granted yet another constitution and proposed an election in 1964 which would move Northern Rhodesia to self-government and then to independence, Gore-Browne asked Kaunda for a legislative place. There were to be sixty-five members elected on the basis of universal suffrage and ten by whites. "I hope there is nothing in [the] rumour," he wrote, "that non-Africans are only to be eligible to stand for reserved [white] seats. Such a restriction is contrary to everything we have been working for these many years, in a country where neither race nor colour counts."[42] Unhappily for Gore-Browne's last years and his hopes of serving, political realities more than sentiment had begun to count, even if color had not—at least not in the precise manner suggested by Gore-Browne.

Kaunda was as frank as he could afford to be, given the ingrained African respect for age and experience and his own personal admiration of Gore-Browne. "I have constantly reminded myself of your desire to serve your country," he wrote, "and I have faithfully

40. Diary, 9 December, 11 December 1962.
41. Creech Jones to Gore-Browne, 10 December 1962.
42. Gore-Browne to Kaunda, 6 September 1963.

carried out my part but found it difficult to get your name through, not because there was anyone who didn't like you, to the contrary, from the warm feelings that were expressed about you by almost all the members of my Central Committee I am able to tell you that they all felt this would be far too taxing a responsibility for you at the moment. They all felt they needed you in public life but with less taxing responsibilities."[43]

Gore-Browne was downcast. "I won't pretend," he confessed, "that I'm not disappointed to find myself out of the struggle." To another he admitted that it had been a considerable surprise not to be allowed to stand—to be left out after such faithful assistance to Kaunda and UNIP.[44] Yet the political realities to which Kaunda alluded so delicately in his letter were, in fact, overriding. Too many hard-working black UNIP officials and workers—each of whom represented the satisfaction of a particular African interest group or amalgam of constituencies—wanted seats for Gore-Browne's efforts to have been rewarded. Giving him a seat—and all would be safe—would deprive Kaunda and the party's central committee of the opportunity to reward others who, in the new black nation, would count for more than Gore-Browne. Cynically, once Africans could glimpse the dawn of a new political era, his services were no longer needed. Yet for Kaunda the decision equally well reflected a realistic appraisal of political requirements, not necessarily the cynicism of some of his colleagues. Early in 1964, with Gore-Browne on the sidelines and the Federation dissolved after ten years, UNIP easily won fifty-five of the sixty-five ordinary seats. Kaunda became prime minister and began leading the country to independence.

When Kaunda transformed Northern Rhodesia into Zambia later in 1964, Gore-Browne attended the inaugural ceremonies of the new nation merely as a much-honored guest. "What impressed me most of all," he wrote, "and what I shall never forget, was the complete and entire absence of any sort or kind of Colour Bar. I felt that the abominable thing had entirely ceased to exist, and it was indeed a good omen for the future." Never starry-eyed, he concluded with a philosophy for the future. "Now I suppose there will be all sorts of minor set-backs and troubles and disappointments. But that is always the way in this world, and we've only to be patient and hope for the best."[45]

43. Kaunda to Gore-Browne, 10 December 1963.
44. Gore-Browne to Kaunda, 18 December 1963; Gore-Browne to Richard Hall, 30 December 1963.
45. Gore-Browne to author, 15 November 1964.

Independence for Zambia marked the commencement of Gore-Browne's final retirement from the political arena. Because of age, but more because his Northern Rhodesia was now in African hands, Gore-Browne's long-time roles as advisor, advocate, and propagandist to and for Africans were no longer relevant. With the Federation dead and only the success or failure of majority rule in question, Gore-Browne had nothing about which to report to the *Guardian, The Economist,* or local newspapers. Politics was now an African pursuit and Kaunda, although a friend, had sources of counsel physically closer and sufficiently weighty to make Gore-Browne's redundant. This was a natural result of the demise of Northern Rhodesia, and a fact accepted by Gore-Browne. His ambitions for Africans having been realized through and by Kaunda, now Zambia's president, he was content to live quietly and gracefully at Shiwa.

Gore-Browne began concentrating more and more on his books, on writing up his reminiscences of aspects of the colonial and farming days, and on providing the lavish hospitality for which Shiwa continued to remain famous. Even with the advent of Zambia, the number of visitors never abated, continuing to average about three hundred a year in the main house, plus many more in the public rest house near the estate offices. Nadine Gordimer, the celebrated South African novelist, was an especially welcomed guest, but her experiences differed only slightly from those of most. "Sir Stewart" she wrote, "is a handsome Englishman of eighty-three, remarkable not in the conventional sense of the grand old man representing the good or bad old past, but in the flexibility of mind that enables him to span, in his personal development, the recorded history of the country he lives in. Few European 'characters' can accept the new Africa; their Africa ends when the soft-footed houseboy gets the vote." "We dined," she wrote of the memorable meals still served by Gore-Browne's staff, "on jugged wart-hog." The next day "I was taken to bathe in the natural pool—turquoise green and surrounded by strange-leaved trees . . . that is fed by warm springs" and in which Gore-Browne's favorites were bidden to soak and gambol.[46] There were picnics at the cottage near the hot springs, and tours of the lake itself for those who liked to fish. Hunting in the hills was still possible, too. After any of these diversions there was sherry in the luxurious library, a view of the distant lake from the adjoining balcony, and sumptuous dinner—whether wart-hog, hartebeest, a goose shot on the wing by a local hunter, estate beef, or ham procured from Lusaka. Breakfast the following day was al-

46. Nadine Gordimer, "Zambia," *Holiday* (June, 1966), 86.

ways the occasion for reminding foreigners, with a sparkle and a slight smile, that only Americans ate toast and jam with their eggs and bacon.

Visitors were caesuric alterations of the rhythmic passage of Shiwa's concluding glory. Aside from a serious bout of bronchial pneumonia in 1965 there were no other major interruptions in these final years. The estate had been transferred legally to the Harveys, so Gore-Browne's own responsibilities were more customary than managerial. He could take an interest in his commercial establishment without necessarily fussing over the accounts or grabbing his gun and racing into the night when lions prowled around the cattle kraals. He proudly showed visitors the new Timba school, the hospital that he had donated to the government, the shut distillery, the remaining limes, the brickworks, the bridges and irrigation works which he had constructed, and the other facets of the vast estate in which he still took appropriate pride. What he had created would, he knew, be cherished by the next generation, and by the grandchildren who were already preparing for university education and a return to Zambia.

Gore-Browne's memory began to fade in late 1966. He could recall the distant past clearly, but not the events of five or ten years previous. He was growing frail, too, but, given Dame Ethel's and his mother's longevity, others hoped that he would be able to enjoy Shiwa and Zambia well into his nineties. This was not to be. Toward the end of the Zambian winter of 1967, having recently been installed by Kaunda as the first and only Grand Officer of the Companion Order of Freedom—the analogy was to a British knighthood—and having settled the writing of his life, he caught pneumonia again, had a heart attack, and was rushed to the Kasama hospital. There he died at eighty-four, at 1 P.M. on 4 August (Dame Ethel had died at 1 A.M. on 5 August 1956).

The announcement of his death, said an old African friend, "was heard like a thunderclap from the air."[47] President Kaunda ordained a state funeral and led a delegation of five ministers, the commissioner of police, the commander of the air force, the head of the army (all of whom had flown from Lusaka), and 500 others to Shiwa. There, with appropriate pomp and reverence, the ceremonies being carried throughout the country on the state television and radio stations, they participated in a short service in the family chapel presided over by the Anglican Archbishop of Central Africa, two Roman Catholic Archbishops (one an African), and the local

47. Paul Bwembya Mushindo, *The Life of a Zambian Evangelist* (Lusaka, 1973), 55.

Gore-Browne at Chisamba, 1967.

African Presbyterian pastor. The 2nd Battalion of the Zambia Regiment then carried the coffin to the burial ground that Gore-
Browne had himself selected high on a hill overlooking the house
and the lake he had so loved. "Born an Englishman," Kaunda said at
the graveside, "he died a Zambian." In him, he continued, God had
"done many things." He had "worked for all because he realized
that no one could claim to love God without loving his fellow men,
that is why he worked for God for he loved all mankind regardless
of colour or creed. . . . The UNIP government has benefited a

great deal from his advice, guidance and, above all, he showed the way which we are following. Sir Stewart stood for equality among all—he stood for Humanism . . . If we remaining Zambians do not learn from him, our future is dark."[48]

48. Kaunda, quoted in Zambian Government Press Release number 1581, 6 August 1967; *Northern News,* 7 August 1967.

X

The Contribution of a
Multiracial Initiative

A BLACK PRESIDENT's graveside eulogy of a white patriarch set Gore-Browne's death, as his life, apart from that of other whites who made their way to Africa in the twentieth century. In Zambia only David Livingstone rivals Gore-Browne in the pantheon of nonindigenous heroes.

Gore-Browne, unlike so many other whites of stature in settler Africa, genuinely sought throughout his long career in Northern Rhodesia and Zambia to integrate the territory's two nations. Tirelessly, he fought against the oppression of Africans, and for the removal of their many taints of inferiority. He advocated a steady increase in African political, social, and economic rights despite the opposition of fellow white settlers, the companies that mined copper in Northern Rhodesia, and the local representatives of the British Colonial Office. As a powerful member of the Protectorate's Legislative Council from 1935 to 1951, he advanced the African cause publicly in debates and by promoting favorable legislation. Even more powerful in private, his accomplishments on behalf of Africans individually and collectively were legion, and widely appreciated. At a time when Africans were otherwise without strong advocates, and had few means of making their own feelings known, Gore-Browne was their champion. Indeed, his own awareness of injustice was at times even more farsighted and perceptive than their own.

An energetic, effective, and unusually incisive speaker, in the chamber of the council Gore-Browne adroitly employed the weapons of sarcasm, shame, and disclosure. In private the logic of his presentations of injustice, as well as his acute awareness of altering trends in African politics, often proved persuasive. So did his letters and articles in British periodicals and his ability, by means of social access or other contacts, to appeal beyond Northern Rhodesia's government to politicians, civil servants, and the jour nalistic and academic communities in Britain. Gore-Browne's persistence mattered, too. Most of all, however, his oft-expressed moral outrage undercut the legitimacy of colonial rule. Only a man of his patrician background and bearing and someone with his gifts of compromise could have so succeeded in moving and manipulating the creaky machinery of colonial reform. The accomplishment of significant change on behalf of Africans—really the righting of wrongs offensive to Gore-Browne and the bolstering of his own chosen advocacy and therefore his own anxious ego—demanded the skills of a politician and, at times, the conviction of an evangelist. It also took courage. Gore-Browne was equal to these challenges, and Africans, and multiracialism in Zambia, ultimately benefited.

Although originally elected to the Legislative Council by working-class whites, Gore-Browne consistently and successfully opposed their prime political solution—amalgamating Northern Rhodesia to self-governing Southern Rhodesia. To a large degree he was responsible for summoning a British royal commission which deferred amalgamation before World War II and effectively ended any lingering enthusiasm for it in conservative British circles. Even more significantly, because of his unquestioned intellectual and moral superiority, judgment, and ability to work with others, Gore-Browne led the whites in the Legislative Council from 1939 to 1946. He deserves credit for detering a ragtag collection of parliamentary racists from following the chimera of pigmentational chauvinism. He worked hard to be a moderating influence on the extremists with whom he was always surrounded and encumbered.

Throughout World War II he helped the Colonial Office chart significant political advances for whites and blacks (he made possible the appointment of blacks to the council) in Northern Rhodesia. In a wider sphere at imperial conferences, and within the local region as a member of transnational war-expediting organizations (he later represented Northern Rhodesia on the Central African Council), as a member of Northern Rhodesia's ad hoc emergency executive council, and as director of manpower and director of war camps and evacuees within Northern Rhodesia, he blurred the usual distinctions between legislative and executive roles in the colonies. He also ran Northern Rhodesia in tandem with governors of the day. In every capacity—almost despite his Afrophile views—he enhanced an international reputation as Northern Rhodesia's premier statesman.

During these years Gore-Browne schooled a railway engine driver as his successor. Roy Welensky, the hefty driver, was an unexpected complement to the balding, monocled, much older and more sophisticated paternalist. But they worked well together and Gore-Browne shifted places with Welensky immediately after

World War II, when whites became more determined than before to forestall the political pretensions of nationalistically-minded Africans. Gore-Browne fought this attempted takeover with reasonable success. In 1948, however, he made the fatal mistake of proposing a less dangerous but still pro-settler constitutional adjustment in order to couple white advances with countervailing, if modest, African gains. Gore-Browne had hitherto successfully found compromises between competing views. This time, however, the cleavage was much sharper than he had realized. His attempt to bridge the gap was widely misunderstood by blacks and dismissed by whites.

The predominant political thrust of the late 1940s in Northern Rhodesia was pro-settler. It coincided with a British determination to rearrange colonial responsibilities in parts of Africa. Together these two initiatives resulted in a proposed federation which was intended to unite both Rhodesia and Nyasaland, thereby giving whites in the two northern territories the greater measure of self-government for which they had long agitated. In this atmosphere Gore-Browne's influence proved much less decisive than previously. Moreover, neither his opposition nor the enmity of Africans succeeded in preventing the British government from imposing Welensky's federal solution in 1953. From his mansion in rural Shiwa Ngandu, Gore-Browne, now retired from politics, watched, waited, and disapproved of the beginnings of the federal experiment. He also observed the rapid rise of African political consciousness. Almost alone among whites in Central Africa, Gore-Browne appreciated that the ascendance of white minorities in Africa would be brief and bitter. Already the Gold Coast and the Sudan had achieved self-government. Soon it would be the turn of the East and Central Africans.

Gore-Browne never shrank from black rule. He had always believed in its ultimate validity and, by the 1950s, accepted its near advent as a justly merited outcome of Northern Rhodesia's complex political convolutions. He therefore refused to indulge in the false panaceas offered by temporizing white "multiracial" liberal alternatives like Moral Rearmament, the Capricorn Africa Society, or the Constitution and Liberal Parties. Instead he joined a handful of other brave whites, none as well-known or as committed to the country as himself, in backing the African National Congress, and, when Kaunda and his other largely Bemba and Lozi followers broke away from the Congress, in supporting the resultant United National Independence Party in its successful drive for independence on black terms. As an old but still vigorous man he journeyed to the United Nations on its behalf and campaigned energetically for a seat in the two 1962 elections.

Gore-Browne's impress on the development of Northern Rhodesia and Zambia was greater than that of any other foreigner. In addition to all of his political triumphs, before the colonial government made the Northern Province easily accessible to wheeled vehicles he designed and built major roads and bridges. By constructing his own aerodrome he also made it possible for the Protectorate to promote aviation earlier than neighboring territories. In 1940 he played a major role in ending a black strike which would have paralyzed the production of copper and led to serious violence. In the Northern Province, from whence many of the mine workers came, he demonstrated that a lone white and his family could farm thousands of acres with the loyal cooperation of hundreds of African employees. He further showed that humane overlordship and aristocratic paternalism would be understood by Africans— that an employer and his employees could live together in what may have begun as a neofeudal harmony but later became a mutually beneficial exchange typified by deference more than subservience. Gore-Browne thus created that rare thing in Africa, a colonial venture where race relations were positive, and within which Africans were not degraded. Shiwa Ngandu was an oasis of humanity during most of Gore-Browne's tenure. There he even managed that equally difficult task, making his agricultural venture—the production of essential oils—pay, if only for a few years.

In all his dealings with Africans, Gore-Browne essentially behaved as an old-fashioned paternalist with a modern heart. His inherited ideals and the concept of noblesse oblige which he had taken early in life as his own, together with a command of Cibemba, enabled him to achieve a rapport with ordinary Africans which was probably unequalled in most Northern Rhodesian circumstances. Equally he was able to accept the rise of an African intelligentsia as natural and welcome. Other whites typically felt threatened by the achievements of Africans. Part of Gore-Browne's ability to move freely among Africans—whether among the militant strikers in 1940, among his own workers, among rural Africans during the Boundary Commission days, at the Lupa Goldfields in 1936, or among the masses at political rallies in the 1960s—as well as with the elite at conferences and in the Legislative Council, was his candor and consistency. He was no bleeding heart. He acted naturally to and among Africans, demanding from them respect if he were their employer or otherwise their superior, and the simplicity of equals if persons of prominence. His ferocious temper was directed at whites as well as Africans. In his early years in Northern Rhodesia he was no more able to suffer white than black fools. Later he became more tolerant, but remained color-blind.

Gore-Browne settled in Zambia because of his attachment to

Africans and Africa. Before World War I he had helped determine Zambia's northwestern boundaries and had then met men to whom he was drawn. When they took him to their homeland in northeastern Zambia he found a lake with hills beyond and realized that he had found Shangri-la and a future home. Nothing in a life that had hitherto consisted of a not very happy upper-middle-class family upbringing and fair success at Harrow had prepared him for his love of Africans and Africa. After Harrow he had become an artillery officer and had served briefly in South Africa after the Boer War. There and at Harrow, and during the battles of World War I, he had close friendships with men of his class. He also became drawn to a childless and inspiring aunt who substituted for his mother and who was to prove his confidant and patron throughout the first six decades of the twentieth century. With her and her husband he shared a fascination with motor cars, then in their infancy, and with the affairs of the far-flung world. Dame Ethel Locke-King encouraged her nephew at every turn and made his African experience possible.

There were two other women in Gore-Browne's life. The first may have loved him but married another. Twenty years later, after her husband's death and her own death in Africa, Gore-Browne married this first love's orphaned daughter. Together in the late 1920s and early 1930s they developed the estate at Shiwa Ngandu until politics, the war, and final estrangement sundered what had at first seemed a prosperous and mutually fulfilling alliance. There was a gulf of age and aspiration which was never fully bridged; what had begun so well deteriorated into a struggle of wills between two gifted, obstinately autonomous individuals. Neither emerged the victor although Gore-Browne always felt himself the loser.

Sir Stewart Gore-Browne was of an age and a character apart. In post-World War I Britain, or in the interwar army, he might have remained a leader of men and a well-respected figure. Going out to Africa gave him more scope, however, and his own force of personality led to unquestioned and unexpected personal prominence, political success, and stature as a national hero. Without him Zambia would have emerged with poorer endowments and more racial bitterness.

At the end of Gore-Browne's life the goals for which he had long worked appeared to have been attained. A black government had emerged under a leader whom Gore-Browne trusted, and for whom compassion and justice were as basic sentiments as they were for him. The multiracialism for which he had long stood had been transmuted into independence, but Gore-Browne was satisfied. Secure in his major contribution to the transition from white to black rule, and confident of the future of Zambia, his last years were welcome ones of contemplation after many decades of active and intimate involvement in the affairs of his adopted country.

The passage of time had mellowed the eruptive anger for which, as the feared Chipembere, Gore-Browne had earlier been known. Yet there was much which had been little eroded. The boundless curiosity which, long before, had been epitomized by his explorations of France in the first motor cars, remained. So did an infectious enthusiasm and an energetic vitality which belied his age and charmed the new friends he made effortlessly. Few, in America as in Britain and Africa, could resist what Gore-Browne himself might, in the years after Harrow, have called the appearance of being well-bred. He was courtly, too, and fastidious in observing the obligations as well as the prerogatives of a gentleman. Yet the erect bearing and proper demeanor could not hide a twinkling, sometimes ribald sense of humor and a rich appreciation of the absurdities as well as the responsibilities of a life of influence. Occasionally, too, the personality of the insecure youth who had matched the achievements of his father and grandfather, pleased his aunt, and surprised himself, dominated that of the egocentric, respectable colonial radical.

Bibliography

ARTICLES BY GORE-BROWNE

"Notes on the Section of the Drakensberg Mountains from Giant's Castle to Cathkin Peak," *Alpine Journal,* XXII (1904–1905), 362–369.

"Instructions for Wagon Lines and Ammunition Columns," 3 November 1915, mimeographed.

"The Relations of Black and White in Tropical Africa," *Journal of the Royal African Society,* XXXIV (1935), 378–386.

"Native Development," January 1936, mimeographed.

"The Federated States of Rhodesia," *Journal of the Royal African Society,* XXXVI (1937), 2–7.

"Colour-Bar," printed address to the annual meeting of the Anti-Slavery and Aborigines Protection Society, 15 June 1944.

"Amalgamation of the Rhodesias and Nyasaland," in Fabian Society, *Four Colonial Questions: How Should Britain Act?* (London, 1944), 17–23.

"Current Problems in Northern Rhodesia," confidential printed address to the Colonial Affairs Study Group of the Empire Parliamentary Association, 10 July 1946.

"Note on the Federation Proposals," unpublished, 20 February 1949.

"Black and White in Africa," *Manchester Guardian,* 10 April 1950.

"Partition in Africa," *Manchester Guardian,* 25 August 1950.

"Central African Problems," *London Newsletter,* 30 December 1951.

"Mpika Road History," *Northern News,* 18 May 1952.

"Partnership in Central Africa," *Manchester Guardian,* 7 February 1952.

"African Aristotle Taken to Task," [Reply to article by Godwin Lewanika], *African Weekly,* 20 February 1952.

"Early History of the Movement for Federation," *Northern News,* 26 April 1952.

"First Federation Conference at Victoria Falls," *Northern News,* 29 April 1952.

"Sir Stewart Reaffirms his Faith in N. R. Partition," *Northern News,* 1 May 1952.

"Central Africa—The Issue," *Manchester Guardian,* 15 May 1952.

"New Draft Constitution Will Simplify Federation Issue," *Northern News,* 24 June 1952.

"Will Federal Constitution's Safeguards for Africans Work?" *Northern News,* 26 June 1952.

"Partition May Be Only Way Out of the Present Deadlock," *Northern News,* 28 June 1952.

"Sir Stewart Gore-Browne Replies to Partition Critics," *Northern News,* 16 August 1952.

"Alternatives to Central African Federation," *Manchester Guardian,* 13 April 1953.

"Legislative Council in Northern Rhodesia Twenty Years Ago," *Northern Rhodesia Journal,* II, 4 (1954), 39–45.

"Real Partnership the Only Key to the Riddle," *Bulawayo Chronicle,* 6 August 1954.

Letters to the *Manchester Guardian,* 20 December 1954, 6 February 1956, 15 August 1961.

"Partnership or Partition," *Northern News,* 21 December 1954.

"Partition May Yet Be the Only Answer," *Central African Examiner,* II, 7 (30 August 1958), 24–25.

"The Political Game in Northern Rhodesia," *Central African Examiner,* III, 13 (7 November 1959), 20.

Foreword to Colin Morris and Kenneth Kaunda, *Black Government?* (Lusaka, 1960).

"Note on Northern Rhodesia," *Dissent,* 20 (7 July 1960), 7–9.

"Urgent: A Fair Franchise," *African Mail,* April 1961.

"Hope through UNIP," *Central African Examiner,* V, 3 (August, 1961), 10.

Foreword to Kenneth Kaunda, *Zambia Shall Be Free: An Autobiography* (London, 1962).

"The Anglo-Belgian Boundary Commission, 1911–1914," *Northern Rhodesia Journal,* V, 4 (1964), 315–329.

BOOKS AND ARTICLES
ABOUT GORE-BROWNE AND HIS TIMES

Anon., "A Forty-Roomed Mansion Built in the Middle of Nowhere," *Rhodesia Herald,* 12 July 1965.

Anon., "Man of the Moment: Lieutenant Colonel Sir Stewart Gore-Browne," *Africa Bureau News,* 2 (1962), 5.

Anon., "Thirty-Room Mansion in Heart of Africa," *Rhodesia Herald,* 19 June 1954.

Anon. ("W.P.A."), "Shiwa Ngandu—The Lake of Crocodiles," *Heathcoat Magazine,* (1955), 43–44.

Allighan, Garry, *The Welensky Story* (London, 1962).

Atteridge, A. Hilliard, *History of the 17th (Northern) Division* (Glasgow, 1929).

Berger, Elena L., *Labour, Race, and Colonial Rule: The Copperbelt from 1924 to Independence* (Oxford, 1974).

Bigland, Eileen, *The Lake of the Royal Crocodiles* (London, 1939).

——, *Pattern in Black and White* (London, 1940).

Brockway, Fenner, *The Colonial Revolution* (New York, 1973).

Brown, Richard, "Anthropology and Colonial Rule: The Case of Godfrey Wilson and the Rhodes-Livingstone Institute, Northern Rhodesia," in Talal Asad (ed.), *Anthropology and the Colonial Encounter* (London, 1973), 173–197.

Carnegie, Sacha, *Red Dust of Africa* (London, 1959).

——, "Stalking a Leopard," *Country Life* (17 October 1957), 815–817.

——, "Introduction to Safari," ibid. (14 November 1957), 1030–1031.

Clegg, Edward, *Race and Politics: Partnership in the Federation of Rhodesia and Nyasaland* (London, 1960).

Davidson, James W., *The Northern Rhodesian Legislative Council* (London, 1948).

Dunn, Cyril, *Central African Witness* (London, 1959).

Epstein, A. L., *Politics in an Urban African Community* (Manchester, 1958).

Franklin, Harry, *Unholy Wedlock: The Failure of the Central African Federation* (London, 1963).

——, *The Flag-Wagger* (London, 1974).

Gann, Lewis H., *A History of Northern Rhodesia: Early Days to 1953* (London, 1964).

Gibbs, Peter, *Avalanche in Central Africa* (London, 1961).

Gladden, Norman, *The Somme, 1916* (London, 1974).

Gordimer, Nadine, "Zambia," *Holiday* (June, 1966), 38–47, 86–89.

Gray, Richard, *The Two Nations: Aspects of the Development of Race Relations in the Rhodesias and Nyasaland* (London, 1960).

Hailey, Baron Malcolm, *Native Administration in the British African Territories. II: Central Africa: Zanzibar, Nyasaland, Northern Rhodesia* (London, 1950).

Hall, Richard, *Zambia* (London, 1965).

Hinden, Rita (ed.), *Local Government and the Colonies* (London, 1950).

Hussey, A. H., and D. S. Inman, *The Fifth Division in the Great War* (London, 1921).

Johnson, Osa (Helen Leighty), *I Married Adventure; The Lives and Adventures of Martin and Osa Johnson* (Philadelphia, 1940).

La Fontaine, Jean S. (ed.), *The Interpretation of Ritual: Essays in Honour of A. I. Richards* (London, 1972).

Leys, Colin, *European Politics in Southern Rhodesia* (Oxford, 1959).

——, and Cranford Pratt, *A New Deal in Central Africa* (London, 1960).

Lunn, Arnold, *The Harrovians* (London, 1913).

Macpherson, Fergus, *Kenneth Kaunda of Zambia: The Times and the Man* (Lusaka, 1974).

Meebelo, Henry S., *Reaction to Colonialism: A Prelude to the Politics of Independence in Northern Zambia, 1893–1939* (Manchester, 1971).

Montagu, Edward, "The Laird of Shiwa," *New Statesman,* 27 February 1960.

Mulford, David C., *The Northern Rhodesia General Election, 1962* (Nairobi, 1964).

———, *Zambia: The Politics of Independence, 1957–1964* (London, 1967).

Mushindo, Paul Bwembya, *The Life of a Zambian Evangelist* (Lusaka, 1973).

Phillips, C. E. Lucas, *The Vision Splendid: The Future of the Central African Federation* (London, 1960).

Ponsonby, Charles, *Ponsonby Remembers* (Oxford, 1965).

Portsmouth, Gerard, Earl of, *A Knot of Roots: An Autobiography* (London, 1965).

Potter, Ursula Barnett, "African Highway. II: Journey Through the Federation," *African World* (April 1960), 5–6.

Richards, Audrey I., *Land, Labour, and Diet in Northern Rhodesia: An Economic Study of the Bemba Tribe* (London, 1939).

Rotberg, Robert I., "The Federation Movement in British East and Central Africa, 1889–1953," *Journal of Commonwealth Political Studies,* II (1964), 141–160.

———, "Race Relations and Politics in Colonial Zambia: The Elwell Incident," *Race,* VII (1965), 17–29.

———, *The Rise of Nationalism in Central Africa: The Making of Malawi and Zambia, 1873–1964* (Cambridge, Mass., 1965).

Anon. (D. Theodore Scannell), "Profile: Sir Stewart Gore-Browne," *Horizon,* VI, 7 (July, 1964), 16–19, 33.

Taylor, Don, *The Rhodesian: The Life of Sir Roy Welensky* (London, 1955).

Thomasson, Kuno, *Phytoplankton of Lake Shiwa* (Bruxelles, 1966).

Welensky, Roy, *Welensky's 4000 Days: The Life and Death of the Federation of Rhodesia and Nyasaland* (London, 1964).

Wills, A. J., *An Introduction to the History of Central Africa* (London, 1967, 2nd edition).

Interviews

With the author:
Sir Stewart Gore-Browne, 9 March 1967 (taped)
Lady Gore-Browne, 1967 (taped)
Robert Gore-Browne, 6 July 1963
Sapphire Gore-Browne Hanford, 18 August 1963
Ronald Bush, 6 July 1963
John Harvey, 10 March 1967 (taped)
Rowland Hudson, 7 July 1963
Lt. Col. H. P. McC. Glover, 29 July 1963
The Rev. Cyril G. Pearson, 4 July 1963
Audrey I. Richards, 27 June 1974

With Todd Matshikiza:
Sir Stewart Gore-Browne, 1 June 1964 (taped)

Index

Neither London, Britain, nor Zambia, which are relevant on most pages, are separately indexed, although some of the more important Zambian categories are listed.

Aaron, medical dispenser, 122–123, 137, 162

Abbeville, France, 83

Abercorn, Zambia, 56, 58, 100, 130, 144, 157, 159, 167, 174, 177, 183, 198, 202n, 204, 206, 235, 237

Abercorn Planters and Settlers Association, 198

Abingdon, England, 69

Accra, Ghana, 263, 309

Acheson, Denis, executive, 304

Achiet, France, 84

Afghanistan, 3, 4

African Administration, in Zambia, 178–183, 189, 239–240, 252

African-American Institute, 318

African Education Advisory Board, 189, 244

African Life, 315

African Mail, 312–313, 315

African Nationalism, xi–xii, 171, 187–188, 191, 224, 226–227, 241–243, 245, 254–255, 265, 273–274, 282, 283, 290, 302. *See also* Congress, African National

African Representative Council, of Northern Rhodesia, 245, 256, 262, 268, 272–273, 275

African War Memorial Fund, of Northern Rhodesia, 295

African Weekly, the, 253

Agriculture, indigenous, 94–96, 114, 138, 143, 177, 183, 188, 239, 277

Air Warfare, in World War I, 66, 72

Aisne River, 63, 64–65, 83

Albert, Lake, 39

Albertville, Zaire, 141

Alcoholism, 40

Aldershot, England, 24, 37, 88

Alexander, Boyd, 6–7

Algeria, 107

All-African People's Conference, 309

Altrincham, Lord, 82n

Amalgamation, of the Rhodesias and/or Nyasaland, 157, 170–172, 174–175, 191–194, 197–198, 202–203, 205–206, 208, 243, 245, 247–249, 250, 256, 260–261, 263–265, 268–271, 274–275, 277, 279–281

Amberley, England, 18

Anglicanism, 3, 6. *See also* Church of England

Angola, 39, 50, 115, 285

Anti-Slavery and Aborigines Protection Society, the, 274, 279, 306

Argonne, France, 83

Armentières, France, 65

Army, British, 3, 4, 6, 16, 18–19, 20–22, 24, 26, 32, 33, 36–37, 48, 61–87, 91–92; artillery, 18, 24, 28, 37, 63–65, 71, 73–76, 78–79, 84

Army and Navy Club, of London, 318

Arnold, E. P., schoolmaster, 9

Arras, France, 76, 77

Artois, France, 73

Asians, in Africa, 300, 304, 318, 321–322

Atlantic Charter, the, 229

Austen, Jane, novelist, 46

Austin, Charles E., and early Shiwa, 92, 103, 104, 105, 106, 110

Australia, 107, 286

Austria, 72

Automobiles and autoracing, 8, 14, 23, 26, 28, 32–35, 137

Aviation and Airports, 147–148, 152, 154, 160, 162–163, 204, 230, 250, 251, 263, 272, 333
Aylesbury, England, 4
Ayrshire, Scotland, 4, 19. *See also* Craigie, Scotland

Bailey, Professor J. O., Hardy specialist, xiii, 26n
Balliol College, Oxford, 12, 19
Balochmyle, Scotland, 6–7
Balovale, Zambia, 259
Bananas, 108
Banda, President Dr. Hastings Kamuzu, 227–228, 256, 267, 274, 279–281, 285–287, 308–309, 310, 313
Bangweulu, Lake, 39, 103, 165, 166, 199
Bapaume, France, 84
Barbados, 234
Barotseland, 157, 187, 194, 245, 268
Barrow, Malcolm, legislator and planter, 250
Barton, Frank, journalist, 304
Battles, of World War I, 62–66, 72, 75, 78, 83
Baya, Zaire, 47, 50
Beckett, Geoff, legislator, 263, 267, 273
Belgium and Belgians, 38–40, 44–45, 55, 65, 67, 70, 72, 75, 87, 108
Belgium Congo. *See* Zaire
Bell, Basil, ichthyologist, 293. *See also* Sutton, Mrs. Xenia Angela Gore-Browne
Bemba, people, 1, 41, 42–44, 49, 50–54, 55–56, 58–59, 95, 162, 199, 221, 306, 307–308, 332; and Shiwa, 97, 98–99, 100, 159; language, 151–152
Benson, Governor Sir Arthur, 307, 310n
Berlin, Germany, 89, 91
Bermuda, 6, 234
Bethune, France, 76
Bicycle Polo, game, 13
Bicycles, in Africa, 42
Bigland, Eileen, author, 201
Billingshurst, England, 19, 90. *See also* Rowner Mills, estate
Bingham's Melcombe, Dorset, 23–26, 28, 69, 133, 135
Bisa, people, 97, 106
Blantyre, Malawi, 299

Bledisloe, Charles Viscount, 205, 207, 209
Boer War, 16, 19
Bonner, Evelyn, and Gore-Browne 127, 132
Botswana, 6
Bosworth Smith, Joan, 25, 26, 28
Bosworth Smith, Neville, 25, 28
Bosworth Smith, Reginald, schoolmaster, 23–24, 28. *See also* Goldman, Lorna; Grogan, Lady
Bosworth Smith, Reginald, Jr., 90
Bosworth Smith, Mrs. Reginald, 133
Boulogne, France, 61
Boundary Commission, Anglo-Belgian, 38–47, 49–55, 117, 333–334
Boxall, Frank, at Shiwa, 112, 119
Boycotts, 295–296, 301, 304, 308–309
Boyd, Lord. *See* Lennox-Boyd
Braine, France, 64
Brelsford, W. Vernon, administrator, 150
Brick and tile making, 106, 137, 146, 150, 164
British South Africa Company, the, 45, 56, 70n, 92, 95–96, 97, 98–99, 113, 282
Broken Hill, Zambia, 102, 124, 167–169, 183, 194, 204, 212, 233; election, 170–173, 175; strike at, 232
Broken Hill Political Association, 168, 197, 205, 206
Brönte, Charlotte, novelist, 14
Brooke, Rupert, poet, 77
Brookes, Senator Edgar H., 230n
Brooklands, Weybridge, estate, 8, 13, 17, 19, 32, 51, 53, 61–62, 66, 69, 82, 112, 133, 134, 137; motor racetrack, 34–35, 132, 306
Browne, Sir Anthony, and King Henry VIII, 3
Browne, Bishop Edward Harold, 3
Browne, General Gore, 3
Browne, John, soldier, 3
Browne, Captain John William, 3
Browne, Louisa, 3
Browne, Maria, 3
Browne, Colonel Robert Gore, 3
Browne, Thomas, merchant, 3
Browne, William, lawyer, 3
Buchan, John, novelist, 150n
Buckingham, Marquis of, 3

Bulawayo Chronicle, the, 197
Bulaya, employee of Gore-Browne, 43, 48, 50, 59, 61, 62, 66, 68–70, 116n
Bulgaria, 107, 126, 276
Buller, General Sir Redvers Henry, 16
Burma, 253
Bush, Ronald, administrator, xiii, 183–185
Bushman River, the, 21
Bussy-les-Daours, France, 79
Butler, Secretary of State R.A., 318
Buxton, Clarence, of Kenya, 297–298
Bwana Mkubwa, Zambia, 237
Byng, General Sir Julian, 84

Cambrai, France, 84
Cambridge, Massachusetts, xii, 318–319
Cambridge, University of, 3, 6, 25, 82–83, 162, 166–167, 199, 230, 256
Campbell, Harriet, 4
Campbell, James, 4
Campbell, Muriel, 13, 19
Campbells, the, 7, 9
Cannes, France, 110
Canoes, transport by, 96, 103, 106
Cape Colony and Province, 6
Capetown, South Africa, xi, 48, 148, 197, 199, 204, 230
Caporetto, Italy, 81
Capricorn Africa Society, the, 296–298, 303, 304, 305, 332
Carnegie, Lady Katherine, 128–129
Carnegie, Sacha, author, 294
Carriers. *See* Porters
Cartmel-Robinson, Harold Francis, administrator, 150, 232, 250
Cary, Joyce, novelist, 147n
Cattle, 58, 95, 96, 100, 105, 106, 146, 164, 276, 292
Caudry, France, 84
Cavendish-Bentinck, Major Sir Ferdinand, legislator, 233, 256
Central Africa Party, the, 305, 313
Central African Council, 248–251, 272, 278, 283, 331. *See also* Interterritorial Conference
Ceylon. *See* Sri Lanka
Chalimbana School, Zambia, 227
Chamber of Mines, of N.R., 231
Chambeshi constituency, in Zambia, 320–321, 323–324

Chambezi River, the, 58, 97, 99–100, 103, 108
Champagne, France, 73
Charleroi, Belgium, 88
Chateau-Thierry, France, 83
Chatham, England, 28
Chibesakunda, Bisa chief, 97
Chickens, 94, 292
Chikwanda, head messenger, 43, 48, 51, 56
Chikwanda, headman, 58, 100, 105
Chilanga, Zambia, 57, 102
Chileshe, Safeli, 256, 267, 304
Chilonga, Zambia, mission station, 57, 58, 96
Chilubi Island, Zambia, 103, 165
China, 292
Chingola, Zambia, 270, 271, 281
Chinsali, Zambia, 56, 58, 96, 100, 113, 148, 150, 183, 201, 283–284, 300, 301, 306, 321
Chinsenda, Zaire, 47
Chipata, Zambia. *See* Fort Jameson
Chipepa, J., provincial councillor, 272
Chipushi, Zambia, 47
Chisamba, Zambia, 102
Chitambo, Zambia, mission station, 57
Chitimukulu, Bemba paramount chief, 97, 178
Chitulika, headman, 243
Cholmeley, Edward Henry, native commissioner, 58
Choma Girls' School, Zambia, 212
Christ Church College, Oxford, 19
Chunya, Tanzania, 184
Church of England, 3, 6, 14, 30, 151, 186, 247
Civil Defence, of Zambia, 211–213
Civil Service Commissioners, British, 16–17
Clarke, R. G., schoolboy, 12
Cochrane, Mrs. Joan. *See* Bosworth Smith, Joan
Cochran-Patrick, Charles, pilot, 162–163
Codes and Ciphers, 46
Coffee, 174, 198, 309
Cohen, Governor Sir Andrew, administrator, xiii, 247, 255, 256, 267, 274, 275, 278, 283
Colchester, England, 36–37
"Cold War," 275
Colonial rule, British, 4, 39, 156, 157, 171, 174, 331

Color bar, in Africa, 214, 218, 223–227, 231, 243, 252–253, 263, 295, 299, 303

Combles, France, 78

Commerce, 3, 95

Commerce, in Zambia, 105, 108, 138–139

Commission, Royal, on Rhodesia and Nyasaland (1939), 205–209

Commission, Royal, on the Federation (1960), 310–311, 313

Concord, Massachusetts, 318, 320

Concrete, use of, 34

Confederate Party, the, 302

Congo. See Zaire

Congo River, 39

Congress, African National (Northern Rhodesia), 262, 274, 275–276, 279, 283, 287–288, 289n, 294–295, 300–302, 304–308, 323, 332

Congress, Nyasaland African, 309

Congress, Zambia African National, 308–310

Conrad, Joseph, novelist, 127

Conservative Party, of Britain, 314, 316

Constitutional Change, in the 1950s and 1960s, 307, 312–313, 316–317, 320, 324

Constitution Party, of Northern Rhodesia, 304–305, 314–315, 332

Cooper, Ruth, and Gore-Browne, 133

Copper, industry, 171, 191, 211–213, 215, 223, 235, 259, 278, 327

Corn. See Maize

Coupland, Professor Sir Reginald, 204

Cowie, Major Walter N., and Shiwa, 92, 102, 105, 106, 108, 110

Craigie, Scotland, 4, 6, 19, 23

Crawfurdland Castle, Scotland, 23

Crickets, tree, 42

Croad, Hector, native commissioner, 111, 114n, 122, 130, 136–138, 144

Cromer, Lord, 147

Crops, in Africa, 94, 95–96, 97, 105, 106, 143, 182

Curragh, Ireland, 88

Danzig, Free City of, 91

Dar es Salaam, Tanzania, 60, 115, 136

Daudet, Alphonse, author, 17

Davidson, Professor James, 256

Davison, Arthur, railwayman, 169, 170, 172–173, 175

Deepcut, England, 26, 28

Defence needs, and Federation, 275, 278

Delaforce, Major Victor, xiii

Denny, S. R., administrator, 150

Depression and Recession, economic, 96, 139, 143, 153–154, 171, 181, 185

Desai, T. L., and UNIP, 318

Devonshire, Duke of (1961), 318

Devonshire, Duke of (1923), 156

Dickinson, Humphrey Neville, novelist, 35–36

Discrimination, in Zambia, 215–216, 218, 227–228, 243, 252

Disease, in Europe and Africa, 20–21, 27, 72, 83, 94, 227, 231

Dobree, Governor Claude Hatherley, 150–151

Dominica, 145

Dorchester, England, 24, 28

Dorset, England, 4, 23–24, 28, 133

Douglas-Home. See Home, Prime Minister Lord

Drakensberg Mountains, 21

Dreyfus, Alfred, 13–14

Dublin, Ireland, 3

Dulwich College, England, 234

Duncan-Sandys, Lord. See Sandys, Duncan

Dundas, Charles Cecil Farquharson, administrator, 181, 182, 185

Durban, Natal, 22

Dusseldorf, Germany, 91

Dutch Reformed Church, 186

Dutton, Eric, administrator, 195

Earl-Spurr, Colonel N. O., 302

Eccles, Launcelot W. G., administrator, 238, 240

Economist, The, 274, 279, 281, 294

Education, of Gore-Browne, 9–17; of Africans, 99, 123, 151–152, 177, 183, 189, 200, 204, 213, 226, 229–231, 258–259, 277, 303

Egypt, 8, 12, 33, 136, 156, 157

Ehrlich, Dr. Paul, 27

Elections, 167–169, 170–175, 303–304, 307–308, 313, 317; of 1962, 320–321, 323–324

Emerson, Ralph Waldo, poet, 318, 320

Emmanuel College, Cambridge, 3

Engineering, 34–35. See also Roadmaking, in Zambia

Ergot, drug, 108
Entebbe, Uganda, 204
Essential oils, 92, 96, 100, 104, 106–108, 110–111, 126, 130, 137–139, 141, 143–145, 199–200, 210, 216, 234–235, 276, 291–292, 327; process of distilling, 107, 143
Escaut River, 84
Ethiopia, 235–236
Eton College, 3
Everett, Captain, and the Boundary Commission, 40, 43
Executive Council, of Northern Rhodesia, 196, 203, 207, 208–209, 210–211, 213, 232, 233, 246–247, 257, 264, 268, 274, 276, 301
Exeter Hall, London, 117
Extrasensory perception, 32

Fabian Society, the, 255, 256
Falcon Steward, Muriel and Will, 19
Federation, idea of and agitation for, 248–249, 275, 277–284; realized, 288, 296
Federation of African Welfare Societies, of Northern Rhodesia, 253, 265, 270, 274, 289n,
Federation of Rhodesia and Nyasaland, xi, 288, 290, 294–296, 297–300, 301, 303, 304, 306–307; riots against, 309–310; breakup of, 313–315, 325
Ferdinand, Archduke Franz, 60
Fife (Isoka), Zambia, 56, 58, 100
Fifth Division, British army, 71, 76–81, 83–85, 87–88, 112, 127
Fives, game of, 13
Fisher, Dr. Charles, legislator, 247, 297, 301, 304, 305
Fisher, Dr. Monica, 304
Fisher, Dr. Walter, missionary, 50
Flanders, France and Belgium, 65, 72, 83
Forestry. See Reafforestation, in Zambia
Forster, Sir John, and his Commission, 223
Fort Hill, Malawi, 299, 309
Fort Jameson, Zambia, 144, 157, 214, 236, 262, 272
Fourth Division, British Army, 61, 73
Fox-Pitt, Commander Thomas, administrator, 150, 306

France, 13–14, 23, 28, 33, 61–67, 72–73, 83–85, 107, 128, 132, 204, 276, 335
Franchise, for Africans, 300, 303, 304–305, 307, 311, 314–317, 318, 320, 323–324
Frankfurt, Germany, 27
Franklin, Harry, Administrator, 301, 302–304, 305
Freiburg, University of, 27
French, Field Marshall Sir John, 65
French, Mrs. Margaret, 267
Fuller, General C. G., 91

Galicia, 72
Gallipoli, Turkey, 72, 77
Gandhi, Mohandas K., 295–296
Gas warfare, 72, 73, 75
Gaunt, John, administrator, 186
Genoa, Italy, 302
Germany, 27, 63, 66, 67, 72, 73, 74, 75, 78, 83, 84, 91, 99, 209, 212–213, 296
Ghana, 228, 263, 291, 295, 308, 309, 310, 332
Gibb, Lady Diana. See King, Lady Diana Charlotte
Gilbert and Sullivan, operettas, 13
Gilkes, Dr. Humphrey, 111–112
Gillam, Major R. A. , 38, 40, 43, 46, 54
Gillum, W. W., boyhood friend, 32, 33, 75
Glover, Lieutenant Colonel H.P. McC., xiii
Glasgow, Scotland, 38
Gloucestershire, England, 8
Goats, 94
Gold, 183–185
Gold Coast. See Ghana
Goldman, Mrs. Agnes Mary, 25, 133
Goldman, Bosworth Monck, 89, 133
Goldman, Maj. Charles Sydney, entrepreneur, 23, 133, 134
Goldman, Dr. Edwin, 26–28, 89
Goldman, Lorna L. Bosworth Smith, 24–28, 89–91
Golf, 8, 14
Gonville and Caius College, Cambridge, 82
Goodall, E. G. H., administrator, 150, 154
Gordimer, Nadine, novelist, xiii, 326
Gordon, Leon, playwright, 70n
Gordon-Walker, Secretary of State Patrick, 283

Gore, the name, 3
Gore, New Zealand, 286n
Gore Browne. *See also* Browne.
Gore-Browne, Sir Francis, 6–7, 9,
　10–11, 14, 21, 34, 109–110, 176,
　251
Gore-Browne, Commander Godfrey
　(Goff), 6, 13, 15
Gore-Browne, Colonel Harold C., 6,
　16
Gore Browne, Lady Harriet, 4–6, 7, 19,
　27
Gore-Browne, Lady Helenor
　Shaw-Stewart, 6–7, 9, 10,
　14–15,17
Gore-Browne, Lady Lorna Goldman,
　xii, xiii, 177, 198, 201, 207, 210,
　234, 293, 334; birth, 89; meeting
　Gore-Browne, 133; and
　Gore-Browne, 133–136, 160–161,
　163–167; marriage, 135;
　developing Shiwa, 137; at Shiwa,
　149, 155, 159, 161–162, 199, 277;
　and Richards, 165–166; medical
　problems, 166–167; divorce, 277
Gore-Browne, Mabyl, 6
Gore-Browne, Mrs. Margaret, xiii,
　108–111
Gore-Browne, Robert, xiii, 7, 9, 35, 61,
　100; and Shiwa, 108–111, 125
Gore-Browne, Lieutenant Colonel Sir
　Stewart, K.B., G.O.C.F.,
　D.S.O., J.P.,
　accused of betraying Africans,
　265–273
　Africans, Gore-Browne's relations
　　with, xi, xii, 22, 40–45, 51–52,
　　54, 57, 92, at Shiwa, 104–105,
　　116–124; in Zambia, 116. *See
　　also* Bulaya
　and African education, 122, 123,
　　151–152, 177, 189, 200, 204, 226,
　　227, 229–230, 240, 258–259, 303
　and African employees, 117–124,
　　143, 153, 201, 333
　on African housing, 190, 223,
　　225–226, 232–233, 259
　and African nationalism, 156, 158,
　　187–188, 189–190, 226–227,
　　241–245, 282–284, 287–288,
　　290, 294, 305, 310
　and African National Congress,
　　294–295
　and African land rights, 237–240, 252
　and African political participation,
　　243–245, 254, 256–258, 262,
　　306, 331–332
　　1948 scheme, 266, 268–269,
　　271, 273, 274
　ambitions of, 48–49, 53–54, 59, 66,
　　209
　and artillery battery, 65–66
　attitude to South Africa, 212,
　　230–231, 238, 282
　attitudes toward the war, 66–67, 75,
　　77, 82–83
　and automobiles, 14, 23, 26, 28,
　　32–35, 123–124, 162, 334
　awarded D.S.O., 80; mentioned in
　　dispatches, 88
　becomes Grand Officer, 327
　birth, 1
　and the Bledisloe Commission,
　　205–209
　and the Boundary Commission,
　　38–47, 49–51, 54–55
　as a bridge and roadmaker, 113, 138,
　　146–149, 154, 157, 159, 166, 200,
　　333
　and the British Army of the Rhine, 91
　the candidate in 1962, 320–321,
　　323–324, 332
　and the Capricorn Africa Society,
　　296–297, 303, 305, 332
　and Cibemba, 46, 58n
　as Civil Defence Commissioner,
　　211–213
　and climate, 41
　and the color bar, 190, 223–224,
　　226–227, 232, 244, 253, 254, 263,
　　271, 284, 295, 299, 303, 325
　as a compulsive, 130
　and the Congress, 302–303, 305,
　　306–307, 332
　constitutional proposals, 193–198,
　　201–204, 207–208, 246–248,
　　256–258; 1948 scheme, 265–274
　as a correspondent, xii, 36, 126,
　　160–161, 293; diaries, xiii, 29,
　　30, 32, 33, 36
　and death, 70, 77–78
　and demobilization, 87–89
　dies, 327
　his dreams, 127
　and dreams of glory, 21, 52, 58, 111,
　　209, 222

and ebbing away of influence, 276, 281, 283, 286–288

and electoral politics, 167–169; 1935 election, 170–175

entering the military, 16–18

and Ethel, 32–33, 36, 38, 45, 48–49, 51–54, 59, 61–62, 66, 71, 77, 85, 88–89, 92–93, 109n, 111, 132, 134–135, 138–139, 144, 157, 160–161, 167, 176, 199, 204, 256, 287–288, 292–293, 334; and his bride, 126–130

the family, xi, 1–3, 4, 7, 17, 23, 52; childhood, 7–9; relations with parents, 8–11, 14–17, 32, 52, 59, 61, 71, 89, 91, 109–110, 126, 132, 176, 251; schooling, 9–15

federal ideas and federation, 157, 175, 194–196, 202, 204, 207, 248–249, 271–272, 274–275, 278–279, 281–282, 284, 286

and the Federation of Rhodesia and Nyasaland, 294–296, 298–300, 306–307, 310–311, 332

with the Fifth Division, 76–81, 83–85, 87–88

as a forester, 153–154

funeral of, 327–328

and Governors, 114–116, 149, 150–151, 154–155, 157, 161, 175–176, 182, 192, 204; Maybin, 210–214, 223, 233, 246; Rennie, 270, 274n; Waddington, 233–235, 238, 246

and his grandfather, 6, 7, 286

help for individuals, 227

and history, 29

as a host, 114–116, 161, 204, 206–207, 310, 323, 326–327

and houses, 14, 23–24, 33, 52, 146, 149–150, 200

as a hunter, 41, 57

on indirect rule, 151–152, 178, 189–190

influencing British public opinion, 284–285, 330–331

on intellectuals, 165

joins UNIP, 315–316, 332

and Kaunda, 311, 313–316, 324–325

and Kerr, 32, 33, 37–38, 43, 70–71.

knighted (K.B.), 251

and the law, 48

as a leader, 38, 41, 65, 76, 79–81

as leader of unofficials, 208–209, 210–211, 214, 233, 246, 250, 255–256, 264, 331; resigns, 261

in Legislative Council, 183, 185; maiden speech, 176–178, 192; agitation for African rights, 188–190, 224–226, 229, 239, 241–242, 251, 258, 259; constitutional change of, 194–197, 203, 207–208, 256; wartime role in, 213; "confession of faith," 251–253; resignation, 287–289; role in, 330–331

letters. See also Gore-Browne, Sir Stewart, as a correspondent

and the "liberals" in Zambia, 301–305, 332

and local government, 158, 181, 240–242

and Lorna I, 24–28, 30, 89–91, 127, 135, 334

and Lorna II, meets, 133; marriage, 135; views on, 135–136; 139, 160–161, 163; tensions between, 164–167, 199–200, 210, 235, 251, 293, 334; divorce, 277

and majority rule, 310, 312

and manpower committee, 211–213

on mines and labor, 57, 59, 98, 153, 154, 183, 217, 223, 231, 259, 327

on miscegenation, 129

and missionaries, 43, 50, 121

and Moral Rearmament, 296, 332

motives of, 124–125, 139, 143–144, 159, 176, 292

multiracial notions of, 157–158, 178, 225, 255, 262–263, 284, 288, 290, 324, 331

and nature, 29, 41, 42, 58, 160

noblesse oblige of, 29–30, 31, 41, 44–45, 49, 56–57, 59, 104, 113, 125, 143, 153, 159, 333

and Northern Rhodesian national politics: before 1935, 113, 114, 150–151, 153–155, 159; after 1935, 170

old age, xii

operations on, 292

and parapsychology, 32

and his parents. See Gore-Browne, Sir Stewart, the family

and partition, 294–295, 299, 300–301

Gore-Browne (cont.)
and partnership, 158, 174, 178, 191, 196, 202, 225, 273, 282, 284, 285, 286, 290, 295, 298–300
as a paternalist, 116–125, 143, 151–153, 177, 207, 239, 255, 257, 262, 305, 331, 333
and the peacetime army, 36–37, 48, 53–54
personal income and finances, 43, 48, 107, 137–139, 144, 153, 236, 276, 293
personal life, xi
and photography, 14
and Portuguese, 81–82
prejudices, 30, 82
promotions, 49, 68, 76, 83
and refugees, 235–237
relations with white partners and employees, 106, 110, 112, 119, 122, 234–235, 276–277, 292
and religion, 14, 69, 78
as representative of Africans, 175–177, 187–188, 209; nominated, 204–205, 226, 241, 243, 261–262, 264, 270–273, 276; resigns, 288
in retirement, 326–327
in retrospect, 330–335
the return to Shiwa (1948–1951), 198, 276–277, 287–289, 290–292
and the 1940 riots, 215–223
and rural development, 239–240, 327
and self-government, 174, 190, 268, 273
with the Seventeenth Division, 68, 71, 73–76
and sex, 15
in South Africa, 19–22
speeches, etc., outside Africa, 157–158, 204
as staff officer, 68, 76–81, 83–85
with the supply column, 64–65
and the surrender, 85, 87
and surveying, 21, 43, 47
tastes in literature and the arts, 13, 14, 17, 28, 33, 46, 91, 114, 127, 138, 158, 163, 200, 211
on tax commission, 185–187
as a teacher, 38, 79, 82, 87
temper, 38, 44, 57, 119, 129–130, 333, 335
with the Third Army, 84–85

to the United States, 318, 320
views of Africans, 143, 150–153, 155–159, 176–178, 179, 194, 196, 214, 252, 258; of African administration, 179–181
views on amalgamation, 157, 172, 174–175, 192–193, 203, 206, 246, 247–249, 261–262, 265, 268–269, 271, 273, 275, 279, 281, 331
views of missionaries, 157, 159, 161–162, 191, 252
views of settlers, 20, 57, 172, 176–177, 181, 183, 208, 263, 285–286
views on South Africa, 100, 112, 119, 156, 157
views of Southern Rhodesia, 206, 271, 278–279, 285, 331
views on white settlers, 112–113, 159–160
views on 1920s Zambia, 103
visit to New Zealand, 5, 286
and War Memorial Fund, 295
and Watson, 45–47
and Welensky, 172–173, 175, 210, 214, 233, 246–247, 256–257, 261, 263–264, 247n, 276–277, 281, 287, 299, 301, 309–310, 312, 313, 331–332
and welfare of Africans, 184–185, 188–189, 206–207, 218, 223–226, 228, 231, 233, 239–240, 259, 330–331
and women (excluding Ethel and the Lornas), 22, 23, 24–29, 30, 89, 100, 127–130
at Woolwich, 18–19
in World War I, 61–87
as a writer, 20, 21n, 35–36
Gore Browne, Governor Sir Thomas, 3, 4, 6, 7, 286
Gore Browne, Bishop Wilfred, 6, 118, 127, 209
Graaff Reinet, Cape Province, 90
Great North Road, 148–149
Greece, 4, 81
Grenada, 145
Grigg, Governor Sir Edward, 82n
Graham, Lord, 302
Greenidge, C. W. W., Anti-Slavery Society Secretary, 278n, 279
Griffith, Secretary of State James, 283–284

Grogan, Lady Effie Bosworth Smith, 26, 69, 133
Guyana, 234

Hailey, William Malcolm Lord, 204, 312, 316
Haiti, 107
Hall, Secretary of State George, 261
Hall, Richard, journalist, 312–313, 315
Hanford, Mrs. Sapphire Helenor Gore-Browne, xiii, 7, 9, 267
Hardy, Thomas, author, 25, 135, 163
Harlech, Lord. See Ormsby-Gore, W.G.A.
Harrow School, 6, 11–18, 23, 35, 61, 334
Harvard University, 318–319
Harvey, John, xiii, 292, 311
Harvey, Mrs. Lorna Katherine Gore-Browne, 146, 163, 166, 209, 211, 235, 276–277, 293, 327; marries, 292
Haslam, Dr. John, 227–228, 302
Henty, G. W., author, 21, 150
Henry VIII, King, 3
Hinden, Rita, of the Fabian Society, 256
High Wycombe, England, 28
Higher Education, 230, 231, 259. See also Education, of Gore-Browne
Hill, William, administrator, 150
Hilton, James, novelist, 200
Holland, Prime Minister S.G., 5
Home, Prime Minister Lord, 312
Hone, Governor Sir Evelyn, 312, 316, 324
Hooge, Belgium, 75
House-building, 59, 105, 139, 146, 149–150, 200
Hudson, Rowland, administrator, xiii
Huggins, Prime Minister Sir Godfrey Martin, 191–192, 197, 201–204, 205, 207–208, 209, 247, 249, 250, 275, 277–280, 283, 298–299
Hunt, Norman, architect, 304
Huxley, Elspeth and Gervase, xiii, 202, 256

Ikelenge, Lunda Chief, 272
Imperial Airways, 147–148
Imperial rule, 4, 175, 242
India, 4, 12, 22, 53, 157, 242, 307. See also Gandhi

Indirect Rule, 151, 187
Indianapolis, Indiana, 34
Inner Temple, the, 6
Insane, treatment of, 177, 228, 250, 259
Institute of Education, London, 204, 259
Ireland, 3, 19, 88, 242
Interterritorial Conference, 208, 246, 247, 249
Isoka, Zambia, 147, 283, 309, 320–321. See also Fife, Zambia
Isonzo River, 72, 81
Italy, 23, 72, 81, 85, 107, 132, 136, 212–213, 235–236, 296, 302
Ivory, 97

Jackson, General H. L., 74
Jackson, Private Samson, 70n. See Bulaya
James, African clerk, 115
James, C. Gordon, 238
Japan, 272
Jelf, General R. A., 18
Joelson, E. S., editor, 204, 300n
Johannesburg, South Africa, 100, 235
Jones, Secretary of State Arthur Creech, xiii, 256, 266–267, 273, 274–275, 280, 283, 285–286, 324
Jones, Sir Austin, xiii, 79–80
Jones, Rowland, clerk, 111, 129
Jong, Josselyn de, administrator, 92
Johnson, Martin and Osa, aviators and writers/photographers, 162
Justice, in Africa, 44, 45, 54–55, 99, 183, 190, 216, 228–229

Kabunda, Zambia, 103
Kabwe, See Broken Hill, Zambia
Kafulafuta, Zambia, 45
Kafue River and Dam, 47, 48, 49, 236, 300
Kakumbi, Mateyo, politician, 273
Kakumbi, messenger, 43, 48, 51, 59, 61, 62, 66, 68–69, 102–103, 121
Kaleñe Hill, Zambia, mission station, 50
Kalepa, R., provincial councillor, 272
Kalikeka, Shiwa cook, 115
Kambole, Zambia, mission station, 121
Kansanshi mine, Zambia, 47, 49, 50, 59
Kaonde, people, 41, 49

Kapombo River, 49
Kapwepwe, Simon, legislator, 307
Kariba Gorge and Dam, Zambia, 250,
    300, 312, 314
Kasama, Zambia, 56, 108, 113, 116, 122,
    129, 137, 150, 151–152, 159–160,
    167, 174, 183, 292, 327
Kasempa, Zambia, 262
Kasokolo, Henry, politician, 279
Katete Stream, the, 57, 113, 114, 150
Katilungu, Lawrence, trade unionist,
    304
Kaunda, President Kenneth, xiii, 283,
    300, 301, 306–308, 309, 310–311,
    312, 313–318, 320–322, 323–325,
    326, 327–329, 332, 334
Kawamba, Zambia, 70n
Kelley, General E. H., xiii
Kenneth of Dene, Lord. See Young, Sir
    Edward Hilton
Kenya, 136, 150n, 156, 163, 202, 233,
    236, 237, 245, 256, 266, 293,
    297–298
Kerr, Captain Cecil, 32, 33, 37–38, 43,
    49, 61, 67, 77, 81, 85, 89; death,
    70–71
Keynes, John Maynard Lord, 154
Khartoum, the Sudan, 160, 204
Kigoma, Tanzania, 136
Kilkenny, Ireland, 19
Kilmarnock, Scotland, 23, 293
Kimberley, Cape Province, 6
King Edward VIII, of Britain, 198
King Henry VIII, of England, 3
King, Lord, 8, 53n, 132, 306
King, Lady Diana Charlotte, 89, 127
King, Frank Jerome Maitland (Peter),
    53
King's African Rifles, 102, 292
King's College, Cambridge, 25, 26
King's Royal Rifles, 6, 16
Kipling Rudyard, 14, 45
Kitawala. See Watch Tower movement
Kitchener, General Horatio Herbert
    Lord, 67, 69
Kittermaster, Governor Harold, 203
Kitwe African Society, 269, 272
Kitwe, Zambia, 214, 218, 269, 312,
    320–321, 323–324
Koblenz, Germany, 91
Köln, Germany, 129
Kumasi, Ghana, 263, 308
Kuruman, Cape Province, 6

Labor, compulsory, 98, 99
Labour Party, of Britain, 306
    204
Ladysmith, Natal, 6, 16
Lamb, Charles, author, 46
Lamba, people, 41
Land, alienation of, 4–5, 240, 245, 252,
    270, 278, 281, 285
Land tenure, African, 213, 237–240, 252
Latham, Geoffrey C., educationist, 151
Latvia, 72, 81
Law and lawyers, 3, 6–7, 8, 9, 10, 14, 48,
    108, 109n
League of Nations, 184, 192
Le Cateau, France, 62–63, 64, 84
Legislative Council of Northern
    Rhodesia, 167–168, 171, 176–178,
    183, 204, 210, 214, 241, 244–245,
    256, 313; African participation in,
    240–245, 256–257, 268, 279, 310;
    changes in, 247, 256, 268, 274, 287,
    307; African members, 279, 287,
    310, 331
Lennox-Boyd, Secretary of State Alan,
    303, 307
Léopold II, King, 39
Léopoldville, Zaire, 263
Lesotho, 90
Lettow-Vorbeck, General Paul von, 99
Liberal Party of Zambia, 303, 313–315,
    317, 323, 332
Liberalism, in Zambia, 301–305, 313,
    332
Ligny, France, 63
Limes, 141, 145, 184, 199, 200, 216, 234,
    276, 291–292, 327
Lincoln's Inn, London, 8
Linguistics, 151–152
Livingstone, Dr. David, explorer, 95,
    97, 330
Livingstone, Zambia, 56, 95, 102, 171,
    191, 212, 228, 270, 271, 295
Livingstone Mail, the, 197, 209
Locke-King, Dame Ethel, xi, xii, 6,
    7–9, 14, 23, 25, 26, 27, 32–33, 36,
    38, 51–53, 61, 65, 66, 69, 70n, 85,
    87, 91–93; awarded D.B.E., 82;
    and Shiwa, 106–107, 125, 137–139,
    149, 156, 256, 286; influence on
    Gore-Browne, 126–128, 132, 134,
    157, 204, 270–271, 292, 334; air
    pioneer, 160; at Shiwa, 163; estate,
    306; dies, 293, 327

Locke-King, Hugh Fortescue, 8, 14, 32–34, 49, 51, 53, 61, 66, 85, 121, 127, 139, 292; dies, 126
Locke-King, Peter John, 8
Lockhart, C. R., administrator, 181–182, 185
Logan, Governor William Marston, 213n, 235
Loire River, 33
Longueval, France, 77
London Missionary Society, the, 121
London School of Economics, 166,202, 227
Lovelace, Countess of, xiii
Lovelace, Earl of, 8, 112
Lowrey, G., batman, 38, 76
Lozi, people, 186, 262, 268, 332
Luangwa River, 97
Luanshya, Zambia, 227, 257, 262, 292, 304, 321
Luapula River, 96, 103
Lubwa Mission, Zambia, 96, 306
Lugard, Frederick Lord, 48, 147, 180, 209
Lunda, people, 41
Lunga River, 49, 50
Lundazi, Zambia, 262
Lupa Goldfields, Tanganyika, 183–185, 333
Lusaka, Zambia, 102, 177, 189, 191, 196, 210–211, 221, 226, 232, 233, 237, 268, 272, 292, 299, 302, 304, 307, 315; Gore-Browne living in, 234–235, 277

McCallum, Governor Sir Henry, 22
MacDonald, Secretary of State Malcolm, 201, 203, 204, 205, 209
MacGillivray, Sir Donald, and the Monckton Commission, 310–311
McKee, Major Hugh Kennedy, legislator, 214
MacKenzie-Kennedy, Governor Henry Charles Donald Cleveland, 168
McMahon, C., administrator, 184n
Macaulay, Rose, novelist, 163
Macleod, Secretary of State Ian, 312, 313–317
Madagascar, 107, 199
Mafeking, Cape Province, 16
Magersfontein, Cape Province, 16
Mair, Lucy, author, 202

Maize, 94, 95, 97, 105, 106
Makasa, Robert, politician, 283
Makerere University, Uganda, 227, 259
Makulu, Reverend Henry, 304
Malawi, 102, 156, 171, 184, 188, 196, 203, 205, 207, 208, 227–228, 248, 249, 250, 258, 271, 273, 275, 280, 285, 291, 297, 299, 308–310, 313,. 315
Malcolm, Dougald, executive, 204
Malimali, herdsman, 100
Malvern, Lord. See Huggins, Sir Godfrey
Manchester Guardian, The, 284–285, 300, 318
Manpower Committee, wartime, 211–213
Marlborough, Duke of, 3
Marshall, Frank, schoolmaster, 13
Mambwe, people, 97
Manioc, 97
Manshya River, 141, 146–147, 316
Maori, people, 4, 5–6, 286
Marne River, 63, 83
Marseilles, France, 61, 128, 204
Mathu, Eliud, legislator, 256
Maudling, Secretary of State Reginald, 317, 320
Maxwell, Governor Sir James Crawford, 161
May, Bishop Alston James Weller, 186
May, Dr. Aylmer, medical administrator, 123
Maybin, Governor Sir John Alexander, 209–211, 213, 214, 217, 220, 223, 233, 234, 242n, 246
Mbala, See Abercorn, Zambia
Mbikusita, Godwin L., 262, 265, 269
Medical treatment, for Africans, 122–123, 137, 162, 177, 188, 227–228, 230. See also Disease, in Europe and Africa
Melcombe, Dorset, 4. See also Bingham's Melcombe, Dorset
Melland, Frank Hulme, district commissioner, 45, 48, 49, 91–92
Mena House hotel, Egypt, 8, 136
Meniane, Bemba cook, 43
Menton, France, 28
Messina, Sicily, 132
Messines, France, 65, 73
Methuen, Field Marshall Lord, 16
Metz, France, 83

Migration, labor, 98–99, 155, 180, 188, 190; and Lupa goldfields, 183–185
Military matters. See Army, British; Navy, British; all of Ch. III
Millennialism, in Africa, 100
Milner, Aaron, legislator, 321
Milton Abbey, Dorset, 25, 28
Mindolo Mine, Zambia, 215, 217
Mines and labor, 57, 59, 94–95, 98, 183, 188, 190, 215–217, 231, 259, 327
Mirongo, Zambia, 58
Miscegenation, 237, 245
Missionaries, 1, 43, 50, 57, 58, 90, 94, 95, 96, 98, 112, 114, 117, 118, 121, 151–152, 157, 159, 161–162, 174, 186, 212, 221, 252, 323
Mitchell, John, politician, 321n
Mitchell, Governor Sir Philip, 236
Moçambique, 272
Moffat, Sir John Smith, administrator and legislator, 239, 295, 301, 302, 312–314, 317
Moffat, Reverend Dr. Malcolm, 162
Moffat, Robert, politician, 321n
Mombasa, Kenya, 136
Monck, Bosworth. See Goldman, Bosworth Monck
Monckton, Lord, 310–311, 313
Monro, Mrs. Violet Vincent, xiii, 23, 32, 293
Mons, Belgium, 67, 73
Mooi River Depot, Natal, 20–22
Moore, Leopold Frank, legislator and pharmacist, 168, 171, 178–179, 191–192, 194, 197–198, 201–205, 213–214, 254, 261; resigns, 208–209
Monte Carlo, 28
Montlhery, France, 34
Moral Rearmament movement, 296–297, 332
Morocco, 124, 126
Morris, Reverend Colin, and UNIP, 304, 311
Morris, James Frederick, legislator, 257, 281
Mpandala Bridge, Zambia, 316
Mpika, Zambia, 49, 56, 57, 96, 108, 116, 148, 149, 150, 292, 321
Mpulungu, Zambia, 116, 136, 137
Mtepuka, E.M.L., editor, 253, 269
Mufulira, Zambia, 215, 217–218, 220, 222, 225, 231, 321

Muggridge, Richard, at Shiwa, 112
Mulemfwe, capitão, 122, 148, 149, 198
Mulenga, Henry, and Gore-Browne, 221–222, 263, 293, 300, 307, 316, 321
Mulenga, Reuben, politician, 283
Muliashi River, 46
Multiracialism, in Zambia, 301–303, 324
Mulungushi, Zambia, 316
Munali School, Zambia, 259
Munday, Edward, administrator, 150
Musonda, Ashton, 270
Mushembe, gardener at Shiwa, 122
Mutemba, Andrew, politician, 312
Mutende, newspaper, 270
Muwamba, Isaac, clerk, 227
Mwango, Shiwa employee, 115
Mwanza, James, clerk, 122
Mweru, Lake, 39
Mwinilunga, Zambia, 50
Myafunshi River, 55

Nairobi, Kenya, xi, 236
Nakonde, Zambia, 321
Nalumango, Nelson, politician, 267, 269–270, 279
Namibia, 56, 72
Namur, Belgium, 87
Namwanga, people, 97
Namwala District, Zambia, 227
Naples, Italy, 132
Natal, 6, 16, 20–22
Native Development Board, 182, 183, 206
Native Education Board, 183
Native Industrial Labour Advisory Board, 176, 183, 190, 213
Navy, British, 3, 6, 15, 72
Nchanga mine, Zambia, 216, 217
Ndilila, Sykes, politician, 321n
Ndola, Zambia, 40, 41, 42, 43, 45, 46–47, 57, 103, 179
Nea, Richard, quoted, 124–125
New College, Oxford, 6
New Statesman, 318
New Zealand, 4–6, 205, 207, 286, 287
Newspapers, 197, 209, 266, 284–285, 299, 300, 312–313, 315
Newton Manor, English estate, 19
Nieppe, France, 65, 83
Niger Co., 48
Nigeria, 209, 263, 273, 310

Nile River, 39
Nkana mine, Zambia, 214, 215, 217–218, 219–220, 222
Nkomo, Joshua, politician, 321
Nkonde, Brian, 256
Nkrumah, President Kwame, 295
Nkula, Bemba chief, 97
Nkumbula, Harry, legislator, 227, 258, 269, 270n, 274, 276, 280n, 295–296, 301, 304, 306–310, 323–324
Noak, Hans, architect, 304
Norris, Gerald Chad, legislator and metallurgist, 168
North Shields, England, 227
Northern News, the, 299
Northern Province Council, 183
Northern Rhodesia. See Zambia
Northesk, Lord, 128
Norton, Mrs. Patricia, and The Economist, xiii, 279, 281, 288
Norwich, England, 61
Novara, Italy, 23
Noyon, France, 64
Nugent, Lord, 4
Nunk. See Locke-King, Hugh Fortescue
Nutrition, African, 183, 188
Nyasaland. See Malawi

Oakley, English estate, 134
Ockham, Viscount Peter, 112
Okehampton, England, 18, 71
Oise River, 64
Ormsby-Gore, Secretary of State William G. A., 201–204, 205, 209
Ostend, Belgium, 72
Oxford, University of, 6, 12, 19, 28, 38, 202, 204, 230, 234

Page, Thomas Spurgeon, legislator, 214, 267
Palermo, Sicily, 132
Paris, France, 33, 61, 83, 110, 133
Paris Evangelical Mission, 90
Parkinson, Sir Cosmo, civil servant, 247
Partnership, notions of, 158, 175, 178, 191, 196, 202, 225, 260, 273, 280, 282, 283, 286, 290, 295, 298–299, 300, 303
Partition idea, 194–198, 203, 206–207, 285–286, 294, 299, 300–301, 309

Passes, for Africans, 190
Passfield, Lord, 156–158, 170–171
Passports, for Africans, 228
Parliament, Houses of, 8, 48
Patel, C.L., and UNIP, 304
Pearson, Dean Cyril G., xiii, 12, 15, 19, 23, 32
Peckham. See Gillum, W.W.
Peel, Viscount, 25
Pretoria, South Africa, 6
Perham, Dame Margery, author, 201–202, 204, 256
Peacock, John, administrator, 150
Perfume, and essential oils, 92, 104, 107, 200
Permanent Mandates Commission, the, 184
Photography, 14
Pigs, 94
Pim, Sir Alan, 256
Plumtree, Rhodesia, 90
Plymouth Brethren, missionaries, 50
Plymouth, England, 3
Poland and Poles, 72, 236–237
Polygyny, 98, 186
Pondoland, Transkei, 21
Ponsonby, General John, 83, 84–85
Port Sudan, Sudan, 136
Porters, 42, 43, 54–55, 96, 100, 102–103
Portugal, 81–82, 285. See also Angola
Prioleau, J. H. (Jack), journalist, 12, 19, 23, 28, 32, 33, 35, 46
Provincial Councils, in Zambia, 158, 181, 182, 183, 203, 241–245, 270
Purvis, General, 68
Pyramids, the, 8, 136

Race Relations: in Africa, xi, xii, 4–6, 20, 22, 40, 43–45, 54–57, 70n; in South Africa, 100; in Zambia, 102, 112, 116, 136, 150, 171, 188, 191, 214–216, 251, 254, 257–258, 284–285, 295–296, 299, 333
Railways, 95, 96, 102, 115, 170–171, 225–226, 259, 292; white workers, 167–169; strike on, 232–233
Raffles, Governor Sir Stamford, 158
Read, Professor Margaret, 204, 256
Reafforestation, in Zambia, 153–154, 303
Red Cross, the British, 9, 62
Red Sea, 136
Refugees, in Zambia, 235–237

Reims, France, 72
Religion, 3, 6, 14, 100. *See also* Moral Rearmament movement
Renfrewshire, Scotland, 7
Rennie, Governor Sir Gilbert, 266, 269, 270, 273, 274n, 275–276, 287–288, 296, 302
Research Institute, its establishment in Zambia, 180–182
Reserves, for Africans, 237–238, 252
"Responsible government," 266–270, 272–275, 331
Rhodes, Cecil, 1, 16, 299
Rhodesia (Southern), 90, 98, 154, 171, 190, 191–193, 197, 202–203, 204, 205–208, 212, 228, 232–233, 236, 237, 245, 246, 248–249, 250, 251, 260, 264, 266, 267, 271, 275, 278–280, 285, 291, 297–298, 299, 304, 309, 316, 331
Rhodesia and Nyasaland, Federation of. *See* Federation of Rhodesia and Nyasaland
Richards, Audrey I., anthropologist, xiii, 162, 165–166, 180, 242n, 256
Richards, Governor Sir Edmund, 250
Rice, 105, 108
Riots, on the Copperbelt, 167, 171, 185, 191, 215–223, 333
Riots, in the Northern and Luapula Provinces, 316–317
Roadmaking, in Zambia, 113, 115, 138, 143, 146–147, 148–149, 154–155, 157
Roan Antelope mine, Zambia, 217, 223, 292
Robinson, Professor Ronald, 256
Roman Catholic missionaries, *See* White Fathers, missionary society
Rome, Italy, 132
Rosebery, Lord, 225
Ross, Reverend James Arthur, missionary, 121, 123
Rowner Mills, estate, 19, 25, 26
Royal Institute of International Affairs, 204
Royal Military Academy, 16, 18–20
Rubber Factory, in Zambia, 103
Rumpi, Malawi, 299
Russia, 72, 81. *See also* Soviet Union
Russell, Bertrand, 165

St. Helena, 4
St. Quentin, France, 64

St. Raphael, France, 132
Salima, Malawi, 297, 303
Salisbury, England, 69, 71
Salisbury, Rhodesia, xi, 236, 299
Salt, 57
Sandford, Thomas F., administrator, 185, 219, 220–221
Sandys, Secretary of State Duncan, 312
Savill, Joe, and Shiwa, 112, 137–138, 141, 149, 200
Scotland, 4, 6–7, 23, 128, 204
Scott, Dr. Alexander, legislator and publisher, 300–302, 303n, 304, 305, 313
Scott, Francis, legislator, 204
Scott, Sir Walter, novelist, 13, 25
Segregation, in Zambia, 99, 190, 208, 237–239, 248, 286
Selano hill, Zambia, 47
Self-government, 274, 295. *See also* "Responsible government"
Serenje, Zambia, 57, 103, 163, 273, 321
Settlers and conflict, 4–6, 20, 22, 40, 43–45, 56–57, 58, 92, 136; in Zambia, 95–96, 112–113, 156–157, 171, 172, 176, 181, 285–286; in Abercorn and Kasama, 174
Seventeenth Division, British army, 67–68, 71, 72–76
Shaw-Stewart, family, 5, 7, 132; John Archibald, 6–7; Helenor, 6
Sheep, 94
Sherborne School, England, 133
Shiwa Ngandu, 1, 60, 62, 66, 69, 97, 100; the house, xi, xii, 59, 130; the Lake, 57–58, 98; Gore-Browne settles at, 92, 103–127; infrastructure, 96; costs and income, 107–108, 111, 125–126, 137–139, 143–145, 150, 199, 235, 264, 276–277, 290–292; Gore-Browne returns with Lorna, 137; developing Shiwa, 137; and airplanes, 147–148; manor house, 149–150, 200; described, 201, by Sacha Carnegie, 294, by Nadine Gordimer, 326; the estate, 211; and riots, 316–317
Shoeburyness, England, 18
Shropham Hall, Norfolk, 133, 134
Sicily, 132. *See also* Stromboli
Sikalumbi, Wittington K., politician, 304
Silicosis, in Zambia, 231

Singapore, 158
Slave trade, the, 97, 99
Smith, Captain A.A., legislator, 214
Smith, Captain E. A. , and Shiwa, 92, 104, 106
Smuts, Prime Minister Jan Christaan, 197, 230, 275
Soils, in Africa, 94, 96, 97, 153, 199
Sokoni, John Malama, politician, 312
Solwezi, Zambia, 262, 272
Somalia, 212–213, 227, 235
Somme River and front, 65, 76–80, 82
South Africa, Union and Republic of, 6, 9, 16, 19–22, 27, 38, 43–44, 56, 72, 89, 98, 100, 108, 112, 148, 156, 190, 192, 197, 202–203, 204, 228, 230–231, 235, 238, 273, 275, 282, 334
Southampton, England, 37, 38
Southern Rhodesia. See Rhodesia (Southern)
Southern Rhodesian Labour Party, 193, 251
Soviet Union, 284. See also Russia
Sri Lanka, 209
Stancioff, Nada, and Gore-Browne, 128, 132–133
Stanley, Governor Sir Herbert James., 70n, 114–116, 126
Stanley, Secretary of State Colonel Sir Oliver, 247–248, 249, 256, 275
Stanley, Governor R.C.S., 267
Stansky, Professor Peter, xiii
Steel, Captain R. G., of the Boundary Commission, 46, 47, 49, 50, 54–55
Stephenson, Colonel Arthur, legislator, 179, 196, 197, 205
Stephenson, John Edward (Chirupula), native commissioner, 129, 288–289n
Steward, Sarah Dorothea, 4
Stirling, Colonel David, and the Capricorn Africa Society, 296–298, 304, 305, 306
Storrs, Governor Sir Ronald, 149, 150, 153–154
Strauss, Richard, composer, 91
Strikes, 232–233. See also Riots, on the copperbelt
Stromboli, 60
Stroud, England, 8
Stubbs, William, administrator, 150
Studdert, General Robert H., xiii, 79, 135
Submarine warfare, 72

Sudan, the, 136, 160, 204, 263, 295, 332
Surrey, England, 8, 62n
Surveys and surveying, 37, 39–41, 47, 49
Sussex, England, 8, 36
Sutton, Mrs. Xenia Angela Gore-Browne, 146, 164, 166, 211, 235, 276–277, 293
Swanage, England, 68
Switzerland, 296

Tagart, R.S.M., district commissioner, 69–70, 114
Tait, Governor Sir Campbell, 250
Tanganyika, Lake, 39, 110, 115–116, 136, 163, 235
Tanganyika Plateau (N.R.) Farmers Association, 113
Tank warfare, 78
Tanzania, 60, 115, 130, 136, 138, 154, 209, 249, 297; Lupa, 183–185, 333
Taormina, Sicily, 132
Taranki, New Zealand, 5
Tasmania, 6, 286
Taylor, Bishop Robert Selby, 247
Taxes, hut and head, 98, 99, 153, 154–155, 167, 183; commission to revise, 185–187
Telegraphs, in Zambia, 95, 116, 147
Temple, Reverend Merfyn, 304, 311, 312, 317
Thiepval, France, 78
Third Division, British army, 73
Thomson, James Moffat, administrator, 57, 155
Thomson, Joseph, Scottish explorer, 1
Thornicroft, Henry, legislator, 304
Thornton, George E., administrator, 266–267, 269
Timba School, the, 200, 316–317, 327
Tippu Tib, slaver, 97
Tobacco, 95, 105, 188
Tonga, people, 240, 251, 252
Traction Engine, the, 50
Trade unions, in Zambia, 215, 217, 223, 231–232, 304, 323
Transport, 104, 115–116. See also Canoes, transport by; Porters; Railways
Transvaal, the, 9, 38
Trapnell, C. G., Soil scientist, 199
Treaties, with Africans, 39
Tredgold, Justice Sir Robert, 232–233

Trench warfare, 64–65, 72, 75
Trentino, Italy, 72
Trinity College, Cambridge, 6
Trusteeship, the concept of, 177–178, 202. *See also* Passfield, Lord
Tsetse fly, 94
Tunisia, 296
Turin, Italy, 23
Turkey, 72
Tweedsmuir, Lord. *See* Buchan, John, novelist

Uganda, 37, 114, 204, 259
Ukraine, 72
United Free Church of Scotland, 96
United Central Africa Association, 275
United Nations, 315, 318, 323, 332
United Federal Party, of Rhodesia and Nyasaland, 304, 375
United National Independence Party, of Zambia, 310–318, 321, 323–325, 332
United Society for Christian Literature, 311
United States, 83, 318
Urban Advisory Councils, of Zambia, 241

Venice, Italy, 136
Verdun, France, 72
Vesle River, 64, 83
Vickers Aircraft Co., 35
Victoria Falls, conferences at, 193, 277–279, 281, 295
Vincent, Violet. See Monro, V. V.
Visitors, wanted and unwanted, at Shiwa, 106, 112–116, 126, 137, 161–162, 201, 293, 323, 326–327
Voluntary associations, in Zambia, 191, 243, 265, 269–270, 283–284

Waddington, Governor Sir Eubule John, 230, 232–235, 238, 239–240, 246, 247–248, 249–250, 251, 256
Wages, African, 104, 106, 215, 217–219, 223, 232, 290
Wagner, Richard, composer, 91
Wales, 36
Walker, Captain, Boundary Commission, 38, 40, 43
Wallace, Sir Lawrence A., administrator, 102
Wankie, Rhodesia, 232

War: World War I, 61–87, 99; World War II, 209, 210, 223, 229, 235–237, 296; "War Cabinet," 247
Warsaw, Poland, 72, 91
Watch Tower movement (Jehovah Witnesses), 100
Watmore, Harold Alexander, administrator, 150
Watson, Tony, Native Commissioner, 45–47, 48, 49
Waugh, Evelyn, novelist, 204n
Webb, Sidney. See Passfield, Lord
Welensky, Prime Minister Sir Roy, xi, xiii, 197, 204, 205, 209, 210, 213–214, 232, 233, 246–247, 249, 250, 251–252, 255, 256–257, 263, 267–270, 273, 275, 277–283, 287–288, 299, 301, 303–305, 309–310, 312, 314, 315–317, 331–332; and 1935 election, 170–173, 175; and Federation, 260–261, 264–265
Welldon, Reverend J. E. C., schoolmaster, 11
Wellesley. *See* Peel, Viscount
Wey, River, 8, 13, 17
Weybridge, England, 8, 13, 85, 293
White Cargo (1924), 70n
White Fathers, missionary society, 58, 96, 112, 151–152
Wicklow, Irish Co., 3
Wilberforce, Bishop Samuel, 3
Williams, A. T., administrator, 219
Williams, Sir Robert, railway builder, 204
Willis, Bunker, administrator, 150, 151
Wilson, President Woodrow, 124
Wina, Sikota, politician, 315
Winchester, England, 69, 71
Wing, Halcyon, and Gore-Browne, 127–128
Wiremu, Kingi, 5
Witwatersrand, University of, 235
Wixenford School, England, 9–10
Woking, England, 8, 18, 19
Wokingham, England, 9
Woolwich, England, 16, 61. *See also* Royal Military Academy
Wynne, Lieutenant, and the Boundary Commission, 40

Yamba, Dauti, politician, 253, 265, 289

Yeta III, Paramount Chief of the Lozi,
    186
Yorkshire, 19
Young, Governor Sir Hubert
    Winthrop, 149, 154, 155, 157,
    179, 181, 182, 185, 205, 211, 237;
    and Amalgamation, 192, 195, 198,
    201, 203, 204
Young, Lake. *See* Shiwa Ngandu
Young, Sir Edward Hilton, 197
Young, Robert (Bobo), Native
    Commissioner, 58, 289n
Young, Reverend W. P., 184–185
Ypres, Belgium, 65, 73, 75

Zaire, 98, 108, 141, 154, 188, 263, 310,
    315, 320; borders, 38–47, 49–55
Zambezi River, 39, 50, 97, 250
Zambia: borders, 38–47, 49–55; early
    settlements, 40; settlers and
    Africans, 42–44; described, 94–99;
    population, 94–95, 112, 171, 265;
    Gore-Browne in (Boundary
    Commission), 102–127, 136–end;
    independence of, 325–326. *See also*
    Shiwa Ngandu
Zanzibar, 136
Zomba, Malawi, 102, 299
Zulu, people, 22